Unlocking OLAP with Microsoft® SQL Server™ and Excel 2000

Unlocking OLAP with Microsoft® SQL Server™ and Excel 2000

Wayne S. Freeze

IDG Books Worldwide, Inc.
An International Data Group Company

Foster City, CA ◆ Chicago, IL ◆ Indianapolis, IN ◆ New York, NY

Unlocking OLAP with Microsoft® SQL Server™ and Excel 2000

Published by
IDG Books Worldwide, Inc.
An International Data Group Company
919 E. Hillsdale Blvd., Suite 400
Foster City, CA 94404
www.idgbooks.com (IDG Books Worldwide Web site)

ISBN: 0-7645-4587-6

Printed in the United States of America

10 9 8 7 6 5 4 3 2 1

1B/RX/QU/QQ/FC

Distributed in the United States by IDG Books Worldwide, Inc.

Distributed by CDG Books Canada Inc. for Canada; by Transworld Publishers Limited in the United Kingdom; by IDG Norge Books for Norway; by IDG Sweden Books for Sweden; by IDG Books Australia Publishing Corporation Pty. Ltd. for Australia and New Zealand; by TransQuest Publishers Pte Ltd. for Singapore, Malaysia, Thailand, Indonesia, and Hong Kong; by Gotop Information Inc. for Taiwan; by ICG Muse, Inc. for Japan; by Intersoft for South Africa; by Eyrolles for France; by International Thomson Publishing for Germany, Austria and Switzerland; by Distribuidora Cuspide for Argentina; by LR International for Brazil; by Galileo Libros for Chile; by Ediciones ZETA S.C.R. Ltda. for Peru; by WS Computer Publishing Corporation, Inc., for the Philippines; by Contemporanea de Ediciones for Venezuela; by Express Computer Distributors for the Caribbean and West Indies; by Micronesia Media Distributor, Inc. for Micronesia; by Chips Computadoras S.A. de C.V. for Mexico; by Editorial Norma de Panama S.A. for Panama; by American Bookshops for Finland.

For general information on IDG Books Worldwide's books in the U.S., please call our Consumer Customer Service department at 800-762-2974. For reseller information, including discounts and premium sales, please call our Reseller Customer Service department at 800-434-3422.

For information on where to purchase IDG Books Worldwide's books outside the U.S., please contact our International Sales department at 317-596-5530 or fax 317-596-5692.

For consumer information on foreign language translations, please contact our Customer Service department at 800-434-3422, fax 317-596-5692, or e-mail rights@idgbooks.com.

For information on licensing foreign or domestic rights, please phone +1-650-655-3109.

For sales inquiries and special prices for bulk quantities, please contact our Sales department at 650-655-3200 or write to the address above.

For information on using IDG Books Worldwide's books in the classroom or for ordering examination copies, please contact our Educational Sales department at 800-434-2086 or fax 317-596-5499.

For press review copies, author interviews, or other publicity information, please contact our Public Relations department at 650-655-3000 or fax 650-655-3299.

For authorization to photocopy items for corporate, personal, or educational use, please contact Copyright Clearance Center, 222 Rosewood Drive, Danvers, MA 01923, or fax 978-750-4470.

Library of Congress Cataloging-in-Publication Data

Freeze, Wayne S.
   Unlocking OLAP with SQL Server and Excel 2000/ Wayne Freeze
       p.   cm.
     ISBN 0-7643-4587-6 (alk. paper)
     1. OLAP technology   2. SQL Server   3. Microsoft Excel (Computer file)   I. Title.
QA76.9D343F74   2000
005.75'85--dc21   00-023393
                                                            CIP

ABOUT IDG BOOKS WORLDWIDE

Welcome to the world of IDG Books Worldwide.

IDG Books Worldwide, Inc., is a subsidiary of International Data Group, the world's largest publisher of computer-related information and the leading global provider of information services on information technology. IDG was founded more than 30 years ago by Patrick J. McGovern and now employs more than 9,000 people worldwide. IDG publishes more than 290 computer publications in over 75 countries. More than 90 million people read one or more IDG publications each month.

Launched in 1990, IDG Books Worldwide is today the #1 publisher of best-selling computer books in the United States. We are proud to have received eight awards from the Computer Press Association in recognition of editorial excellence and three from Computer Currents' First Annual Readers' Choice Awards. Our best-selling *...For Dummies®* series has more than 50 million copies in print with translations in 31 languages. IDG Books Worldwide, through a joint venture with IDG's Hi-Tech Beijing, became the first U.S. publisher to publish a computer book in the People's Republic of China. In record time, IDG Books Worldwide has become the first choice for millions of readers around the world who want to learn how to better manage their businesses.

Our mission is simple: Every one of our books is designed to bring extra value and skill-building instructions to the reader. Our books are written by experts who understand and care about our readers. The knowledge base of our editorial staff comes from years of experience in publishing, education, and journalism — experience we use to produce books to carry us into the new millennium. In short, we care about books, so we attract the best people. We devote special attention to details such as audience, interior design, use of icons, and illustrations. And because we use an efficient process of authoring, editing, and desktop publishing our books electronically, we can spend more time ensuring superior content and less time on the technicalities of making books.

You can count on our commitment to deliver high-quality books at competitive prices on topics you want to read about. At IDG Books Worldwide, we continue in the IDG tradition of delivering quality for more than 30 years. You'll find no better book on a subject than one from IDG Books Worldwide.

John Kilcullen
Chairman and CEO
IDG Books Worldwide, Inc.

*Eighth Annual
Computer Press
Awards ≥1992*

*Ninth Annual
Computer Press
Awards ≥1993*

*Tenth Annual
Computer Press
Awards ≥1994*

*Eleventh Annual
Computer Press
Awards ≥1995*

Credits

ACQUISITIONS EDITORS
John Osborn
Judy Brief

PROJECT EDITORS
Valerie Perry
Andy Marinkovich

TECHNICAL EDITOR
David M. Williams

COPY EDITORS
Victoria Lee
Amy Eoff

MEDIA DEVELOPMENT SPECIALIST
Jason Luster

PERMISSIONS EDITOR
Lenora Chin Sell

MEDIA DEVELOPMENT MANAGER
Stephen Noetzel

PROJECT COORDINATORS
Linda Marousek
Marcos Vergara

GRAPHICS AND PRODUCTION SPECIALISTS
Robert Bihlmayer
Jude Levinson
Michael Lewis
Victor Pérez-Varela
Dina F Quan
Ramses Ramirez

BOOK DESIGNER
Jim Donohue

ILLUSTRATORS
Mary Jo Richards
Clint Lahnen
Karl Brandt

PROOFREADING AND INDEXING
York Production Services

COVER DESIGN
Joann Vuong

About the Author

Wayne S. Freeze is a full-time author and computer technology consultant. He has written eight different books on Visual Basic and SQL Server, since he began his career three years ago.

Wayne learned to program in BASIC back in 1969 on an old Teletype terminal connected to a faceless mainframe computer located far way. Since then, computers have ruled his life. Wayne has worked on computers ranging in size from tiny 8080-based embedded systems to large-scale IBM mainframes. His formal education includes degrees in engineering, computer science, and business management.

During his career, Wayne has worked in various capacities on many different sizes and brands of computers. Before he became a full-time writer, Wayne was the Technical Support Manager at the University of Maryland, where his responsibilities included long-range strategic planning and managing the day-to-day crises that arise in a multi-million dollar organization.

Wayne's experience with personal computers began in 1977 when he built the original personal computer, the Altair 8800, from a kit. Since then, Wayne has used nearly every major type of personal computer ever made, many of which are still sitting around his house, waiting for him to establish a personal computer history museum.

Besides working with computers, Wayne loves to collect cars ranging in size from a 1:144 Dodge Viper that sits on his desk to a 1:1 Porsche Turbo driven only when there is no rain in sight. He also loves photography and can often be found at air shows taking pictures of World War II fighters. He also hopes to get his pilot's license, and then get certified to fly a P-51 Mustang.

Wayne lives in Beltsville, Maryland with his lovely wife, Jill, and their wonderful children, Christopher, age seven, and Samantha, age five. Jill is a well-respected writer and Microsoft beta tester, specializing in Microsoft Office, Internet Explorer, and Windows. Chris is perhaps the youngest person to beta test software for Microsoft, having tested both Windows 98 and Microsoft Millennium in his short career. Sam, on the other hand, loves to just sit on Dad's lap, and one day hopes to write a book just like her Mom and Dad.

Together, they live in a house full of animals including a golden retriever name Lady Kokomo, and four cats, named Pixel, Terry, Dusty, and Cali. Wayne also has a pet stingray, Raymond, named after his father-in-law, who is learning to eat worms from his hand (the stingray, that is, not my father-in-law).

Wayne maintains a web site at www.JustPC.com, containing information about the various books he and his wife have written. Please take the time to visit their web site and sign their guest book.

This book is dedicated to my readers, editors, and everyone else who was patient enough for me to finish it

Preface

The traditional books about data warehousing and Online Analytical Processing (OLAP) focus on the management techniques and issues related to building a data warehouse and selecting an OLAP tool. They discuss issues such as how to choose a database vendor, and how to compare the different analysis tools. The also spend a lot of time helping you develop checklists, project plans, and evaluation guidelines.

While this type of information is appropriate in many situations, I feel it ignores a large group of people that need a data warehouse, but don't have the resources to put together a massive project to develop one. Your time is valuable. Do you have time to spend three months trying to pick a database vendor for your data warehouse, or should you use the Microsoft SQL Server database you already have? Why should you spend lots of time evaluating and choosing an OLAP analysis tool, when you already know Excel?

I believe that by showing you how to use commonly available tools like SQL Server and Excel, you can implement your data warehouse and OLAP solution faster and cheaper than you could if you went the traditional route. In this book, I'm going against tradition. I'm ignoring the management issues in favor of showing you how to use some commonly available tools like Microsoft SQL Server 7 and Microsoft Office 2000 to implement a real world data warehouse.

Since the best way to show you how to do something is to build a concrete example, I've included a complete database for a company known as JustPC – a mom and pop computer retailer with three locations. You'll be able to use this database to create a data warehouse, and then learn how to use Microsoft's tools to extract information from the data warehouse.

To make this example even more realistic, the production database contains the detailed transactions of over 15,000 JustPC customers over a period of four years. The total database size is about 50 megabytes, which means your queries won't run in the blink of an eye. Rather, when you extract the data from your production database for your data warehouse, you will have time to walk down the hall for coffee and still make it back in time to wait some more.

Audience

This book is aimed at a knowledgeable computer user who needs better information to make better business decisions. You should have a working knowledge of Windows 2000/NT Server and Excel 2000. A working knowledge of SQL Server 7 is highly desirable.

What This Book Covers

This book shows you how to use SQL Server and Microsoft Office to create and use your own data warehouse. It introduces the key concepts behind data warehousing and OLAP, without getting bogged down in the management and theoretical aspects. While Microsoft's framework for data warehousing is discussed, most of the book focuses on the practical side of data management, by showing you in detail how to use:

◆ **Microsoft SQL Server 7, Enterprise Manager** to build and maintain your data warehouse.

◆ **Microsoft SQL Server 7, Data Transformation Services** to convert data from your production database to your data warehouse.

◆ **Microsoft SQL Server 7, Query Analyzer** to answer simple questions using your data warehouse.

◆ **Microsoft SQL Server 7, English Query** to build a simple application that allows non-technical people to ask English language questions against your data warehouse.

◆ **Microsoft SQL Server 7, OLAP Manager** to design and create OLAP cubes.

◆ **Microsoft Excel 2000** to analyze the information in your data warehouse and OLAP cubes.

◆ **Microsoft MapPoint 2000** to analyze geographical information from your data warehouse.

The accompanying CD-ROM includes an evaluation copy of SQL Server, so all you need to do to test the examples in this book is to find a computer with a gigabyte of free disk space running Window 2000 Server or Window NT Server. Plus you'll need a copy of Microsoft Excel 2000 to work through the Excel examples and Microsoft MapPoint if you want to try analyzing your data geographically.

Also on the CD-ROM is a copy of the production database and a copy of the data warehouse I used for all of the examples in the book. I strongly encourage you to load the databases and try to use them as you read the book.

What This Book Doesn't Cover

You should have a working knowledge of Excel before you start this book. While I'll cover how to import data from the data warehouse and how to create and use PivotTables, I'm going to assume that you already are comfortable using the rest of the features.

Also, I'm not going to get into details about how to install and use Windows, Windows 2000/NT, or SQL Server 7. There are a number of good books on this subject. Despite their name, the Dummies books will teach you want you really need to know without making you feel dumb in the process.

Hardware and Software Requirements

While it's possible to run SQL Server and Excel on a single machine, you'll be happier if you dedicate one machine to SQL Server and use a second for Excel. If you do choose to use a single machine, you should have a lot of memory (128 megabytes should be fine for Windows NT Server, while 256 megabytes are really needed on Windows 2000 Server) and a lot of processing power (any Pentium processor over 400 MHz should be fine). If you want to use multiple machines, I suggest that the one with more memory be used for the database server. Performance of the database is controlled more by the amount of available memory than by any other factor.

I wrote this book using two computers: one (called Mycroft) for running Excel and MapPoint, and the other (known as Athena) to run the database server. Mycroft is a Gateway 9100 laptop with a Pentium 200 processor and 64 megabytes of main memory, along with Windows 98, Office 2000, and SQL Server 7. The database server is a Gateway desktop computer with a Pentium 120 processor and 80 megabytes of main memory, running Windows NT Server 4.0. Besides NT Server, the NT Server Option Pack is installed. It also has Service Pack 4 installed, which is a requirement for SQL Server 7. Obviously SQL Server was installed, plus the Internet Information Server (IIS) 4.0. Just for good measure I also installed Office 2000 on this machine. The two computers were connected using a 10 MHz Ethernet LAN. The combination was slower than I would have liked, but it worked for me.

Visit My Web Site

I maintain a Web site at http://www.JustPC.com with additional information about the books that my wife and I have written. Each book has its own web page on which I answer frequently asked questions and point you to other resources you may find interesting. If you get a chance to stop by, please sign my guest book to let me know you were there.

You're also welcome to send me e-mail at WFreeze@JustPC.com. Let me know what you liked about the book and what you didn't. I've made friends with readers from all over the world by doing this. However, please understand that I make my living from writing and consulting, so asking me to be your unpaid consultant isn't fair to you or me. I know what it is like having a critical project and not being able to get the answers I need in a hurry. If I can help, I will try. However, my priorities are my family, my current book (though my editors may think it should have a higher priority), my readers, my web site, and then everyone else. So don't be surprised if you send me a note and a few weeks (or even months) later you hear from me. Writing a book such as this one takes a considerable amount of time and many things, like sleeping, eating somewhere other than my desk, and answering e-mail, are often put off until after the book is finished.

Now don't be afraid to send me e-mail. I enjoy reading every note I get and I do read every single note. I've always enjoyed teaching people how to do things, and writing a book allows me to teach more people than I've ever had the opportunity to do before. Unfortunately, I miss the feedback that you get from teaching someone in person. E-mail is my link to you. So, while I can't meet everyone in person, hearing from you via e-mail is the next best thing.

Acknowledgments

Nearly everyone thinks being an author is a wonderful job. You get to work at home, to set your own hours, and have the freedom to do what you please. The only people who don't believe this are the authors, their family, and the people who take the manuscripts I write and magically transform them into a book. They know that writing is hard work, and that the few minutes of joy in seeing the new book on the shelf doesn't always make up for the months of 16-hour days.

Sometimes things happen in your life that you can't anticipate. I want to thank John Osborn for being so understanding while I was distracted by personal problems in the middle of writing this book. While it seemed like forever, at least I was able to bring it to a close. I also need to acknowledge the help from Bill Ray, who filled in for me while I wasn't able to write. I want to thank Jill for her assistance in wrapping up this book. It is much appreciated. Thanks also go to project editors, Andy Marinkovich and Valerie Perry, and to copyeditors, Victoria Lee and Amy Eoff, whose contributions in putting this book together are greatly appreciated. Thanks for the help!

My agent, Laura Belt certainly earns her commissions. She does her best to insure that I have money for the things that most writers don't have, like electricity to run my computer and a roof over my head. Now if I could only afford something to eat.

Because of the demands on my time, I don't get to visit my friends as often as I would like. But I do think of them often. Shaun, Elwyn, Rick, Ariane, Dr. Bob, Veronica, Scott, Bob K., and Ian, I'll be in touch soon. I promise.

Bucky and Goose are two of the most interesting people you can ever meet and I feel privileged to have them as my in-laws. We miss you both and wish you were living across the street.

It seems like I never get to see my mother and father as often as I wish. I hope that changes in the future, since they are both very special people to me. I want to especially thank you for your support while writing this book. It was much appreciated.

If you read this book carefully, you will find occasional references to Christopher, Samantha, and Jill. Chris, who is seven, knows more about computers than some well-paid people I used to work with and has tested more beta software on his computer than most adults. While Samantha is only five, she already wants her own computer so she can write books like her mommy and daddy. My lovely wife, Jill, is a very respected writer and beta tester in her own right, having written books on Microsoft Office, Internet Explorer, and Windows. If you believe in yourself, anything is possible! I love you all!

Contents at a Glance

Contents

Part I

Introduction to OLAP

Chapter 1

Introducing OLAP

IN THIS CHAPTER

◆ Data warehouses

◆ Online analytical processing

◆ Choosing OLAP tools

THE NEED FOR SOME computer applications is obvious. Accounting applications perform exacting calculations to manage your business's money. Inventory applications manage the stock levels in your warehouse so that you may fill customers' orders promptly. Human Resources systems insure that your employees receive their paychecks on a regular basis, as well as help you with all of the paperwork associated with having employees.

So, what do these applications have in common? They are *tactical applications* that help you run your business on a day-to-day basis. However, they don't answer this question: "How can I improve my business?" To answer that, you need a *strategic application* that looks at your business from a broader perspective. This type of application collects information about your business and helps you analyze it so that you can make better, more educated decisions.

Strategic applications are also called *decision support systems*, which work by helping you collect and analyze information that enables you to make better business decisions. There are two primary components of a decision support system: the *data warehouse* and the *online analytical processing (OLAP)* tools.

Data Warehouses

If you read the trade press, you know that everyone is implementing data warehouses. A *data warehouse* generally refers to the collection of data taken from tactical applications, such as your accounting system and your inventory control system. Then, this data is transformed into a more useful format and made available for anyone that wants to use it. Unlike tactical applications, there is no specific, planned use for this data. Instead, it simply is stored in the data warehouse until someone wants something — just like a warehouse is used to store inventory until someone needs it. Building a data warehouse is often a complex task, but it doesn't have to be if you have the right tools.

Data Warehouses versus Data Marts

You may wonder what the difference is between a data warehouse and a *data mart*. Both gather data from tactical applications and both make it available for detailed analysis. However, data warehouses try to capture every piece of data available from all of the tactical applications for analysis. Building a data warehouse usually involves mammoth projects and lots of time and resources to complete.

A data mart, on the other hand, is a lightweight version of a data warehouse. Initially, it usually collects only a subset of the information stored in tactical applications. Then, over time, data from other tactical applications is added as needed. While I personally favor the data mart for collecting data, I believe the term data warehouse more accurately describes the concept of storing data until it's needed.

No matter how you build a data warehouse, you should build it on top of a relational database system. A *relational database system* is an extremely flexible way to store your data. Most modern relational database systems can access other database systems even if they come from different vendors. In many cases, you can even access non-relational databases that may be resident on the corporate mainframe. This easily enables you to collect data from your tactical applications and keep it in one location. You also can take the time to translate the data into more meaningful terms.

See Chapter 2 for details about relational database systems.

Having a single location for your data warehouse values is very important. This enables you to look at data that spans multiple applications. Without this capability, you miss the opportunity to see relationships that exist between data in different applications. For example, you may know that a particular individual is a top salesperson in a particular store. However, by combining Sales data with Human Resources data, you may be able to determine that the sales for the entire store during the time the leading salesperson is actually working are less than they are for another group of people working at another time.

Online Analytical Processing

While collecting data for a data warehouse is useful, the data is meaningless unless you use it. You need to be able to analyze the data in order to understand how your business operates today and how it may operate in the future. In the past, this type of information was generated using reams of paper, but now the trend is toward building interactive tools that help you analyze your data. This process often is referred to as online analytical processing or OLAP.

While it is easy to produce simple statistics – such as the number of items sold or the average cost to produce something from a data warehouse – with the right tools, you can find far more information than you thought might be available. The results of these statistics are presented in the form of multidimensional reports.

Viewing Multidimensional Reports

An OLAP tool typically presents data in the form of a *multidimensional report.* While a multidimensional report sounds ominous, it's just the name used when you compare two or more columns of information. Each dimension in a report corresponds to a data axis. Thus, a *two-dimensional*, or *cross-tabulation*, report has two axes and takes the shape of a rectangle. A three-dimensional report looks like a cube. Don't ask me what a four-dimensional report looks like – my brain doesn't work that way. However, the OLAP tools in SQL Server supports cubes with up to 65,535 dimensions.

CROSS-TABULATION REPORTS

As just mentioned, a multidimensional report with only two dimensions is known as a *cross-tabulation* or *crosstab* report. The data is arranged in the form of a rectangle, with a set of rows and columns containing summary information about the data (see Figure 1-1).

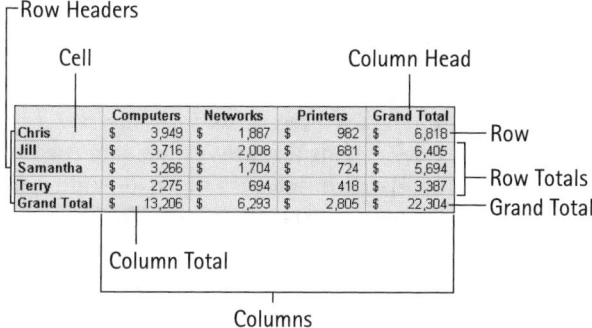

Figure 1-1: Cross-tabulation reports have only two dimensions.

As you can see, the report consists of a number of different parts (see Table 1-1). The columns in this report (Computers, Networks, and Printers) contain information about sales of each of the individual product lines. The rows in this report (Chris, Jill, Samantha, and Terry) contain information about how much each of the various salespeople sold. The first cell (which has a value of $3,949) shows the total computer sales for Chris. The Grand Total column and Grand Total row contain the total sales for the various products and salespeople, except for the value in the lower-right corner. This value represents the total sales for all products and the total sales for all salespeople.

TABLE 1-1 PARTS OF A CROSS-TABULATION REPORT

Part	Description
Cell	The intersection of a row and a column in the report
Column	The series of values arranged vertically
Column Head	The label at the top of a column that uniquely identifies the data in the column
Column Total	The value at the bottom of a column that represents information for the entire column
Grand Total	The value at the bottom of the last column, and at the end of the last row, that represents information for the entire report
Row	The series of values arranged horizontally
Row Header	The label at the start of a row that uniquely identifies the data in the row
Row Total	The label at the end of a row that represents information for the entire row

To create a crosstab report, you need to identify three fields from the raw data table, plus a statistical operation. (Listing 1-1 contains a subset of the data used to create the crosstab report in Figure 1-1). The first two fields (salesperson and product) are used as subscripts to select a single cell into the crosstab table. The third field (total sales) is used as input into the statistical function that is displayed in the selected cell. In this case, the values are added together to create a single sum for each cell.

Listing 1-1: Some of the raw data used in the crosstab report

```
Salesperson    Product       Total Sales
Chris          Computers      777.00
Samantha       Computers      870.00
Jill           Computers      987.00
Terry          Computers      567.00
Chris          Printers       234.00
Samantha       Printers        54.00
Jill           Printers       123.00
Terry          Printers       145.00
Chris          Networks       335.00
Samantha       Networks       453.00
Jill           Networks       444.00
Terry          Networks       222.00
Chris          Computers      897.00
Samantha       Computers      774.00
Jill           Computers      987.00
Terry          Computers      587.00
```

SUM is probably one of the two most common statistical functions. For each line of data in the input file, the SUM function adds the value of the third field the cell in the crosstab report indexed by the values in the first and second columns. It will also update the appropriate row, column, and grand totals (refer back to Figure 1-1).

Beyond these statistical functions, you usually can use functions such as AVERAGE, COUNT, MINIMUM, MAXIMUM, STANDARD DEVIATION, and VARIANCE to compute the crosstab values. Of course the exact mix of functions will depend on the tool you use to build the crosstab report.

A Trip Back to My Roots — OLAP Where Were You?

Many years ago when I first stared working with computers, I worked for the Maryland State Department of Education. I spent much of my time creating statistical reports (mostly crosstab reports) based on data collected from high school graduates. A complete copy of the report used several dozen boxes of paper. Even though the reports covered most of the questions people asked of the high school graduates, I often received special requests for information that wasn't in the standard reports. If the OLAP tools available today were available then, I could have avoided months of specialized programming to create the reports. Additionally, the educators could have queried the data directly to get their information. Not only would they have been able to answer their questions faster, but they also might have been able to identify trends from a closer examination of the data so that they could change their curriculum to benefit future high school graduates.

CUBE REPORTS

A *cube report* has three dimensions. Because it's difficult to represent a three-dimensional object on a two-dimensional computer screen, cubes usually are represented as a series of crosstab reports. In this situation, each crosstab report is known as a slice of the cube.

Here's another way of looking at a slice. If you hold one of the fields that define the axes constant, you're left with a crosstab report. The remaining two axis fields define the row headers and column headers.

GENERAL MULTIDIMENSIONAL REPORTS

If you go beyond three dimensions, you have even more problems. Of course you can choose specific values for all but two of the axes and display a crosstab report. However, there is another option. You can choose to group rows within rows and columns within columns. This leads to a hierarchy in which the values from one field are repeated for each of the values in the other field. This often leads to a confusing arrangement, like the one shown in Figure 1-2.

Salesperson	Product	Q1	Q2	Q3	Q4	Grand Total
Chris	Computers	$ 777	$ 897	$ 1,323	$ 952	$ 3,949
	Networks	$ 335	$ 568	$ 437	$ 547	$ 1,887
	Printers	$ 234	$ 234	$ 256	$ 258	$ 982
Chris Total		$ 1,346	$ 1,699	$ 2,016	$ 1,757	$ 6,818
Jill	Computers	$ 987	$ 987	$ 890	$ 852	$ 3,716
	Networks	$ 444	$ 645	$ 321	$ 598	$ 2,008
	Printers	$ 123	$ 321	$ 111	$ 126	$ 681
Jill Total		$ 1,554	$ 1,953	$ 1,322	$ 1,576	$ 6,405
Samantha	Computers	$ 870	$ 774	$ 870	$ 752	$ 3,266
	Networks	$ 453	$ 127	$ 439	$ 685	$ 1,704
	Printers	$ 54	$ 125	$ 231	$ 314	$ 724
Samantha Total		$ 1,377	$ 1,026	$ 1,540	$ 1,751	$ 5,694
Terry	Computers	$ 567	$ 587	$ 541	$ 580	$ 2,275
	Networks	$ 222	$ 87	$ 129	$ 256	$ 694
	Printers	$ 145	$ 89	$ 88	$ 96	$ 418
Terry Total		$ 934	$ 763	$ 758	$ 932	$ 3,387
Grand Total		$ 5,211	$ 5,441	$ 5,636	$ 6,016	$ 22,304

Figure 1-2: A report with three dimensions can be confusing.

Manipulating Multidimensional Reports

The online part of the OLAP analytical tools implies that you should use these reports interactively. In fact, without the interactive component, you miss a lot of the information in an OLAP report. A good OLAP tool enables you to switch dimensions dynamically. Thus, on a crosstab report, you can swap the fields used for columns and rows. On a cube, you can swap all three dimensions around to radically change how you see the data. On a report with more than three dimensions, you can choose which values to fix and which to display on each dimension.

In addition to being able to manipulate the fields displayed on each axis, you also can choose to drill down into a particular field and uncover more details. This helps you to identify situations in which you might draw the wrong conclusion from the data. Consider a government agency that finished its year under budget. However, when you examine the divisions within the agency, you find that all of them except one were significantly over budget. The one division that was under budget had no expenditures starting part of the way through the year. The savings from that one division allowed the others to spend more than their budget. Is this a problem? Maybe, maybe not. But it's definitely a situation worth investigating further.

Choosing OLAP Tools

Until recently, building a decision support system required a number of different tools from several different vendors. These tools often were expensive, hard to use, and difficult to adapt to changing needs. Microsoft has recognized this problem and now offers a complete solution: SQL Server 7 and Excel 2000.

SQL Server 7

One of the major goals of this Microsoft's SQL Server 7 was to create a scalable product that runs well on a typical Windows 98 desktop machine with limited resources. Another goal was for it to run equally well on a Windows NT server with multiple processors, gigabytes of main memory, and practically unlimited disk space.

Another important goal for Microsoft was to reduce the total cost of ownership. Modern relational databases often are served by a group of specialists known as *database administrators*. These people are expensive to hire and difficult to keep due to the increasing demand for their skills. SQL Server 7 addresses this problem by including a number of wizards that make it easy to perform routine tasks. Also, you can use the SQL Server Agent to run various activities when your machine is unattended.

Microsoft addressed decision support systems by including two key features in SQL Server 7. The first is the *Data Transformation Services (DTS)*. This feature makes it easy to move data from one place to another. This is particularly important because the data in a data warehouse usually is taken from tactical applications such as accounting and inventory systems – even if they exist on the corporate mainframe.

The second key feature is *OLAP Services*. These services bridge the gap between the data warehouse and the analysis tools running on the user's workstation. The data warehouse data is preprocessed in the OLAP server before the results are presented to the analysis tool. Microsoft has made available the *application programming interface (API)* to OLAP Services so that other companies can design client tools to analyze OLAP data.

Excel 2000

Microsoft Excel 2000 arguably is the premier data analysis tool available in the marketplace today. Individuals and corporations rely on its ability to manipulate data and extract useful information.

The key to performing complex data analysis is the *PivotTable* feature of Excel. Unlike regular worksheets, PivotTables enable you to look at multidimensional reports interactively (see Figure 1-3). You can drag columns from one place on the worksheet to rearrange how your data is presented, or drill deeper into the data to reveal more of its details.

Quarter	(All)			
Sum of Total Sales	Product			
Salesperson	Computers	Networks	Printers	Grand Total
Chris	3949	1887	982	6818
Jill	3716	2008	681	6405
Samantha	3266	1704	724	5694
Terry	2275	694	418	3387
Grand Total	13206	6293	2805	22304

Figure 1–3: PivotTables enable you to view hierarchical data.

PivotTables by themselves are relatively limited in size. However, Excel has the ability to communicate directly with SQL Server's OLAP Services. This means that Excel can manage much larger PivotTables than ever before and the work is split between Excel and the computer running OLAP Services.

The concept of PivotTables in Excel 2000 has extended to charts. Much like you manipulate PivotTables by dragging information around on the screen, you can do the same with PivotCharts.

Also new in Excel 2000 is the ability to manipulate your worksheets, PivotTables, and PivotCharts using a Web browser. Essentially, you can analyze your data using Excel and publish the results on your local intranet so that others in your organization may use it.

See Chapters 4 and 25-28 for details about PivotTables.

Other Useful Tools

Besides the SQL Server database and Excel 2000, there are a few other tools you may find interesting to use for data analysis. Some of these tools are found in SQL Server, while others are tools available for an extra charge from Microsoft. Each is designed to approach the problem of data analysis from a slightly different angle.

QUERY ANALYZER
Query Analyzer is a standard component of SQL Server 7 that enables you to execute SQL queries and retrieve their results interactively. While not as sophisticated as some of the tools available, it is nonetheless ideal for answering simple questions such as, "How many employees are in my company?"

ENGLISH QUERY

Another standard component of SQL Server 7 is *English Query*. It takes English questions such as, "How many students attended a math class last year?" and translates it into the equivalent SQL statement for execution. This tool is ideal for people who are intimidated by tools like Query Analyzer.

MAPPOINT 2000

The newest standalone member of the Office 2000 family is known as *MapPoint 2000*. It is designed to help you visually analyze geographically oriented data so you can determine the geographic distribution of your data. This can help you to identify key customers, which you can target with specialized mailings. It also can help you identify trouble spots where more attention is needed.

ACCESS 2000

Access 2000 is another tool you might find useful. You can use the rich assortment of wizards in Access to create your own forms and reports using the data from your data warehouse.

VISUAL BASIC

If you're a programmer, you may be interested in using *Visual Basic* from time to time. No matter how powerful the tool, nothing beats a real programming language when you run into a really complex situation analysis. Often, Visual Basic is hidden away as the macro language in Excel and Access, or you can use Visual Basic as a conventional programming language and access the database directly.

THIRD-PARTY TOOLS

A number of *third-party* tools also are compatible with SQL Server 7 and OLAP Services. You can check Microsoft's Web site at http://www.microsoft.com/sql for more information about these vendors.

Why Do I Need OLAP?

If you believe everything you see in advertisements, the answer to this question is to make better business decisions. However, OLAP is really only worth the time and effort you are willing to put into it. The more time you spend understanding your data, the better the information you can extract from it.

Consider a Little League baseball team that collects information about every pitch during every game. From this information, you can produce statistics such as batting average, home runs hit, walks, and strikeouts. However, if you're willing to dig a little deeper, you might find out that your leading hitter isn't very good against left-handed pitchers. Therefore, when it's the bottom of the ninth, two outs, the winning run is on third, and you're facing a left-handed pitcher, you might want to put in a different batter. While this doesn't guarantee that you'll win the game, the odds just got a little better.

In the Little League example, I doubt whether the coach will make a decision based on detailed analysis of data. Many other factors, besides the statistics, also have an impact on the outcome (such as how the player is feeling, who the "hot" player is at that moment, and so on). But this example does illustrate an important point – that looking at simple statistics often can be misleading. The more you understand the underlying data, the more likely you will be able to make a better decision based on the data.

Summary

In this chapter, I introduced you to a few basic concepts such as OLAP and data warehouses. Hopefully, I've answered the question of "What is OLAP?" As for "Why do I need it?" only you can answer that for yourself. In the rest of this book, however, I'm going to do my best to convince you that OLAP is critical for educated decision-making in your business. Unless you can understand what is happening with your business now and what has happened in the past, you cannot expect to predict – or even plan for – its future with confidence.

In the next chapter, I review the fundamentals of relational databases, including such items as databases, tables, columns, rows, indexes, data types, and normalization. This will help you as I begin talking about building a data warehouse using SQL Server and analyzing the data using OLAP Services and Excel 2000.

Chapter 2

What Is a Relational Database?

IN THIS CHAPTER

- ◆ Inside a relational database
- ◆ Clients and servers
- ◆ Other objects in a database
- ◆ Relationships among tables
- ◆ Normalization
- ◆ Database design tricks

STATED SIMPLY, A *database* is a collection of computer records that an application program can access. A *relational database* is a type of database that uses mathematical set theory to describe how the various pieces of data in the database are related to one other. Over the last ten years, relational database systems effectively have displaced all other types of database systems in the marketplace. Primarily, this is due to three different factors: the flexibility of the data model, the increasing availability of inexpensive computers, and the standardization of the technology.

The primary advantage of a relational database is the flexibility of the data model. You easily can change your database design on the fly to meet your changing needs. Other types of databases are harder to change, which makes it harder to adapt existing databases to meet new business challenges.

Originally, the primary disadvantage of relational databases was the amount of resources they consumed. However, as computers have become faster and cheaper, it is now more practical to devote the resources necessary to use a relational database. Today, the average PC has far more computing power than the largest mainframe of 20 years ago. Combined with the availability of high-speed networking, it's possible to manage databases that people couldn't even begin to think about only ten years ago.

The final reason that relational database systems have come to dominate the marketplace is the fact that nearly all of these systems are based on the *Structured Query Language* or *SQL*. People who learn SQL on one database system can apply that knowledge to other database systems. This means that there is a large pool of people with the right skills available for hire; for employers, this equates to less cost in hiring and training new people to work on database projects.

Inside a Relational Database

A relational database contains a collection of objects that hold your data using information you supply to the database system. You describe these objects using a series of SQL statements or by using high-level database design tools. Collectively, this information is known as a *schema*.

The Database Object

A database is the highest level object that a *DBMS (database management system)* manages. It holds a collection of *tables* and *indexes*, both of which are discussed below. Disk storage generally is allocated to a database, which in turn makes it available for use by tables and indexes.

The Table Object

Each table consists of a set of *columns* and a set of *rows* (see Figure 2-1). Each column contains a unique attribute of the data, such as an employee name or item description. Each row contains a unique instance of the data, such as the information about an employee or a part in the inventory.

Salesperson	Date	Product	Quantity	Total Sale	Customer
Chris	5-Jan	Server	1	$ 25.00	Pixel Web Design
Chris	6-Jan	Workstation	7	$ 35.00	Tracy's Training
Samantha	8-Jan	Server	2	$ 50.00	Bob's Lab
Samantha	8-Jan	Workstation	10	$ 50.00	Bob's Lab
Jill	10-Jan	Server	4	$ 100.00	Cali's Internet Service
Chris	12-Jan	Workstation	2	$ 10.00	Koko's Accounting
Terry	15-Jan	Printer	1	$ 2.00	Tribble's Auto Shop

Figure 2-1: A table has horizontal rows and vertical columns.

Each table contains a set of one or more columns that uniquely identify a row. This is known as the *primary key*. Thus, you need to know the primary key to retrieve a particular row. For example, assume that you have a table that contains information about your customers. You can't use name as a primary key, since it's possible that you might have two customers named John Smith. A better choice for the primary key would be CustomerNumber, where each value of CustomerNumber would uniquely identify a particular customer. Using this value, you will always be able to identify which John Smith you are talking about.

Even though a table contains a set of rows, the order of those rows is arbitrary. In other words, you don't know which row from a table will be retrieved next unless you explicitly request that the rows be sorted so that they returned in a particular order. In practice, most database systems store the rows in the same order you insert them into the table.

Horizontal Rows

A row contains information about a specific instance of an object. For example, a row may contain information about a single item in the inventory or information about a single employee. Sometimes a row is referred to as a *record.*

All of the basic operations work on sets of rows. You can select rows from a table, insert rows into a table, delete rows from a table, or update rows in a table.

Vertical Columns

A column contains a single piece of information, such as a person's name or the description of an inventory item. These contents also are called *fields* or *data elements,* but these terms are holdovers from older database technologies. A column should contain an *atomic* piece of information (you can't break the information into smaller pieces) about an object. In practice, some values, such as a date, are treated as atomic values even though they can be broken into year, month, and day.

Data Types

Associated with each column in a table is a *data type,* which describes the type of information the column may hold. For instance, the name of an employee contains a sequence of characters, while the list price of an item obviously is numeric. Table 2-1 lists some common data types.

TABLE 2-1 COMMON DATA TYPES

Data Type	Description
Bit	Contains either TRUE or FALSE
Binary	Contains a fixed length string of binary data
Char	Contains a fixed length string of characters
Datetime	Contains a date or time value
Decimal	Contains a number with the specified number of decimal places
Int	Contains an integer number
Real	Contains a floating-point number
Varbinary	Contains a variable length string of binary data
Varchar	Contains a variable length string of characters

The data types you'll use most often are those that hold character information. You can use the Char and Varchar data types to store textual information, such as a person's name or an item's description. Binary and Varbinary data types are useful for storing unusual types of information, such as an image or a sound clip. The Datetime data type stores information about dates and times. There are only two possible values in the Bit data type: TRUE and FALSE. You might use this data type to store information in which you only have two possible values (such as ON and OFF, YES and NO, or TRUE and FALSE).

There are three different data types that can hold numeric information: integer, floating point, and decimal. An integer value is an exact number that doesn't have any fractional part (for example, 12,345). This data type is useful for storing values, such as quantities or identification numbers. A Real data type is a scaled value with a fixed number of digits of accuracy (for example, 1.2345×10^{12}). It can represent a wide range of values. This data type is mostly used in engineering and statistical calculations, and not commonly used in most databases. Decimal data types, on the other hand, store the fractional part of a number exactly (for example, 123.54). You should use decimal values anytime you deal with money.

Many of the data types require additional information, such as the length of a Char string or the precision of a Decimal number. With a fixed-length data type, such as Binary or Char, the length determines the amount of storage that is reserved in the database for the column. Variable-length data types, such as Varchar and Varbinary, use this information to determine the maximum number of characters or bytes of information stored in the column. The actual storage depends on the actual amount of data stored in the column.

In most cases, the maximum size of the Binary and Char columns is limited to a few thousand bytes of storage. However, this is a big limitation when it comes to images and sound clips whose length is measured in megabytes. So most database systems implement special data types that enable you to store much larger values. In many cases, these values can exceed a gigabyte of storage.

Null Values

Besides containing a value, a column can have a flag that indicates whether a value is stored in the column. This is called a *null flag*. If a column is null, then you know it doesn't contain any information. Therefore, you shouldn't use it to perform any calculations.

An empty string ain't null: A character string, which has a length of zero, is called an *empty string* because there are no characters in the string. However, an empty string is not the same thing as a null value. If a column is null, it means that it doesn't have a value. Even though an empty string doesn't have any characters in it, it still has a value. Hence, an empty string ain't null.

One reason that nulls are important is that you often insert rows into a table by specifying a list of values for individual columns. If you don't specify a value for a column, the column is set to null.

Indexes

Because the rows in a table do not have a particular order, you may have to search through every record in the table to locate a specific row. Adding an index can reduce the time it takes to locate a particular record. While an index can be created independently, it is tightly coupled to a table and takes advantage of knowing exactly where in the table each row is located.

When you create an index, you specify one or more columns that form a *key*. As you insert rows into the table, the key value is stored in the index along with the location of the row. Then, you easily can get the location of all of the rows associated with the key value.

While a table can have as many indexes as you want, each index increases the time it takes to insert a row into the table. During the insert process, each index on the table must be updated to reflect the new row. The more indexes you have, the longer it takes to insert a row. The same problem occurs when you update a row; however, only the indexes with changed columns are updated.

It's primarily about speed: You always should have an index on the primary key of your table. Many database operations rely on the ability to retrieve a row from a table based on its primary key. Using an index on the primary key will make a big difference in performance.

One interesting aspect of an index is that while an index is closely associated with a table, you add or delete indexes on the fly without affecting a table. That means you can add or delete an index to see if it improves performance.

Clients and Servers

Relational databases are controlled by a piece of software known as the *database server*. The database server receives requests from a *database client* and processes the request. It then returns a status code, which indicates whether the request was processed successfully and returns any results the request may have generated (see Figure 2-2).

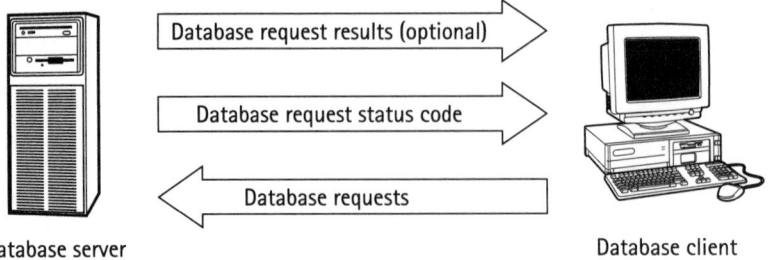

Figure 2-2: A database client communicates with a database server.

While the database server and client may reside on the same computer, this generally is not the case. For large databases, an entire computer system usually is dedicated to running the database server. For smaller databases, other functions, such as a file server or a print server, may reside on the same machine.

Database Servers

A database server is a very specialized computer program. Unlike many programs that interact with a user by displaying a window and responding to the keyboard, a database server doesn't interact with a user – at least not directly. The database server listens for requests from the database client and responds to them. It even can handle multiple requests simultaneously.

The database server is designed to manage multiple databases. In fact, the database server stores all of its own internal information in a *master database*, which contains a number of database tables that hold information about the other databases in the system.

Database Clients

A database client is simply a program that communicates with a database server. It can be nearly anything from a general-purpose program that accepts SQL statements from the user and passes them onto the database server for execution to custom-built applications that perform very specific functions (such as running a cash register at a sporting goods store).

Other Objects in a Database

Besides the fundamental objects in a database, such as tables and indexes, there are many other objects that work in conjunction with one other in the database.

Views

You can think of a *view* as a virtual table that is constructed from one or more other tables. Views are useful when you want to restrict the columns or rows that someone sees in the table. Views also can compile several tables into one big table that is easier for users to manipulate. The only drawback to views is that, depending on how they are constructed, you may not be able to update them.

If you have a view of a single table and it doesn't include all of the Not Null columns, any attempt to insert or update the data in this table may create an error because the unreferenced fields are assumed to have null values. If you try to insert a row into this view, the Not Null columns raise an error condition.

Constraints

A *constraint* is a rule associated with a column that determines which types of values can be stored in the column. The information in constraints is defined when you create your table. If you attempt to insert a value into a column that violates a constraint, an error is returned and the insert operation is canceled. Table 2-2 lists the five basic types of constraints.

TABLE **2-2 BASIC TYPES OF CONSTRAINTS**

Constraint Type	Description
Not Null	Ensures that there is a value in the column. This prevents situations in which a critical column doesn't have any information.
Check	Enables you to specify an equation that returns either TRUE or FALSE. A TRUE value means that the value is acceptable, while FALSE means that the value is unacceptable. Typically, this equation specifies a range of values that are acceptable — such as verifying that the column's value is greater than zero or between zero and ten.
Unique	If the value isn't null, it must not exist already in the table. This prevents duplicate values in the column.
Primary Key	Identifies the column or columns that make up the primary key. It ensures that the value or values are unique in the table and that they also are not null. A table can have only one primary key.
Foreign Key	Identifies a set of one or more columns that reference a value in another table. Typically, this is the primary key of another table. The value must exist in the second table before you can insert the row into the first table.

Stored Procedures

A *stored procedure* is a small program that runs in the database server. It contains a series of SQL statements that perform whatever task you wish. An advantage of using a stored procedure is that it minimizes the amount of traffic between the client and server. This means that fewer resources are required to run the stored procedure than to run the individual SQL statements on the client.

Triggers

A *trigger* is a special type of stored procedure that is executed automatically whenever a row is inserted, deleted, or updated in a table. If the trigger fails, the operation is canceled. Triggers are useful in verifying your data before you insert it into the table. You might consider using a trigger to update the information in another table.

Relationships Among Tables

Two tables are *related* if a row in one table has something in common with a row in another table. There are three basic types of relationships: one-to-one, one-to-many, and many-to-many.

One-to-One Relationships

In a *one-to-one relationship*, a specific row in one table matches exactly one row in the other table based on the value in one column. This isn't a very common relationship because it usually makes sense to combine the two tables into a single table. One situation where you might want to break a single table into two tables is when you want to store pictures in your database. By keeping the picture separate from the rest of the information, you can often improve overall performance. To create the second table, you would take the primary key from the first table and add the image column. Since the primary keys are identical, the two tables have a one-to-one relationship.

One-to-Many Relationships

In a *one-to-many relationship*, one row in one table can match zero or more rows in another table. Unlike the one-to-one relationship, the one-to-many is a very common relationship in databases. For example, consider a mail-order form. At the top of the form is a lot of information such as the person placing the order, the address it will be shipped to, and an order number. At the bottom of the form is a grid containing information about each item you plan to order. The top of the form fits naturally into one table, while the bottom part of the form fits into another. The top part of the form represents just one row in the first table, while the information on the bottom occupies one row for each item ordered. However, since each of the rows in the second table is related only to the one row; this is a one-to-many relationship.

Many-to-Many Relationships

In a *many-to-many relationship*, one row in the first table is related to many rows in the second, while one row in the second table is related to many rows in the first table. Consider the relationship between authors and books. One author may write many books, while one book might have several authors.

Many-to-many relationships can't be modeled directly in a relational database. So you have to break the many-to-many relationship into two one-to-many relationships by adding a *junction table*. A junction table contains one entry for a combination of book and author; for a given book, you can find all of the authors that wrote the book and for a given author, you can find all of the books they wrote.

Normalization

Normalization is a set of rules that describe a database design. From a theoretical viewpoint, the higher the normalization, the better the database design. However, this isn't always practical, nor is it often desirable. The most common types of normalization are listed below.

- ◆ **Unnormalized:** No rules are imposed on the database structure.

- ◆ **First normal form:** Each field must be atomic. Repeating groups and composite fields are not permitted.

- ◆ **Second normal form:** Every non-key field must depend on the entire primary key. A field must not depend on only part of a composite primary key. The database also must be in first normal form.

- ◆ **Third normal form:** A non-key field can't depend on another non-key field. The database also must be in second normal form.

And that ain't all folks: Relational database theory also describes a fourth normal form, a fifth normal form, and a Boyce/Codd normal form. However, trying to describe these forms without dipping into mathematics is very hard and really doesn't add much to this discussion. If you really want to learn more about normalization, check out *An Introduction to Database Systems 7th ed.* (Reading, MA: Addison-Wesley, 2000) by C.J. Date. This is the best source for the mathematics behind relational database theory.

The most important thing to understand is that, as you move up the normalization ladder, the database's large tables become broken down into an increased number of smaller tables. This is done in the name of reducing data duplication. So while database theory says this is good, practical experience has shown that the more normalized a database is, the slower it performs. This is obvious when you think about it because the database server has to access more tables to retrieve the data.

First Normal Form

You can't build an unnormalized relational database because there isn't a way to define repeating groups and composite fields when you create a table, so your relational database is always (at least) in first normal form. *Composite fields* (fields that are created from several independent pieces of information) and *repeating groups* (fields that can hold multiple values) aren't permitted in a table. Composite fields simply are broken into separate pieces that become columns in your table. A repeating group is organized into a one-to-many relationship. This involves creating a separate table using the primary key from the main table and one of the values from the repeating group.

Second Normal Form

A database in *second normal form* introduces the concept of *dependency*. One field is said to depend on another field if there is only one possible value for the field. For example, consider a table containing information about an employee. For a particular employee number, there is only one possible employee name. Hence, employee name depends on employee number.

To be considered in second normal form, the database must be in first normal form. In addition, each field in each table must depend on the primary key. Consider the case of a college course such as CMSC 101-0101. It consists of three parts: the department (CMSC), the course number (101), and the section number (0101). Assume that there is another course called CMSC 101-0201. While each course is assigned a unique instructor, the number of credits offered for the course only depends on the department and the course number. Thus, this information needs to be separated into two tables — one containing the department, the course number, and the number of credits and the other containing the department, the course number, the section number, and the name of the instructor.

Third Normal Form

In *third normal form*, every field in a table must depend only on the table's primary key. This differs slightly from the second normal form in which the fields must depend on the primary key, but also can have a dependency on another field or set of fields in the table. For example, assume that you have a customer table with name and address information, with a primary key of `Customer Number`. Obviously all of the columns depend on `Customer Number`. However, the `State` column also depends on `Zip Code`, meaning that this table is not in third normal form.

Reality

Normalization is an important database concept. It formalizes many of the ideas about how a relational database should be designed to minimize duplicate information. However, normalizing a database usually increases the number of tables in the database. This makes it harder to use because you now need to get information from multiple places. It also makes many applications slower because gathering data from multiple tables always takes more time than grabbing data from just one place. In practice, most production databases are created in second normal form.

TIP

Theory versus Reality: After spending many years studying database theory, while building complicated databases, I've decided that the theoreticians can't build a practical database no matter how hard they try. Don't feel you should build completely normalized databases. Many other factors come into play that force you to denormalize your databases in order to make them practical.

Database Design Tricks

As you design your database, there are some things you can do to help improve your design. These tricks will make your database easier to use, faster, or more efficient.

Smaller Is Better

Probably the most important design decision after choosing the level of normalization you need is to determine the data types you want to use for each field. In general, the less space you use for each field the better. This enables you to pack more information into less space. While disk drives are cheap, disk I/O isn't. The less space a row takes up, the more rows you can retrieve with a single I/O. This means that fewer I/Os are required to read the table, which makes many queries run faster.

Store Only What You Need

Along the lines of "smaller is better" is the concept of storing only what you need. The largest fields in your database usually hold character data. Simply using `Varchar` rather than `Char` for these fields saves a lot of space in most fields. For example, consider a field that holds someone's name. You have to reserve enough space for the largest name, while (in practice) most names are significantly shorter.

This trick doesn't work well when the information in each field is almost always the same size or the fields are very small. Using a `Varchar` field to hold a two-character state abbreviation wastes space because the extra information to hold the length of the field may be larger than the two characters in the field.

Codifying Your Data

One very common technique is to *codify your data*. To do this, take fields such as `Male` or `Female` and translate them into the values M & F or the numbers 1 and 2. The advantage of codifying your data is that it takes up less space in the database. While this isn't as important today as it was ten years ago, many databases use codified values.

Besides saving space, codifying fields makes it easier to change their values. For instance, consider a field called `department id`. This field is included in a lot of rows in the database. If you need to change the name of the department, all you have to do is to change the translation value rather than the codified value.

Summary

In this chapter, I talked about the major parts of a relational database including tables, columns, and rows. I also presented some common data types and discussed null values. I also covered how most database systems use client/server architecture and some supporting objects in a database such as constraints, stored procedures, and triggers. After finishing the basics, I ran quickly though more advanced concepts, such as how tables are related to one other and the basic concepts of normalization.

While a data warehouse is built using relational database technology, there are a lot of design differences between a data warehouse and a typical tactical application. I discuss these differences in Chapter 3, with detailed coverage of data warehousing and why you need it.

Chapter 3

Introducing Data Warehousing

IN THIS CHAPTER

- ◆ What is a data warehouse?

- ◆ Before you build your data warehouse

- ◆ Determining your information needs

- ◆ Designing your data warehouse

- ◆ Populating your data warehouse

- ◆ Using your data warehouse

- ◆ Management issues

- ◆ Security considerations

IN ORDER TO ANALYZE data using OLAP tools, you need to have the data stored in a place where you can access it conveniently. The most natural place to store this information is in a *data warehouse*. A data warehouse is not merely a set of data randomly collected from tactical applications, but is rather a collection of information stored in a uniform and consistent fashion.

There are many different ways to build a data warehouse. All of them require a detailed knowledge of your organization and its business practices, plus in-depth knowledge of the tactical applications that support its day-to-day operations. You need to translate this knowledge into the database structure and the set of computer tasks that populate the structure.

Once the data warehouse is designed, you must collect the information from the available data sources, validate it, and store it into the databases that make up the data warehouse. Then you need to worry about teaching users how to access the information and ensure that only authorized users have access to the information.

What Is a Data Warehouse?

A *data warehouse* is a collection of information stored in a database that supports an organization's decision-making processes. Information is gathered primarily from existing tactical applications. However, it also is reasonable to gather data from other sources, such as your competitors and data from information research firms. The collected data then is validated and restructured and stored in the data warehouse. This centralization enables decision-makers to go to one place to access data that spans their organization.

The data in a data warehouse typically is stored in a *relational database management system (RDMS)*. This means that you have all of the flexibility of a relational database and the ability to use the database tools with which you already are comfortable. However, a data warehouse is designed differently from a database for a tactical application because of the way you use it.

The biggest difference between a tactical application and a data warehouse is that the user can't update the information in a data warehouse. The user only can read the data. Updating the strategic information in the data warehouse using the data from tactical applications and other data sources is performed outside of the normal hours when the data warehouse is used by one or more batch jobs.

Another key difference between the data warehouse and a tactical application is that tactical users almost always use custom applications to access their data, while strategic users almost always use general-purpose tools to access their data. While this difference may not seem important, you need to take this information into consideration when designing your database for the data warehouse. If the design is too complex, it may be too difficult to use.

 See Chapter 1 for an explanation of tactical and strategic applications.

Before You Build Your Data Warehouse

Building a data warehouse is an iterative process (see Figure 3-1). You begin by analyzing your information needs. Rather than focussing on business processes, you need to focus on business concepts. It is much more important to understand how sales are made rather than how an invoice is printed. From this analysis, you determine the information you need from your tactical databases and external data sources.

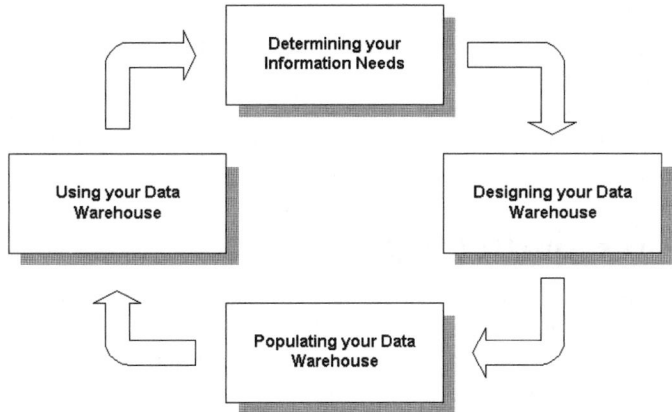

Figure 3-1: Designing a data warehouse is an iterative process.

 **Don't do it all at once:** When building your data warehouse, you should take it one step at a time. Don't be afraid to repeat the process many times. By taking small steps, you can get comfortable with the processes involved and learn from your mistakes. The biggest cause of failure in a data-warehousing project is being too aggressive and trying to tackle too much in the first step.

There are three basic approaches you can use when building a data warehouse:

◆ Start from the top-level concepts and work your way down to the implementation details.

◆ Begin at the bottom by looking at the information you have available and working our way up to the top to determine the kinds of questions you can to answer.

◆ Blend the first two approaches to create a third one that uses the best techniques of both.

All of these approaches have their advantages and their disadvantages. You should choose the approach that best suits your situation.

Building from the Top Down

A top-down approach begins by defining a set of rules to which all data stored in the data warehouse must adhere. This ensures that you can use data seamlessly, even though it may span multiple data sources. Also, some preprocessing may be performed to reduce the amount of resources required to answer a particular question.

This approach requires a strong commitment from everyone involved in the project, especially those in management. Building a useful data warehouse involves many different people at many different levels in your organization.

This is the approach favored by most data warehousing books because it results in the most structured data warehouse. This approach also leads to fewer problems and makes it easier to use when many people are involved.

Building from the Bottom Up

Building a data warehouse from the bottom up means that you look at the data you have available and add it to the data warehouse. The main advantage to this approach is that it is easy and quick to implement. It also has the ability to answer more types of unplanned questions.

However, the bottom-up approach has the drawback of being harder to use because the data elements may be inconsistent between data sources. Additionally, this approach may require more resources to answer a question because the data generally is stored in its raw form rather than being preprocessed.

This approach generally is best if you are trying to demonstrate the value of data warehousing. It works best when only a small number of data sources are involved and a small number of people use it.

Building from Both Directions

I believe the best way to build a data warehouse is to combine the best features of the top-down approach with those of the bottom-up approach. In the top-down approach, you spend a lot of time defining rules that to govern how the data warehouse is built. These rules are important, but they need not be complete before you start building your data warehouse. Likewise, in the bottom-up approach, you examine the databases from your existing tactical applications to determine which information you wish to include in your data warehouse.

When you combine these approaches, you pursue designing the rules while you actually build your data warehouse based on data that you already know about. This has the obvious benefit of implementing something quickly, giving you a quick return on your investment.

The key to making this approach work is to perform several iterations of the data warehouse design process in the time you normally would take for a single iteration of the top-down approach. By taking very small steps, you can receive feedback quickly and correct the flaws in your design. While you might avoid these flaws with a comprehensive top-down implementation, a top-down design takes more time to implement and there is no guarantee that you'll avoid the flaws anyway.

The biggest drawback to building your data warehouse from both directions at the same time is that your data warehouse remains in a state of change as you add new features and change existing features. I suggest that you limit the number of people who can access the data warehouse while it is in the early stages of development to those who can provide constructive feedback. The fewer people involved with the project, the faster each iteration of the project proceeds. Just be sure to include a sufficient number of people so that all aspects of the design are reviewed and tested; otherwise you may miss something important that can hurt you later.

Determining Your Information Needs

Once you choose your approach, you need to understand how your organization works. This means knowing its structure and how the various units interact. Then you need to determine the scope of the data warehouse. You do this by identifying the unit or units of your organization on which you want to focus.

With the top-down approach, you also must think about the information needed to help your organization make decisions. From this, you can determine a set of data elements that provide the information you need. At the same time, you also begin to determine dimensions and metrics that are used to describe the data in a consistent fashion. In order to analyze your data, it is very important that you use the same unit of measure in both, otherwise you cannot compare two different pieces of information.

You must determine the four following factors in order to discover your information needs:

- ◆ Your organization's structure
- ◆ Scope of the data warehouse
- ◆ Dimensions and metrics
- ◆ Data elements

The following sections discuss the steps involved in determining each of these factors.

Determine Your Organization's Structure

The first step in determining your information needs is to identify all of the units in your organization. This is important, even if all of the units initially do not participate in the data warehouse. This information helps you design the data warehouse's database so that it easily can be expanded to cover other segments of your organization as they are added to the data warehouse.

You should be concerned most about how the various units within your organization interact. In many cases, you may find that it is difficult to view the activities of one unit independently of another unit. In fact, in many organizations the various units are so interdependent that you can't separate them.

Determine the Scope of the Data Warehouse

The next step in designing a data warehouse is to determine the scope of the data that you are handling. This step identifies the organizational units that use the data and those that supply the data. Note that the units supplying the data may not be the units that necessarily use the results.

When focusing on an organizational unit, you need to consider how it interacts with the other units in the organization. If you can't functionally separate the unit from another unit, then you must handle both of them simultaneously when you design your data warehouse.

If possible, you should try to choose a unit whose data is both important to the organization and simple enough to model in the first iteration of your data warehouse. While this doesn't mean you should ignore the rest of your organization, it makes it easier to focus on your immediate task at hand – which is building a useful data warehouse.

Determine the Dimensions and Metrics

One of the hardest parts of designing a data warehouse is ensuring that all information in the data warehouse is stored in a consistent fashion. One of the key elements in ensuring consistency is defining what dimensions metrics to use. This information is used when analyzing your data.

The *dimensions* are used to choose the subset of information from the data warehouse that you want to analyze. The *metrics* represent the values that you wish to analyze. For example, when analyzing automobile sales, some typical dimensions are car model, size of the car, and the sales quarter. Meanwhile, the number of units sold and average sales price are the metrics you analyze.

Use the same metrics and dimensions. This is critical for the success of your data warehouse. If you don't believe me, walk through the laundry detergent aisle of a grocery store that features unit pricing. Try looking for the best deal. You may find some items marked with the price per pound, and others marked with the price per load. You can't tell anything about the two different products based on this information.

Determine the Data Elements

In the bottom-up approach, you review the data elements from your tactical databases and from external sources, and choose those that you think will be the most useful in the decision-making process. In a top-down approach, you identify the data elements from your tactical databases that can help you answer the types of questions you identify. In both cases, you end up with a list of data elements that are used in your data warehouse.

 **Too much is too much:** A popular strategy for implementing a data warehouse takes every scrap of information from your tactical databases and saves it in your data warehouse. This isn't a good idea. Two things result from this. First, you store a tremendous amount of data in your data warehouse. Second, not only do you spend more money on disk drives, but you also spend a lot more resources to search through all of this information to find specific information. By determining the information you really want, you save time and effort in the long run.

Recall that not all of the data elements need to come from internal tactical systems. You may need to look outside your organization for additional information. This type of information may come from many different places, such as from researching independent reporting groups or observing your competitors' actions. For instance, you may want to collect information about your competitors' sales from an independent reporting agency or you may want to scan your competitors' advertisements and Web sites to seek current pricing information.

Designing Your Data Warehouse

No matter which approach you choose, you need a list of data elements to include in the data warehouse. This information is used to design or redesign the databases that hold your data warehouse. Unlike a traditional relational database that is normalized, data warehouses tend to be much less normalized. This makes it easier to access the information you want by reducing the number of operations needed to find the information.

 **Updating read-only data:** Because the data in the data warehouse is updated only through a small set of tasks, you can optimize the data warehouse for read-only performance. Using denormalized tables and lots of indexes hurts the performance of a tactical database. However, these techniques improve the performance of your data warehouse. They reduce the time it takes to process a query; anything you can do to improve query performance improves the effectiveness of your data warehouse.

See Chapter 2 for more in-depth detail about normalization.

Star Schema

Many data warehouses are organized using a Star Schema. A *Star Schema* is a relational database design consisting of a central fact table, which holds the metrics, surrounded by a series of dimension tables (see Figure 3-2). Each of the dimension tables holds detailed information that helps you summarize the information in the fact table in different ways.

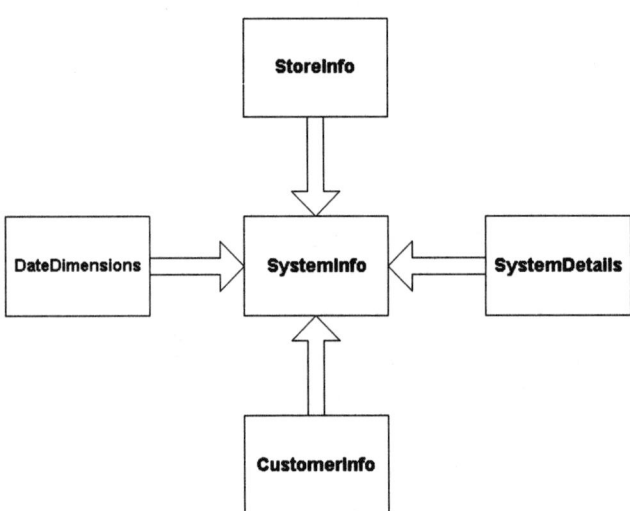

Figure 3-2: A Star Schema has a central fact table surrounded by a set of dimension tables.

Snowflake Schema

A *Snowflake Schema* (see Figure 3-3) is another way for you to organize your data warehouse. It retains the central fact table and dimension tables from the Star Schema, but other dimension tables can reference these dimension tables.

Summary Tables

While fact and dimension tables can solve most queries, sometimes the amount of data to be processed can result in long-running queries. To help address this situation, you may want to keep summary tables to help answer some of the more common questions.

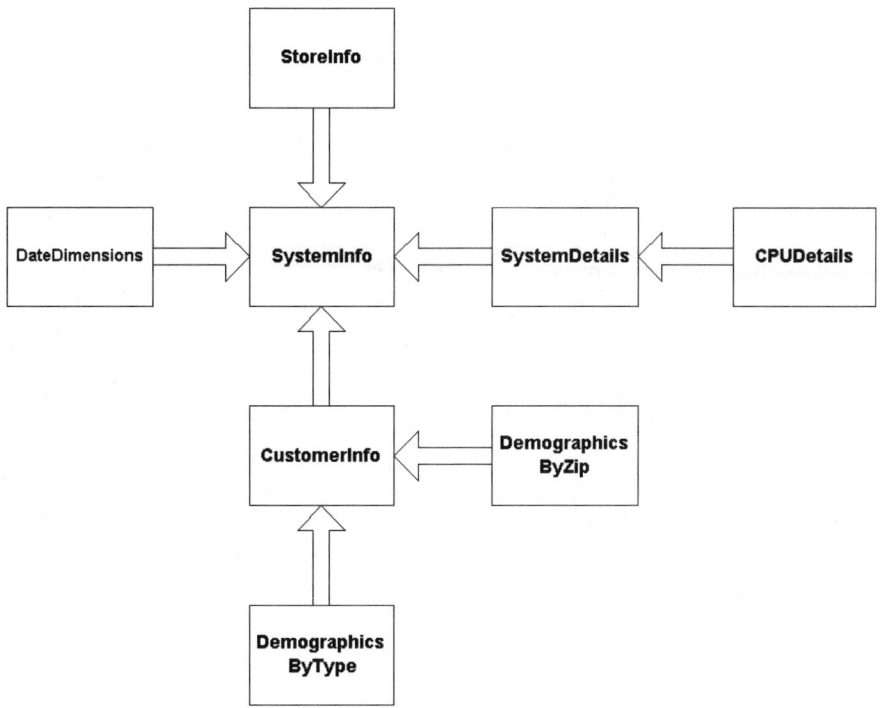

Figure 3-3: A Snowflake Schema is just a Star Schema in which the dimension tables have dimension tables.

 **Duplicate data:** When designing a tactical database, you should try not to create duplicate data. This not only means the simple case of the same information stored in more than one location, but also storing information that summarizes other information in the database. This can cause problems if the duplicate data values aren't kept in sync. However, duplicating data in a data warehouse is a totally different situation. It often is desirable to store summary data and the details to speed up processing in the database.

 **Consistent data:** While keeping summary data in your data warehouse is a good idea, the summarized data must be consistent with the rest of the data in your data warehouse. If it isn't, then people can arrive at two different answers running queries against the summary data and the detail data. The best way to ensure that this data is consistent is to update the detailed data and then re-create the summarized data from the newly updated detail data.

History Tables

In addition to summary tables, another useful way to store information in your data warehouse is by using history tables. *History tables* store information about how the dimension tables change over time. For example, as your company adds new products and changes prices on existing products, only the most current information is usually stored in the tactical database.

Your data warehouse may contain data that spans several years, so it is important to keep track of these changes over time. This is where history tables come in handy. You can use them to isolate a particular dimension in time and then analyze the metrics associated with that particular dimension.

Rules and Metadata

One of the most important parts of building a data warehouse is developing a set of rules that govern the data warehouse. Things such as consistent naming conventions, measurements, physical attributes, and semantics are critical because it is difficult use the data warehouse without these rules.

Having these rules isn't everything, however. Unless the end user (or the end user's tools) can access the information derived from the rules, it's useless. This information is known as *metadata* and is stored in a repository. The metadata contains all of the information an end user needs to understand each of the fields in the data warehouse.

Populating Your Data Warehouse

Populating the data warehouse is not merely a matter of getting values from your tactical database, but it also includes verifying and validating the information to ensure that it meets your expectations. You don't want incomplete or misleading data in your data warehouse because you make business decisions based on this data. Many tactical applications allow incomplete or incorrect data into the system, knowing that it will be corrected at a future time. Also, with any large application, errors can creep into the database as time passes. These errors can be caused by data entry mistakes or by errors in the application itself. This can cause serious problems in your data warehouse. If you don't take the time to check the information as it comes in, then the errors in the tactical databases can creep into your data warehouse as well.

Once the data warehouse is populated for the first time, you need to develop processes to ensure that the data is kept current. While there are a number of ways to update your data warehouse, all of them fall into two broad categories. You either erase all of the data from the data warehouse tables you plan to load and get a fresh copy of the data from your tactical databases, or you load only the data that has changed in the tactical database since the last time you updated your data warehouse.

Loading Everything

The easiest way to populate your data warehouse is to erase everything in it periodically and get a fresh copy from your tactical database. This means that you don't have to decide what data has changed since the last time you ran the update job. The biggest downside to this approach is that loading all of the data takes longer than loading only the changes.

Another downside to loading everything in a single task is that you may lose historical data in the data warehouse. For instance, your tactical application may keep only detailed information about a transaction for a period of several weeks or months. This may be insufficient for analyzing trends in your data.

Loading Changed Data

While loading only the changed data probably is more desirable than loading everything, it also is more difficult. You need to be able to identify which rows in your tactical database were updated since the last load. This can be difficult unless the tactical database was modified to track this information. The easiest way to track this information is to include the date and time that the row was modified or the transaction was executed.

 **New app:** If you build a new application, you may want to build in the facilities to help collect the data for a data warehouse. A little work in the beginning can save a lot of work down the road.

Other schemes may be available depending on the database system you choose to use. In SQL Server 7, you can include a time stamp column at the end of a row that SQL Server updates. It uniquely identifies when that row was updated last.

Using Your Data Warehouse

Once your data warehouse is populated, you can begin to use it. Chances are you will use a lot of different tools with your data warehouse because no single tool can do everything you require. The key to choosing your tools is to find those that give you the greatest flexibility. You need everything from simple query tools that execute SQL statements on the fly to complex tools that extract geographical information from your data warehouse.

As you use your data warehouse, you may find that it doesn't quite meet your needs. Perhaps you need to support a new business function or you have a question that you can't answer with the current information in the database. This means that you need to go back to the first step and repeat the design process.

Management Issues

Building a data warehouse is primarily an issue in project management. The larger the scope of the project, the more people that need to be involved. As more people get involved, their personal and organizational biases tend to slow down the implementation process. Anything that slows down the implementation process greatly hurts the entire project. The best way to implement a successful data warehouse is to take many small steps quickly rather than try to implement it as a single, monolithic step.

To prevent this from happening, you need to keep the number of people directly involved in the project as small as practical. Assigning a few good people to the project produces far better results than staffing it with everyone who has an interest in the project.

Security Considerations

A data warehouse may be the most important information asset your company owns. As such, you need to ensure that the information is well protected. You may not want everyone to access everything in the data warehouse.

See Chapter 10 for details on securing your data warehouse.

Summary

In this chapter, I answered the question "What is a data warehouse?" Then I introduced you to the various steps it takes to build a data warehouse. This includes determining your information needs, designing your data warehouse, and populating your data warehouse. I went into detail about the various design concepts such as dimensions and metrics and star and snowflake schemas. This information will prove useful later in this book, when it comes time to learn how to design and build a data warehouse.

While I didn't go into many details about the management issues related to building a data warehouse, you should be aware that this is where most data warehouse projects fall apart. The best way to deal with this issue is to limit the scope of your data warehouse project to minimize the number of people that could adversely impact your project. By starting with a small project and proving that a data warehouse can be implemented and offer value to your organization, you can gain support for expanding its scope.

In the next chapter, I'm going to introduce you to SQL Server 7 and the tools included with it. Then I'll discuss some of the other tools that are available from Microsoft that you can use with your data warehouse, including Excel 2000 and MapPoint 2000.

Chapter 4

Introducing Microsoft's OLAP Tools

IMPLEMENTING A DATA WAREHOUSE can be quite a challenge. It is very important to choose the right software packages so that they all work together. Microsoft has made this process a little easier by providing a complete set of tools to help you build your OLAP solution.

There are many benefits to having a single vendor solution to a problem. The key benefit is the ability for the collection of applications to work together in a consistent manner. Multivendor solutions may rely on competing standards for many areas of software operation. Even though vendors claim that they comply with a specific standard, you shouldn't assume that you could interchange components easily.

Besides the right software, you also need to ensure that you have the right hardware for the job. Microsoft's hardware recommendations usually are optimistic. While technically you can run the software on their recommended configuration, you probably don't want to use it. A data warehouse is a large investment – not only in development time and effort, but also in shared resources, such as computing power, massive storage, and network assets.

Microsoft OLE DB

The key to making the database tools work is the underlying technology called OLE DB (Object Linking and Embedding Database). OLE DB is a set of Component Object Module (COM) interfaces that enable you to access information from many data sources using the same general-purpose interface. Because OLE DB can access many different data sources, it is possible to build general-purpose tools, such as English Query and the Data Transformation Services.

All that is required to access a data source is a supported OLE DB driver. There are drivers for several different database systems (such as Microsoft SQL Server, Microsoft Jet, Oracle, plus a generic ODBC driver that enables you to access other databases, such as FoxPro, dBASE, and Paradox). In addition, there are OLE DB drivers for non-database files, such as text files, Excel workbooks, and Microsoft's new Active Directory Server. Third-party developers provide data source drivers for additional database systems.

Microsoft SQL Server 7

Microsoft SQL Server 7 is the latest generation of Microsoft's premiere database system. It's designed to run on a variety of systems — everything from a Windows 95–based system with a Pentium 166 processor and 32 megabytes of RAM up to a Windows NT Server Enterprise Edition system with eight processors and two gigabytes of RAM using the same code base. SQL Server 7 enables you to choose the solution that best suits your needs now and to know with confidence that whatever you develop today can be moved to a larger platform as your application grows.

SQL Server 7 comes in three editions:

◆ **Small Business Server Edition** is designed to run on the BackOffice Small Business Server system. It is limited in the number of connections and total size of the database it supports and doesn't support any of the OLAP features.

◆ **Standard Edition** runs on Windows NT and can service an unlimited number of users. There is also no limit on the total size of the database. Both the Small Business Server Edition and the Standard Edition can use up to two gigabytes of memory and four CPUs.

◆ **Enterprise Edition** of SQL Server requires the Windows NT Server Enterprise Edition. This edition of Window NT supports up to three gigabytes of main memory and up to 32 processors. It also has the ability to create user-defined partitions in an OLAP cube.

From any of these three editions, you can install a special desktop edition of SQL Server. This edition is targeted primarily for Windows 98 users and doesn't support parallel queries, read-ahead scans, or other advanced features.

Database Server

At the heart of SQL Server is the database server itself. It is a rock-solid offering that combines high performance and high reliability in a very stable package. The database server runs as an independent program in Windows. It listens to the network for requests from database clients, interprets these requests, and returns the results back to the database client. Besides the normal functions found in a database server, SQL Server also implements some special features, such as *database replication*, the SQL Server Agent, *full-text indexes,* and a real-time performance monitor. I discuss all of these features below. SQL Server operates as a service of the Windows NT operating system, which allows it to take advantage of NT's integrated security and performance-monitoring features.

The database server now supports databases in the terabyte range. This is important because data warehouse databases tend to be rather large. New query optimization techniques are available that can take advantage of multiple indexes. This is also important for data warehouses because the tables in a data warehouse generally have multiple indexes. Also, the ability to break a large query into smaller queries to permit an increased level of parallelism can make a big difference when you run large queries against the data warehouse database.

REPLICATION

Database *replication* is an important feature in SQL Server 7. It enables you to keep multiple copies of your databases synchronized so that they reflect the same information. Replication is based on the *publisher* and *subscriber* model. The publisher is a server that makes data available for replication. The subscriber receives data from a publisher. Because the publisher and subscriber do not need to be in constant contact with each other, it is practical to use replication to copy information automatically from the publisher to your data warehouse database.

You also can use replication to distribute your data warehouse across your organization. The data warehouse typically is updated on a regularly scheduled time period, so you can use replication to synchronize the data warehouse across multiple servers.

SQL SERVER AGENT

Another useful SQL Server 7 tool is the *SQL Server Agent.* This tool enables you to schedule tasks to run unattended, such as database backups and other periodic maintenance activities. It also can respond to events as they occur inside the database by notifying an operator, running a job, or passing the event to another server for handling. However, one use that is particularly important for data warehousing is its ability to run Data Transformation Services, programs that load data from a tactical computer to your data warehouse.

FULL-TEXT INDEXES

While a conventional index is created using the entire contents of the columns, a *full-text index* breaks the contents of the columns into individual words that are used in the index. You can search on any word or combination of words in the full-text index using the facilities in SQL Server. While a full-text index may not help all applications, it may prove useful if your database contains lots of words in one or more columns.

PERFORMANCE MONITOR

SQL Server 7 includes the tools that enable you to understand how your database is performing in real-time. You can look at the database as a whole to determine bottlenecks, or you can look at individual queries to tune them for better performance.

Enterprise Manager

The SQL Server *Enterprise Manager* is the primary tool that you use to create and manage your database. The Enterprise Manager provides a *graphical user interface (GUI)* for database management and administration. While there are other ways to perform many of the tasks that the Enterprise Manager can perform, most are more complicated. By using the Enterprise Manager, you can create databases, tables, and other database objects; edit information in tables; manage the database server by scheduling database backups and other maintenance functions; maintain database security; and monitor the database server's performance. You can perform all of these activities programmatically or by using a command line, but using the Enterprise Manager is more intuitive and easier to learn.

The Enterprise Manager is capable of managing multiple SQL Server 7 database servers from a single workstation. It includes a large number of wizards to help you administer your database server. You use the wizards to create processing schedules for database backups and other maintenance functions. You also can use them to create databases.

Another component of the Enterprise Manager is the ability to design databases graphically. You begin with a database diagram, and then add tables. You can view many or few of the details of the table while you are designing the database. You also can specify foreign key references by linking the primary key in one table to the appropriate columns in another table. Facilities are included to enable you to define triggers and other stored procedures.

Query Analyzer

The *Query Analyzer* is a tool that enables you to enter and execute SQL statements on the fly. This is primarily a quick and dirty tool for examining the information in your database. You need a good working knowledge of SQL before you can use it. However, once you have this knowledge, you can use the Query Analyzer to help you create and test SQL statements and study how SQL Server processes your query.

English Query

English Query is a useful tool that translates natural language questions into SQL statements and executes them. This lets people who don't know SQL retrieve information from your database. It enables you to ask questions such as, "How many Beach Boys albums were sold in the Midwest?" Before you can permit someone to use English Query, you must define information about your database to English Query. This allows English Query to translate the nouns and verbs into the database objects and relations used in your database.

The standalone program English Query is included with SQL Server 7. It accepts English language queries and executes them. You can also integrate English Query into your own application program or Web site by using English Query's COM interfaces.

Microsoft Decision Support Services

Although technically part of Microsoft SQL Server 7, the Microsoft Decision Support Services adds a number of facilities to support data warehousing and online analytical processing. It consists of an OLAP server, OLAP Manager, PivotTable Service, Data Transformation Services (DTS), and the Microsoft Repository.

OLAP Server

The *OLAP Server* provides support for pre-aggregation of frequently queried data. This allows a tool like Excel 2000 to handle larger volumes of data, while at the same time displaying the results quicker than if Excel had to perform the aggregations itself. OLAP Server also includes a way to create different views of the data, and the facilities to manage the data and its security. Both Multidimensional OLAP (MOLAP) and Relational OLAP (ROLAP), which are the two primary forms of an OLAP database, are supported, along with the ability to use both ROLAP and MOLAP in the same cube. This combination is known as Hybrid OLAP or HOLAP. Also important to the performance of the OLAP server is its ability to cache data to respond more quickly to requests for data.

OLAP Manager

OLAP Manager is a graphical tool for managing your OLAP resources. Because it uses the same interface as the SQL Server Enterprise Manager, it is easy to operate. The OLAP Manager provides a hierarchical structure in which you can view and manipulate your data warehouses, OLAP cubes, and the attributes of the cubes. You can use OLAP Manager to control the dimensions, measures, partitions, and roles for a cube.

PivotTable Service

The *PivotTable Service* is a specially designed query tool that sits between the OLAP Server and any OLAP client (such as Excel 2000) that supports the OLE DB OLAP Extensions. It doesn't provide any user interface on the server, but controls traffic between the server and the client OLAP cube. It passes along requests received from the OLAP client to the OLAP server for processing and returns the response from the server to the client.

The PivotTable Service provides caching on the client side of the system, enabling users to perform data analysis even when they are not connected to the server.

Data Transformation Services

The Data Transformation Services (DTS) exploits the OLE DB technology to interact with many different data sources to load the information into your data warehouse. Besides performing a straight copy of the data, it can perform complex data validation and translation as part of the copy process to make the data compatible with your data warehouse database.

A DTS wizard enables you to create and use packages, which contain scripting language from VBScript, to automate the data transfer process. You also can use DTS with the SQL Server Agent to perform DTS transfers at a predetermined time. DTS enables you to integrate data from SQL Server sources, as well as from many other data sources.

Microsoft Repository

The *Repository* is a place where information is kept about your database. This information is shared among multiple applications through a set of common ActiveX interfaces. It is used to store the database schema, information used by DTS to translate the data from your tactical database into your data warehouse, plus *metadata* that describes the data in your database in detail.

Microsoft Excel 2000

Microsoft Excel is the most widely used spreadsheet product in today's market. It has evolved from relatively simple numeric applications to complex data management and analysis. Excel 2000 easily can retrieve information from a SQL Server database and is designed to work with the PivotTable Service to manage much larger PivotTables than was possible in previous versions.

Also new in Excel 2000 is the ability to publish Worksheets, PivotTables, and PivotCharts as HTML documents on a Web server. You can publish them as static documents that can be viewed only using a Web browser, or you can create an interactive document that can be manipulated just as if the user was running Excel.

Worksheets

Excel has the ability to extract information directly from a database using the Microsoft Query tool. This information may be inserted directly into a worksheet where you can use Excel's tools to sort, group, and subtotal this information. Then Excel's full range of numerical functions, formatting tools, and charting features are available for working with the data.

PivotTables

A *PivotTable* is the name given in Excel 2000 for a multidimensional report that you can analyze interactively. You can choose to work with PivotTables entirely in Excel or to split the workload between Excel and the PivotTable Service. The advantage of using the PivotTable Service is that you can take advantage of the resources of the server to speed up your processing and to handle larger amounts of data.

PivotCharts

If you cross a regular Excel chart with a PivotTable, you get a *PivotChart*. You can manipulate the information displayed along each axis just like you can on a PivotTable. The only difference is that the information is presented graphically instead of using a crosstab report.

Microsoft MapPoint 2000

The newest member of the Microsoft Office family of products is Microsoft *MapPoint 2000*. MapPoint is designed to create maps based on your business data. You can use these maps to help identify new trends for your business. MapPoint can handle data organized by complete street address, zip code, metropolitan statistical area, county, state, or country.

In its simplest form, MapPoint is designed to plot locations on a map. However, because you can plot these locations from data stored in your database, you can see the geographic distribution of your information. MapPoint 2000 also includes demographic data for such variables as population, households, average household income, median age, and population broken into different age ranges. This data is available for 1980, 1990, the current year, and a five-year projection into the future. You can compare your data with the demographic information to help you identify trends in your data.

Microsoft Windows

Microsoft Windows comes in three basic flavors: Windows 98, Windows 2000 Professional, and Windows 2000 Server. All three of these operating systems can run SQL Server 7 and Excel 2000. Knowing the limitations of each of these systems enables you to choose the one that best fits your needs.

 **Not Serving 98:** While you can install SQL Server 7 on a Windows 98 computer system, you can't install any of the OLAP server-side tools. Also SQL Server 7 has other limitations, such as lack of support for NT Authentication, asynchronous I/O, and the performance monitor when run on a Windows 98 platform.

Windows 98

Windows 98 is Microsoft's consumer operating system. It uses fewer resources and is less expensive than Windows 2000 Professional. While it doesn't have all of the capabilities of Windows 2000, it offers a fine solution to running OLAP client-side tools, such as Excel 2000 and English Query, when connected to a Windows 2000 system running SQL Server 7.

Windows 2000 Professional

Windows 2000 Professional is targeted at professional users. Unlike Windows 98, it offers such advanced features as security and a more efficient file system. Windows 2000 also is designed to provide a very stable operating platform, allowing it to operate around the clock without needing to reboot the system. Windows 2000 Professional can run all of the SQL Server 7 components, including the OLAP Server. However, Microsoft has optimized Windows 2000 Professional so that it benefits the interactive user, not the background server. This may have a negative impact on performance if you run complex tasks interactively, while also making heavy use of the database server.

Windows 2000 Server

If you need to support a number of connections to your SQL Server 7, you should consider using Windows NT Server instead of NT Workstation. NT Server has the tools to monitor the server's performance and tune the system to provide the best possible performance. NT Server is optimized to run server applications like SQL Server 7.

Windows 2000 Server comes in three flavors: Windows 2000 Server, Windows 2000 Advanced Server and Windows 2000 Datacenter Server. The primary difference between the three editions is that the Advanced Server and Datacenter Server support additional processors and memory, plus offer support for clustering. These features are useful if you have a very large database with a large number of users, but for most people, Windows 2000 Server will be more than sufficient.

 **The best of both worlds:** It's possible to use Windows 2000 Server interactively. Anything that you can do with Windows 2000 Workstation, you can do with Windows 2000 Server. I frequently do this when testing new software. The biggest downside to using Windows 2000 Server in place of Windows 2000 Workstation is the extra cost of the software. However, having all of the tools on a single machine sometimes is worth the extra cost.

Other Microsoft Tools

Occasionally, you find yourself in a situation in which your current suite of tools can't handle the job. You might consider using Access 2000 or Visual Basic to deal with these problems.

Access

Sometimes you want to view information in your data warehouse directly, without the use of query tools like English Query and Query Analyzer. Access 2000 offers an easy-to-use database programming tool that comes complete with a number of wizards to help you build programs with which you can access your SQL Server 7 database.

There are two basic types of tools in Access 2000: *forms* and *reports*. Forms provide a way to view and edit information in your database. While you don't want to change the contents of the tables in your data warehouse, you may need to view and update other tables in your database from time to time. If you need to do this, Access 2000 is a good option. Access's ad hoc querying and reporting tools, supported by a collection of wizards, provide a flexible platform for interacting with your SQL Server 7 data.

Visual Basic and VBA

Visual Basic is Microsoft's premiere *Rapid Application Development (RAD)* tool. Occasionally, you will run into circumstances that you can't solve without creating a custom program. Sometimes you will encounter this because you need a very complex report, while other times you might need to do something special to move your data into the data warehouse.

Visual Basic (VB) is a key strategic programming tool for Microsoft. Its wide popularity has led to the growth of an enormous third-party community of add-ins for the Visual Basic environment. Using VB, you can create standalone applications for virtually any purpose in Windows, including database querying and reporting applications.

Visual Basic for Applications (VBA) is the application macro language that Microsoft includes as part of the major Office 2000 applications, including Excel and Access. VBA uses the same programming syntax as VB, while supporting the functionality of its host applications through a rich object model. You can use VBA to automate your client-side activities.

VBScript is yet another dialect of Visual Basic. It is the language you can use to automate components, such as Microsoft Internet Explorer and *Active Server Pages (ASP)*.

Hardware Considerations

Having all of the right software is meaningless if you don't have the right hardware to run it. Essentially, two different scenarios enable you to unlock OLAP. The first scenario uses a single PC system running Windows 2000 Professional, SQL Server 7, and Excel 2000. This approach enables you to build a complete OLAP solution on your desktop. The second approach uses a dedicated Windows 2000 Server running SQL Server 7 and one or more clients with Excel 2000.

All on One

You can use all of the principles I discuss in this book to perform data analysis on a single machine. You can run all of the tools I discuss in the book on a single PC with Windows 2000 Professional. Of course, it helps to have a big enough system to run all of the tools at the same time. While you might think in terms of getting the fastest processor available, you might want to think about getting the largest and fastest disk drives available. Also, the more main memory you have the better.

Workstation doesn't mean single user: Even though you run SQL Server 7 on Windows 2000 Professional, it doesn't mean that only you can access your database. As long as your computer runs on a network, others can access your databases if you choose to let them. While sharing your database with others slows down your computer, it enables you to service a small workgroup of users or help you test your prototype system.

Microsoft recommends a minimum of a Pentium 133 with 64 megabytes of RAM. Don't believe it. While the processor speed isn't that critical, available memory is important. In practical terms, you should have a minimum of 128 megabytes of memory. Beyond this minimum configuration, I recommend adding more memory (256 or 512 megabytes of memory makes a big difference when running larger databases and dealing with larger worksheets in Excel).

While CPU speed is not very critical, use a Pentium III processor if possible because it has a 100 or 133 MHz bus compared to the normal Celeron bus. The Pentium III processor helps SQL Server 7 move data around faster, which leads to better overall performance.

SQL Server 7 itself only needs about 250 megabytes of space in addition to whatever else the rest of the system requires. I suggest using two 4.5-gigabyte SCSI (Small Computer System Interface) drives for better performance. You should load the operating system and SQL Server 7 itself on the first drive and your database files on the second. This segregates the operating system's disk activity from that of the database server. Additional disk drives may be helpful because you can place your database files on them to split the database disk activity (and the page file on a disk of its own, if it is particularly large).

Choosing a SCSI disk drive over an IDE (Integrated Drive Electronics) drive gives you better performance over the long run. This doesn't mean that you can't run SQL Server 7 using IDE disk drives. In fact, this book was written using a system that doesn't have a SCSI disk drive – but I wasn't worried about performance. You will be because heavy database activity negatively impacts Excel's performance.

 **Proving the concept:** Sometimes, before you can get funding to implement a large data warehouse/online analytical processing project, it's necessary to prove the concept will work. Building a prototype data warehouse on a single machine enables you to show that your organization can benefit from this technology.

Dedicated Computers

While you can implement a small data warehouse on a single computer with all of the OLAP tools, you are better served by dedicating a single computer to running SQL Server 7. This means that you can optimize the server for just one thing – responding to database requests.

 **Dedicated to the pursuit of speed:** When designing client/server systems, you always should try to dedicate a computer system to a specific purpose. Sharing heavily used resources, such as disk drives and memory, always slows a computer down; a database server's speed depends mainly on the speed of its disk drives and the amount of main memory available.

The optimal solution to running SQL Server 7 on a dedicated computer is to run it under Windows 2000 Server and throw a lot of hardware at it. While I recommend a minimum of 128 megabytes of memory for a smaller Windows NT 2000 Professional configuration, you may want to start with a 256 to 512 megabytes of main memory. Windows NT Server can address up to two gigabytes of main memory, while Windows NT Server Enterprise Edition can support up to three gigabytes of main memory.

As with the Windows 2000 Professional, having SCSI disk drives is very important. The same basic principles discussed there also apply here. However, if you truly are building a server to handle a large number of people, you may want to consider using RAID (Redundant Array of Inexpensive Disks) technology to improve the reliability of your system.

 RAID technology automatically generates error-correcting information and spreads your data and the error-correcting information across multiple disk drives. Then if any of the disk drives fails, there is enough information on the rest of the disk drives to reconstruct the data that was stored on the disk drive that failed.

Earlier I suggested using the 100 or 133 MHz bus-based Pentium III processors because of the faster speed between main memory and the processor. That speed becomes even more important here. Also, you may want to consider using multiple processors. While SQL Server 7 is not very CPU bound, you can find a system that supports more than one processor. That way you can expand your system by adding another processor when you need it, rather than upgrading to a new system. It will improve performance should you choose to use Windows 2000 Server interactively. Cache size is also an important consideration.

Networking

Both a single computer solution and one involving dedicated computers require high-speed network connections. Building a data warehouse means that you will move large volumes of data on a regular basis. Because the data comes from other computers, all of the data has to come from other systems. This means that your network connection is as important as your system's disk drives. Unlike the disk drives in your system, your company probably dictates the type of network you use.

If you have a choice, you should use the fastest possible network connection that is available to you. While a 10 MHz Ethernet is fine for many users, consider using a faster connection if you expect to move a lot of data among your tactical applications. The 100 MHz Ethernet hardware is fairly common and can make a significant improvement in performance when you have to move a lot of data, and gigabyte Ethernet hardware is rapidly coming down in prices.

Summary

All of Microsoft's database tools revolve around a new standard called OLE DB. This technology is designed to provide a universal interface to all of the data you need. It is at the heart of SQL Server 7 and has been implemented on many other database and non-database applications.

SQL Server 7 is a comprehensive tool that comes with a set of features that make it a first-class enterprise database server. Included with the list of features is a complete set of OLAP server-side tools. Excel 2000 and its PivotTable facility can exploit the OLAP server tools. The Data Transformation Services and the Repository help you create a process to populate your data warehouse. This process can be run automatically by the SQL Server Agent on a schedule you define.

Excel 2000, English Query, and MapPoint 2000 are just three of the many tools that you can use to analyze the data in your SQL Server 7 database. Excel 2000 has the ability to analyze the multidimensional data from the OLAP server by using PivotTables. English Query enables non-technical people to submit questions to your database and get results. MapPoint 2000 has the advantage of turning geographical data into a visual format to help you identify trends in your business.

In terms of hardware, I presented the workstation approach that supports a handful of users and the dedicated server approach that can handle many users. These approaches really represent the two extreme ends of the possible hardware configurations. Your needs dictate the actual hardware configuration. It's possible that you can have a multipurpose server attached to your network, which has sufficient resources to handle the database and OLAP servers.

In the next chapter, I cover Microsoft's Data Warehousing Framework. This framework shows you how the tools work together as part of a comprehensive solution for data analysis.

Chapter 5

Introducing Microsoft's Data Warehousing Framework

IN THIS CHAPTER

- ◆ Goals of the Framework
- ◆ Components
- ◆ Data warehouse management
- ◆ Metadata and the Repository
- ◆ Operational data sources
- ◆ Data warehouse design
- ◆ Information Directory
- ◆ End-user tools

MICROSOFT DEVELOPED THE Data Warehousing Framework in order to provide its customers with some guidelines to help them build a data warehouse. It is a complete solution that is based on real products currently available for purchase.

I abstracted much of the material for this chapter from various white papers found on Microsoft's Web site at http://www.Microsoft.com/SQL. You can monitor this site for news on product updates and technical support for SQL Server 7.

Goals of the Framework

Designing a data warehouse is a complex task, which means that it can be time consuming and expensive to implement. To address this problem, Microsoft has worked with industry leaders to develop technology and products that are designed to simplify the implement process and reduce overall costs. Quoting from

Microsoft's Data Warehousing Strategy document, the Data Warehousing Framework is designed to provide:

◆ An open architecture that is integrated easily with, and extended by, third-party vendors

◆ Heterogeneous data import, export, validation, and cleansing services with optional data lineage

◆ Integrated metadata for warehouse design, data extraction/transformation, server management, and end-user analysis tools

◆ Core management services for scheduling, storage management, performance monitoring, alerts/events, and notification

Not all of the tools for your data warehouse need to come from Microsoft. Microsoft has made the standards that make up the framework open to the public. However, as you saw in Chapter 4, Microsoft has all of the tools you really need to build your data warehouse.

Components

The Microsoft Data Warehousing Framework is shown in Figure 5-1. It identifies eight major areas of importance:

◆ Data Warehouse Management

◆ Repository

◆ Operational Data Sources

◆ Data Transformation and Cleansing

◆ Data Warehouse

◆ Information Directory

◆ End-User Tools

◆ Data Warehouse Design

These components are connected in two directions. Metadata that describes the data warehouse flows from the data warehouse management to the data warehouse design. This is considered the *management process*.

Building the data warehouse begins with the actual data itself at the operational data source, or OLTP application. The data then flows through the data transformation and cleansing process and into the data warehouse database. Then, the end user uses the information in the Information Directory to locate the information from the data warehouse and to load it onto the end user's machine and analysis tools.

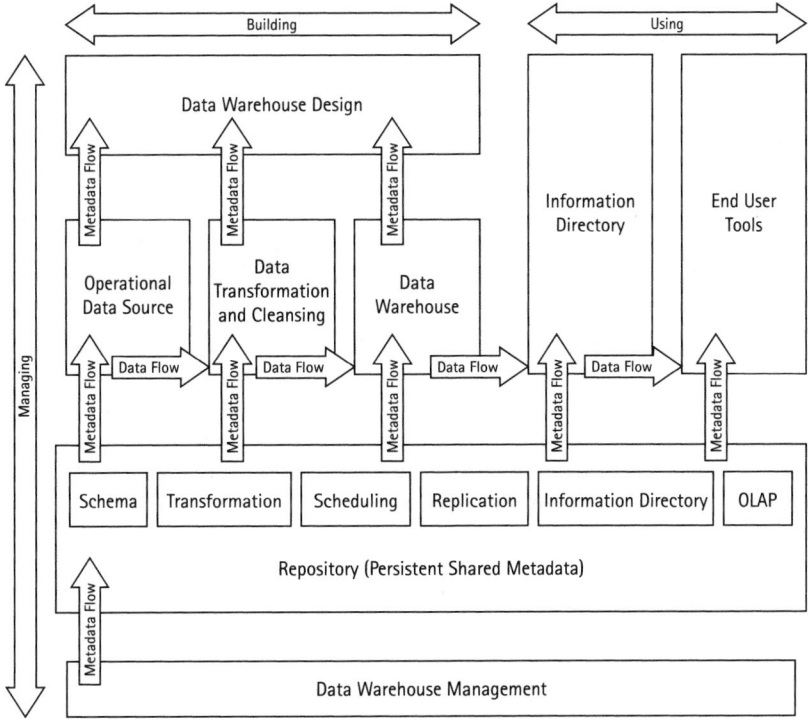

Figure 5-1: The components of the Data Warehousing Framework

Data Warehouse Management

Managing the data warehouse is a hidden cost that sometimes shows up only after the data warehouse is built. Specialized skills are required to design and maintain a modern relational database server. However, Microsoft has spent a lot of time and effort in attempting to minimize the amount of work required to manage a SQL Server 7 database server. The Enterprise Manager includes a large number of wizards to help you perform routine functions. These functions include:

◆ Creating databases, views, indexes, and stored procedures

◆ Backing up a database

◆ Restoring a database

◆ Performing routine database maintenance

◆ Managing database security

◆ Defining database replication publishers

In addition to the wizards, SQL Server 7 also provides the SQL Server Agent. This enables you to create schedules for running many routine tasks, such as running a database backup or performing routine database maintenance while the server is unattended. You can review the status of these tasks after execution by using the Enterprise Manager.

Metadata and the Repository

One of the most important concepts in a data warehouse is *metadata*. This information is critical to the success of a data warehouse. Unlike a tactical application in which only a handful of tools access a database, a lot of different tools access a data warehouse. This means that a central repository of information about the data in the database is very important. Each tool can access the Repository to find the information about the data elements in the data warehouse. Without this common information, you would have to define all of the data elements in the data warehouse according to each tool you use. The more tools you use, the more complex this process becomes.

Accessing the Repository is done through an *Open Information Model (OIM)*, which is a set of COM object definitions. Currently, OIMs for the database schema, data transformations, and OLAP are defined. OIMs are planned for the future for replication, task scheduling, semantic models, and an information directory combining business and technical metadata.

Database Schema

In order for a client tool to offer choices to the user, it needs to be able to determine information about the user's database design. This information is found in the database *schema*. The schema holds information about the database including tables, indexes, columns, stored procedures, triggers, and constraints.

Data Transformation

The Data Transformation and Cleansing section of the Repository contains information about how DTS transforms the data from the data source (the tactical database) to the data warehouse.

Task Scheduling

This information is used by the SQL Server Agent to run various tasks in the database, such as database backups, database maintenance, and database transformation jobs.

Replication

Replication is an important way to duplicate the contents of a database, which enables you to keep multiple data warehouses in sync with a central data warehouse or to move information from a tactical database into another database under control of the data warehouse. For instance, in a geographically distributed organization, you may want to keep a centralized data warehouse and multiple geographically distributed data warehouses. In this case, replication is used to keep all of the data warehouses synchronized.

Information Directory

The *Information Directory* contains references for the various objects that are located in the Repository such as stored procedures, predefined queries, forms, and reports that are available for use by the end user.

OLAP

The OLAP section of the Repository contains information about the OLAP cubes and other objects defined in the data warehouse.

Operational Data Sources

What Microsoft refers to as an Operational Data Source, I call operational databases. But no matter what term you use, it represents the source of the data for your data warehouse. Any OLE DB–compatible database can be a source of data for your data warehouse under the Microsoft framework. Thus, you can use a database from Oracle, Sybase, or IBM, as well as any OLE DB–compliant vendor as a data source.

Data Transformation and Cleansing

The process that occurs between the operational data source and the data warehouse is the data transformation and cleansing process. It's important to understand that you can't just copy the data from an operational data source to the data warehouse. The obvious reason is that because the data structures are different, simply copying one row from the tactical database into the data warehouse doesn't work.

However, the real reason is that the data may not be complete. It is very important to make sure that the data you load into the warehouse is correct. Simply because a record exists in one tactical database table doesn't mean that the rest of the records related to it exist. It's common to map multiple tactical database records into a single data warehouse record, so any missing records result in a single incomplete record in your data warehouse.

The approach used by Microsoft in their Data Warehousing Framework is to employ a new tool called Data Transformation Services (DTS). This tool is designed to:

♦ provide better importing, exporting, and transformation of data using OLE DB to communicate with different data sources

♦ provide an extensible architecture

♦ share rich metadata about the data sources, data destinations, and transformations through integration with the Repository

The key to DTS is the OLE DB interface. It enables you to communicate with many different types of databases and even non-database files, such as Excel workbooks and ASCII text files that are treated as data sources.

The DTS Architecture

The DTS architecture is straightforward (see Figure 5-2). The *DTS data pump* is at the heart of the process. It reads data from the data source, transforms it according to the information in the Repository, and writes it to the destination.

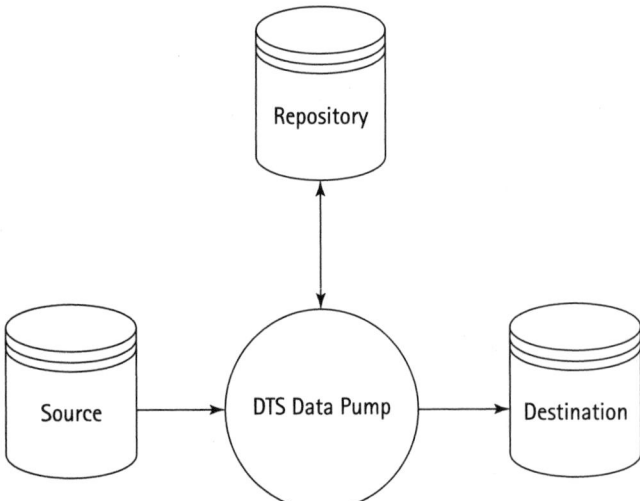

Figure 5-2: The DTS architecture

In the simplest case, DTS can copy one table into another. You can choose which fields in the source records are mapped onto the fields in the destination records.

However, sometimes a simple transformation isn't sufficient. DTS accommodates this requirement by integrating into the data pump the ability to use an ActiveX scripting engine. This means you can write VB Script or JavaScript programs to help you verify and transform your data. These programs also are stored inside the Repository with the rest of the DTS package. For example, you may want to change the coding scheme for incoming data. Because individual source applications can use different product codes, write a scripted application that converts the codes during the data transfer process.

The DTS Package

Each transformation process using DTS is known as a *package*. A DTS package contains a series of one or more tasks, each of which perform a useful function. Each task can be either a simple transformation, a transformation that uses a VBScript program, or a call to an external program.

You can sequence tasks in a DTS package so that they run in a particular order. You also can define a finish-start relationship in which one or more tasks must finish successfully before the next task starts. You even can define tasks that run at the same time.

Once you have built a package, you can create an execution schedule. The SQL Server Agent knows the schedules and automatically starts the package at the appropriate time.

Data Warehouse

This is the physical database where the information is stored. In Microsoft's framework, this is a SQL Server 7database probably running on a dedicated computer system somewhere on your local area network.

Information Directory

Just because you have all your data in one location doesn't mean that you are able to find the information you are looking for. An Information Directory contains the tools and utilities that are used to extract information from the data warehouse such as stored procedures, predefined queries, forms, and reports. Having these tool available make it much easier for the end user to use and get the information they require.

End-User Tools

Having the data in the data warehouse isn't sufficient unless the users have easy ways to access the information. While it is always possible to write traditional database programs to access the data, these programs often are limited in their capabilities and are difficult to adapt to changing needs. Providing the end users with general-purpose tools enables them to answer their own questions.

Excel 2000

Microsoft Excel is probably the most common tool used for data analysis today. There are two main ways to use Excel 2000 with your data warehouse: with worksheets and PivotTables. You easily can load data into an Excel worksheet. From there, you can use the regular features in Excel to analyze your data. While you can load data from the database into a PivotTable and work with it locally, you also can connect a PivotTable to the OLAP server and access the data directly. This makes it very easy to work with large PivotTables and enables you to split the work across multiple computers.

English Query

English Query enables end users to ask for information from the data warehouse by asking questions in English. While this tool can be difficult to set up initially, the benefit of reaching users who aren't trained in SQL easily outweighs the difficulties.

Query Analyzer

Query Analyzer accepts SQL statements from a user and executes them on the fly. In addition to executing the statements, Query Analyzer also can perform a detailed analysis of a query. It can explain how the query is executed, which can help you to rewrite the query so that it takes fewer resources.

Data Warehouse Design

This aspect of the framework is an ongoing task. As new operational data sources are added and existing ones are changed, this implies that changes will be needed in the design of the data warehouse. Also, depending on how the data warehouse is used by the end users, other changes will need to be made to the physical design. These changes will reflect ways to improve performance and make the data warehouse easier to use.

Summary

In this chapter, I gave you a brief overview of the Microsoft Data Warehousing Framework. The Microsoft Data Warehousing Framework is designed to give you a high-level design with which you can build your data warehouse. I identified the major components that a data warehouse should have and which tools from Microsoft can help you build that component.

While you need not build your data warehouse around Microsoft's ideas, you'll get the largest return on your investment by using these tools. If you already own SQL Server 7 and Office 2000, you already have these tools – it's merely a matter of using them to create your data warehouse.

In the next section of the book, I discuss how to build a data warehouse by determining the data you need to keep, designing the physical databases, building the databases, and then populating the data. This makes the data available for analysis by using standard database query tools, and by accessing the OLAP Service and Excel 2000's PivotTables.

Part II

Creating a Data Warehouse

Chapter 6

Identifying the Data Requirements

IN THIS CHAPTER

- ◆ Understanding your needs
- ◆ Analyzing tactical applications
- ◆ Building the Data Repository

DESIGNING A DATA WAREHOUSE is just like designing any other database application — you must understand the types of information you need from the data warehouse before you can determine which data elements you require. Once you do this, you can work backwards to determine the data elements that you can use to create this information. Finally, from these data elements, you can analyze the different sources you have available to determine where and how to collect the raw data.

Understanding Your Needs

When designing any application system, the first thing you want to do is identify the problem you are trying to solve. A data warehouse is no exception. The difference between a tactical application and a data warehouse is that a tactical application addresses a more concrete problem such as, "I need to process orders placed over the Internet," while a data warehouse addresses problems such as, "I need to know more information about where my customers are located."

Grasping the Scope of the Project

The first step to understanding your needs is deciding where you want to focus your attention. While it is possible to design a data warehouse for your entire organization as a single project, you are better off picking one aspect of your organization and focusing your attention there.

This doesn't mean that you can't build an organization-wide data warehouse as a single project. As the scope of the project increases, so do the number of people who want to get involved. The more people who are involved, the more complex the project becomes. Eventually, the project can become so unwieldy that it collapses under its own weight. While this isn't guaranteed to happen, it is probably the number one cause of failure for data warehousing projects.

A small data project, on the other hand, involves fewer people with fewer needs. This translates into a higher probability of success. Once you build a successful data warehouse, you can expand and change it to meet new requirements over time.

Identifying Questions

The best way to understand your needs is to identify typical questions that you want your data warehouse to answer. These questions can give you insight into the types of information you need to make available in your data warehouse, plus it gives you a way to measure the success of your data warehouse.

I like to collect these questions during a brainstorming session. The goal is to identify as many questions as possible that the user wants to ask. Do not criticize any of the questions and do not edit them during the session. Some of the best questions often are the most off-the-wall ones asked.

After the session, someone with computer skills should organize the questions into categories and then attempt to eliminate duplicate questions. Then distribute this list to each of the participants for review and comments. Additional questions may be included. Once this list is complete, you can begin looking at various data sources to try to find the information necessary to answer these questions.

Pinpointing Sources of Data

The data for a data warehouse generally comes from the tactical applications already used by your organization. Thus, you don't have to worry about how to collect the various data elements you need to answer your questions – simply get them from an existing database.

Data also can come from outside your organization. There are a number of places where you can obtain demographic information, which you may want to combine with data you create internally. This type of information can help determine where your organization is doing well and where it needs some additional work. It also can help you identify new opportunities and places for expansion.

You also can obtain information about your competitors via their Web sites. For retailers selling merchandise over the Internet, you can extract price and discount information from their Web sites and use it to compare against your own information.

The JustPC Data Warehouse

Throughout this book, I use a fictitious company known as JustPC as an example of how to build an operational data warehouse and how to use Microsoft's tools to analyze the data in the data warehouse. JustPC is a small ma-and-pa computer store based out of Beltsville, Maryland. It sells its own line of computer systems, assembled from components purchased from parts wholesalers. JustPC sells computers primarily to neighboring businesses and consumers, although it occasionally sells computers to out-of-state customers.

JustPC's goal in implementing a data warehouse is to better understand the purchasing habits of its customers. Therefore, the scope of the data warehouse is limited to information about JustPC customers and the items they purchase. Other functions in the tactical application system – such as payroll, personnel information, and accounting information – are not included in the initial data warehouse, although this information may be included in a future implementation.

Analyzing Tactical Applications

When analyzing a tactical application, you need to keep a number of things in mind. The design of a tactical database is much different from that of a data warehouse. Also, the data stored in a tactical database must meet different quality standards than those needed for a data warehouse.

Tactical Database Design

A *tactical database* is designed to support a large number of people reading and updating small numbers of records at a time, compared with a data warehouse that has a small number of people reading a large number of records at a time. Tactical databases keep only active information online. In a tactical database, information on transactions that are completed for a relatively short amount of time are deleted routinely or archived so that only the active data is stored in the database. Conversely, a data warehouse often needs historical data that spans several years to enable its users to identify historical trends.

In order to improve performance, tactical databases often store data in multiple tables to minimize redundant data. This allows values in the tables to be updated more easily. In a data warehouse in which updates are not a common practice, data is stored in fewer tables even though the same data may be stored multiple times. This helps performance since it typically is faster to search one large table than multiple smaller tables.

Quality of Data

Tactical databases also need a different level of quality than a data warehouse. A tactical database deals in transactions affecting only a small number of records at a time, so it is quite possible that you can have some incomplete or inaccurate records in the database and not realize it. In many cases, these records can sit in the database for months or even years before you encounter them. However, once an error is found, it can be corrected easily.

If the data is moved into the data warehouse in the meantime, it is quite likely to be encountered anytime someone runs a query. Depending on the type of error, at best your query returns inaccurate results. The worst case is that your query does not run at all.

Here are the three main types of errors found in a database:

Incomplete Data Errors

Only part of the data is present in the database when you encounter an incomplete data error. This generally happens if an application program doesn't work properly. The user may begin a transaction to update the database and later change his or her mind and abort the transaction. This can leave some information in the database, but not other information. It is possible that this type of error may not affect any of the tactical application programs, so the people responsible for the application may not even consider it an error. For example, a customer may enter his or her name and address information into a database when placing an order and then choose to cancel the order. The name and address information may remain, while the order information is deleted. Therefore, when you build your data warehouse, you can't assume that every customer in the database actually placed an order.

Inaccurate Data Errors

All of the data is present in the database, but some of the values are wrong when you encounter an inaccurate data error. This can happen if a customer enters a wrong address or telephone number or in any number of other ways. This type of error is hard to find and correct. Generally, this problem is found and corrected only when the end user spots that the data is wrong and corrects it. Consider what happens if someone enters an invalid zip code. You don't know for certain if he or she entered a bad zip code or entered the wrong name for the city. However, you get different results by assuming that both values are correct and then processing data by zip code and by city name.

Inconsistent Data Errors

All of the data is present in the database, but for various reasons some records may not be consistent with other records when you encounter an inconsistent data error. This may happen for various reasons. For example, when dealing with data collected from several time zones, an application may record local time for various values rather than a standardized value. This also can happen because items are measured in different units, such as meters and feet or liters and gallons.

To prevent this problem, you must verify and correct any errors in the data from the tactical database before you load it into the data warehouse.

FIXING THE ERRORS

For incomplete data, you have to determine if the data is incomplete and then discard it. Another option is to design your data warehouse so that incomplete data does not pose a problem. For inaccurate data, you may want to discard it also, assuming that you can detect the inaccuracy. Most likely, however, you can assume that the data is correct until you run into a problem with it and then decide to delete it. For inconsistent data, all you may need to do is translate the values into a consistent set of values – although this may be harder to accomplish than you may expect.

The JustPC Tactical Database

The JustPC tactical database (see Figure 6-1) is a fairly complex database that covers all aspects of business including order tracking, customer information, payroll, accounts payable, and accounts receivable. Altogether, the database supports 17 different tables. A list, with a brief description, of these tables follows.

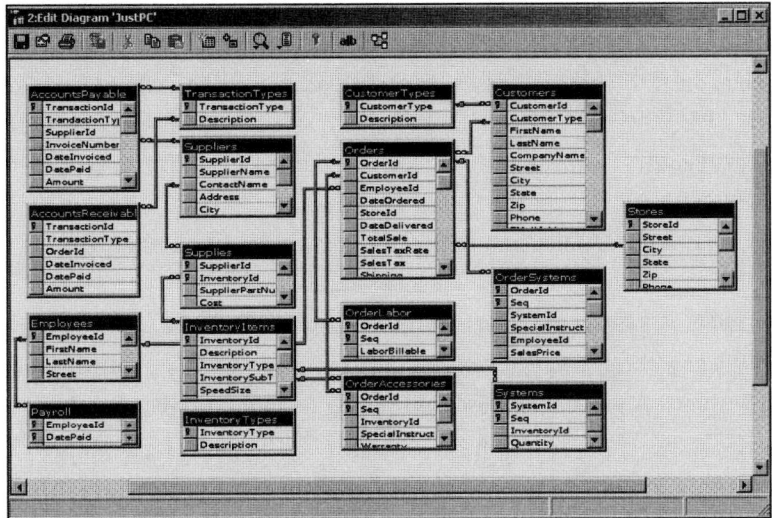

Figure 6-1: Viewing the JustPC database

 **See JustPC-DB.** This database is available on the CD-ROM for you to use. Follow the directions in the Appendix to restore the database to your SQL Server system.

 **What you need.** Only the data relevant for this book is included in the JustPC-DB database. Therefore, some of the tables that aren't important to the data warehouses are empty. These tables include: **AccountsPayable, AccountsReceivable, Payroll, Suppliers, Supplies** and **TransactionTypes**.

◆ **AccountsPayable:** A table containing information about invoices that JustPC must pay

◆ **AccountsReceivable:** A table containing information about invoices that JustPC has sent to its customers

◆ **Customers:** A table containing information about the customers of JustPC, including the customer's name, address, and e-mail address

◆ **CustomerTypes:** A table that translates the codified field CustomerType into its descriptive text

◆ **Employees:** A table containing information about the employees at JustPC

◆ **InventoryItems:** A table containing information about the parts available for sale at JustPC. This includes both parts that are sold directly and parts that are incorporated into a computer.

◆ **InventoryTypes:** A table that translates the codified field InventoryType into its descriptive text

◆ **OrderAccessories:** A table containing information about an ordered accessory

◆ **OrderLabor:** A table containing information about the labor costs associated with an order

◆ **OrderSystems:** A table containing information about an ordered system

◆ **OrderTypes:** A table that translates the codified field OrderType into its descriptive text

◆ **Payroll:** A table containing information about the money paid to an employee

◆ **Stores:** A table containing information about one of the JustPC stores

◆ **Suppliers:** A table containing information about the vendors that supply parts to JustPC

◆ **Supplies:** A table containing information about the parts purchased from various suppliers

◆ **Systems:** A table containing information about the systems sold by JustPC

◆ **TransactionTypes:** A table that translates the codified field TransactionType into its descriptive text

Using the Data Repository

Once you understand how the tactical application works, you need to compile a list of the tables and data elements that are available for you to use. SQL Server 7 includes a facility called the *data repository*, which enables you to track information about the tables and columns in your database. Using the data repository, it is possible to import the list of tables and columns from a database and use the information to begin documenting the database design. This information also is referred to as *metadata*.

Importing Database Information into the Repository

To import a database into the repository, you need to use a tool called SQL Server Enterprise Manager. This is a very powerful tool used frequently in creating and maintaining SQL Server databases.

STARTING ENTERPRISE MANAGER

To run this tool, click the Window Start button and choose Start → Programs → Microsoft SQL Server 7.0 → Enterprise Manager. After a few moments, a display similar to the one shown in Figure 6-2 appears on your screen. The Enterprise Manager display has two main panes – the left pane contains a series of icons arranged in a tree view, while the right pane contains data related to the selected icon in the tree view.

In the tree view pane, expand the icon tree until you locate the database server where your database is located. Then, expand the database server icon so that your display looks like the one shown in Figure 6-3. Most of the tasks you perform using Enterprise Manager are launched from this view.

TO IMPORT INFORMATION INTO THE REPOSITORY

Expand the Data Transformation folder to show the list of icons beneath it and click the Metadata icon. This displays the Repository metadata screen shown in Figure 6-4. This screen lists each of the databases that are defined to the Repository.

 **About metadata.** The Repository metadata is global for the entire database server. Information is kept separate by database name.

Figure 6-2: Starting Enterprise Manager

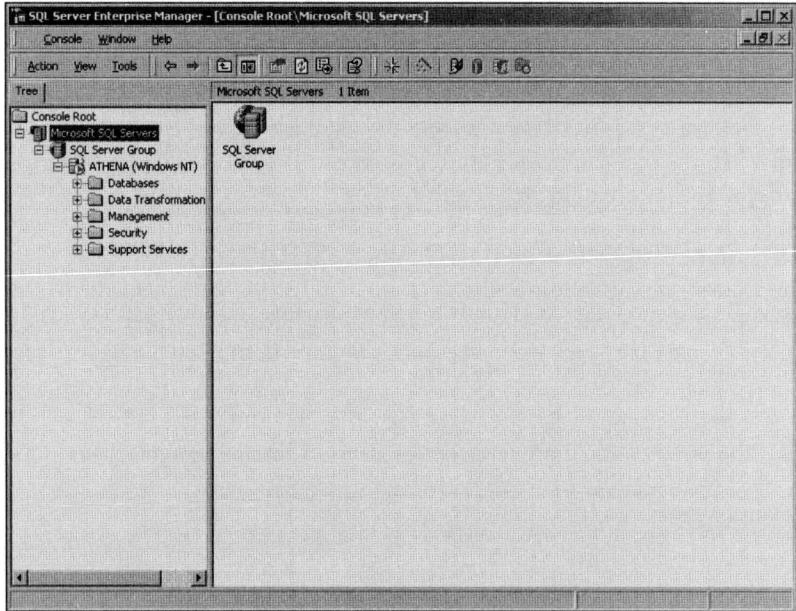

Figure 6-3: Looking at the icons available for your database server

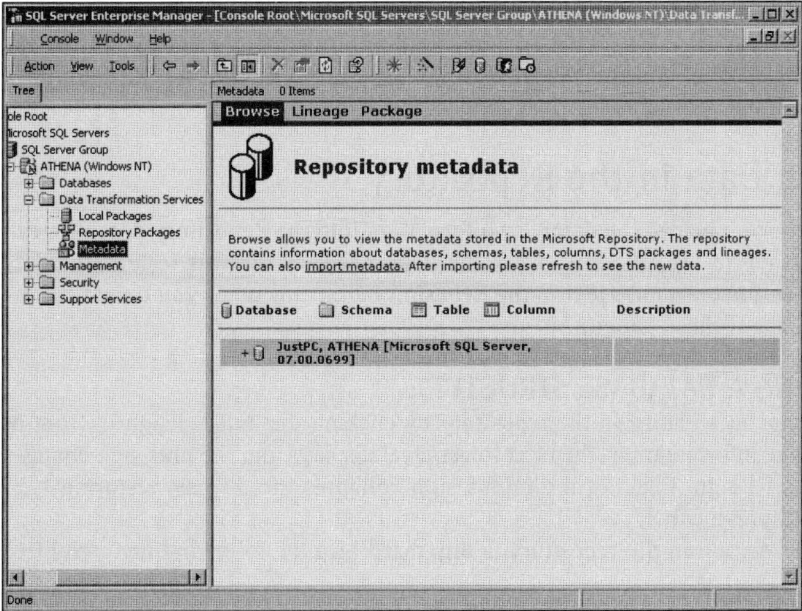

Figure 6-4: Viewing the Repository metadata screen

You can import the information from a particular database by right-clicking the Metadata icon in the tree view and selecting Import metadata from the popup menu, or by clicking the Import metadata hyperlink in the Repository metadata display. In either case, you are prompted to supply the information needed to connect to the database you wish to import. Specify the name of the database server, insert valid authentication information to access the database server and the name of the database you wish to import, and press the OK button (see Figure 6-5).

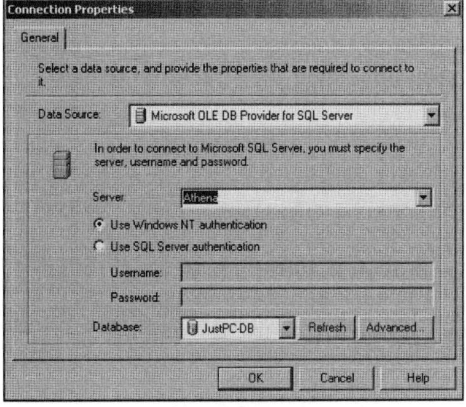

Figure 6-5: Specifying connection information for the database you wish to import

After pressing OK, be prepared to wait for a while as the database server gathers the information from the database and loads it into the repository. When the process is complete, you are returned to the Repository metadata window with a new listing for the database you just added.

Editing Data in the Repository

Just because you loaded the database information into the Repository doesn't mean that it is ready to use. The only work the import facility did was to load the data structures inside the database into the Repository. It is now up to you to add the information about those structures.

SELECTING A DATABASE STRUCTURE

You can expand an entry in the repository by clicking the plus (+) sign in front of the icon. The information at the next lower level displays and the plus sign changes to a minus (-) sign. Clicking the minus sign collapses the display, restoring it to what it was previously.

The information in the repository is organized into the following hierarchy (see Figure 6-6):

◆ **Database:** The highest level item in the Repository (ex: JustPC-DB)

◆ **UserID:** The UserID that created tables within the database. Typically, this UserID is dbo.

◆ **Table Name:** The name of a table within the database (ex: Customers)

◆ **Column Name:** The name of a column within a table (ex: FirstName)

◆ **Column Structure:** The physical attributes of a column

EDITING THE STRUCTURE'S INFORMATION

By clicking the name of a database structure such as database, UserID, table name, or column name, you see a display similar to the one shown in Figure 6-7. This display enables you to edit two pieces of information about the structure: the description and comments.

You can enter a short description for an item that is displayed beside it when it is listed. This area is extremely useful if the original name of the data element or table is somewhat cryptic, such as FN instead of FirstName or Cust instead of Customers.

You should use the comments section to provide a more complete description of the field. This may include information such as how and where the data is collected for this field and any special considerations about how to use the item.

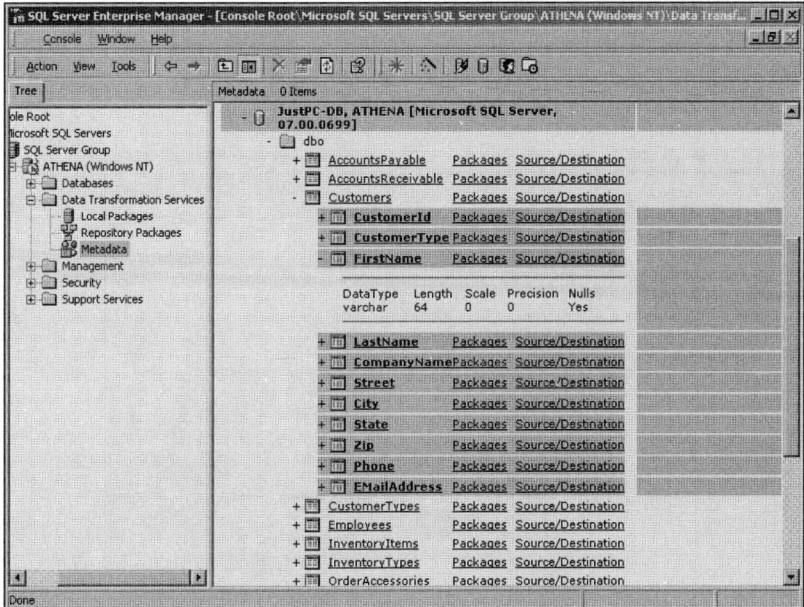

Figure 6-6: Viewing the database's structure

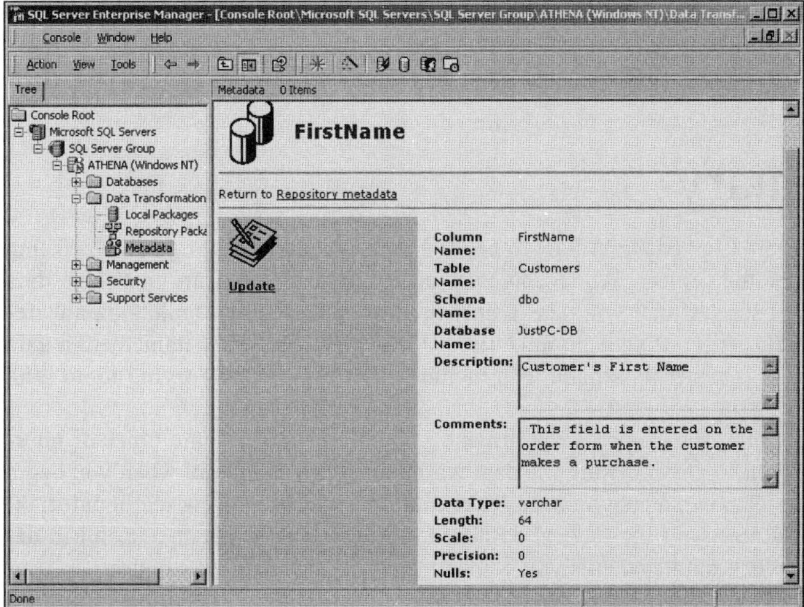

Figure 6-7: Adding a description and comments for an item in the repository

When you have finished entering this information, click the Update hyperlink and then click the Return to Repository metadata hyperlink to return to the list of metadata items in the Repository (see Figure 6-8).

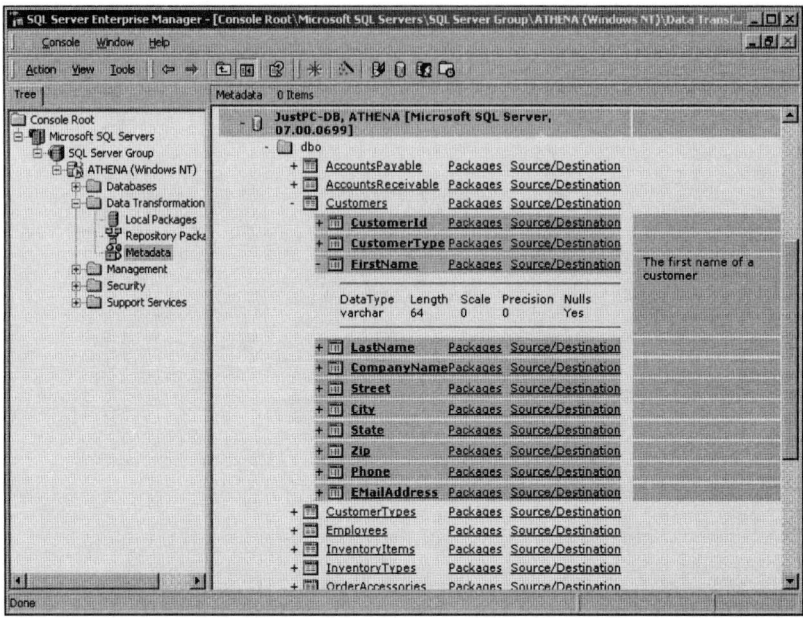

Figure 6-8: Viewing the update information in the Repository

Summary

In this chapter, I talked about how to begin a data-warehousing project by defining the scope of the project. While you may be tempted to build an enterprise data warehouse, I suggest that you take a more modest approach and build a data warehouse for one aspect of your organization. Once you successfully implement a data warehouse, it is easier to expand it to include other aspects than trying to do it all at once.

After defining the scope of the project, you should identify the types of questions you want to answer using the data warehouse. This is helpful when you begin to select the data elements you need for the data warehouse. Likewise, the information you collect about the tactical database in the Repository is also useful in determining which data elements you want to keep in your data warehouse.

In the next chapter, I cover how to take the information gathered here and turn it into a database design. I also outline some of the basic design techniques and discuss why your data warehouse should look different from your tactical database.

Chapter 7

Designing the Data Warehouse

IN THIS CHAPTER

- ◆ Entity/Relationship modeling
- ◆ Identifying data elements
- ◆ Designing your data warehouse
- ◆ Building your data warehouse

IN THIS CHAPTER, I show you how to take the scope and other information about your data warehousing needs and translate them into a database design. As I design the database, I explain why the design for the data warehouse is different from a tactical database.

Entity/Relationship Modeling

Entity/Relationship (E/R) modeling is my favorite way to design a database. It is based on the concept of identifying relationships among multiple entities. It enables you to think about your data logically, without necessarily being restricted by the structures you can define in a database.

Key Terminology

An *entity* is a thing that can be identified uniquely, such as a computer, a customer, an order, and so on. Associated with the entity is a set of *attributes,* which help to describe the entity. A customer has a name and an address. A computer system has attributes such as a CPU, memory, and a monitor.

Relationships are formed between two entities. For example, a customer places an order for a computer system. Not every entity is related to every other entity in a database – at least directly. Sometimes two entities may be related though a third entity. Other times an entity may stand alone.

If two entities are related, then you can characterize their relationship as one-to-one, one-to-many, or many-to-many. (Chapter 2 reviews these concepts.)

Mapping E/R Concepts to a Database

An entity generally is mapped onto a database table, while attributes are mapped onto the columns in a table. Relationships are a little bit more complex. How a relationship is implemented in your database depends on the type of relationship between the two entities.

Implementing a one-to-one relationship is fairly straightforward. There should be a common attribute or set of attributes between the two entities; this common attribute or set of attributes forms the basis for the relationship. This attribute or set of attributes also uniquely identifies any particular instance of either entity.

You can use the set of common attributes in a one-to-one relationship as the primary key for both tables.

A one-to-many relationship also has an attribute or set of attributes that is common to both entities. Unlike a one-to-one relationship, the common attribute or set of attributes in a one-to-many relationship only uniquely identifies an instance of one of the entities. The collection of attributes can identify any number of instances of the second entity.

Many-to-many relationships are the most complex of all. However, there is a trick that makes it easier to implement this type of relationship. You can break the many-to-many relationship into a pair of one-to-many relationships. Each of the main entities is on the one side of the one-to-many relationships; if you're lucky, you have an entity that you can use on the many side of relationships. However, you can create an artificial entity that consists of the set of attributes the two main entities have in common.

See Chapter 2 for details about different relationships.

Normalization

When designing a database, most people seek to avoid redundant data. *Normalization* is an entire discipline of database theory devoted to analyzing database designs to minimize redundant data. While there is a lot of mathematical theory behind normalization, the basic idea is to identify columns that contain redundant data and split a table in such a way as to eliminate as much of the redundant data as possible.

For example, a table containing a normal address consisting of a person's name, street address, city, state, and zip code contains redundant data. If you know the person's zip code, you can identify the city and state in which he or she lives. Therefore, if you completely normalize this table, you delete the city and state columns and add a second table that consists with zip code as the primary key and city and state names that apply to the zip code.

Normalization typically helps tactical databases in which having redundant data can cause performance problems. However, data warehouses aren't updated like tactical databases. Consequently, many of the reasons why you would normalize a database simply don't apply to a data warehouse database. In fact you generally are better off not normalizing a data warehouse database because retrieving the data from the second or third table requires an extra disk I/O or two for each row you retrieve. Unlike a tactical database in which you may retrieve a dozen or two dozen rows to satisfy a single database request, you may have to retrieve thousands or tens of thousands rows to satisfy a single request within a data warehouse. Anything you can do to eliminate extra disk I/O greatly improves the performance of your data warehouse.

Identifying Data Elements

At this point, you should have a general idea about the information you want to keep in your data warehouse based on the scope of the project and the types of questions you expect to answer. You also should be familiar with the raw material that you will use to build your data warehouse – the data from your tactical databases and the data that you can extract from external sources.

Choosing Data Elements from a Tactical Database

The next step in the process of creating your data warehouse is comparing the list of questions you identified during the brainstorming session (described in Chapter 6) with the list of data elements from the tactical databases. The main idea is not so much to identify the data elements you want as to identify the data elements you don't need.

For example, in the JustPC application, a possible question is "How many customers live in a particular zip code?" To answer this question, you need the CustomerId and the Zip data elements. The CustomerId represents a unique customer, while Zip contains the customer's zip code information. To answer the question, "What were the total system sales to Virginia in 1997?" you need the SalesPrice, State, and DataPurchased data elements.

 At this stage of designing your data warehouse, you don't need to worry about tables. It is more important to identify the data elements needed to answer your questions.

In some cases, you may not be able to answer a question with the data elements from the tactical applications. If not, examine some of the external data sources for information. Consider the question, "How do the prices of my computers compare with equivalent computers from my competitors over time?" This question is particularly nasty from several angles. Obviously, one key piece of information – the price of the competitor's computer systems isn't available in the tactical database. Of course, you also need to identify which competitor you're talking about.

However, the real headache is determining when two computers are equivalent. You have to examine a number of fields – such as CPU speed, memory, disk drives, video cards, monitor size, and other accessories – to ensure that you aren't comparing apples to oranges (or Macs to Pentiums so to speak). Then you need to track this information for both your computers and those of your competitors.

Finding this information for your computers is easy because all of the information is available in the tactical database. However, getting this information for the competition is more difficult because you must try to capture the information directly off the Internet or manually enter the information directly into the data warehouse.

Choosing Data Elements from an External Source

Choosing data elements from an external data source is not as complicated as you may think. In general, each data element you obtain from an external data source is compared with a value already in one of your tactical databases. After all, part of the reason that you want data from an external data source is to see how your organization is doing relative to another.

The trick here is to identify your local values first, then model the data elements for your external data elements in the same fashion. This ensures that you easily can compare both data elements down the road.

Data Elements for the JustPC Data Warehouse

When designing the JustPC data warehouse, I chose to focus on information related to sales of computer systems and computer parts. For the most part, I selected data elements directly from the JustPC tactical database without changing the type or meaning. I also included a few new data elements, such as HardDiskCount and TotalHardDiskSpace, which contain consolidated data from other fields. Table 7-1 includes the list of data elements I selected, with a short description of their contents.

TABLE 7-1 DATA ELEMENTS FOR JUSTPC DATA WAREHOUSE

Data Element	Description
City	contains the name of a city
CompanyName	contains the name of a company
CPUSpeed	contains the speed of a CPU in a system
CustomerId	uniquely identifies a customer
CustomerType	describes the type of customer using a two-character codified value
CustomerTypeDescription	describes the type of customer using a text string
DatePurchased	contains the purchased date of something
EMailAddress	contains the customer's e-mail address
FirstName	contains the customer's first name
HardDiskCount	contains the total number of hard disks in a system
InventoryDescription	contains a description of the item in inventory
InventoryId	contains the inventory ID number
InventoryType	contains the general type of an inventory item
ItemCost	contains the cost of a sold item
LaborCost	contains the cost of the labor associated with the sale of an item
LastName	contains the customer's last name
Memory	contains the number of megabytes of memory in a system
MonitorSize	contains the size of a monitor
Month	contains a month value
Phone	contains a telephone number
QuantitySold	contains the number of units sold
Quarter	contains the calendar quarter
SalesPrice	contains the amount paid for an item

Continued

TABLE 7-1 DATA ELEMENTS FOR JUSTPC DATA WAREHOUSE *(Continued)*

Data Element	Description
SpeedSize	contains a value describing the major characteristic of an item in the inventory
State	contains a two-character state abbreviation
StoreId	uniquely identifies a JustPC store location
Street	contains a street address
SystemId	uniquely identifies a computer system sold by JustPC
TotalHardDiskSpace	contains the total hard disk space on a system
Warranty	is TRUE if the item sold was handled as a warranty replacement
Week	contains the week of the year
Weekday	contains the day of the week
Year	contains a year value
Zip	contains a valid zip code

Designing the Data Warehouse

Designing the data warehouse is merely a matter of taking the information about the data elements you already obtained and grouping them together according to some rules for building a data warehouse. The rules for designing a data warehouse are similar to those you use to design a tactical database, but there are some key differences. These differences reflect how the databases are used.

Data Warehouses versus Tactical Databases

In a tactical database, users typically retrieve a few dozen rows of information from the database and then update some of them. In a data warehouse, users typically retrieve thousands of rows of information, but never update anything. In general, data warehouses have fewer tables than a tactical database, but these tables have more columns and more rows of information.

Yet, just like in a tactical database, you should combine data elements together only when they are related logically. Grouping unrelated fields together causes problems with a data warehouse just as it causes problems with a tactical database.

Entities and the Data Warehouse

Once you have a list of data elements to work with, it's time to begin arranging them into entities. Typically, you begin this process by looking at your data elements and trying to identify the common entities. However, you want to proceed a little differently in a data warehouse.

There are two types of entities in a data warehouse: facts and dimensions. A *fact* entity contains information that can be summarized, such as the cost of an item or the number of items sold. *Dimensions* characterize the individual facts – such as when the item was sold or to whom the item was sold.

The relationship between a dimension and a fact is always one-to-many. Both the fact entity and the dimension entity contain a set of attributes that you can use to link the two entities together, such as the date the item was sold or the ID of the customer who purchased the item. This type of arrangement also is referred to as a *Star Schema*.

You can use an alternate arrangement, known as a *Snowflake Schema,* for a data warehouse. This arrangement is similar to the Star Schema, except that you can link dimensions to dimensions. This arrangement isn't common in small data warehouses, but it can be useful when you have a large data warehouse.

See Chapter 3 for details about the Star and Snowflake Schemas.

Each of the entities becomes a table in your data warehouse and the attributes associated with each entity become columns in the table, which makes it easy when you're ready to design the database.

Choosing Data Elements for the Fact Tables

A *fact table* is composed of two parts: one or more key values that uniquely identify an entry in the fact table and a set of values known as *measures*. Each key value is a link to a dimension table.

The measures, on the other hand, typically contain numeric values that you can add together to form meaningful values, such as sales price or quantity sold. Other types of numeric values, such as zip code or department number, represent information that should appear in a dimension.

Each row in the fact table typically contains information associated with an event, such as a particular sale or other transaction. However, a fact also may contain summary information on a group of sales or transactions in which the lower level of detail may be unimportant. For example, in a fast food restaurant, it may be unnecessary to track each individual transaction because of the shear volume of data that is generated. Instead, you may summarize each of the items on the menu in 15-minute intervals. This reduces the amount of data in the data warehouse and allows queries that run against this data to execute faster.

Choosing Data Elements for the Dimension Tables

Each *dimension table* has two parts: a key value that links to a group of rows in a fact table and a series of attributes related to the key value. The *key value* uniquely identifies a row in the dimension. It also is used to link to a group of rows in the fact table.

While you may want to retrieve information based on a key value from the data warehouse, more likely you may want to retrieve information based on one of the attributes. The attributes should be related to the key value and should contain information that you can use to select a group of related facts. For instance, in the JustPC data warehouse, you may be interested in tracking sales by various customer types. This can help you decide where you want to place advertisements to reach the majority of your customer base.

Sometimes a group of attributes in a dimension table may represent a collection of hierarchy data. This provides an easy way to examine data at one level and then drill-down to look at the details at the next lower level.

The classic example of a hierarchy in data warehousing is date information. Assume that the table contains a column holding the purchase date of something. It is useful to extract the year that the object was purchased from the date value. This way enables someone using the data warehouse to retrieve information based on a value for a year, rather than try to select a range of date values corresponding to a year. This is not only easier for the user, but it also is more efficient.

Typically, a date value is expanded into year, quarter, month, and week. However, other hierarchies are possible. The only requirement is that one level of the hierarchy must be contained wholly in the next higher level, as month is inside a year. Note that weekday is not part of a true hierarchy involving year, month, and day because weekdays span the entire year.

The JustPC Data Warehouse

In the JustPC example, there are two main fact tables: SystemInfo and SalesInfo. SystemInfo tracks information about the sales of complete computer systems (see Figure 7-1). Four dimension tables — SystemDetails, StoreInfo, DateDimensions, and CustomerInfo — surround the SystemInfo table.

The SystemInfo fact table (see Table 7-2) contains only three measures: SalesPrice, ItemCost, and LaborCost. From these three values you easily can derive a value for profit (SalesPrice – ItemCost – LaborCost). The rest of the columns in this table are links back to the various dimension tables.

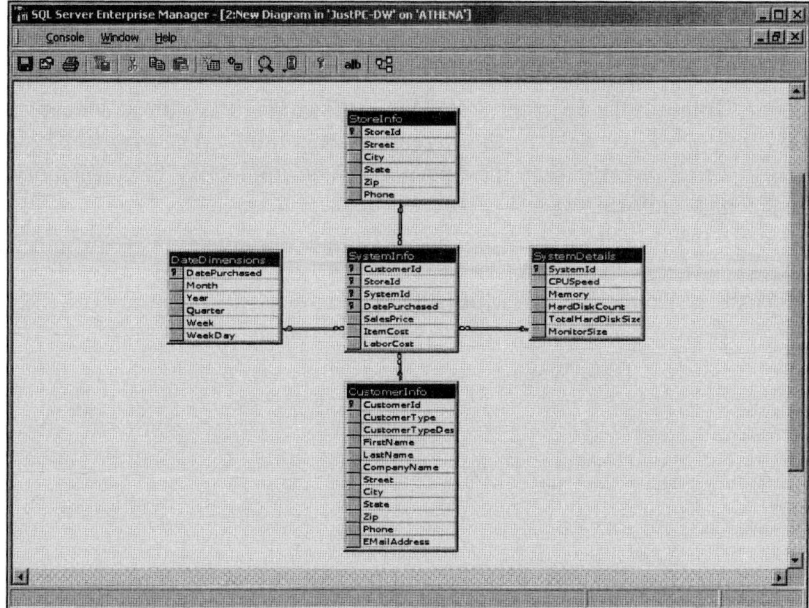

Figure 7-1: Viewing the SystemInfo table and related dimension tables

TABLE 7-2 DATA ELEMENTS IN SYSTEMINFO

Data Element	Data Type
CustomerId	Int
StoreId	Int
SystemId	Int
DatePurchased	Datetime
SalesPrice	Money
ItemCost	Money
LaborCost	Money

 See Chapter 2 for an explanation of the various data types.

The data elements chosen for the SystemDetails dimension table (see Table 7-3) include the link back to the fact table (SystemId), plus several key indicators that describe a computer system. These indicators include CPUSpeed, Memory, HardDiskCount, TotalHardDiskSpace, and MonitorSize. Each of these values is derived from the SpeedSize field in the InventoryItems table. The InventoryType field is used to determine whether the SpeedSize field applies to CPU, Memory, HardDiskSpace, or MonitorSize.

TABLE 7-3 DATA ELEMENTS IN SYSTEMDETAILS

Data Element	Data Type
SystemId	Int
CPUSpeed	Int
Memory	Int
HardDiskCount	Int
TotalHardDiskSpace	Int
MonitorSize	Int

The StoreInfo dimension table (See Table 7-4) contains descriptive information about a store. While some of these fields – such as Street and Phone – aren't likely to be used as search values, it is quite possible to incorporate the information from these fields into a report. The remaining fields – such as City, State, and Zip – all reflect information that may be useful when searching for the sales in a particular geographic area.

TABLE 7-4 DATA ELEMENTS IN STOREINFO

Data Element	Data Type
StoreId	Int
Street	Varchar(64)
City	Varchar(64)
State	Char(2)
Zip	Int
Phone	Varchar(32)

The DateDimensions dimension table (see Table 7-5) is probably the most unusual table in the design. While at first it contains a lot of redundant information, you soon find that having these extra fields makes running queries against the data in the data warehouse much easier.

TABLE **7-5 DATA ELEMENTS IN DATEDIMENSIONS**

Data Element	Data Type
DatePurchased	Datetime
Month	Int
Year	Int
Quarter	Int
Week	Int
WeekDay	Int

The CustomerInfo dimension table (see Table 7-6) contains the information from the tactical database's Customers table. All of the fields are carried over without change; also, the CustomerType field is translated into a more descriptive field just in case you want the text description of CustomerType rather than the two-character code.

TABLE **7-6 DATA ELEMENTS IN CUSTOMERINFO**

Data Element	Data Type
CustomerId	Int
CustomerType	Char(2)
CustomerTypeDescription	Char(10)
FirstName	Varchar(64)
LastName	Varchar(64)
CompanyName	Varchar(64)
Street	Varchar(64)

Continued

TABLE **7-6** DATA ELEMENTS IN CUSTOMERINFO *(Continued)*

Data Element	Data Type
City	Varchar(64)
State	Char(2)
Zip	Int
Phone	Varchar(32)
EmailAddress	Varchar(128)

The SalesInfo table tracks information about sales of accessories and labor (see Figure 7-2). Like the SystemInfo table, four dimension tables surround the SalesInfo table: InventoryInfo, StoreInfo, DateDimensions, and CustomerInfo.

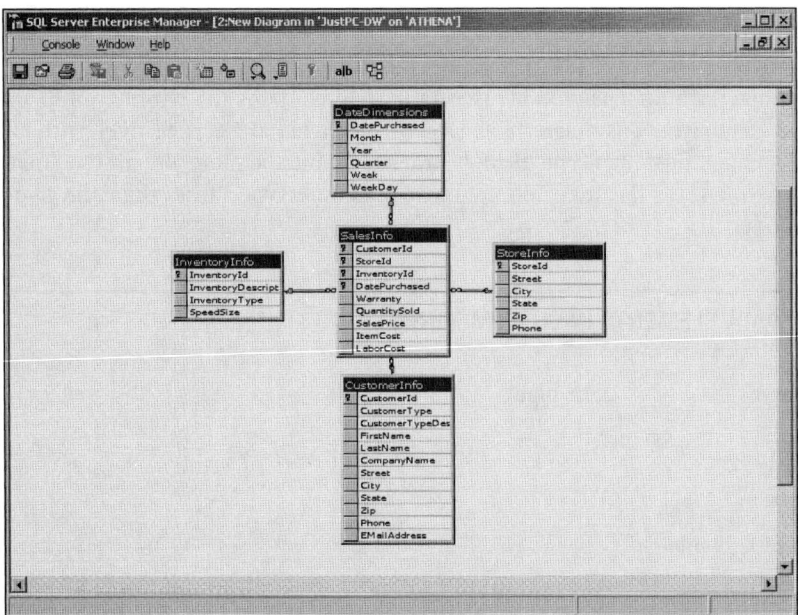

Figure 7-2: Viewing the SalesInfo table and related dimension tables

The SalesInfo fact table (see Table 7-7) is very similar to the SystemInfo fact table. It contains links to three shared dimensions (CustomerId, StoreId, and DatePurchased) along with a link to the InventoryInfo dimension. Unlike the SystemInfo table, it is possible that a customer purchased more than one component so a QuantitySold field also is included. The Warranty field indicates whether the costs included in the SalesPrice, ItemCost, and LaborCost fields actually are charged to the customer (FALSE) or covered as part of a warranty repair (TRUE).

TABLE 7-7 DATA ELEMENTS IN SALESINFO

Data Element	Data Type
CustomerId	Int
StoreId	Int
InventoryId	Int
DatePurchased	Datetime
Warranty	Bit
QuantitySold	Int
SalesPrice	Money
ItemCost	Money
LaborCost	Money

The InventoryInfo dimension table (see Table 7-8) provides information about the inventory item found in the SalesInfo fact table. The InventoryType and SpeedSize fields classify the type of item sold, while the InventoryDescription field primarily provides a text description of the item referenced by InventoryId.

TABLE 7-8 DATA ELEMENTS IN INVENTORYINFO

Data Element	Data Type
InventoryId	Int
InventoryDescription	Varchar(64)
InventoryType	Char(2)
SpeedSize	Int

Of the five dimensions used in this design, three of them are common to both fact tables. By sharing the common tables, the final design for the data warehouse looks like the example shown in Figure 7-3.

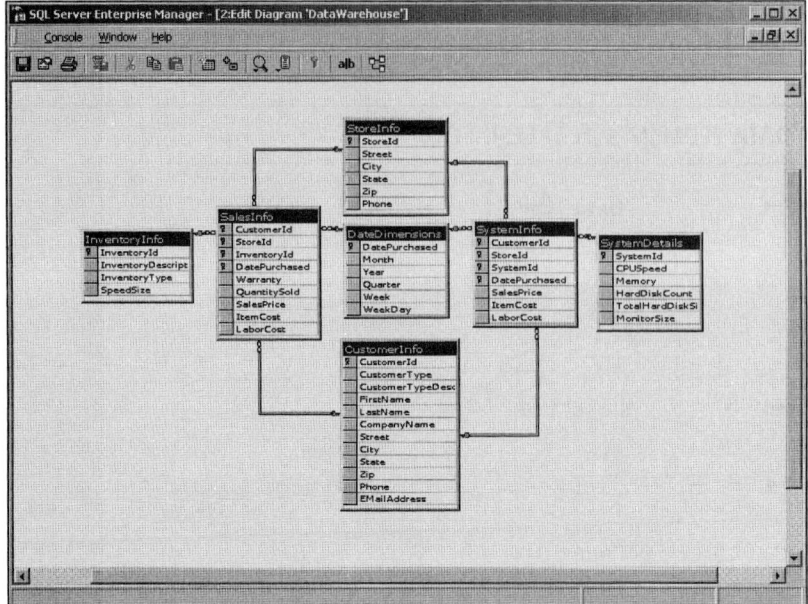

Figure 7–3: Viewing the entire data warehouse design

Figures 7-1, 7-2, and 7-3 are drawn using the Database Diagram facility in Enterprise Manager, which I discuss in Chapter 6 and elaborate on in Chapter 8. Using this tool, you can view your database as an Entity/Relationship model. This view of your database is extremely useful to have when you query the database for information.

Summary

In this chapter, you learned about how to design your data warehouse – which probably is the single most complex task you will have to do. While the process discussed in this book is complete, it also is simplified somewhat. However, the complexity of the task comes not from the technical tasks but from the management tasks. I purposely ignore the management tasks in this book because there are many different books that cover these issues in much more detail. One such book is *Data Warehousing For Dummies* by Alan R. Simon (published by IDG Books). Very few data warehousing references address the real issues behind the technical design of a data warehouse.

In the next chapter, I'm going to cover how to build your data warehouse using SQL Server 7's Enterprise Manager tool. At the same time, I'm also going to cover how to perform some routine tasks that are necessary for every database server.

Chapter 8

Building the Data Warehouse

IN THIS CHAPTER

- ◆ Creating a database
- ◆ Creating a database diagram
- ◆ Creating tables
- ◆ Performing scheduled database backups
- ◆ Recovering a database

THIS CHAPTER SHOWS YOU how to build your data warehouse using SQL Server 7's Enterprise Manager utility. Topics include creating an empty database, building each of the tables to hold your data, creating indexes, and performing routine operations such as database backup and recovery.

Building Your Data Warehouse

Once you know which tables and columns in the tables you want to create, you're ready to begin building your database. The SQL Server Enterprise Manager is a powerful tool used to administer your database server. Chapter 6 showed you how to use this tool to enter information about a database into the Repository. Now I show you how to use it to create your database.

Creating Your Database

Creating an empty database is a relatively simple process. Just log onto your SQL Server database server (or with another login that has the equivalent authority) and run the Create Database Wizard and you'll have a brand-new, empty database ready to use in a matter of minutes.

INFORMATION NEEDED TO CREATE A DATABASE

Before you create your database, you should know the following information:

- ◆ The name for your new database

- ◆ The location where you want to place the database files

- ◆ The approximate size of the database

- ◆ How your database will grow over time

 **Estimate.** While the size of the database and how the database grows over time are important, don't worry if you do not have exact values. You should take your best guess and adjust them later if you feel the need.

SELECTING THE CREATE DATABASE WIZARD

Creating a database using SQL Enterprise Manager is a very straightforward process. You begin by expanding the icon tree in the tree view and selecting the database server where you want your database to reside (see Figure 8-1). Then select Tools → Wizards from the main menu. This displays the list of available wizards in Enterprise Manager (see Figure 8-2).

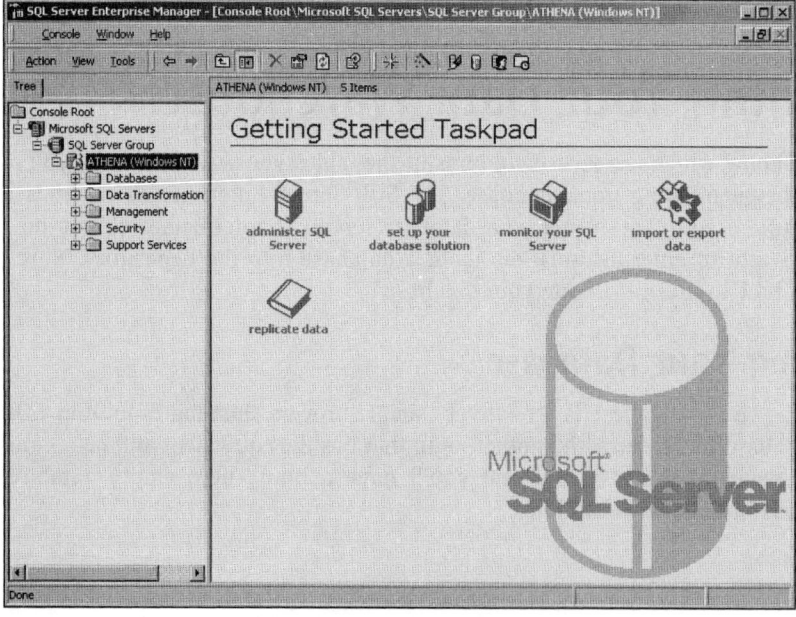

Figure 8-1: Choosing a database server for your database

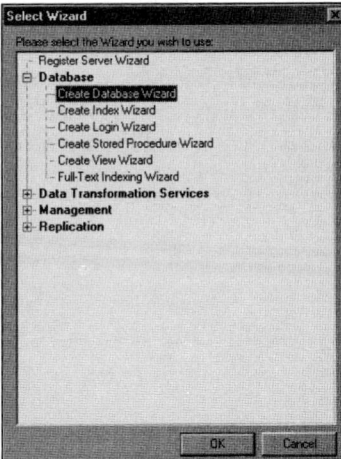

Figure 8-2: Selecting the Create Database Wizard

 **Which wizard?** A number of available wizards in SQL Server 7 help you administer and maintain your database server and your databases. While you may perform all of these functions directly, you should take advantage of these wizards until you are comfortable enough with the information they request to use the direct methods.

RUNNING THE CREATE DATABASE WIZARD

When you first start the Create Database Wizard, a dialog box is displayed listing the information you need to run the wizard (see Figure 8-3). Press Next to continue.

Figure 8-3: Starting the Create Database Wizard

SPECIFYING THE DATABASE NAME

The wizard then prompts you for the name of the database and the location of the database file and transaction log file (see Figure 8-4). Enter the name for your database and the drive and directory where you want to keep the database files and the database log files. The default directories for the database server are displayed for both file locations.

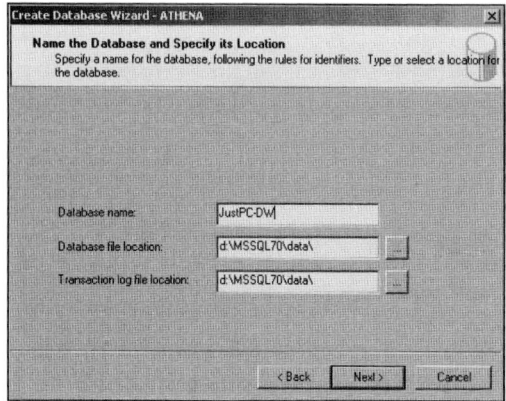

Figure 8-4: Entering the database name and specifying file location information

The database files hold the actual data for your database, while the database log files hold all changes to your database. In the event of a disk failure, you can use the database log file to rebuild your database from the most recent database backup.

The more, the merrier: If you have two or more drives available, try to place your database log files on a separate disk drive from the database files themselves to protect yourself from a hard disk failure. If one of the drives with your database on it fails, you can rebuild your database using a database backup and the current database log file. If the drive with the database log on it fails, you can back up your current database files and then rebuild your database. Either way, your data is safer than if you place all of your files on a single disk drive.

CHOOSING DATABASE FILE NAMES

Pressing Next displays the form shown in Figure 8-5. You can specify the name of the file where you want to keep your database and its initial size. A file name is created using the name of your database followed by _Data. An initial file of one megabyte is assumed. If you wish, you can split your database across multiple files; but unless you have multiple disk drives, this probably isn't worth the effort. However, specifying a larger than default database size is desirable because it saves the database server from having to expand the size of the file later.

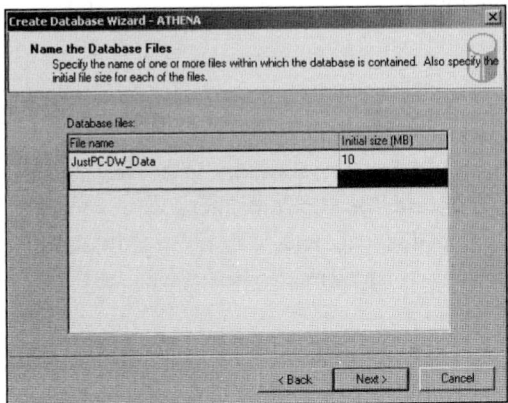

Figure 8-5: Entering file names for your database

GROWING YOUR DATABASE FILES

In the next step of the wizard, you specify if the database should increase the space in the files automatically and, if so, how it should go about doing this (see Figure 8-6). Unless you have a specific reason not to let the server automatically grow the database files, let SQL Server handle it. Otherwise, one day you may find that an overnight data update fails due to insufficient space available in the files.

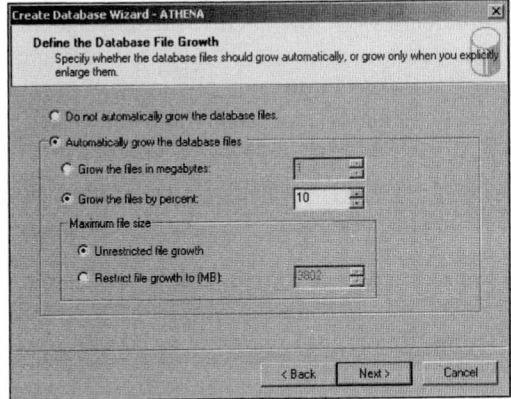

Figure 8-6: Defining database file growth parameters

Once you decide to let SQL Server manage the size of the files, you need to decide whether you want to increase the available space by a fixed number of megabytes or by a fixed percentage. Both approaches are equally valid and it doesn't really matter that much which option you pick. Choose the one with which you feel the most comfortable.

Finally, you need to decide if you want to limit the growth of the files to a specific size. Otherwise, SQL Server automatically grows a file until there is no more space on the disk drive.

 **Watch your space!** While SQL Server can manage the space for your data warehouse database files automatically, it is no substitute for actively monitoring how much space you really use. If you don't monitor your disk space usage, you may find yourself out of disk space for a relatively small database just because SQL Server automatically added more space than needed.

NAMING AND GROWING YOUR DATABASE LOG FILES

The next two steps of the wizard repeat the same forms shown in Figure 8-5 and 8-6, but this time they ask for information about your database log files. The default name for the database log file is the name of the database followed by _Log. You can have multiple database log files, just as you can have multiple database files. Likewise, you can choose to grow your database log files automatically when they run out of space.

FINISHING THE CREATE DATABASE WIZARD

In the final step of the wizard, you see a list of all of the parameters you supplied to the wizard (see Figure 8-7). If you think they are correct, press Finish to create your database. A message box saying, "The database was successfully created" is displayed if the wizard encounters no problems. Press OK to close the message box and exit the wizard. The wizard then asks you if you want to create a maintenance plan. If you press Yes, the Maintenance Plan Wizard automatically starts. Pressing No ends the wizard. (I cover the Maintenance Plan Wizard later in this chapter).

If you wish to change one or more of the parameters, simply press the Back button until you reach the form containing the parameters you want to change. Then you simply follow the remaining steps again until you reach the last step in the wizard.

If the wizard runs into a problem, the message box contains the error or errors causing the problem. Simply press the Back button until you reach the step containing the information you need to change, follow the remaining steps, and reenter the information as needed.

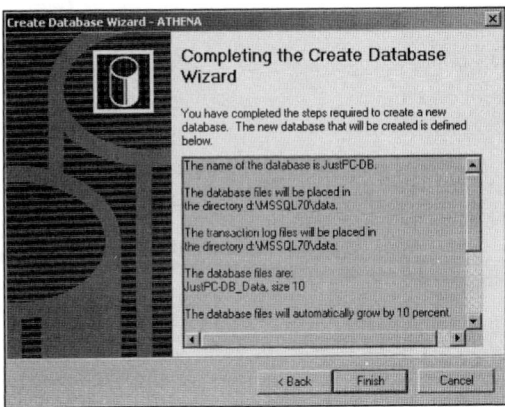

Figure 8-7: Verifying your selected parameters

Creating a Database Diagram

A *database diagram* is a graphical way to view the data structures in your database using a format similar to an Entity/Relationship diagram. You can use a database diagram to create and edit tables in your database, draw relationships between tables, and add text annotations.

CREATING A BLANK DATABASE DIAGRAM

To create a blank database diagram, expand the tree view of the database server to show the list of available databases. Expand the Database icon to show the icons below it and choose Diagrams. Right-click Diagrams and select New Database Diagram from the popup menu. This starts the Database Diagram Wizard. If your database doesn't have any tables, a message box appears saying "There are no tables to be added to the diagram. You can create new tables from within the diagram."

ADDING EXISTING TABLES TO A DATABASE DIAGRAM

If there are tables in your database, the Create Database Diagram Wizard displays an initial screen outlining what it will accomplish. Pressing Next displays a list of tables in the database and asks you to choose which tables to include in your diagram (see Figure 8-8).

Choose the tables you want to include in the diagram and press Next. On the next screen, review these selected tables and press Finish to create the database diagram. The wizard automatically adds the tables to your diagram, draws the appropriate links between the tables if they are defined, and automatically arranges the information on the screen.

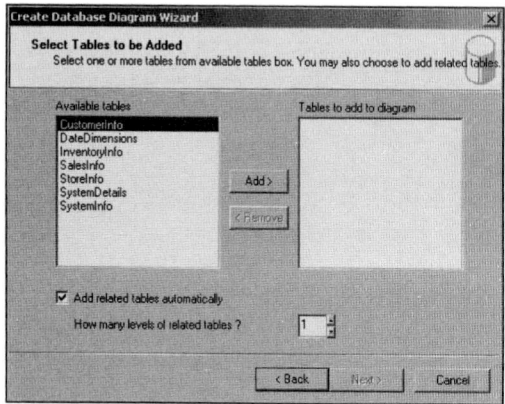

Figure 8-8: Selecting tables for inclusion in your database diagram

Save your diagram. The database diagram is not saved until you press the Save button or try to close the window containing the diagram. The first time you save the diagram, you are prompted for its name. Choose a descriptive one and press OK to save the diagram.

EDITING AN EXISTING DATABASE DIAGRAM

A database diagram is a work in progress; it reflects the current design of your database. You are free to make any changes you want to your database design. To select the database diagram, simply expand the icons in the tree view until you find the database containing the database diagram. Then expand the Database icon to show the various elements beneath it. Select the Diagrams icon to display the list of database diagrams in the pane on the right side of the form (see Figure 8-9).

When you save the diagram, Enterprise Manager analyzes the changes and builds a change script. It then lists the tables that are affected by the changes (see Figure 8-10). If you click Yes, the changes are made to your database. If you click No, the changes you make to the database diagram are discarded. Clicking Save Text File saves the script as a text file that you can use to update the database at a later time.

Adding New Tables to Your Database Diagram

After you create a database diagram, you easily can add new tables to your database from within the diagram.

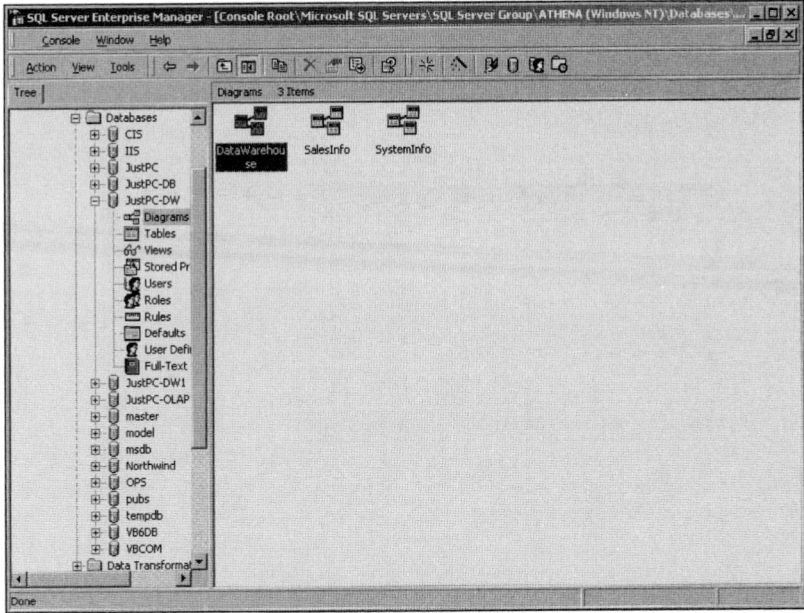

Figure 8-9: Selecting a database diagram

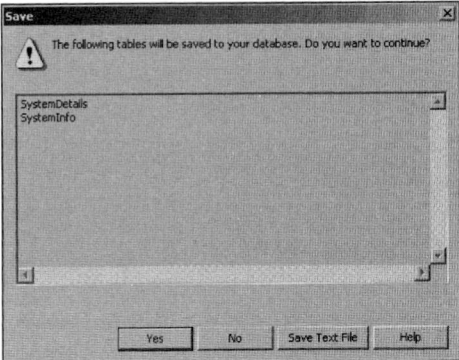

Figure 8-10: Saving changes to your database

CREATING A NEW TABLE

Right-click the diagram and select New Table from the popup menu. You then are prompted for the name of the table. Enter the name and press OK. The view of your table is displayed on the database diagram (see Figure 8-11).

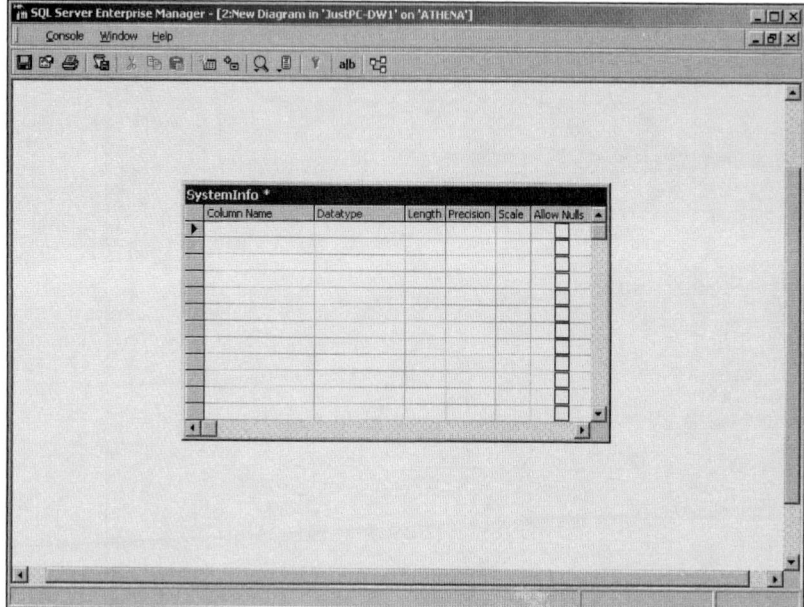

Figure 8-11: Creating a new table in your data diagram

Note that the name of the table is displayed at the top of the view, followed by an asterisk (*). The asterisk indicates that the table has been modified since you opened the database diagram.

ADDING COLUMNS TO YOUR TABLE

You can add a column to a table simply by entering the appropriate information in the topmost blank row in the table view (see Table 8-1). You only need to enter those fields marked as required to define a column. If you forget a required field, you'll receive an error message when you move to the next row. You must assign values for Column Name, Datatype, and Allow Nulls. Depending on the data type, you may have to enter values for Length, Precision, and Scale.

TABLE 8-1 COLUMN INFORMATION

Field	Required	Description
Column Name	Yes	Contains the name of the column.
Datatype	Yes	Contains the data type of the column.
Length	Depends on data type	Specifies the length of a variable length data type.

Field	Required	Description
Precision	Depends on data type	Specifies the total number of digits in a numeric value.
Scale	Depends on data type	Specifies the number of digits to the right of the decimal point.
Allow Nulls	Yes	When TRUE, the column is accepted.
Default Value	No	Supplies a value that automatically is used if the user doesn't assign a value to this column. Do not use this field if Allow Nulls is TRUE.
Identity	No	When TRUE, the column automatically is assigned a new unique value based on the Identity Seed and Identity Increment values.
Identity Seed	No	Used to determine the first identity value inserted into the table. Defaults to 1 if Identity is TRUE.
Identity Increment	No	Added to the highest identity value in the table to create a new identity value. Defaults to 1 if Identity is TRUE.
Is RowGuid	No	When TRUE, the column contains a globally unique identifier value. Used primarily for database replication.

While the rest of the fields in a column definition may be useful in some databases, try not to use them in your data warehouse unless you really understand how they work.

 See Chapter 2 — and the next section of this chapter — for details about data types.

CHOOSING DATA TYPES

A column can consist of any one of a number of different data types. Table 8-2 lists some of the more common data types in SQL Server 7. Unless you have a reason to choose a different data type, always use the same data type that your data source uses.

TABLE 8-2 COMMON DATA TYPES IN SQL SERVER

Data Type	Description
Binary	Contains a binary string of data, up to 8,000 bytes long. Must specify the maximum size of the string using the Length field.
Bit	Contains only two values: TRUE or FALSE.
Char	Contains a string of characters, up to 8,000 characters long. Must specify the maximum size of the string using the Length field.
Datetime	Contains a date/time value in the range of 1 January 1753 to 31 December 9999 with an accuracy of 3.33 milliseconds.
Decimal	Contains a numeric value. The Precision field specifies the total number of digits in the value, while the Scale field specifies the number of those digits that are displayed to the right of the decimal point.
Float	Contains a 64-bit floating-point value.
Int	Contains a 32-bit integer value.
Money	Contains a money value ranging in size from −922,337,203,685,477.5808 to +922,337,203,685,477.5807 with an accuracy of 4 decimal places.
Real	Contains a 32-bit floating-point value.
Varchar	Contains a variable-length character string up to 8,000 characters long. Must specify the maximum size of the string using the Length field.

Which type? Picking the right data type can be difficult when you have too many from which to choose. If you are tracking the number of something, use an Int. If you need to store text about something, use a Varchar with a large enough value for Length to hold the largest possible value. If you are dealing with money values, use Money. When assigning a unique identifier for an object, use Int if the identifier is always numeric or Char if the identifier can contain non-numeric values. Nearly all of the columns you use in your data warehouse fall into one of these four categories.

SETTING THE PRIMARY KEY ON A TABLE

The *primary key* of a table is a set of one or more columns whose values are unique for a particular row. Setting a primary key is a good idea because SQL Server automatically assigns an index to the primary key and it tries physically to order the data in the table by primary key. Setting the primary key has a positive impact on your database's performance.

To set the key, select the column or columns that make up the primary key (see Figure 8-12). To mark these columns as the primary key, right-click while the mouse pointer is over the table and select Set Primary Key from the popup menu. Note that if you have more than one column in your primary key, you need to hold the Shift key to select multiple columns.

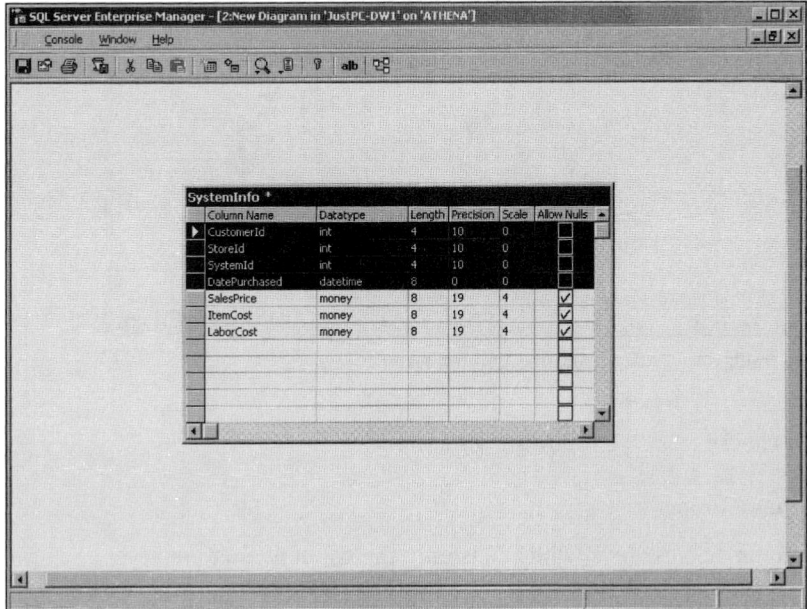

Figure 8-12: Selecting the table's columns that make up the primary key

 **Null values.** Any column included in the primary key must not leave the Allow Nulls field unchecked because null values are not permitted in the primary key.

CHANGING THE VIEW OF A TABLE

When drawing a database diagram, you can display your table using various levels of detail. The view that I'm working with is known as the Column Properties view. This view shows all of the details of all of the columns in the table. However, there are several other views that you may want to use from time to time.

My favorite view is the Column Names view (see Figure 8-13). This view contains the name of the table and just the Column Name field. It enables me to see all of the columns in the table in the minimum amount of space. This is especially useful when your database diagram displays several tables at the same time.

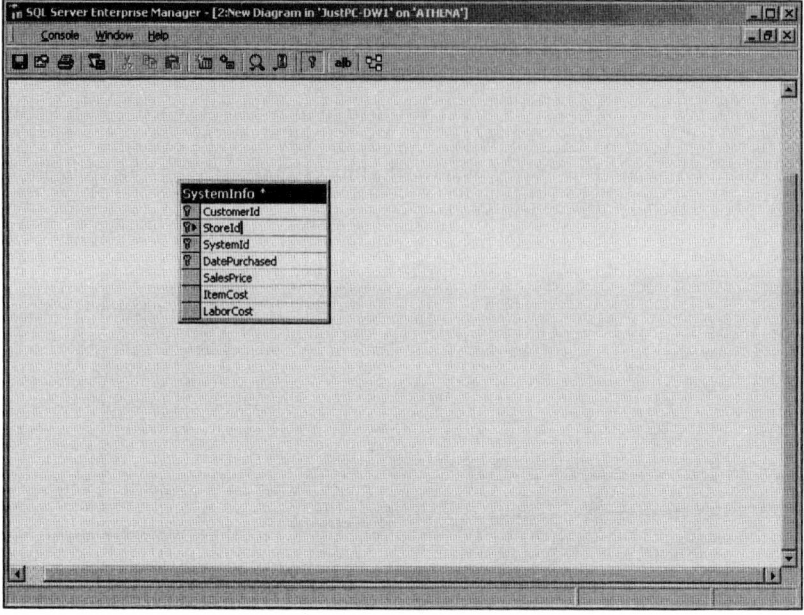

Figure 8-13: Displaying a table using the Column Names view

You can choose from the following views:

- ◆ Column Properties
- ◆ Column Names, Keys (which lists only the columns that are keys)
- ◆ Name (which lists only the name of the table)
- ◆ Custom (which displays a view in which you can select the fields to display from Column Properties). You can select the columns displayed in the Custom view by choosing Modify Custom View from the popup menu.

To change views, simply right-click while the mouse pointer is over the table and select the view you want from the popup table.

 **Changing window size.** You can adjust the size of the window used to display the table to fit your needs. Scroll bars appear automatically when there is more information than can fit in the window.

> **TIP** **Applying views to multiple tables.** Hold down the Ctrl key and click the name of each table. Then move the mouse pointer over a table and select a table view as normal. The view is then applied to all selected tables.

Creating Relationships between Tables

You can instruct SQL Server to enforce a one-to-many relationship between two tables by creating a relationship between those two tables in your database diagram. The relationship links the primary key of one table to a column in a second table. The column in the second table is known as a *foreign key*. Every value of the foreign key must exist already as the primary in the first table. If you attempt to add a row into the second table whose foreign key value is not in the first table, SQL Server refuses to add the new row.

To add a relationship between two tables, select the row or rows corresponding to the primary key in the first table. Press and hold the left mouse button while over the selected rows and drag the mouse pointer to the second table. While you drag the mouse around, notice a dashed line linking the current position of the mouse pointer with the primary key in the first table. Move the mouse pointer over the foreign key and release the left mouse button. The Create Relationship dialog box is displayed, as shown in Figure 8-14.

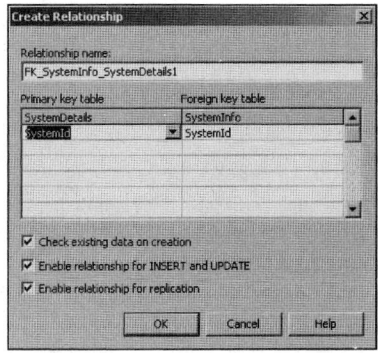

Figure 8-14: Creating a relationship

You can change the relationship name by filling in a different value in the corresponding text box or you can leave the default name. I like the default name because it identifies the relationship as a foreign key relationship (FK) and contains the name of both tables involved.

Below the relationship name is the list of columns that participate in the relationship. If you notice that the wrong columns are listed, you easily can change them by clicking the column name below the table name and pressing the arrow at the end of the field. This displays a drop-down list of the table's column names from which you can choose. You can add a column by selecting an empty field and pressing the arrow at the end, and you may delete a column by erasing all of the characters in the field.

At the bottom of the dialog box are three checkboxes. By default, they all are checked:

◆ Check Existing Data on Creation: When this option is checked, Enterprise Manager checks the tables to ensure that any existing data is compatible with the new relationship. An error occurs if any of the data doesn't meet the requirements of the relationship.

◆ Enable Relationship for INSERT and UPDATE: When this option is checked, it instructs the database server to check the relationship each time a row is inserted into the foreign key table or when the contents of the foreign key change during an update. If the foreign key value is not found in the primary key table, the insert or update fails.

◆ Enable Relationship for Replication: Database replication goes beyond the scope of this book. You safely can leave the checkbox checked because this field is meaningless unless you use database replication.

 **Staying in sync.** Database replication is a way to keep the contents of two or more databases synchronized. Replication is typically used to improve performance by allowing applications to access multiple database servers, or to provide reliability when you need a backup database ready in case of an emergency. You can find more about database replication by checking out the *Microsoft QL Server 7 Secrets* by David K. Rensin, published by IDG Books.

When you're satisfied that the information about the relationship is correct, press OK to create the relationship in the database diagram.

Saving Your Database Diagram

Just because you make changes to your database diagram doesn't mean that your database diagram actually reflects your database. You must save your changes in order to make the changes to your database. To save your changes, simply press the Save button. If you haven't saved your database diagram before, a Save As dialog box prompts you for the name of the database diagram.

If you have more than one table in your database, another dialog box is displayed listing all of the tables that you have to change in the database diagram (see Figure 8-15). This dialog box gives you three choices for saving your changes. Pressing Yes immediately applies the changes to your database. Pressing No discards the changes you just made. Pressing Save Text File enables you to save a SQL script that you can use to make these changes at a later time.

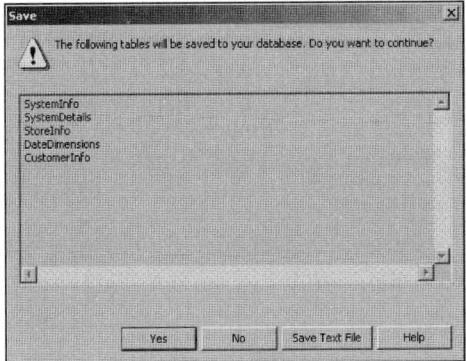

Figure 8-15: Saving the changes to your database

Other Database Diagram Functions

The Database Diagrams facility has a number of other functions that you may find useful. You can access these functions (see the following list) by right-clicking over the database diagram and selecting the appropriate item from the popup menu.

- ◆ **New Text Annotation** enables you to add comments to your database diagram.

- ◆ **Show Relationship Labels** displays the relationship name near the relationship arrows that are drawn between the tables.

- ◆ **View Page Breaks/Recalculate Page Breaks** enables you to partition your database diagram over multiple pages, which makes it easier to print large, complex databases.

- ◆ **Arrange Tables** automatically rearranges the tables and relationship arrows on your database diagram.

- ◆ **Zoom** enables you to increase or decrease the magnification of your table. Sometimes zooming to a smaller percentage value enables you to see your entire database in the database diagram window.

- ◆ **Print/Page Setup** enables you to send your database diagram to the printer.

- ◆ **Properties** enables you to set the view and set various attributes about a table.

Performing Database Maintenance

A database is not something you install and forget. There are a number of tasks you need to perform on a periodic basis to ensure that your database stays healthy. Microsoft makes it easy by providing some wizards that help you define a maintenance plan, then the database server automatically executes the maintenance plan as scheduled. Each time the maintenance plan executes, a report is generated notifying you whether additional attention to your database is required.

Defining a Maintenance Plan

A database maintenance plan automatically performs a number of different functions against one or more databases on a scheduled basis. These functions include:

◆ Optimizing database resources

◆ Recomputing optimization statistics

◆ Performing database integrity checks

◆ Performing database backups

The Database Maintenance Plan Wizard works by asking you to select various functions to be performed and then packages them into jobs that execute according to a schedule you define. Then a tool known as SQL Server Agent monitors the scheduled jobs and starts them at the proper time.

 **Running the SQL Server Agent.** In order to run any scheduled tasks, including a database maintenance plan, the SQL Server Agent must be running. To start the SQL Server Agent, open the tree view for the database server and expand the tree view under Management. Right-click the SQL Server Agent icon and select Start from the popup menu.

STARTING THE DATABASE MAINTENANCE PLAN WIZARD

You can start the Database Maintenance Plan Wizard by choosing Tools ÿ Database Maintenance Planner. When the wizard starts, it shows a welcome form that describes what the wizard can do. Press Next to start the wizard.

SELECTING DATABASES

The first step in the wizard enables you to select the databases you want to manage with this maintenance plan (see Figure 8-16). You can choose to manage all of the databases on your database server, or only the databases that comprise your data warehouse.

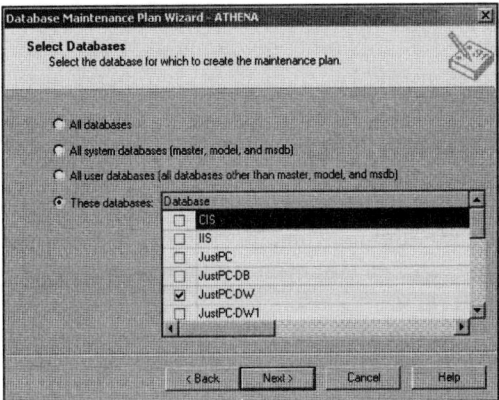

Figure 8-16: Selecting the databases for the maintenance plan

Ensuring proper backup. A maintenance plan should cover every database on your database server to ensure that the database is backed up properly. This includes databases used for testing, plus databases used to manage SQL Server itself.

OPTIMIZING YOUR DATABASE

In the Update Data Optimization Information step, the Database Maintenance Plan Wizard enables you to select several different ways to optimize your database (see Figure 8-17). You also can schedule how often this job runs.

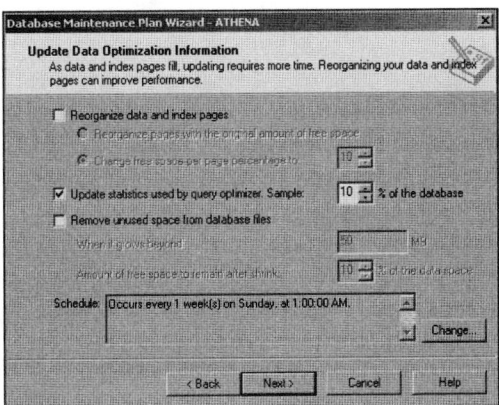

Figure 8-17: Choosing data optimization information

Checking the *Reorganize data and index pages* checkbox drops and re-creates all of the indexes in the selected database. While this function can make a big difference in a tactical database in which rows are added and deleted continually in the tables, it isn't that useful in a data warehouse.

Checking the *Update statistics used by query optimizer* option analyzes the data in your tables and indexes, and provides information for the query optimizer to use in determining the best way to answer a complex query. Performing this task is very important in a data warehouse because running complex queries are the norm. However, you only need to update statistics when you update your data warehouse.

You also can remove unused space from a database when it exceeds a certain threshold. In general, this function isn't important in a data warehouse since you rarely, if ever, will delete information from a data warehouse database. This means that the database only increases in size, so there shouldn't be any free space to remove.

At the bottom of the form is the default execution schedule for this function. You can revise the schedule by pressing the Change button next to the schedule. This displays a form called the Edit Recurring Job Schedule, which schedules any job in SQL Server. The default time to run this job is once a week on Sunday morning at 1:00 a.m., which is fine for most database servers.

SCHEDULING A JOB

The Edit Recurring Job Schedule form enables you to define a job to the SQL Server Agent (see Figure 8-18). Using this form, you can schedule a job to run daily, weekly, or monthly. If you specify a weekly job, you can choose to run the job every week or skip a specified number of weeks between each execution. You also can select which days of the week you want the job to run. Selecting Daily or Monthly in the Occurs area displays a different set of scheduling options in place of the Weekly area.

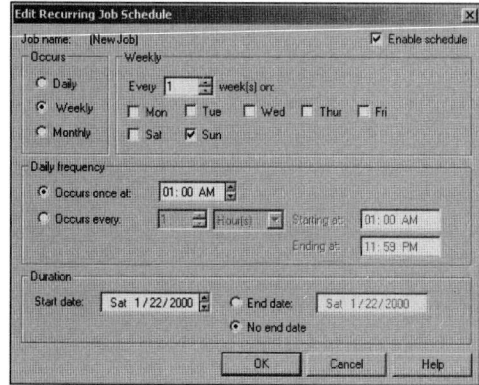

Figure 8-18: Creating a job schedule

Under the Daily frequency area, you can specify the time of day the job starts. You also can instruct the SQL Server Agent to run the job multiple times during the day at the specified intervals, optionally specifying the starting and stopping times. By default, this job runs forever; however, you can specify an optional end date for the job to prevent the job from running indefinitely.

CHECKING DATABASE INTEGRITY

In the next step of the wizard, you can choose to check the database integrity (see Figure 8-19). I highly recommend this option because it is desirable to know if your database does or does not have a problem. You can choose to include or exclude the indexes and optionally repair minor problems. I strongly recommend including the indexes and allowing SQL Server to repair minor problems. The primary downside to doing this is that the job runs longer.

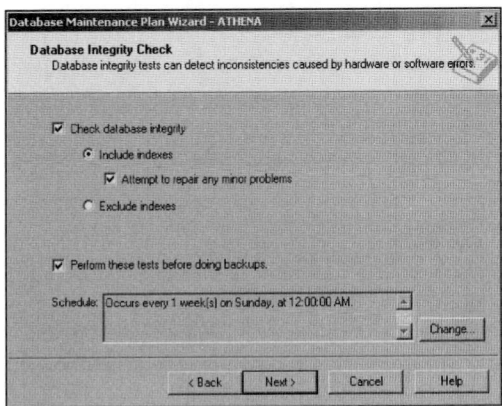

Figure 8-19: Checking database integrity

If you select *Perform these tests before doing backups*, the tests are run before the database is backed up. If there are any problems found, the backup does not run. I prefer to back up my databases even if there is a problem because it's possible that I can corrupt the database even more while trying to correct the problem. Having a backup available enables me to try to restore the database and try to fix it again.

BACKING UP YOUR DATABASE

In the Specify the Database Backup Plan step of the wizard, you can include a database backup as part of your maintenance plan (see Figure 8-20). Of all the things you can do as part of your maintenance plan, this is the most important. There are thousands of ways your database can get corrupted, and there is only one real way to fix it – by restoring your database from a backup copy.

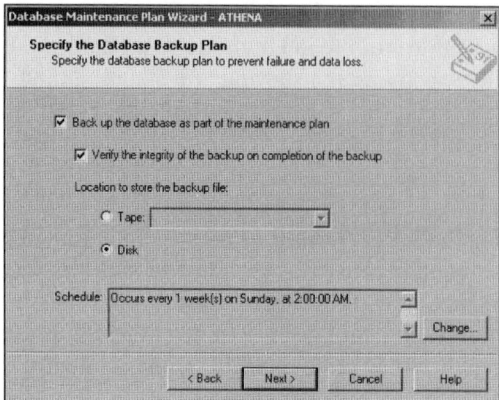

Figure 8-20: Backing up your database

TIP

Verify integrity. I highly recommend that you verify the integrity of your database backup, especially if you choose to back up your database to tape. The last thing you need is a database backup that you can't read.

As with the other jobs created with the Database Maintenance Plan Wizard, you can specify how often to run a database backup. The default schedule is to run it once a week on Sunday morning. This is fine for most databases because as long as you have your database transaction log, you can recover changes made to your database up until the time you stop recording changes in the database log.

You can back up your database to either a disk file or a tape file. If you choose to back up your database to tape, you need to specify the name of the tape drive you want to use. If you choose to back up your database to a disk file, you need to specify where to store the backup files. This information is entered in the next step of the wizard.

TIP

Backing up to a disk file. Try to locate the file on a disk drive that isn't used for your database files or your database log files. That way you still can access your database backups even if the hard disk containing your database or your database transaction log files crashes.

If you choose to back up your database to disk, you need to specify where to keep your database backups (see Figure 8-21). You can specify the location of the backup directory and choose to use a separate directory for each database. You even can specify the file type associated with each database backup.

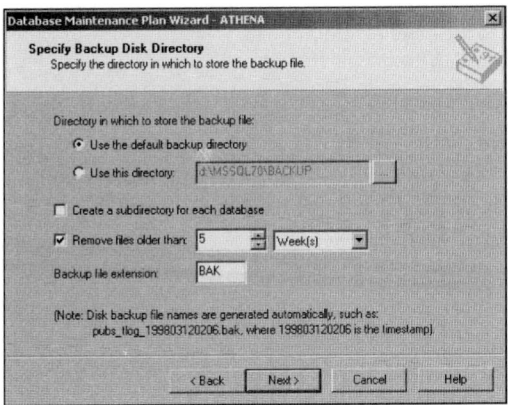

Figure 8-21: Specifying information for disk-based database backups

One problem with backing up your database to disk is that you accumulate a lot of disk files. You can choose to let the backup process delete all backups of your database that are older than the specified amount of time. I prefer to keep five weeks of backups around because I can retrieve a backup taken during the previous month at any time.

Reducing backup files. Database backups to disk create a simple disk file that you can copy to another location. Therefore, you keep five weeks of database backups on disk; then once a month, you can copy the oldest backup to a different location. This means you can keep a year's worth of backups using only 17 files (12+5), rather than 52 files.

BACKING UP THE DATABASE TRANSACTION LOG

Along with backing up your database, you should back up the transaction log (see Figure 8-22). The database transaction log contains only the changes to your database, so it typically is much smaller than the database itself. Thus, the time and space required to back up the transaction log is much less. This means that it is practical to do this backup more frequently than backing up your database. The suggested default is once each day, except for Sunday, at midnight. This works for most databases.

You also have the option to save your transaction logs to either tape or disk. If you choose to back up your logs to disk, then the next step of the wizard prompts you where to store the backups using a form that resembles the one shown in Figure 8-21.

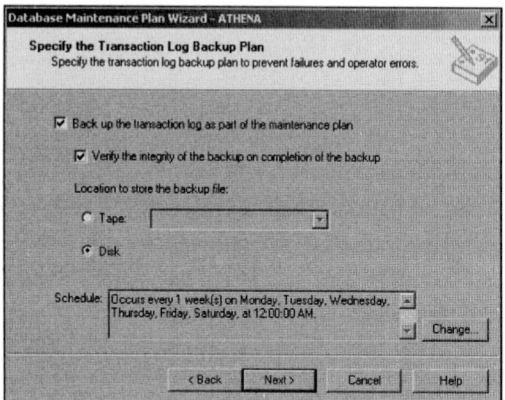

Figure 8-22: Backing up your database transaction logs

Pros of daily backup. Even though you don't update your data warehouse on a daily basis, there is information in the system tables of your database that is updated on a daily basis. Therefore, I believe that a daily backup of your transaction log is a good idea.

GENERATING REPORTS AND TRACKING HISTORY

In the next step of the wizard, you can choose to generate a report for each job performed by the maintenance plan (see Figure 8-23). I strongly recommend selecting this option. After all, you never can be sure if there was a problem or not without a report. Always save the report as a disk file just to be certain that a copy exists, and keep as many reports as you keep database backups. While you can choose to e-mail your reports to a SQL Server operator, it isn't worth the effort as long as you write the report to a disk file.

Figure 8-23: Generating a report for your maintenance jobs

You also can keep a history of the activities performed by the maintenance plan in your database (see Figure 8-24). This is a good idea. The default limit of 1,000 rows is sufficient for most databases. You can use Query Analyzer or another database tool to view the table msdb.dbo.sysdbmaintplan_history.

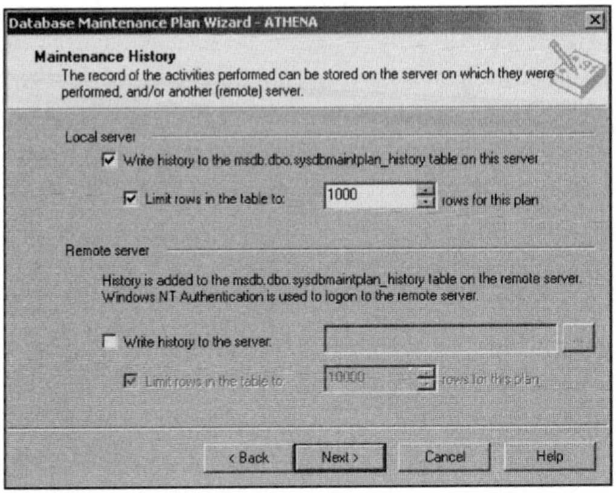

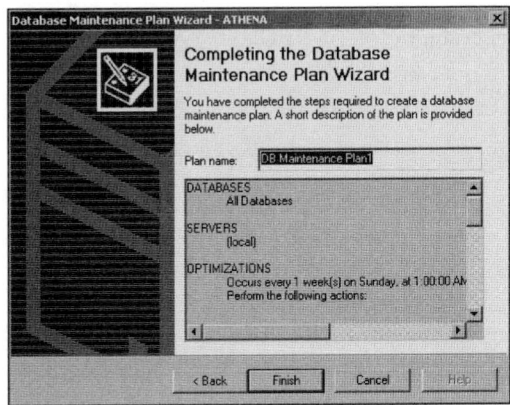

Figure 8-24: Keeping a history of your maintenance activities

COMPLETING THE WIZARD

In the last step of the wizard, you are asked to review all of the selected options and to assign a name for the maintenance plan (see Figure 8-25). If everything appears OK, press Finish to create your jobs and schedule them for execution. Otherwise, press Back to go back and correct your mistake.

Figure 8-25: Reviewing the selected options

After pressing Finish, the wizard creates the maintenance plan and displays a message box saying that it has created the maintenance plan successfully.

EDITING THE DATABASE MAINTENANCE PLAN

Once you create your maintenance plan, you can go back and change it at any time. Choose the database server you want to modify in the icon view in Enterprise Manager and select the Database Maintenance Plans. A list of database maintenance plans is displayed in the right pane of the display.

Double-clicking the name of the maintenance plan displays its Properties window (see Figure 8-26). All of the information you enter in the wizard is displayed under the various tabs. You easily can review and change any of the information already entered.

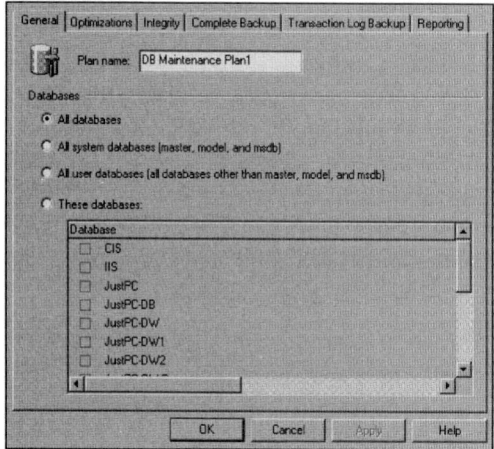

Figure 8-26: Viewing the maintenance plan

 **Viewing history.** On the Reporting tab of the Database Maintenance Plan Properties window is a button labeled View History. Pressing this button enables you to quickly view the maintenance history for this plan.

Recovering a Database

Having a backup of your database is useless unless you know how to restore it. Unlike some database servers, SQL Server 7 makes it very easy to restore your database. You simply identify the database backup you want to use, set a few options that control how the restore runs, and click OK. The database server handles the rest.

 **Restore at your own risk.** Restoring a database is always a dangerous operation. The restore process deletes your current database and re-creates it using the information stored in the backup. If for some reason the restore process fails, you may lose your current database and all of its information. Deciding to restore a database takes a lot of consideration.

STARTING THE RESTORE PROCESS

To restore a database, expand the icon view under the database server and select the database you want to restore. Then right-click the database and choose All Tasks → Restore Database from the popup menu. This displays the dialog box shown in Figure 8-27. This form contains information about the most recent backup of your database.

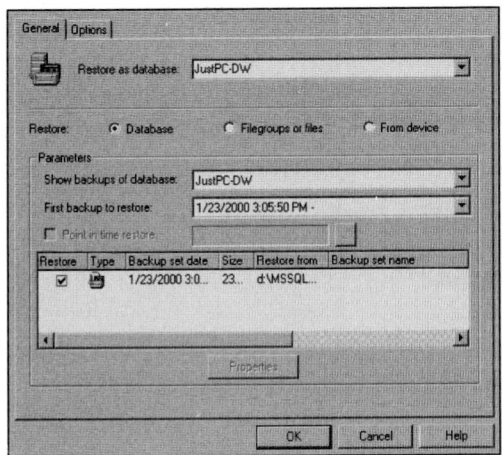

Figure 8-27: Reviewing backup information before restoring your database

The General tab on the Restore Database form specifies the name of database to restore in the *Restore as database* field. The Restore field should have the Database option button selected. You use the other option buttons – not recommended for beginners – when you want to do a more complicated restore.

 **Making a copy.** You can restore an existing database backup into a new database, creating an identical copy of the database as it was at the time it was backed up. This can be useful if want to test the restore process or if you want to create another copy of a database. I also use this technique to install the sample JustPC databases.

In the Parameters area, you select the backups you want to use. First, you must identify the set of database backups you want by using the *Show backups of database* field. These backups include both normal database backups and backups of your transaction log files. Normally, choose to restore both the database backup and the transaction log that you may have saved.

SETTING RESTORE OPTIONS

The Options tab has a few choices that you may want to review before restoring your database (see Figure 8-28). There are three checkboxes at the top of the form:

- ◆ Eject tapes after restoring each backup
- ◆ Prompt before restoring each backup
- ◆ Force restore over existing database

Of these options, the only one that is important is the *Force restore over existing database*. Unless the box is checked, you can't restore your database until you delete the old database.

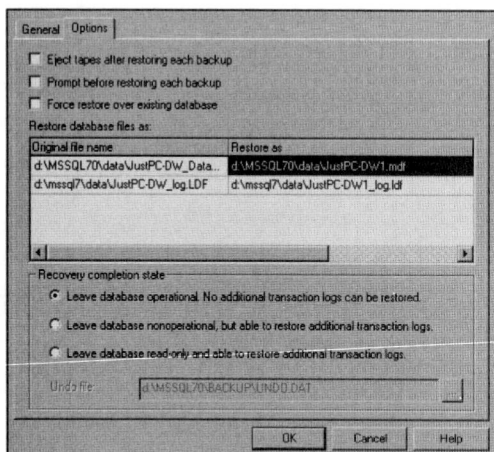

Figure 8-28: Setting database restore options

In the middle of the form is a series of rows indicating the file names associated with the database backup as well as the file names that are used to restore the database.

 **Moving your database to a different disk drive.** Simply specify the new disk drive and file path in the *Restore database files* area on the Options tab of the Restore database dialog box.

On the bottom of the form is the *Recovery completion state* area. This section gives you three options on how to leave the database at the end of the restore process. In general, always select the *Leave database operational* option unless you plan to restore additional transaction log files after the backup is finished.

RUNNING THE RESTORE

After you set all of the appropriate option buttons, press the OK button to begin the restore process. Obviously, pressing the Cancel button aborts the restore without doing anything. When the restore process begins, you see a dialog box that tracks its progress (see Figure 8-29).

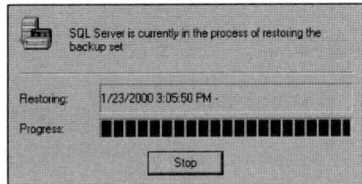

Figure 8-29: Watching the restore run

If the restore is successful, you receive a message box letting you know this. Otherwise, you see an error message and you need to take the appropriate action to try and restore it again.

Summary

This chapter discussed how to create a database and the various database structures inside the database using SQL Server 7 Enterprise Manager for your new data warehouse. I also discussed how to instruct SQL Server to back up your database automatically and how to restore it in case of emergency.

In the next chapter, I cover the Data Transformation Services (DTS). This tool, which also is part of SQL Server 7, makes it easy to copy data and transform it from existing data sources into your data warehouse.

Chapter 9

Using Data Transformation Services

THIS CHAPTER DESCRIBES HOW to use Data Transformation Services (DTS) to move data from the corporate database to the reader's data warehouse. It also discusses how to use the Data Import and Data Export Wizards to build your DTS package and how to use the Query Builder to perform a complex data transformation.

Introducing Data Transformation Services

Of all the new features in SQL Server 7, the *Data Transformation Services (DTS)* is my favorite. DTS is a utility program that enables you to copy data from one source to another. It also has the ability to use a SQL query to select only the rows you want to move.

 **Wait, there's more.** There are many other options in DTS, including the ability to validate and transform your data using a VBScript program. Unfortunately, this topic involves programming and lies outside the scope of this book. For more information about this facility, see the *Microsoft QL Server 7 Secrets* by David K. Rensin, published by IDG Books.

DTS Data Sources

DTS relies on the data access facilities provided by OLD DB, which allows it to talk to many different data sources. It also includes support for both ODBC data sources and provides the ability to read and write to flat files. This means you can move data among any of these data sources:

◆ Microsoft SQL Server 7 databases

◆ Microsoft SQL Server 6.5 and earlier databases

◆ Microsoft Access databases

◆ Microsoft Excel worksheets

◆ Microsoft FoxPro databases

◆ IBM DB2 databases

◆ Oracle databases

◆ dBase databases

◆ Paradox databases

◆ Comma-separated value files

◆ Fixed field length files

DTS Architecture

I like to think of the Data Transformation Services as a fancy version of the DOS Copy command. You need to specify the source file and the destination file, plus any options you use during the copy. This information is combined into a single entity called a *Package*. Then the package is stored in a database, or regular disk file, for execution.

Unlike the Copy command, DTS needs a lot more information about the source and destination than just the file name. In the case of database files, you need to specify the database server, the database, and the table that you want to access. In the case of other types of files, you still have to specify additional information such as the name of the worksheet in a workbook for Excel or a table name in an Access database.

DTS is designed to deal with columnar data, so you need to ensure that each column in the data source is matched with the correct column in the destination. You may call a VBScript program to transform your data, column by column.

There are two ways to create a DTS package: with the Import/Export Wizards or with the DTS designer. The Import/Export Wizards enable you to create a single task of copying one set of data, while the DTS Designer enables you to create complex copy and transformation processes.

Creating a Simple DTS Package

I often find it useful to copy a table from my database into Excel for data analysis. While there are a lot of ways to do this, DTS makes this process very easy. In the following example, you discover how to copy the InventoryItems table from the JustPC-DB database to an Excel worksheet on the hard disk.

RUNNING THE EXPORT WIZARD

Using Enterprise Manager, expand the icon tree by selecting the database server where your data resides to expose the list of databases. Then right-click the database containing your data and choose All Tasks → Export Data. This starts the Data Transformation Services Export Wizard (see Figure 9-1).

Figure 9-1: Starting the DTS Export Wizard

Export or Import? The only difference between the Export Wizard and the Import Wizard is that the Export Wizard uses the database you select before you start the wizard as your default data source, while the Import Wizard uses the database as the default data destination.

SELECTING A DATA SOURCE

In this step of the Export Wizard, you specify the location of the data you want to export (see Figure 9-2). In the source area, you can choose from a list of various data sources. In this case, I want to access the database server so I use the default value of Microsoft OLE DV Provider for SQL Server.

In the area beneath the data source provider is a set of information used to gain access to the database server. You need to provide login information and choose the default database you wish to use. I choose to use the Export Wizard, so all of these values are set to access the database I select before I start the wizard.

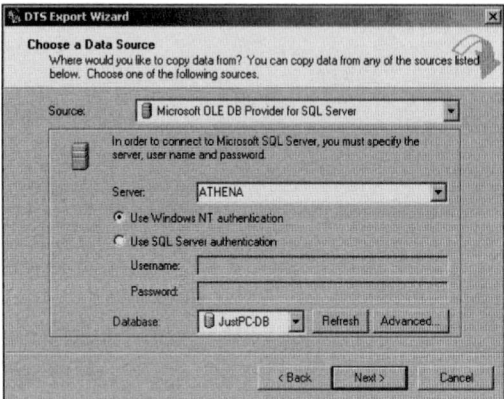

Figure 9-2: Selecting a data source

SELECTING A DATA DESTINATION

The next step in the wizard asks you to choose a destination for the data (see Figure 9-3). I select Microsoft Excel 8.0 (which is the real version number of Excel 97) as the provider. After selecting Excel, the area beneath the drop-down box is replaced with the information needed to access an Excel worksheet. In this case, all I really need to provide is the name of the file to hold the worksheet.

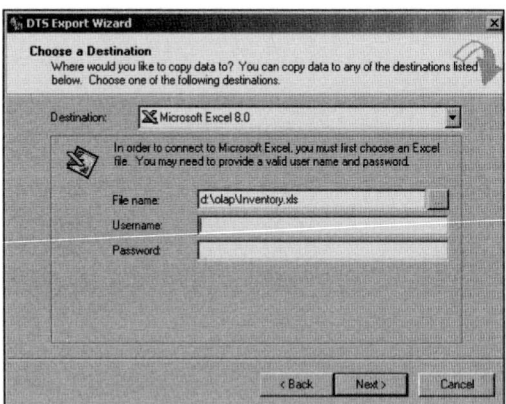

Figure 9-3: Selecting a data destination

 **Excel 8.0?** Excel 97 and Excel 2000 use the same file format for . XLS files, so it is safe to specify Excel 8.0 when you want to create an Excel 2000 workbook.

SPECIFYING A COPY METHOD

After choosing the data source and destination, you need to specify how to copy
the data (see Figure 9-4). While all I want to do is copy the complete table from the
database to a worksheet, you can choose from any of these approaches to copy
your data:

◆ **Copy tables(s) from the source database** copies all rows and columns
   from the selected table or tables to the destination location.

◆ **Use a query to specify the data to transfer** copies the data returned by a
   SQL **Select** statement. (See Chapter 11 for more information about the SQL
   Select statement.)

◆ **Transfer objects and data between SQL Server 7.0 databases** copies
   any of the selected data objects or tables between databases. This option
   is available only when both the data source and destination or both SQL
   Server 7 databases.

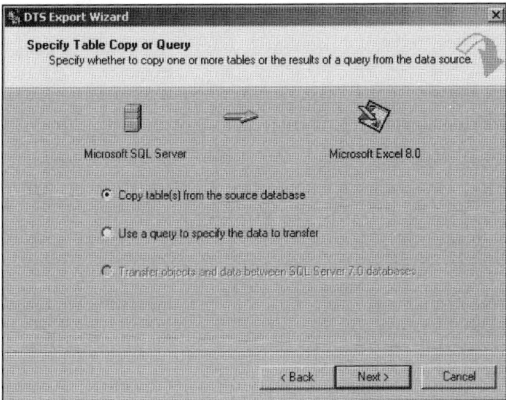

Figure 9-4: Selecting the copy method

 **Select statements.** When creating a data warehouse, you may find using a
SQL **Select** statement more appropriate because you can use it to identify
only the rows you want to be copied. Also, it enables you to create a single
table with data extracted from multiple tables.

SELECTING SOURCE TABLES

If you choose simply to copy your data, the wizard displays a list of tables in your
database (see Figure 9-5). Each table you select is copied to a different worksheet in
your Excel workbook. You can copy as many tables as you wish in a single DTS

package. Simply place a checkmark next to each source table you want to copy. You also can choose the name of the destination table. I'm creating an Excel workbook, so this name represents the name of a worksheet in the workbook.

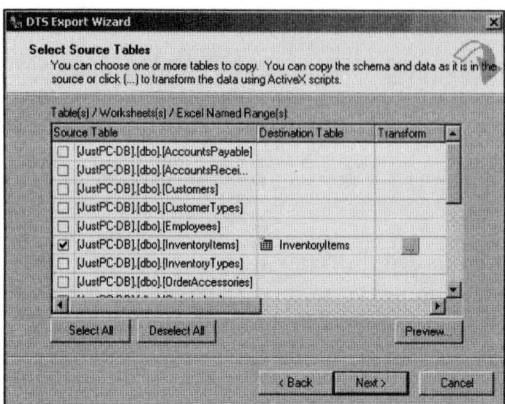

Figure 9-5: Choose the table or tables you want to copy.

In the Transform column is a button you can press if you want to transform the data. Pressing this button will display the Column Mappings and Transformations window (see Figure 9-6). There are two ways to transform your data – you can specify how the source columns are mapped onto the destination columns or you can write a VBScript routine to create a value for each column.

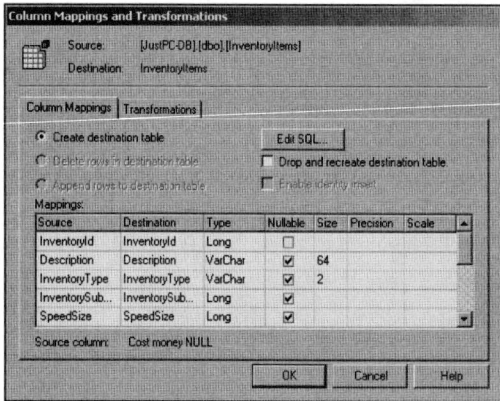

Figure 9-6: Transforming your data

Pressing the Preview button displays up to the first 100 lines of the data source (see Figure 9-7). This is a good way to verify that you are copying the correct information. If the information isn't correct, you may need to select a different table. Close the preview window and then press the Back button on the wizard to change some of the earlier information you provided to the wizard. Press the OK button to return to the wizard.

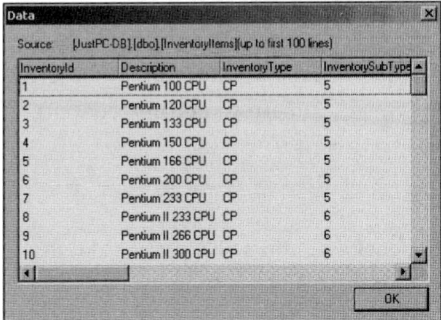

Figure 9-7: Previewing the data you want to be copied

SAVING AND RUNNING THE PACKAGE

After you define what you want the package to do, the wizard asks you when you want to run it and if you want to save it (see Figure 9-8). You can run the package immediately after the wizard is finished.

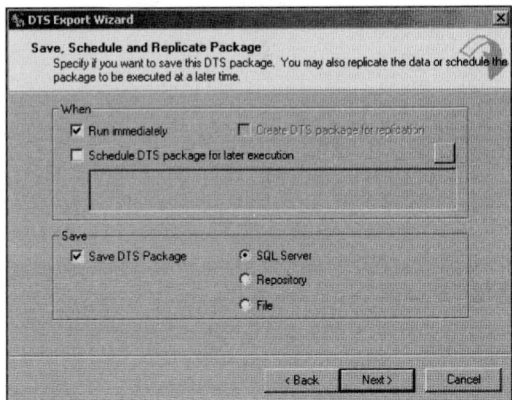

Figure 9-8: Setting save and execution options

You also can schedule the package for execution using the same SQL Server Agent scheduling utility that you used to schedule your database maintenance plan. You can choose to run the package at a specified time. However, you should run the package after your database maintenance jobs finish to avoid impacting their work.

See Chapter 8 for details on maintenance plans.

Run on a schedule. You also can schedule your DTS package to run on a schedule. This can be very useful when you have to update your data warehouse with the latest data from your tactical database.

On the form is an option to save your DTS package into a SQL Server database, the Repository, or a file. You must save the package if you choose to use SQL Server Agent to schedule its execution. However, saving your DTS package is a good idea even if you don't want to schedule its execution. Saving it enables you to execute on request or edit the package later to change the way it works.

If you choose to save your package in SQL Server or in the Repository, the next step of the wizard prompts you for additional information, such as the name of the package, a short description, and database login information to save the package (see Figure 9-9). If you choose to save the package as a file, the wizard asks you for the file name.

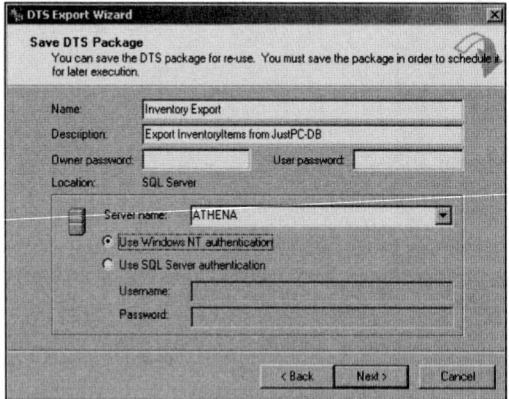

Figure 9-9: Providing information to save your DTS package

FINISHING THE WIZARD

In the last step of the wizard, you see a summary of the information you entered. Here you have the option to press the Back button to correct any mistakes (see Figure 9-10). Pressing Finish ends the wizard.

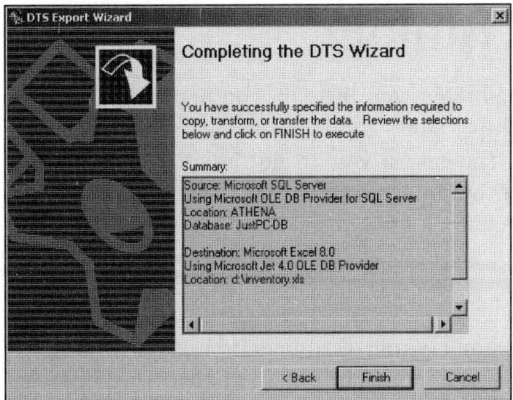

Figure 9-10: Completing the DTS Export Wizard

If you opt to save the package, it is saved. Then if you opt to run the package, the wizard starts the package. In this case, this is a three-step process – saving the package, creating the worksheet, and copying data from the database to the worksheet. As each step is run, its status is displayed on the window shown in Figure 9-11.

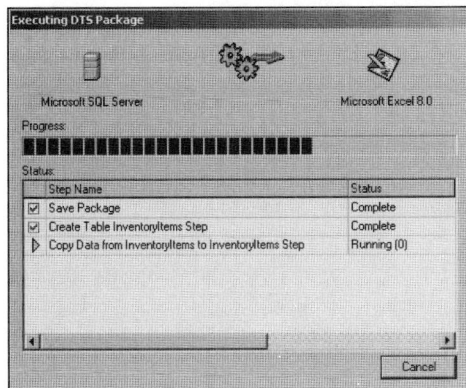

Figure 9-11: Running the package

When the package finishes running, a message box is displayed letting you know if the data successfully transferred or an error occurred while the package was running. If an error occurred, the message box contains a description of the error. Pressing OK returns you to the last step of the wizard. From there, you can press the Back button to correct the problem.

Using the Query Builder

Sometimes copying a table doesn't really give you the data you need. There may be times when you want to combine multiple tables from your tactical databases into a single table in your data warehouse. The easiest way to do this is by using a SQL query to specify the data you want to insert into your data warehouse. Building a SQL query can be difficult, so Microsoft includes a utility called Query Builder in DTS.

Defining the Problem

Tables 9-1 and 9-2 describe the Customers and CustomerTypes tables from the JustPC-DB database. The Customers table contains information about JustPC's customers, while the CustomerTypes table contains a translation for the value in the CustomerType field in the Customers table. However, these tables are combined into a single table in the data warehouse called CustomerInfo (see Table 9-3). There are a number of ways to solve this problem, but the easiest way is to build a SQL query.

TABLE 9-1 DATA ELEMENTS IN CUSTOMERS

Data Element	Data Type
CustomerId	Int
CustomerType	Char(2)
FirstName	Varchar(64)
LastName	Varchar(64)
CompanyName	Varchar(64)
Street	Varchar(64)
City	Varchar(64)
State	Char(2)
Zip	Int
Phone	Varchar(32)
EmailAddress	Varchar(128)

TABLE 9-2 DATA ELEMENTS IN CUSTOMERTYPES

Data Element	Data Type
CustomerType	Int
Description	Varchar(64)

TABLE 9-3 DATA ELEMENTS IN CUSTOMERINFO

Data Element	Data Type
CustomerId	Int
CustomerType	Char(2)
CustomerTypeDescription	Varchar(64)
FirstName	Varchar(64)
LastName	Varchar(64)
CompanyName	Varchar(64)
Street	Varchar(64)
City	Varchar(64)
State	Char(2)
Zip	Int
Phone	Varchar(32)
EmailAddress	Varchar(128)

See Chapter 2 for a detailed explanation of data types.

Running the Query Builder

The Query Builder is called from the Import and Export Wizards. After selecting the data source and destination, you should select the option *Use a query to specify the data to transfer* (see Figure 9-4). This displays the form that enables you to enter a SQL query statement (see Figure 9-12).

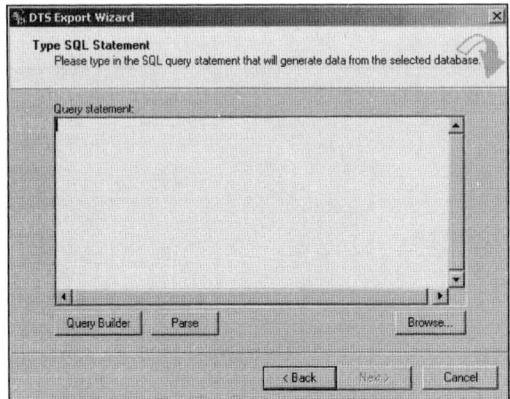

Figure 9-12: Entering a SQL query to select the data to be transferred

SELECTING COLUMNS

If you press the Query Builder button, Query Builder starts and displays a form that enables you to select the columns you want from your default database (see Figure 9-13). You can move an entire table by selecting the table and pressing the > button, or you can expand the table to see all of the individual columns in the table. Then you can add a column by selecting the column and pressing the > button.

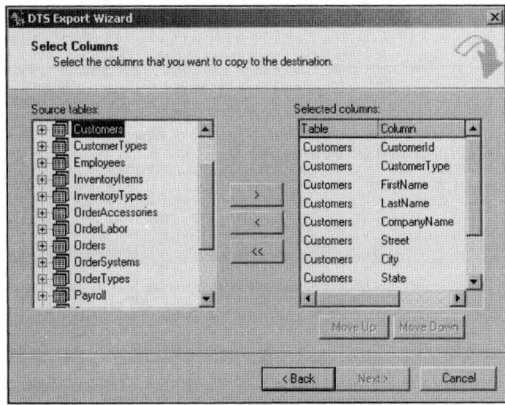

Figure 9-13: Starting Query Builder

If you aren't happy with the columns listed under the Selected columns section of the form, press the << button to remove all of the columns or select the column you don't want and press the < button to remove it.

SPECIFYING SORT ORDER

In the next step of the Query Builder, you can specify how the data is sorted (see Figure 9-14). While this isn't important when your destination is another table, it may be useful to sort your data if you export it to an Excel file. If you want to skip this step, press the Next button.

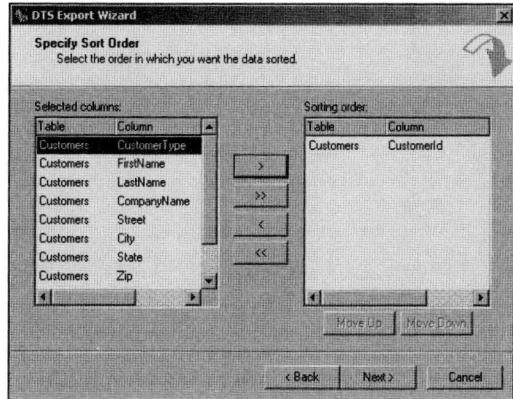

Figure 9–14: Specifying the sort order

To add a column to the sort key, simply select the column listed under Selected columns and press the > button. To add all of the columns, press the > button. The << button removes all of the columns under the Sort order section of the form, while the < button removes a single column.

You also can adjust the relative priority of a column in the sort key by pressing the Move Up and Move Down buttons. These buttons move the currently selected column listed in the sort order in the specified direction.

SPECIFYING SEARCH CRITERIA

You can limit the rows you retrieve by specifying one or more search criteria. This is an optional step. If you wish to retrieve all rows from the table, just press the Next button.

You specify search criteria by building a simple equation using a column, an operator, and another column or value. For instance, the following equation instructs DTS to return all rows in which the CustomerId column isn't zero.

```
[Customers].[CustomerId] <> 0
```

To enter this equation into the form, click the *Only Rows meeting criteria* radio button (see Figure 9-15). This enables the drop-down boxes under the Column, Oper (Operator), and Value/Column headings. Select [Customers].[CustomerId] under Column, <> under Oper, and type 0 under Value/Column. You also can press the ... button to see the list of values in the database for the selected column.

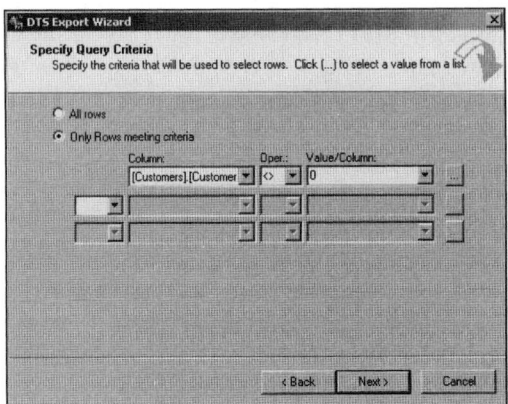

Figure 9–15: Specifying the query criteria

You can specify multiple search criteria by choosing And or Or in the drop-down boxes in front of the second and third criteria. This helps to build a rather complex search condition.

 See Chapter 11 for more information about using multiple search criteria with the SQL Select statement.

LINKING TABLES WITH QUERY CRITERIA

Another use for query criteria is to link multiple tables. This only works for tables related to each other through two columns that share a common value. In the JustPC example, you want to link the two tables using the CustomerType column. For each row in the Customers table, the value of CustomerType will be used to extract the corresponding row from the CustomerTypes table. Thus the two tables will be combined into a single one, which has the same definition as the CustomerInfo table.

To actually create the link, you must make sure that the value for CustomerType is the same in both the Customers and CustomerTypes tables. You accomplish this using the following criteria (see Figure 9-16).

```
[Customers].[CustomerType] = [CustomerTypes].[CustomerType]
```

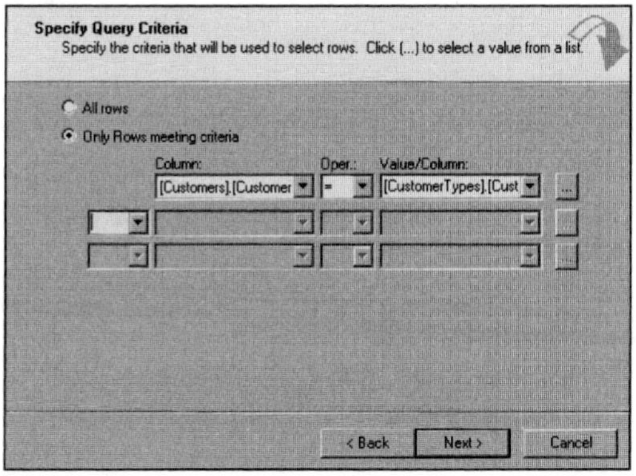

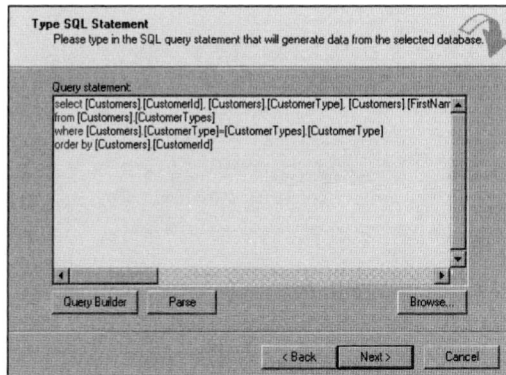

Figure 9-16: Linking two tables using query criteria

RETURNING TO THE SQL STATEMENT

After entering the query criteria and pressing the Next button, you are returned to the Type SQL Statement window with your newly built SQL statement (see Figure 9-17). You can modify the statement if you wish and press the Parse button to verify that the SQL statement is valid. Note that this doesn't mean you will get the proper results, only that the statement is formatted properly.

Figure 9-17: The finished SQL statement

The Browse button enables you to load a SQL statement that is stored in a disk file. This can be useful if you use the Query Analyzer tool – which I cover starting with Chapter 11 – to build and test your queries.

JUSTPC QUERIES

The JustPC data warehouse was built using DTS and either simple table copies or SQL queries. Sometimes the queries can get rather complex, as in the following query used to load the SystemInfo table.

```
Select Distinct SystemId,
   (Select Max(SpeedSize)
      From Systems As CPU, InventoryItems
      Where CPU.SystemId = OUT.SystemId
         And InventoryType =CP
         And CPU.InventoryId = InventoryItems.InventoryId) CPUSpeed,
   (Select Sum(SpeedSize * Quantity)
      From Systems As MEM, InventoryItems
      Where MEM.SystemId = OUT.SystemId
         And InventoryType =ME
         And MEM.InventoryId = InventoryItems.InventoryId) Memory,
   (Select Sum(Quantity)
      From Systems As HD1, InventoryItems
      Where HD1.SystemId = OUT.SystemId
         And InventoryType =HD
         And HD1.InventoryId = InventoryItems.InventoryId)
            HardDiskCount,
   (Select Sum(SpeedSize * Quantity)
      From Systems As HD2, InventoryItems
      Where HD2.SystemId = OUT.SystemId
         And InventoryType =HD
         And HD2.InventoryId = InventoryItems.InventoryId)
            TotalHardDiskSize,
   (Select Max(SpeedSize)
      From Systems As DIS, InventoryItems
      Where DIS.SystemId = OUT.SystemId
         And InventoryType =DI
         And DIS.InventoryId = InventoryItems.InventoryId)
            MonitorSize
From Systems As OUT
```

This query is very complex because I want to radically transform the data from the JustPC tactical database into the JustPC data warehouse. This single statement summarizes a large number of rows of information into a single entry, making it easier for the end user to get information from the data warehouse.

Building this type of query is not something you can do without practice. However, it is something you can do without programming. This type of transformation isn't needed in many data warehouses. However, the type of query I used to combine the Customers and CustomerTypes tables is common when building most data warehouses.

Summary

The Data Transformation Services utility is one of the key components of building a data warehouse. Nearly all of your data already exists somewhere. Your job is to move it as quickly and as efficiently as possible. This is where DTS shines. It enables you to populate your data warehouse quickly and is easy enough to use without doing any programming. Although you don't need to be a programmer to load information into your data warehouse using DTS, having a good working knowledge of SQL is very helpful.

In the next chapter, I briefly cover some of the security issues related to running your data warehouse on a SQL Server database.

Chapter 10

Securing the Data Warehouse

IN THIS CHAPTER

◆ The SQL Server 7 security architecture

◆ Adding logins and user names to the database

◆ Adding users to a database

◆ Defining roles

◆ Securing tables and views

SECURITY IS SOMETHING THAT you may easily forget when designing a data warehouse, especially because the data is read-only. You may assume that as long as no one can modify your data, your data warehouse is secure. However, nothing is further from the truth. One of your organization's most valuable assets is the information in your data warehouse and one of your most important tasks is to prevent unauthorized access to your data.

The SQL Server 7 Security Architecture

Security in SQL Server 7 revolves two phases: authentication and authorization. *Authentication* is the process of establishing a user's identity to the database server, while *authorization* determines what resources an authenticated user may access.

Authentication

SQL Server 7 supports two methods to authenticate a user. The first is known as Windows NT Authentication Mode; the second is known as SQL Server Authentication. A SQL Server 7 database server operates in either Windows NT Authentication Mode or Mixed Mode, which supports both Windows NT Authentication Mode and SQL Server Authentication Mode. This user ID becomes known inside SQL Server 7 as the login ID.

WINDOWS NT AUTHENTICATION

In Windows NT Authentication Mode, a user must log on to a Windows NT domain successfully before attempting to log on to SQL Server 7. SQL Server then assumes that the user ID is valid and uses it as the SQL Server login ID. No other passwords are exchanged between the database server and user.

Microsoft recommends using Windows NT Authentication Mode because the security mechanisms in Windows 2000/NT far exceed those in SQL Server. When users log on to the domain, their passwords are verified using a sophisticated encryption algorithm. Windows automatically provides services that enable you to set password expiration dates, minimum size restrictions, and various auditing tools. Windows also provides you with the ability to disable a user ID after multiple invalid login attempts. When the user attempts to access SQL Server, SQL Server uses Windows security mechanisms to get the authenticated user ID and then determines if the user is permitted to access the database.

 **Disadvantage.** The downside to using Windows NT Authentication Mode is that only users with a Windows 95, 98, NT, or 2000–based computer can access the database server.

 **Security groups.** You can use Windows security groups with NT Authentication to simplify security administration.

SQL SERVER 7 AUTHENTICATION

In SQL Server 7 authentication, users must supply a special login ID and password when they attempt to log on. This information is verified against the master list of login IDs and passwords stored in the Master SQL Server database. If there is a match, then the user is permitted to access the database server.

In mixed mode access, SQL Server 7 examines the information supplied to it. If the user name is blank, SQL Server uses Windows NT Authentication to determine if the user name is valid – otherwise the information is checked with SQL Server Authentication. If the user ID doesn't match the information in Windows or SQL Server 7, then the user is denied access.

Authorization

Once the users are authenticated, the next step is to determine which resources they can access. This is a two-step process. First, the login ID is used to determine which databases the users can access. During this process, the login ID is mapped onto a user name for each database he or she can access. In the second step, the user name is used to determine which resources within the database the user is permitted to access.

 **About user names.** With this architecture, a particular user may have a different user name in each database that he or she accesses. Also, it is possible to have multiple login IDs mapped to a single user name.

This two-step process helps to ensure that certain databases, such as the SQL Server Master database, are protected from unauthorized access. It also allows one database server to support your production database as well as your data warehouse, yet keep them totally independent.

Roles

Roles are used to simplify database security. A role represents a group of users that you can manage as a single entity. You can add and remove users from a particular role and modify the permissions assigned to a role. Some roles are applied at the database level, while others apply to the whole database server. Those roles at the database server level are associated with logins, while those at the database level are associated with a database user name.

FIXED SERVER ROLES

When you install SQL Server 7, a number of roles are supplied automatically . These roles are used to perform various security-related functions (see Table 10-1). You should exercise caution when assigning these roles to someone because they all can affect the integrity of your database to a large degree.

TABLE 10-1 FIXED SERVER ROLES

Role	Role Name	Description
Security Administrators	`sysadmin`	Can perform any activity in SQL Server, including those activities associated with the rest of the roles listed in rest of this table.
Server Administrators	`serveradmin`	Can configure server-wide settings.
Setup Administrators	`setupadmin`	Can add or remove linked servers.
Security Administrators	`securityadmin`	Can add or delete logins.
Process Administrators	`processadmin`	Manages the processes within SQL Server 7.
Disk Administrators	`diskadmin`	Manages the disk files associated with SQL Server 7.
Database Creators	`dbcreator`	Can add and delete databases.

THE SYSTEM ADMINISTRATOR LOGIN

Every SQL Server 7 system includes one special login called sa, which is short for system administrator. This login is assigned to the sysadmin role, which is permitted to add and delete databases and add and delete logins.

Microsoft recommends that you create other logins that are assigned to the sysadmin role and use the sa login only in cases of emergency. My philosophy is less strict. If you have multiple people that are performing system administrator activities, then each person should have his or her own unique login assigned to the sysadmin role. However, if your database server has only one system administrator, then it is acceptable to use sa.

The sa login. By default, the sa login does not have a password. The first step in securing your database should be to assign a password to this login. If you don't, you run the risk of someone breaking into your database server and causing serious problems.

The sa login is hard-coded to the sysadmin role and cannot be changed.

Do not forget the password you assign to sa; otherwise you will have to reinstall SQL Server 7 to recover it.

FIXED DATABASE ROLES

Table 10-2 lists some roles that are used to manage functions inside a database. Within a database, the database owner is king. Anyone with this user name can determine who can access certain resources in the database.

TABLE 10-2 FIXED DATABASE ROLES

Role	Role Name	Description
Owner	db_owner	Can perform any operation in the database, including those activities associated with the rest of the roles listed in the rest of the table.

Role	Role Name	Description
Access Administrator	db_accessadmin	Can add and delete groups and users in the database.
Data Reader	db_datareader	Can see all data from all user tables in the database.
Data Writer	db_datawriter	Can update data from all user tables in the database.
Data Administrator	db_ddladmin	Manages the database objects in the database.
Security Administrator	db_securityadmin	Manages the roles and statement and object permissions in the database.
Backup Operator	db_backupoperator	Can backup the database.
Deny Data Reader	db_denydatareader	Cannot see any data in the database.
Deny Data Writer	db_denydatawriter	Cannot update any data in the database.

THE DATABASE OWNER USER NAME

All tables in a database are qualified by the user name and table name. Thus, if someone with the user name Christopher created the table MyTable, it would be known in the database as Christopher.MyTable. While Christopher can access the table as simply MyTable, anyone else using the database must reference it as Christopher.MyTable.

However, the user name dbo is special. If you use a table name without specifying the user name that created it, SQL Server 7 looks for the table under your user name, then checks if it was created by the dbo user name. Thus, if Samantha tries to use YourTable, SQL Server 7 checks to see if Samantha.YourTable exists. If it doesn't, then it checks to see if dbo.YourTable exists. If it doesn't, then SQL Server 7 returns an error. If it does, then Samantha can proceed to use the table (assuming that she has access to the table, which I cover later in this chapter).

 **About the dbo user name.** It's a good idea to create all of your tables using the dbo user name in your data warehouse and not allow any other users to create tables. This way, the user only needs to specify the name of the table when writing a query.

CUSTOM ROLES

While SQL Server 7 has a collection of fixed roles, as discussed earlier, you also can create your own roles. Roles are useful because you can define a role and assign a set of standard permissions to it. Then you can associate a user name with a role, just like one of the fixed roles. The user name automatically inherits all of the role's security permissions.

Permissions

Within a database, security permissions are used to grant or deny various types of access to a database object such as a table or a view. The actual object determines the exact set of permissions available. Table 10-3 lists some of the most common permissions.

TABLE 10-3 COMMON DATABASE PERMISSIONS

Permission	Description
Delete	The user can delete records from a table or a view.
Execute	The user can execute a stored procedure.
Insert	The user can add records to a table or a view.
Select	The user can retrieve records from a table or view.
Update	The user can change records in a table or a view.

Managing SQL Server Logins and Users

There are several tools available in SQL Server 7 that enable you to manage your logins. The easiest tool to use is Enterprise Manager. You can use a wizard to build your login, or you can enter the login directly (see Figure 10-1).

 **Query Analyzer.** If you wish, you also can use Query Analyzer to enter the appropriate SQL statement or to call the appropriate stored procedure to perform the desired security function.

If you look carefully, you can see that some of the logins listed come directly from Windows. These have a type of NT Group or NT User. Any user with a type of Standard uses SQL Server Authentication to access the system.

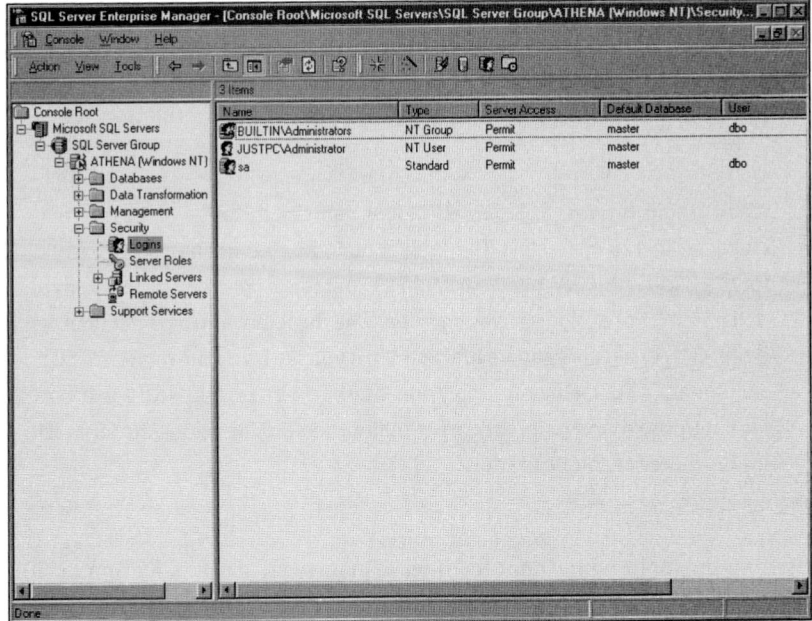

Figure 10-1: Viewing the list of logins

Adding a New Login ID

To add a login ID, right-click the Logins icon or the right side pane of the Enterprise Manager window and then select New Login from the popup menu. This displays the Login Properties dialog box (as shown in Figure 10-2).

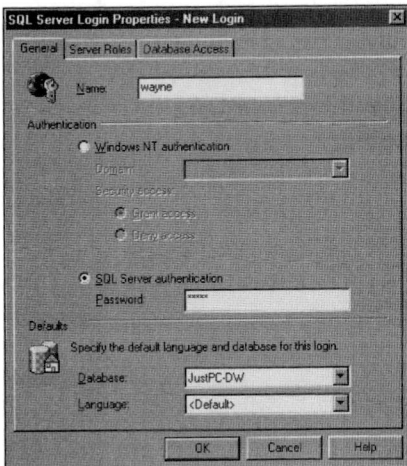

Figure 10-2: The General tab of the SQL Server 7 Login Properties dialog box

ENTERING A LOGIN NAME

In the Name text box on the General tab, you must specify the login ID you want to create. This can be the Windows user ID of the user (if you want to use Windows NT Authentication) or a name created for use with SQL Server Authentication.

 **About login names.** SQL Server 7 login names can range in size from 1 character to 128 characters. They can contain any set of characters, except for the backslash (\). When your login ID contains a space, or begins with a dollar sign ($) or at sign (@), you must enclose the login with a pair of double quotes ("") or a pair of square brackets ([ ]) if you are using the name in a SQL statement. Of course, if you simply are entering your login ID into a text box for Enterprise Manager or any other utility, then don't enclose the login ID inside quotes or square brackets.

After entering the login name, choose either Windows NT Authentication or SQL Server Authentication. If you specify Windows NT Authentication, you have a choice whether to grant access to the database server or deny access. If you select SQL Server Authentication, you need to specify a password for the login.

At the bottom of the General tab, you can specify the default database and language for the login. For the default database, specify the database that the login will use the most. You should never leave the default database set to master, model, msdb, or tempdb – even for system administrators. This helps to prevent someone accidentally modifying the wrong database.

SELECTING SECURITY SERVER ROLES

On the Server Roles tab, you can choose which of the fixed server roles the login is granted (see Figure 10-3). As you select each role, a brief description is displayed in the Description frame. Normally, you shouldn't select any of these roles because most users should not have this ability. Only individuals whose job responsibilities absolutely need these roles should be assigned to them.

Pressing the Properties button near the bottom of the form displays a Permissions dialog box that lists both the users that already are assigned to this role, plus the individual commands that anyone who is granted this role may perform.

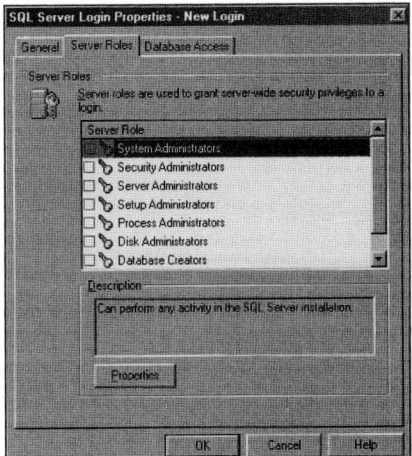

Figure 10-3: Choosing security roles for your new login ID

 **How many admins?** Finding the correct balance between too many and too few administrators is always a challenge. In general, the fewer people that have access to the administrator roles the better. However, it is always a good idea to have at least two people that have administrator privileges because there will be times when you need to make a change to your database and the only person with administrator privileges is on vacation in the Rockies without a phone.

GRANTING ACCESS TO DATABASES

On the Database Access tab, you can select which databases the login may access (see Figure 10-4). Placing a checkmark in the box next to the database name implies that the login has access to that particular database. To the right of the database name is a field where you need to specify the user name that the individual assumes when he or she accesses that database. When you place the checkmark next to the database name, the Enterprise Manager automatically puts the same name in the User column.

 **Security alert.** Never grant access to the master, model, msdb, or tempdb databases to a user who is not involved directly with managing the database. This can cause a potential security problem.

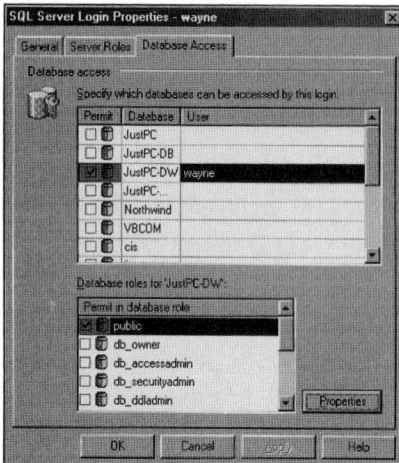

Figure 10-4: Granting access to one or more databases

TIP

Same name? While the user name need not be the same as the login name, using two different names can lead to confusion on the part of the user and the security administrator. By using the same name, the user never realizes that the login name and the user name are two distinct values.

Once you permit the login to access a database, the list of database roles in that database is displayed below the list of databases. Check the appropriate role or roles that the user should have. Next to the roles section of the Database Access tab is a button labeled Properties. Pressing this button displays the users who are currently in the role.

SAVING YOUR NEW LOGIN

Once you finish choosing which databases the user should have access to, press OK to create the new login. If you create a login using SQL Server Authentication, you are prompted to reenter the password to ensure that the password is correct. When you press OK on the Confirm Password dialog box, the login will be saved.

Modifying a Login

After you create a login, you may have to change some of its characteristics from time to time. Simply select the Logins icon on the tree view area of Enterprise Manager and double-click the login name you want to modify in the data area. The same property window that you used to enter the login information is displayed. You then can change any of the properties associated with the login, except for the authentication method.

Securing Tables and Views

In addition to the fixed roles for the server and for a database, you also can define your own roles for use in controlling access to tables and views in your database.

Creating a Role

To create a database role, expand the tree view in Enterprise Manager to show the database you want to secure. Expand the Database icon to show the details below it. Right-click the Roles icon and select New Role from the popup menu. This displays the Database Role Properties window, as shown in Figure 10-5. Fill in the Name field with a descriptive name for the role. Then select Standard role as the database role type.

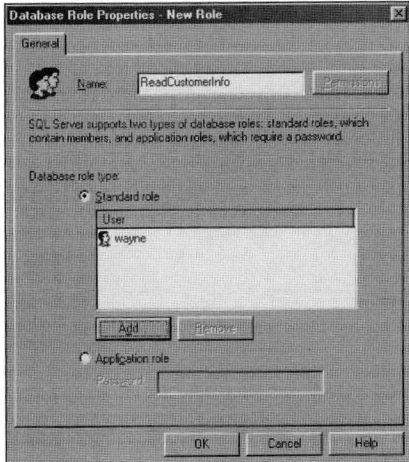

Figure 10-5: Adding a new standard role to a database

 **About role names.** The name of a role must not duplicate the name of another role or a user already in the database.

ASSOCIATING DATABASE PERMISSIONS WITH A ROLE

Pressing the Permissions button displays the dialog box shown in Figure 10-6. You can choose to list all of the objects that can be secured in the database or list only those objects that already are part of the role. To add a new table or view, you must list all of the objects in the database.

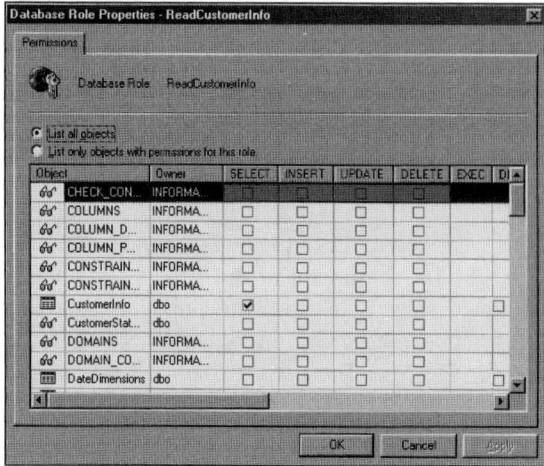

Figure 10-6: Assigning permissions to a role

For each table or view, you can select from a set of permissions including Select, Insert, Update, and Delete. Choose Select if you want to allow the members of this role to read the table. Choose Insert, Update, and Delete if you want to permit the members of this role to modify the table. (Note that the other permissions listed, such as Exec, don't apply to a table).

Insert, Update, and Delete. Many database objects hold information about the database itself. Do not allow normal database users to access any of these tables with Insert, Update, or Delete. Should they change values in some of these tables, your database can become corrupt.

ADDING USER NAMES TO A ROLE

Pressing the Add button on the Database Role Properties dialog box (see Figure 10-5) displays the list of user names in the database, which currently are not added to the role (see Figure 10-7). Choose the names that you want to add and press OK. The names are added to the role and the display is updated to reflect the newly added names. To remove a name from the list, select the name and press the Remove button (not shown in the following figure). When you finish adding names to the list, press the OK button to create the role.

Two different roles. Don't confuse standard roles and application roles. Application roles are intended for use by application programs when handling special security problems that can't be solved using standard roles.

Figure 10-7: Adding user names to a role

Modifying and Deleting Roles

Modifying a role involves listing the roles in your database and double-clicking the role you want to modify. From there you can see the same dialog box you saw when you created the role. The only difference: where you entered the name of the role into a text box, the name of the role can't be changed.

To delete a role, you first must remove all of the users in the role. You do that by opening the role's Properties window and explicitly removing all of the users by selecting them and pressing the Remove button. After pressing the OK button to close the property window, right-click the role and select Delete from the popup menu. The Enterprise Manager displays a message box asking if you really want to delete the role. Pressing Yes removes the role from your database.

Summary

In this chapter, I talked about how to create logins, user names, and roles to prevent unauthorized access to your database. If you don't secure your database, you're just asking for someone to try to break in and steal your data.

Believe it or not, the people you need to worry the most about breaking into your application are the folks that already have access to your network. If you leave your database unsecured, someone on your staff who shouldn't have access to the data may try to do something with it. They can modify the data so that your data warehouse helps you make bad decisions or they can copy your data and sell it to a competitor who might use it to better understand how you operate your organization.

This chapter also wrapped up the part of the book devoted to creating your data warehouse. In the next part, I introduce you to the SQL language and Query Analyzer. Together, these tools enable you to perform queries to your newly created database.

Part III

Using the Data Warehouse with Query Analyzer

Chapter 11

Creating Simple Queries with Query Analyzer

IN THIS CHAPTER

- ◆ Introducing Query Analyzer
- ◆ Introducing the Structured Query Language
- ◆ Creating simple Select statements
- ◆ Using the Where clause
- ◆ Sorting with the Order By clause
- ◆ Complex SQL queries

IN THIS CHAPTER, I introduce you to Microsoft's Query Analyzer. Query Analyzer provides the ability to edit and execute Structured Query Language (SQL) statements. At the same time, I introduce you to the most commonly used SQL statement, the **Select** statement, which is used to retrieve data from your databases.

Introducing Query Analyzer

Now that you know how to put data into your data warehouse, let's discuss how to extract information from your data warehouse. While there are other tools you can use to access your database, the most fundamental tool is the Microsoft Query Analyzer.

A *query* generally is a request for information from a database. Sometimes, people use the term query to refer to any database operation. In the case of Query Analyzer, queries are written in a language known as the Structured Query Language or SQL.

Query Analyzer enables you to enter and execute SQL statements interactively. While Query Analyzer is a relatively primitive tool, it is one of the most important database tools you have. SQL Server 7 is also based on the Structured Query Language; the ability to work in the native language of the database server is important. Many of the tools that I cover in the rest of the book rely on the SQL language for their internal processing and some (such as Data Transformation Services) require you to write SQL statements.

In this chapter, and in those that follow, I use the sample data warehouse on the CD-ROM. If you load the data warehouse onto your database server, I strongly recommend that you try some of the examples using Query Analyzer. While some people think the SQL language may be difficult to learn, I believe that the more queries you execute the more comfortable you will be with the language.

Introducing the Structured Query Language

SQL originally was developed in the 1970s (by researchers working for IBM to access information stored in a relational database. Since then it has evolved to become an industry standard. All major database vendors support this language and it has evolved into an ANSI standard. Essentially, if you know how to use SQL on an Oracle system, you easily can transfer it to SQL Server 7.

SQL is a rich and complicated language. I do not discuss all of the details of the language in this book. Instead I focus on some of the statements you are most likely to use. However, it is worth the time to learn about. I recommend reading *SQL For Dummies,* written by Allen G. Taylor and published by IDG Books Worldwide, to get all of the real details.

Set Theory

SQL is based on set theory. When using SQL statements, don't think about individual rows of data but rather sets of data; all of the statements I talk about deal with sets of data. Sometimes a set of data consists of a single member, while other times a set deals with thousands of members. Regardless, there is no difference in how you write the SQL statements.

Each set corresponds to a table and each member of the set corresponds to a row in the table. A set can contain zero or more members. If the set doesn't have any members, it's known as the *empty set.* A set with the members A, B, and C usually is written as:

```
{A, B, C}
```

OPERATIONS AGAINST A SINGLE SET

You can perform a number of operations against a single set. First, you can determine if something is a member of a set using the IN operator. This returns a value that is either TRUE (meaning the item is in the set) or FALSE (meaning the item is not in the set). Other operators include COUNT, which counts the number of items in a set; MIN, which determines the smallest member in the set; and MAX, which determines the largest member in the set.

```
A In {A, B, C} = TRUE
Count {A, B, C} = 3
Min {A, B, C} = A
```

The DISTINCT operator returns a set in which all of the members are unique. Any duplicate members are discarded.

```
Distinct {A, B, B, C} = {A, B, C}
```

OPERATIONS AGAINST TWO SETS

You also can perform operations using two sets. The AND operator compares the members in two sets and lists the members in common. This also is known as the INTERSECTION operator. The OR operator, on the other hand, returns the set of values that are found in both sets. This operator also is known as a UNION.

```
{A, B, C} And {B, C, D} =  {B, C}
{A, B, C} Or {B, C, D} = {A, B, C, B, C, D}
```

Note that the OR operator may leave duplicate values. If you then apply the DISTINCT operator, the duplicate values are eliminated.

```
Distinct {A, B, C} Or {B, C, D} = {A, B, C, D}
```

By combining these operators, you can perform some very complex set manipulations. These types of operations become very important when I start talking about the Where clause later in this chapter.

Types of Statements

The SQL language defines a series of *statements,* which basically are commands that perform specific functions in the database. There are statements that you use to create databases and tables. Other statements enable you to add, delete, and update records from tables. Yet another statement enables you to retrieve records from the database. This statement is known as the Select statement. (I discuss it in detail later in this chapter.) Other key statements, which I talk about in Chapter 12, include:

- ◆ **Create Table** creates a table in a database.
- ◆ **Create View** creates an alternate way of looking at a database.
- ◆ **Drop View** deletes a view.
- ◆ **Insert** adds one or more records to a table.
- ◆ **Delete** deletes one or more records from a table.
- ◆ **Update** changes values in one or more records in a table.

Referencing Tables and Columns

SQL statements perform operations against databases, tables, and columns. Within each table, every column is unique. Each combination of table name and user name is unique within a database. Thus, if you have a column called CustomerId within a table called CustomerInfo created by the user dbo in a database called JustPC-DW, you can reference a table like this:

```
JustPC-DW.dbo.CustomerInfo
```

and a field within the table like this:

```
CustomerInfo.CustomerId
```

The key is that you separate each name with a period and you list the names from most general (database name) to most specific (column name).

You only need to include a reference to a database if you are accessing a table in a database that is outside your current database. SQL Server 7 checks for a table referenced by the user's name and tries dbo if it doesn't find the table, so you usually can omit the user name as well.

In the Enterprise Manager, it is easy to create table names and column names that include special characters, such as a space. While this is legal in SQL, it also causes problems when parsing the language. For instance, if you choose to use the following table name,

```
Customer Info
```

the parser in SQL sees two words instead of a single word referring to a table. This creates a ton of problems for the parser. The SQL language has a special way to handle this situation. You must enclose the name in a pair of square brackets like this:

```
[customer info]
```

You can even use them to qualify multiple names such as:

```
[customer info].[customer identifier]
```

Note that you don't want to try writing the statement this way:

```
[customer info.customer identifier]
```

The original case refers to a table name and a column name in the table. The second case refers to a single name that has two spaces and a period in the middle.

A Brief Introduction to Query Analyzer

In order to use Query Analyzer, you need to know how to write SQL statements. However, the best way of learning is by doing, so you really need to learn a little about Query Analyzer in order to run some of these samples.

Starting Query Analyzer

To run Query Analyzer, choose Start → Programs → Microsoft SQL Server 7.0 → Query Analyzer. When the program first starts, you see the main Query Analyzer window in the background and a SQL Server logon window (see Figure 11-1) in the front. Select the database server you want to use, enter your user information, and press OK.

Figure 11-1: Logging into SQL Server

Parts of a Query Analyzer Form

After you finish with the logon window, you see a window similar to the one shown in Figure 11-2. The first thing you should notice is that Query Analyzer is a *multiple-document interface (MDI)* program similar to Excel. The main program offers an area where you can have multiple open documents. In this case, each document holds a single query session.

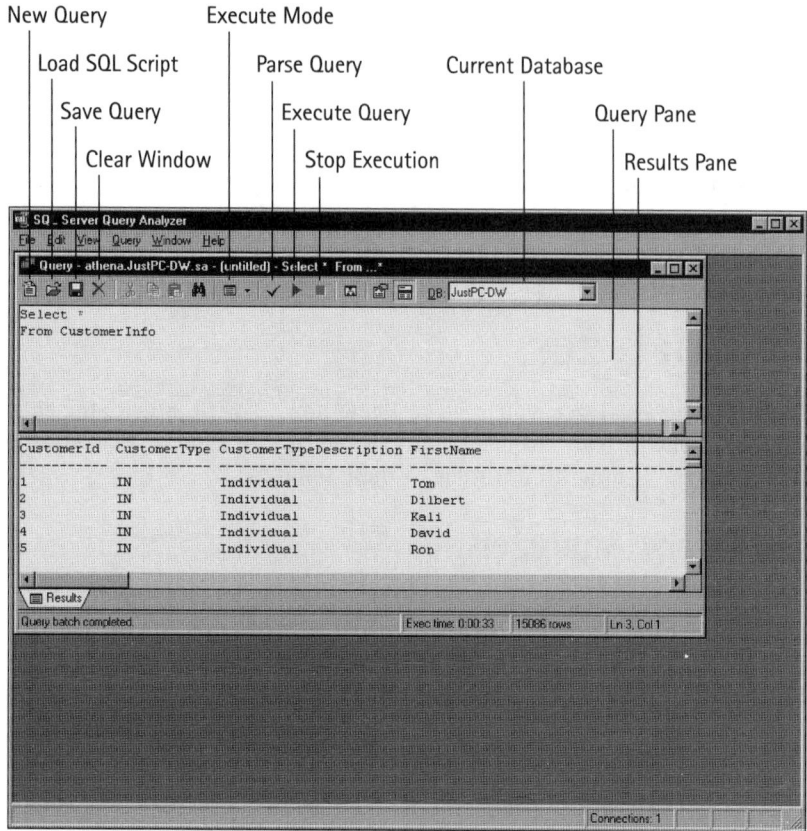

Figure 11-2: Viewing a Query Analyzer window

Each query window has a toolbar, a Query Pane, and a Results Pane. While you can see the Results Pane in Figure 11-2, it normally is not visible until you execute your query. You can find everything you need to execute your queries in the toolbar. Following is list of the most important buttons and what they do.

♦ **New query** opens a new query window.

♦ **Load SQL script** enables you to choose a text file (usually with a file type of .SQL) and load it into the query window.

♦ **Save query** enables you to save your current SQL query into a text file with a file type of .SQL. If your cursor is in the Results Pane, pressing this button saves the results to a report file (.RPT) which is really just another text file.

- **Clear window** clears the current window and leaves it ready for you to enter another query.

- **Execute mode** determines how the results of the query are displayed in the Results Pane. By default, it is displayed as a series of text lines. However, you also can choose to display the results in a *data grid*. Additionally, you can choose to see the details of how the query was executed by viewing the execution plan.

- **Parse query** enables you to verify that the structure of your query is correct before you attempt to execute. Parsing your query does not find some types of errors, such as misspelled table names and column names, but it can find out if you managed to put all of the symbols and keywords in the right place.

- **Execute query** actually runs your query. It begins by parsing your query, then resolving all of the column and table names. If everything is correct, it executes the query and returns the results in the Results Pane.

- **Stop execution** stops a query while it's executing. Because a query can take minutes or hours to run, the Stop button can be a very useful thing.

- **Current database** contains a drop-down list of databases that you can access on your database server. The one displayed is your current default database. You can change your default database by picking another one from the list.

 It is very important that you check the current database drop-down box when you start Query Analyzer. By default, it tries to pick the database called Master. Unfortunately, this is the worst possible default database because SQL Server 7 uses it to store information about all of the other databases in the database server. I do not recommend you access this database at all; if you manage to update a table or delete it, you may get some firsthand, practical experience on how to restore a corrupted database server.

The Select Statement

The **Select** statement is the most commonly used statement in SQL. Its purpose is to enable you to retrieve information from your database. You can use it to retrieve one row or an entire table. You also can use it to combine tables into a new table. Finally, you can use it to sort and summarize the data you retrieve.

The **Select** statement also happens to be the most complicated statement in SQL. The following syntax represents only part of the full **Select** statement syntax. However, you rarely need more than what I cover here.

```
Select [<selectoption> ] <selectexpression> [, <selectexpression>]
....
[Into <newtable>]
From <tableref> [, <tableref>] ...
[Where <expression>]
[Group By <column> [, <column>] ... [With Rollup]
[Having <expression>]
[Order By <expression> [Asc|Desc] [,<expression> [Asc|Desc] ]...
```

Where

```
<selectoption> ::= All | Distinct | Top <number>
<selectexpression> :: = * | <selectitem> [ [As] <alias> ]
<selectitem> ::= <column> | <function> ( [Distinct]<expression> ) |
<expression>
<function> ::= Count | Max | Min | Sum
```

And

```
<alias> is an alternate name of a column or table.
<expression> is a valid expression.
<newtable> is the name of a table that will hold the result of the
query.
<number> is a valid number.
```

A **Select** statement is composed of a series of clauses such as **Into**, **From**, **Where**, and so on. Only the **From** clause is required. Next, I discuss how the basic **Select** statement works, and then I discuss each of the clauses that work with it.

The Basic Select Statement

To use a basic **Select** statement, you simply need to identify the table and the columns you want to retrieve from the database. For the StoreInfo table in the JustPC data warehouse, the **Select** statement looks like this:

```
Select StoreId, Street, City, State, Zip, Phone
From StoreInfo
```

Immediately following the **Select** statement is the list of columns you want to retrieve. Each column is separated from the previous column by a comma. The **From** clause specifies the table you want to use. Running this statement in Query Analyzer generates the results shown in Figure 11-3.

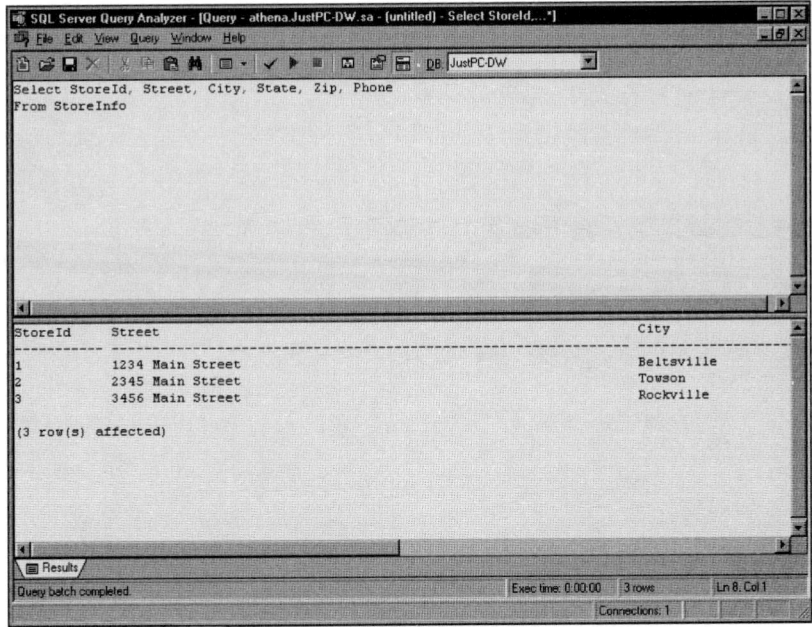

Figure 11-3: Running a simple query

It is very common to retrieve all of the columns of a table in a query, so the SQL language enables you to use an asterisk where you normally would have a list of column names. This shortcut enables you to rewrite the previous query like this:

```
Select *
From StoreInfo
```

Executing this query returns the exact same results.

COUNTING WITH FUNCTIONS

In addition to retrieving columns, you also can perform some basic calculations using a basic **Select** statement. For instance, the following query returns the number of records in a table).

```
Select Count(CustomerId)
From StoreInfo
```

In addition to COUNT, you can use other functions such as MIN, MAX, and SUM. These functions return the minimum value for the column, the maximum value for the column, and the sum of all of the values in the column. For the COUNT function only, you can use an asterisk in place of a column (see Figure 11-4).

```
Select Count(*)
From StoreInfo
```

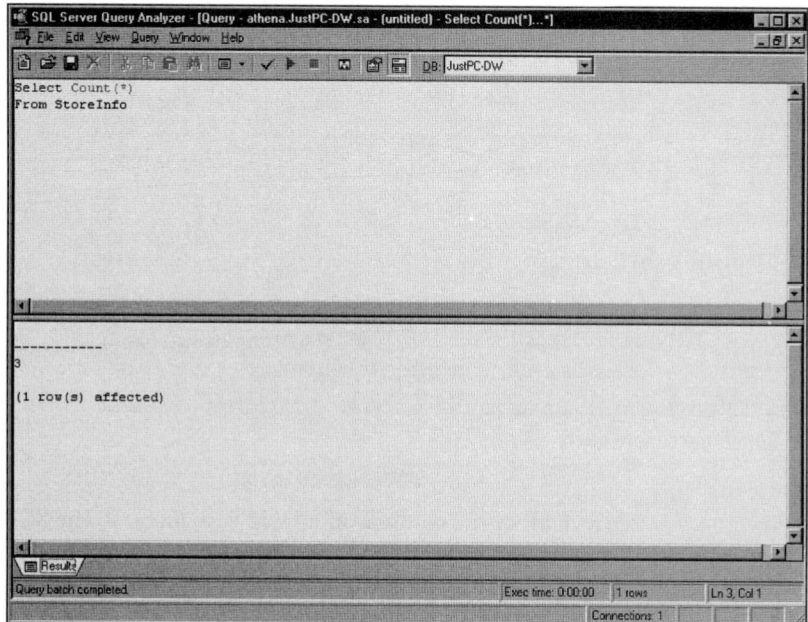

Figure 11-4: Counting the number of rows in a table

Remember the **Select Count(*)** statement. You will use it frequently when you want to find the number of rows in a table.

If you try to use a formula and a column name in the same **Select** statement, you get a cryptic error message that says something about a missing **Group By** clause. This happens because the COUNT function returns one row, while the column name returns one row for each row in the table.

COLUMN HEADERS

One problem, as you may have noticed in Figure 11-4, is that the results of a query displayed in the Results Pane do not have a column header. While this isn't a problem with the simple queries I've presented so far, it does become a problem with more complex ones.

The solution to this problem is to add column headers (formally known as *aliases*) to each column. You include an alias by adding a second identifier after the formula. The alias must be enclosed in double quotes ("Record Count") or in square brackets ([Min Store]) if the identifier has a space or a special character inside it, or you may simply write the identifier as a single identifier (MaxStore) if it doesn't contain any spaces or special characters (see Figure 11-5).

```
Select Count(*) Record Count, Min(StoreId) [Min Store],
   Max(StoreId) MaxStore
From StoreInfo
```

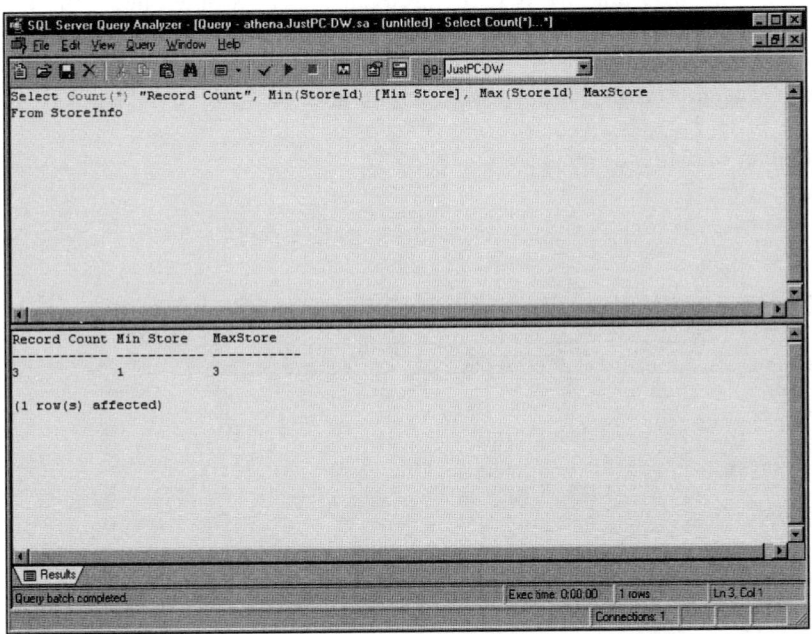

Figure 11-5: Counting the number of rows in a table in a different way

While the above example uses functions, you also can use an alias with any column. Thus, you can employ this facility to create reports with nice column headings. To do this, access the print facility by going to the main menu and choosing File → Print. Selecting Subsets of a Table

One nice thing about using a small table is that the queries are manageable. They run very quickly and don't return a lot of information. However, it is far more common to use queries with large tables. In most cases, you don't want to return all of the rows in a table; you want to see the records that are related to a particular customer or a particular item in inventory. You do this in a **Select** statement by using the **Where** clause to isolate the records you really want to retrieve.

USING SIMPLE SEARCH EXPRESSIONS

When you code a **Where** clause, you need to supply an expression that is TRUE only for the records you want to retrieve. A simple case using the StoreInfo table is to retrieve all the rows for a particular StoreId, as in the following statement.

```
Select *
From StoreInfo
Where StoreId = 1
```

In this example, only one row is returned because there is only one row in the table with a StoreId value of 1. (Remember that any value stored in StoreId must be unique within the table). However, if I run the same query against another table, such as the SystemInfo table, I retrieve a greater number of records (see Figure 11-6).

```
Select Count(*) Records Found
From SystemInfo
Where StoreId = 1
```

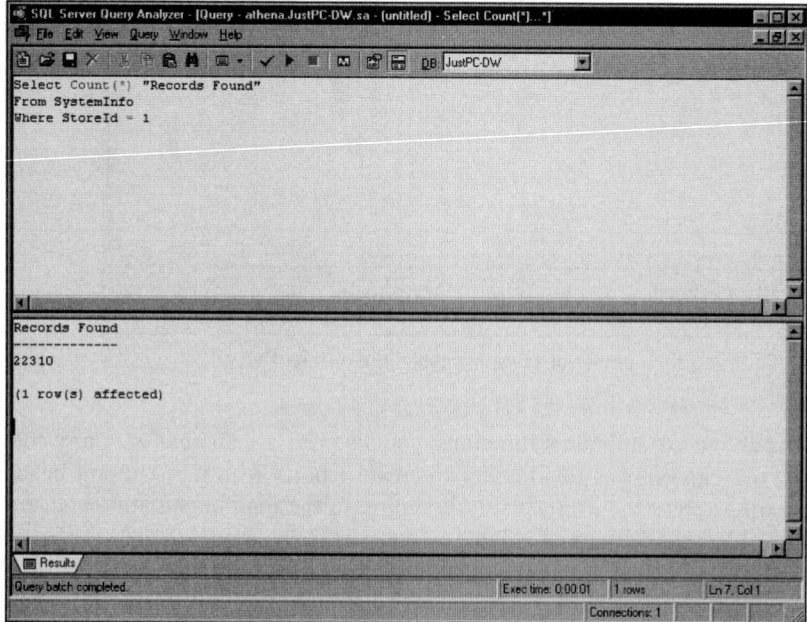

Figure 11-6: Retrieving numerous records

Putting this in terms of set theory, you are creating a set using the **Select** statement whose members have a particular value for an attribute for each member.

MORE COMPLEX SEARCH EXPRESSIONS

Let's assume that you want to find the number of computers sold in April 1999. You have a complete list of systems and purchase dates in the SystemInfo table. The easiest way to find this number is to use a more complex expression in the **Where** clause (see Figure 11-7). For example:

```
Select *
From SystemInfo
Where DatePurchased >= "1-April-1999" And DatePurchased <= "4/30/99"
```

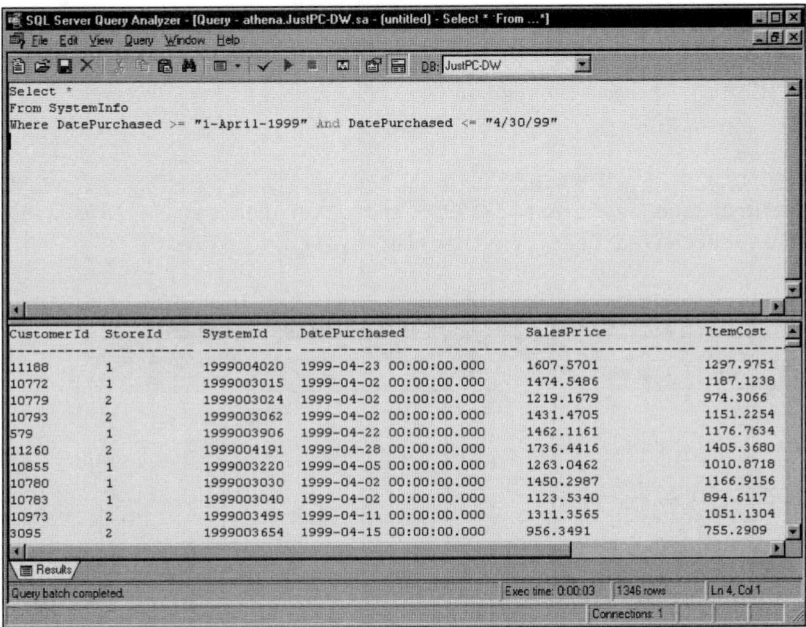

Figure 11-7: Finding a particular group of records in a table

This query retrieves all records in the SystemInfo table whose DatePurchased value is greater or equal to April 1 and less than or equal to April 30. Another way of approaching this is to consider that there are really two subsets we're dealing with. The first subset includes all of the systems purchased on or after April 1, while the second set contains all of the systems purchased on or before April 30. Then, take the intersection of the two sets by using the And operator.

While the above example uses the same column multiple times, you just as easily can use multiple columns. For instance, to answer the question, "How many computers did customer 11111 purchase in 1999?", write the following query.

```
Select Count(*)
From SystemInfo
Where DatePurchased >= "1/1/1999" And CustomerId = 11111
```

Sorting the Results

If you look carefully at the results listed in Figure 11-7, notice that the information isn't displayed in any particular order. Look particularly at the values in the CustomerId and DatePurchased fields. Also note that this set contains over 1,300 records. If you printed this list and tried to find a particular customer on a particular date, you would have to search a bunch of pages.

Wouldn't it be nice to sort the results in some meaningful way? Well, you can use the Sort clause. The Sort clause enables you to specify a list of one or more columns that you want to sort. If you want your data sorted from the highest value to the lowest, simply use the keyword Desc to return the rows in descending order (see Figure 11-8).

```
Select *
From SystemInfo
Where DatePurchased >= "1-April-1999" And DatePurchased <= "4/30/99"
Order By DatePurchased Desc, CustomerId, SystemId
```

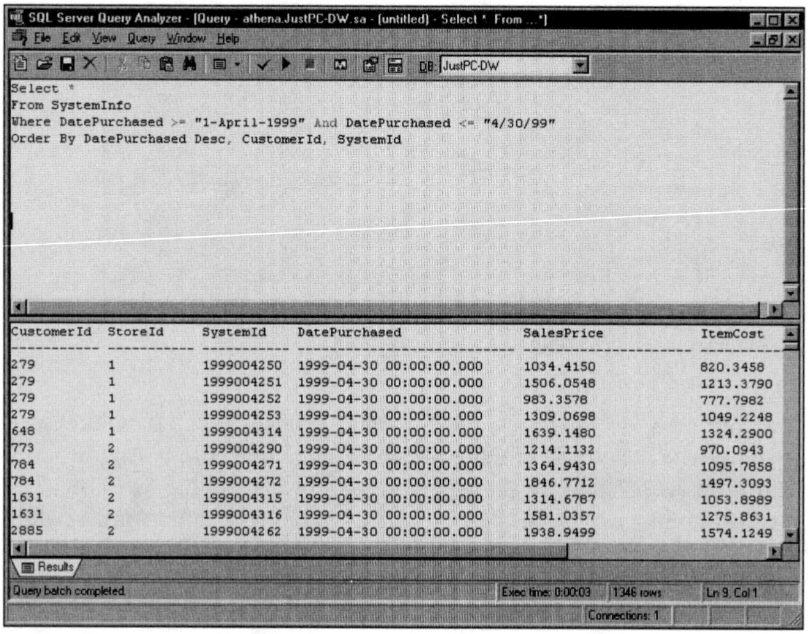

Figure 11-8: Sorting your results

Summary

In this chapter, I introduced you to Query Analyzer and the **Select** statement. While you may or may not believe it, the material I covered in this chapter is sufficient to answer most of the questions you are likely to ask of your data warehouse. For instance, you can write **Select** statements that answer questions such as, Who is customer 12345? (Hint: Customer=12345), What is the total value of the systems sold in December 1998? (Hint: **Sum**(SalesPrice), and How many customers live in Beltsville? (Hint: **Count**(City).

I strongly encourage you to load the sample database from the CD-ROM accompanying this book and try to run some of these queries. There is enough information here for you to have some fun and learn at the same time.

In the next chapter, I dig deeper into the **Select** statement and cover issues such as creating totals and subtotals and accessing more than one table in the same statement. I also talk about how to create a table, which isn't a table, to help you solve other problems when you become more comfortable using your data warehouse.

Chapter 12

Writing Complex Queries

IN THIS CHAPTER

- ◆ Using the Group By clause
- ◆ Using the Having clause
- ◆ Using two or more tables in the same Select statement
- ◆ Nested queries

IN THIS CHAPTER, I continue my discussion of the **Select** statement and how to use it with Query Analyzer. I also cover how to access multiple tables in a single query and how to extract totals and subtotals from your query. Finally, you learn about views, which enable you to define a table based on tables that already exist.

Creating Reports

In Chapter 11, I talked about how you can use the **Where** and **Order By** clauses to create simple reports. Now I want to show you how to get more information from your tables than you can by running simple queries.

Performing Calculations

The first area I want to address is how to perform calculations. Quite often, you find that you have information in your database that isn't quite the value you want. You can run the query and drag out your calculator to perform the final calculations, or you can use the **Select** statement to do the dirty work for you.

CALCULATING WITH CONSTANTS

One of the simplest **Select** statements is shown below. It computes the value for 1+1 and returns it as a single row (see Figure 12-1).

```
Select 1+1
```

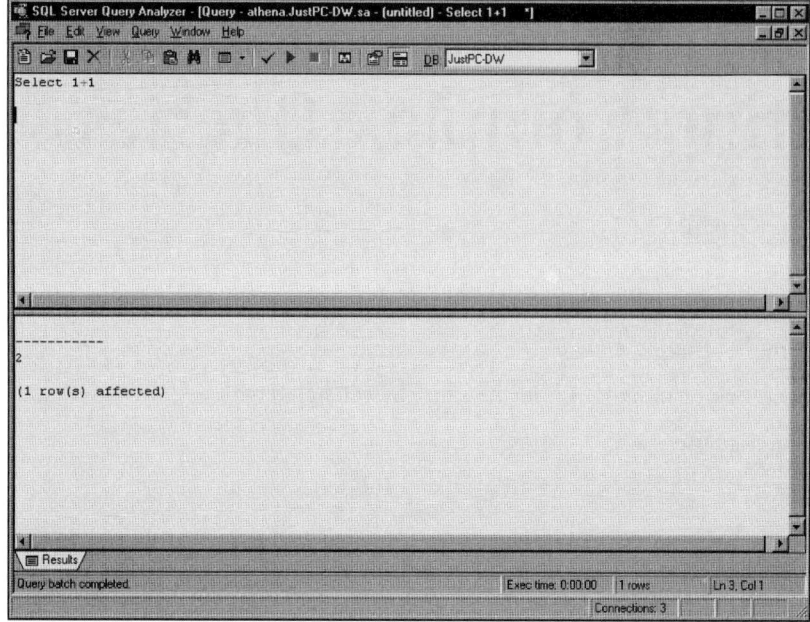

Figure 12-1: Proving 1+1 equals 2

In this case, I don't need the **From** clause because I'm not accessing any tables. The single column I compute is returned as a single row. Note that I can perform calculations with more complex expressions; if I separate the expressions with commas, I return one column for each expression (as in the following statement).

```
Select 2+2, 2*2, 2/2, 1+2-3*4/5
```

CALCULATING WITH COLUMNS

Suppose you want to find out how much profit JustPC made selling computers in a particular month. While you don't have a field containing the profit, you do have the information you need to calculate profit in the SystemInfo table. If you subtract ItemCost and LaborCost from SalesPrice, you get the profit as shown in the following query.

```
Select SalesPrice-ItemCost-LaborCost
From SystemInfo
```

 When performing calculations using a **Select** statement, the server uses the most exact data type available. This isn't a problem until you realize the expression 1/2 returns a value of 0, not 0.5. You need to restate the expression as 1/2.0, 1.0/2, or 1.0/2.0 to get a resulting value of 0.5. Usually, the data type chosen for the calculations is driven by the data types of the columns included in the calculation.

You can use the aggregation functions SUM and COUNT (discussed in Chapter 11) with calculations. For that matter, you can even use aliases and the **Where** clause, as in the following example (see Figure 12-2). Note that I can include the calculations inside the SUM function or perform the calculations outside the SUM function. The results are the same.

```
Select Sum(SalesPrice)- Sum(ItemCost)- Sum(LaborCost) "Total 1",
    Sum(SalesPrice-ItemCost-LaborCost) "Total 2"
From SystemInfo
Where DatePurchased >= "1-April-1999"
    And DatePurchased <= "4/30/99"
```

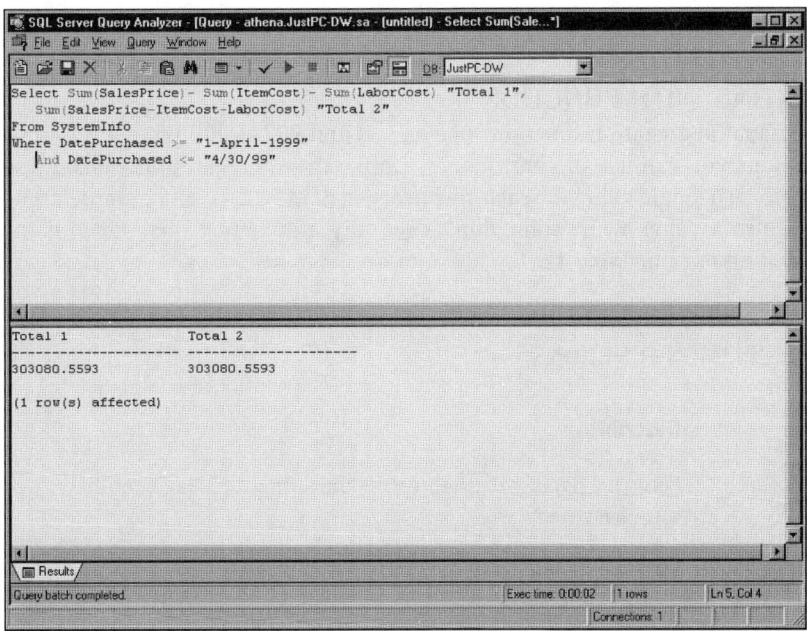

Figure 12-2: Computing profit two different ways

Formatting SQL Statements

I should mention that there are no formatting requirements for SQL statements. You can write a statement as a single line or one line per keyword, identifier, or quoted string. However, here are a few tips I've learned over the years.

First, always start each clause on a new line. This makes it easy to find each clause in your query.

Second, if a clause doesn't fit on a single line, indent the next line of the clause and any lines after that, until you reach the start of the next clause. Again, this serves to identify the major sections of your query.

Third, start each condition on a new line in a **Where** clause and end the previous line before the logical operator (for example, And and Or) begins. Typically, the **Where** clause is the longest clause in a query and it is also the place where you're most likely to find a problem. Finally, this clause makes it easy to add or delete additional conditions.

While you may not think that formatting your SQL statement is important, most queries will tend to grow longer and more complex than you expect. Proper formatting also helps to find syntax errors in your query. By now, you probably have learned that the error messages Query Analyzer returns are, at best, cryptic.

CALCULATING WITH FUNCTIONS

I've talked about aggregation function such as SUM and COUNT, but there are a lot of other functions you can use in your queries. Unlike the aggregate functions, these functions return a single value for each row processed. Most take one or more arguments to return a value, while some don't need any arguments. I list some of the more interesting ones in Table 12-1.

Table 12-1 COMMON FUNCTIONS

Function	Description
ASCII	Returns a number that represents the leftmost character in the specified string.
CAST	Converts an expression to a different data type.
CURRENT_USER	Returns the name of the current user.
DATEADD	Adds a number to a date/time value.

Function	Description
DATEDIFF	Subtracts two dates.
DATENAME	Returns a string containing the specified value from a date/time expression.
DATEPART	Returns a number containing the specified value from a date/time expression.
DAY	Returns the day of a month from a date/time expression.
GETDATE	Returns the current date and time.
MONTH	Returns the month value from a date/time expression.
RAND	Returns a random number between 0 and 1.
ROUND	Returns a numeric value rounded to the specified length or precision.
STR	Converts numbers to their equivalent characters.
STUFF	Inserts a string into another string.
SUBSTRING	Retrieves a string from the middle of another string.
YEAR	Returns a year value from a date/time expression.

Let's suppose you want to find the number of computers purchased in the year 1998. As I showed you earlier, you can write a **Select** statement that looks like this:

```
Select Count(*)
From SystemInfo
Where DatePurchased >= "1-January-1998"
   And DatePurchased <= "31-December-1998"
```

However, it's easier to write it like this:

```
Select Count(*)
From SystemInfo
Where Year(DatePurchased) = 1998
```

Both **Select** statements return the same values, but the second one is much easier to write.

Here's another example that you may find interesting. Create a list of all the computers purchased in the last 90 days. While you can figure out what the date was 90 days ago and enter that value into your query, the following query uses the DATEDIFF function and the GETDATE function to compute the date automatically.

```
Select Count(*)
From SystemInfo
Where DateDiff(Day, DatePurchased, GetDate()) <= 90
```

Summarizing Data

In Chapter 11, I talked about how to get totals from a set of data. However, it is often desirable to get subtotal values as well. To do this, you use the **Group By** clause. The **Group By** clause is a bit more complicated than other clauses because it imposes some restrictions on the values you retrieve from the database.

HOW GROUP BY WORKS

The **Group By** clause works by taking the data retrieved from the table and breaking it up into subsets in which each set of values for the columns listed in the **Group By** clause is unique. Then, for each subset of the data, it outputs a single row of information using the list of columns specified after the **Select** keyword. These columns can contain references to the columns in the **Group By** clause and may use aggregation functions containing references to the other columns available in the table.

Does this sound confusing? Then let's consider the following query, which generates the results shown in Figure 12-3.

```
Select DatePurchased, Sum(SalesPrice) "Total Sales"
From SystemInfo
Where DatePurchased >= "1-September-1999"
Group By DatePurchased
Order By DatePurchased
```

I use the **Where** clause to exclude all of the data before September 1, 1999 from the query. Then I break the remaining data into subsets using the values in DatePurchased. Next, I retrieve the values from the DatePurchased column and add up the total sales for each group using the SalesPrice column. Finally, I use the **Order By** clause to place the final set of data in order by the value in the DatePurchased column.

GETTING TOTALS AND SUBTOTALS

One of the options available with the **Group By** clause is `With Rollup`. This keyword instructs the database server to return additional rows containing subtotals and a grand total for each of the subsets. Null values are used to distinguish between normal summary rows and the subtotal and grand total rows. Thus, the grand total row has null values for each of the **Group By** fields and the subtotal rows have null values in at least one of the **Group By** fields.

Consider the following query. It summarizes the sales information from the SystemInfo table by year and month. In Figure 12-4, you can clearly see the null values that represent the totals and grand totals.

```
Select Year(DatePurchased) "Year Purchased",
   Month(DatePurchased) "Month Purchased",
   Sum(SalesPrice) "Total Sales"
From SystemInfo
Group By Year(DatePurchased), Month(DatePurchased) With Rollup
Order By Year(DatePurchased), Month(DatePurchased)
```

FILTERING GROUPED DATA

The **Having** clause works like a second **Where** clause, except that the **Having** clause applies only to the subsets created by the **Group By** clause. This can be used to find good sales months (a good month means that more than $2.5 million dollars worth of computers are sold). The results in Figure 12-5 show that only four months meet the definition of a good month.

```
Select Year(DatePurchased) "Year Purchased",
   Month(DatePurchased) "Month Purchased",
   Sum(SalesPrice) "Total Sales"
From SystemInfo
Group By Year(DatePurchased), Month(DatePurchased)
Having Sum(SalesPrice) > 2500000
Order By Year(DatePurchased), Month(DatePurchased)
```

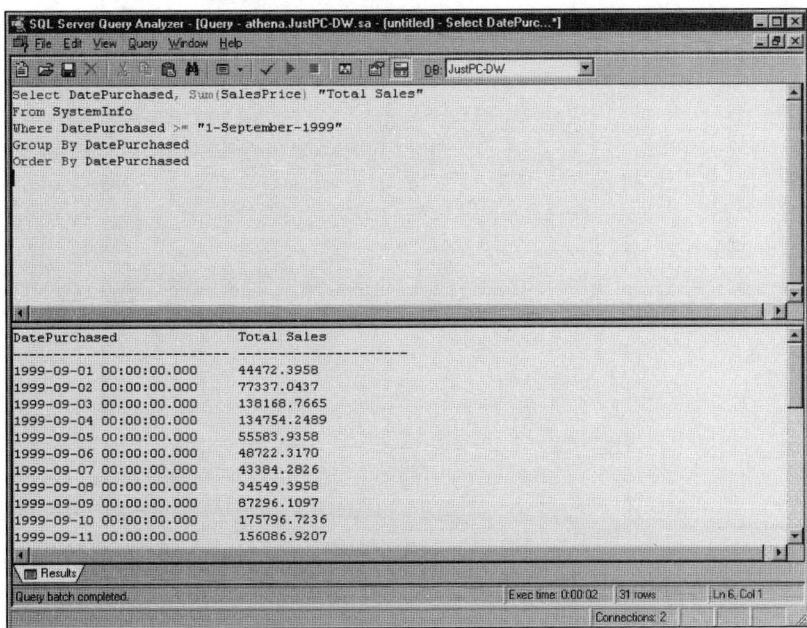

Figure 12-3: Getting the daily sales totals

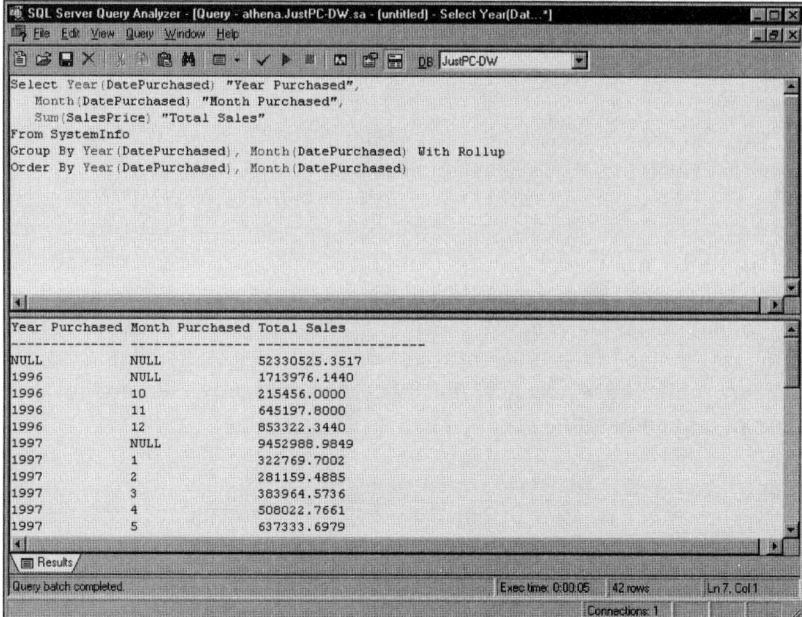

Figure 12-4: Creating totals and grand totals

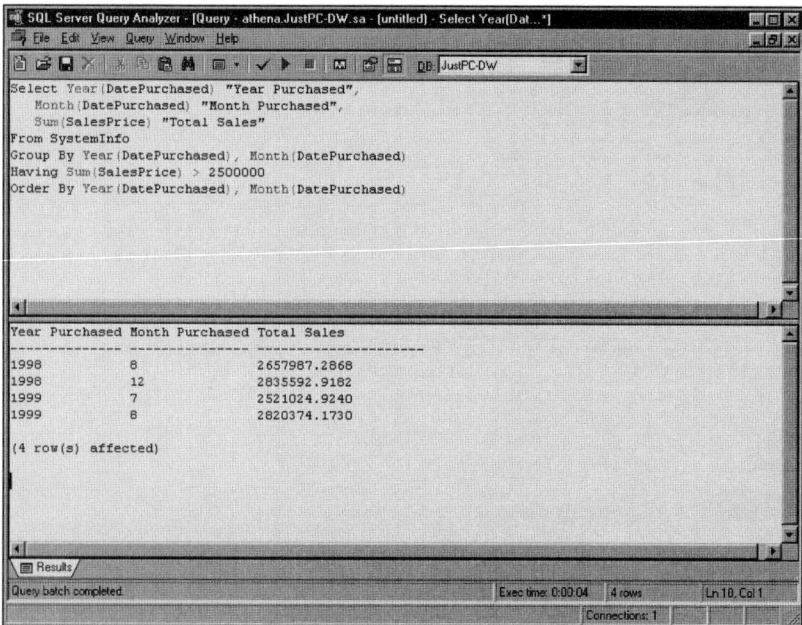

Figure 12-5: Selecting specific totals and grand totals

ORDERING CLAUSES

The clauses in a **Select** statement must be listed in the following, specific order:

- ◆ From specifies the tables where the data is extracted.

- ◆ **Where** discards any unneeded data.

- ◆ **Group By** breaks the data into subsets and then returns a single row for each subset.

- ◆ **Having** enables you to discard some of these subsets.

- ◆ Order By sorts the rows in the specified order.

This is also the same order in which the clauses are processed. Keeping this flow in mind when you write **Select** statements can be very helpful.

You should use the **Where** clause, rather than the **Having** clause, to filter out anything unnecessary.

Accessing Multiple Tables

Up until this point, all of the queries I showed you accessed only a single table. While there are many questions you can answer from your data warehouse using a single table, there are many more questions that you can't answer. This is something easily handled with the **Select** statement.

 The technical term for combining the rows and columns in two or more tables is known as a *join operation*.

The Wrong Way to Use Two Tables

The **Select** statement enables you to specify a list of tables in the **From** clause. However, the results probably are not what you may expect. Consider the following tables. Each table has three rows, with two columns in each row. Each letter in the set represents a specific value in a column.

```
Table A: {{A, I}, {B, J}, {C, K}}
Table B: {{X, I}, {Y, J}, {Z, K}}
```

If you perform a **Select** statement like this:

```
Select *
From A, B
```

you get the following result. Note the **Select** operation matches every row in the first table with each row in the second. This creates a table with nine rows and each row having four columns. While there may be cases in which you want this result, I can't think of any off the top of my head.

```
{{A, I, X, I}, {A, I, Y, J}, {A, I, Z, K},
{B, J, X, I}, {B, J, Y, J}, {B, J, Z, K},
{C, K, X, I), {C, K, Y, J}, {C, K, Z, K}}
```

The Right Way to Use Two Tables

Generally, when you want to use two tables, it is because the two tables are related to each other. This means that the tables have one or more columns in common. In the JustPC data warehouse, the SystemInfo and CustomerInfo tables have the CustomerId column in common.

Suppose that Table A and Table B have the same column in common. For the purposes of this example, let's call this column Column2, which is in the second position of both tables. The following **Select** statement enables me to combine the two tables together, but only those rows that have a common value in their second column are selected.

```
Select *
From A, B
Where A.Column2 = B.Column2
```

The **Select** statement returns only the following rows. Note that even though Column2 values are identical, they are repeated twice because the rows are appended to each other. Also, if you look back at the previous set of results, you find these three rows buried. The **Where** clause merely filters out the rows that aren't meaningful.

```
{{A, I, X, I}, {B, J, Y, J}, {C, K, Z, K}}
```

 A join that uses the **Where** clause to match column values in different tables is known as an *equijoin*, which is short for *equality join*.

Trying Joins in a Real Database

If you're like most people, understanding the theory behind something often can make things more confusing. However, a real example usually clears up the confusion. Let's suppose you want to create a list of customer names and the SystemIds they purchased. You need to access the CustomerInfo table to get the customers' names (the LastName and FirstName columns) and you need to access the SystemInfo to get the SystemId field. The field in common with the two tables is the CustomerId field. Your **Select** statement should look like the following one and the results should look like Figure 12-6.

```
Select LastName, FirstName, SystemId
From CustomerInfo, SystemInfo
Where CustomerInfo.CustomerId = SystemInfo.CustomerId
```

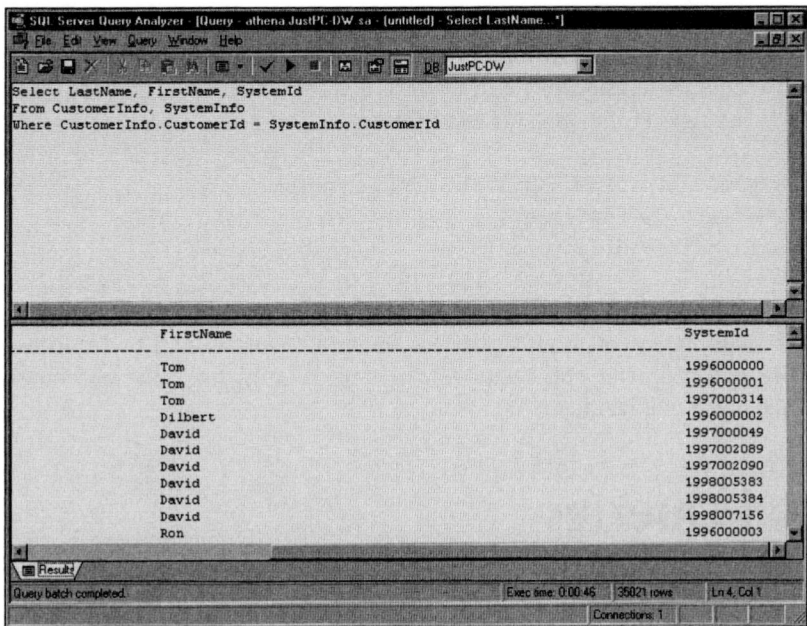

Figure 12-6: Joining two tables together

Of course, you can improve the results considerably by adding an **Order By** clause. But you can see that the appropriate SystemId column from the SystemInfo table is listed beside the FirstName column from the CustomerInfo table.

Resolving Duplicate Column Names

The following query has a problem. Because the CustomerId field is in both the CustomerInfo and SystemInfo tables, the server doesn't know which CustomerId value to return.

```
Select LastName, FirstName, SystemId, CustomerId
From CustomerInfo, SystemInfo
Where CustomerInfo.CustomerId = SystemInfo.CustomerId
```

To solve this problem, you must qualify the column name with a table name. Note that because both columns always have the same value (this is forced by the **Where** clause), it doesn't matter which table name you use.

```
Select LastName, FirstName, SystemId, CustomerInfo.CustomerId
From CustomerInfo, SystemInfo
Where CustomerInfo.CustomerId = SystemInfo.CustomerId
```

Using Table Aliases

To make life easier, you may want to use *table aliases*. Table aliases enable you to define an alternate name for your table. While they aren't displayed in the result of the query like column aliases, they can be very helpful when writing queries. For instance, you can rewrite the previous example as:

```
Select LastName, FirstName, SystemId, C.CustomerId
From CustomerInfo C, SystemInfo S
Where C.CustomerId = S.CustomerId
```

The table aliases are specified in the **From** clause by following the table name with the alternate name you want to use for the table. Personally, I prefer to use short (one or two character abbreviations) for table aliases, but you can choose whatever size name you want.

Nested Queries

Of all the things you can do with the **Select** statement, *nested queries* are the most complex. In a nested query, you actually use a second (or third or fourth) **Select** statement nested inside your main statement. There are two basic types of nested **Select** statements: those that return a set of values and those that return a single value.

In a Set

Sometimes you may want to compare a column to a list of values — as shown in the following query. While this is fairly easy to write, imagine the problems you may have with a list of 15 or 20 different values.

```
Select LastName, FirstName
From CustomerInfo
Where Zip = 20705
   Or Zip = 21045
   Or Zip = 21234
```

An alternative to writing a bunch of different clauses is using the `In` operator. The `In` operator enables you to compare a column against a set of values, as shown in the following query. It returns a list of customer names that live in the following zip codes: 20705, 21045, and 21234.

```
Select LastName, FirstName
From CustomerInfo
Where Zip In (20705, 21045, 21234)
```

SETS OF VALUES

You also can create a set of values using a **Select** statement in conjunction with the `In` operator. Consider the following query that answers the question, "Which small business customers are in the same zip code as an educational customer?" Figure 12-7 shows the results.

```
Select LastName, FirstName
From CustomerInfo
Where CustomerType = "SB"
    And Zip In (Select Zip
                From CustomerInfo
                Where CustomerType = "ED")
```

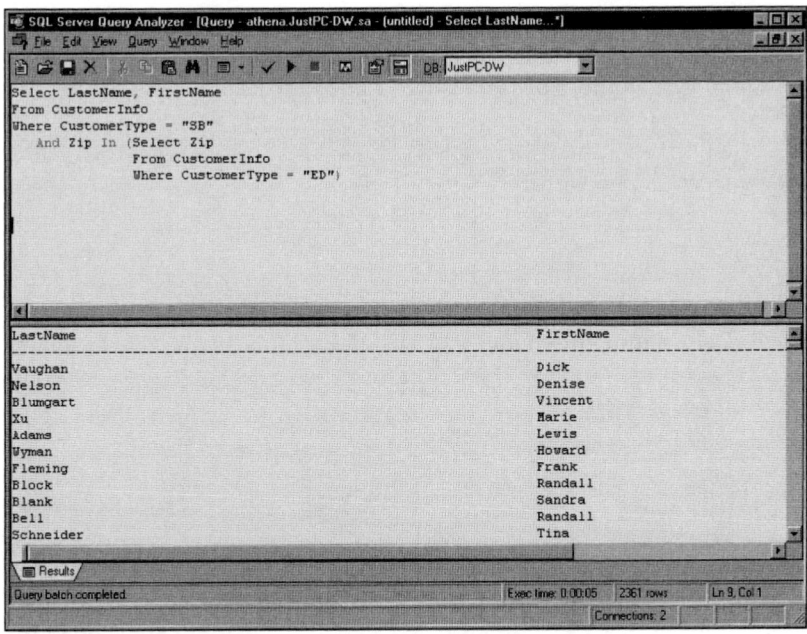

Figure 12-7: Choosing from a set of values

The In operator determines if the Zip value from the first CustomerInfo table matches one of the Zip values found in the nested **Select** statement. While this query is somewhat contrived, it gives you an alternative way to create a set of values.

Retrieving a Single Value

You also can use a nested query as one of the values returned by the **Select** statement. In the example below, I retrieve statistics for sales by zip code. The statistics include the total number of systems sold, their sales price, and the number of customers.

```
Select Zip, Sum(SalesPrice) SalesPrice, Count(SystemId) SystemCount,
   (Select Count(*)
    From CustomerInfo X
    Where X.Zip = Z.Zip) CustomerCount
From CustomerInfo Z, SystemInfo Y
Where Z.CustomerId = Y.CustomerId
Group By Zip
Order By Zip
```

This query is really two independent queries that are coupled together by zip code. The first query retrieves the number of systems sold and the total volume by zip code. It uses a two-table join on CustomerId to relate the Zip column to the information in the SystemInfo table. Then I use the **Group By** clause to reduce the information in the SystemInfo table to a single value for each zip code.

```
Select Zip, Sum(SalesPrice) SalesPrice, Count(SystemId) SystemCount
From CustomerInfo Z, SystemInfo Y
Where Z.CustomerId = Y.CustomerId
Group By Zip
Order By Zip
```

The second query returns the number of customers in each zip code as shown below:

```
Select Zip, Count(*)
From CustomerInfo
Group By Zip
```

Combining these queries is a real challenge. I want to retrieve the number of customers in each zip code while I process the other statistics. The easiest way to do this is to rewrite the query to retrieve a single value for the current zip code in the main query, so I give each table an alias. This clarifies whether I am referring to the zip value in the nested CustomerInfo table or the CustomerInfo table in the outer query.

Thus, all I have to do is count the customers in the inner query whose zip code matches the zip code in the outer query (**Where** X.Zip = Z.Zip). This query, in turn, returns only a single value, which is returned as part of the outer query (see Figure 12-8).

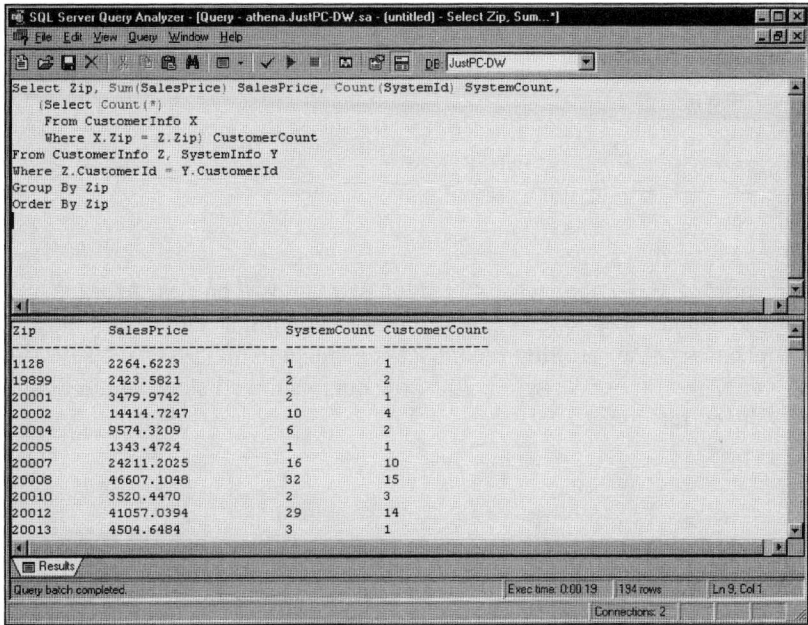

Figure 12-8: Building a complex nested query

TIP

Nested queries often take a while to debug. The syntax errors can drive you nuts. I suggest avoiding using them unless you can't perform the query any other way. Unfortunately, there are some questions that you may want to ask that can only be answered using nested queries.

Questions and Answers

Now that you have a basic understanding of the **Select** statement, I want to work through some examples of questions that you may encounter when using your data warehouse. I usually build queries in small increments. For instance, I add an **Order By** clause last – once I'm satisfied that the rest of the query is correct. In a query with multiple tables, I generally start by retrieving the data that I want from the first table and add the rest of the tables one at a time – when I'm satisfied with the previous results.

Which Customers Purchased Systems with More Than 64MB of Memory?

At first glance, this appears to be a rather simple query. The only complicated part is that I have to join three tables together. Here is my first attempt at solving this query:

```
Select LastName, FirstName
From SystemDetails SD, SystemInfo SI, CustomerInfo C
Where SD.Memory >= 64
   And SD.SystemId = SI.SystemId
   And SI.CustomerId = C.CustomerId
Order By LastName, FirstName
```

However, running this query results in a lot of duplicate entries. After all, it's possible for a customer to purchase more than one computer. The easiest way to eliminate duplicates in the resulting record set is to include the Distinct keyword immediately after the Select keyword. Thus, the query shown below, and in Figure 12-9, shows the correct answer.

```
Select Distinct LastName, FirstName
From SystemDetails SD, SystemInfo SI, CustomerInfo C
Where SD.Memory >= 64
   And SD.SystemId = SI.SystemId
   And SI.CustomerId = C.CustomerId
Order By LastName, FirstName
```

Which Customers Spent More Than $10,000 on Computers in 1998?

The first step in this query is to identify those customers who purchased a computer in 1998.

```
Select CustomerId
From SystemInfo
Where Year(DatePurchased) = 1998
```

Then I summarize the results by CustomerId to eliminate duplicate customers.

```
Select CustomerId
From SystemInfo
Where Year(DatePurchased) = 1998
Group By CustomerId
```

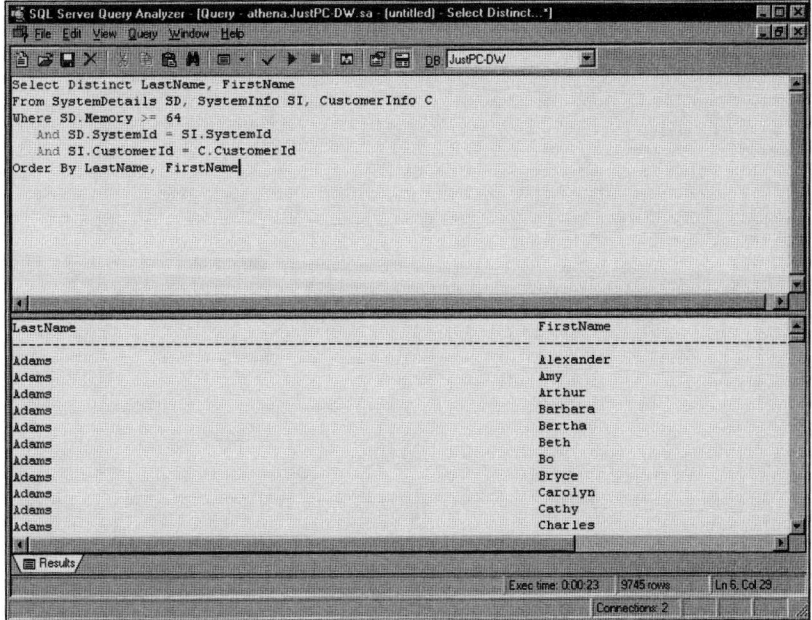

Figure 12-9: Answering a complex question with a nested query

Next, I add a **Having** clause to select only those customers who have purchased more then $10,000 in computers.

```
Select CustomerId
From SystemInfo
Where Year(DatePurchased) = 1998
Group By CustomerId
Having Sum(SalesPrice) > 10000
```

I add a reference to the CustomerInfo table to replace the CustomerId column with the FirstName and LastName fields. This is somewhat tricky because I also need to carry these fields in the **Group By** clause as well as add the relation to the **Where** clause. Finally, I throw in an **Order By** statement to present the data in alphabetical order (see Figure 12-10).

```
Select LastName, FirstName
From SystemInfo S, CustomerInfo C
Where Year(DatePurchased) = 1998
    And C.CustomerId = S.CustomerId
Group By S.CustomerId, C.LastName, C.FirstName
Having Sum(SalesPrice) > 10000
Order By LastName, FirstName
```

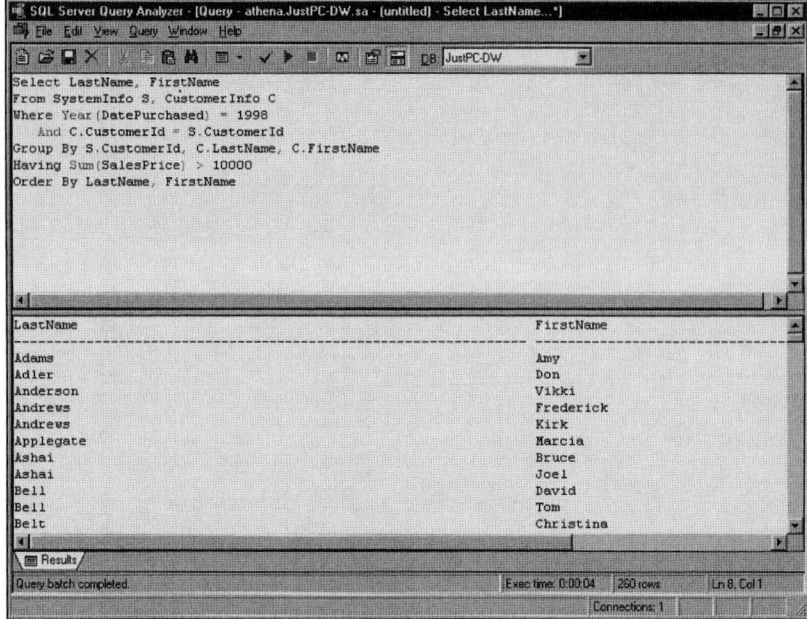

Figure 12-10: Choosing from a set of values

Summary

In this chapter, I discussed some techniques for building complex queries. Joining two or more tables together is a very common activity and one that you will find very easy to perform once you understand how to do it. While you may not need the rest of these techniques now, chances are that you probably will need them sooner or later.

In the next chapter, I discuss a few other SQL statements that you may find useful, plus I spend a little time talking about how to improve the speed of your queries.

Chapter 13

Using Query Analyzer for Other Tasks

IN THIS CHAPTER, I finish talking about Query Analyzer and touch briefly on some of the other statements you may use. Then, I talk about why some queries run longer than other queries and discuss some changes you can make to significantly improve their performance.

Inserting Rows into a Table

By now, you know several different ways to put data into a table. For instance, you can use the Data Transformation Services to copy data into a table from an external source. You also can use the Enterprise Manager utility to open a table and add data at the bottom of a worksheet-like grid. However, all of these tools rely on the SQL **Insert** statement, which has the following syntax:

```
Insert [Into] <table> [(<column> [, <column>} ...)] Values (<value>
[,<value>]...)
```

Where

```
<table> is the name of where you want to insert new rows.
<column> is the name of a column in the table.
<value> is a value that you wish to insert into a column.
```

The **Insert** statement adds a record into the specified table. You can specify a list of columns for which you assign the values, or use the list of columns specified when the table was created. Then in the **Value** clause, specify the list of values you want inserted into the table. The position of each value corresponds to order of the columns specified in the **Insert** statement; if the list columns are not specified, the values correspond to the order of the columns in the table definition.

Here's a very simple **Insert** statement. It adds a single row of information into the InventoryInfo table (see Figure 13-1).

```
Insert Into InventoryInfo
    (InventoryId, InventoryDescription, InventoryType, SpeedSize)
Values (99999, "Dummy inventory item", "CP", 9999)
```

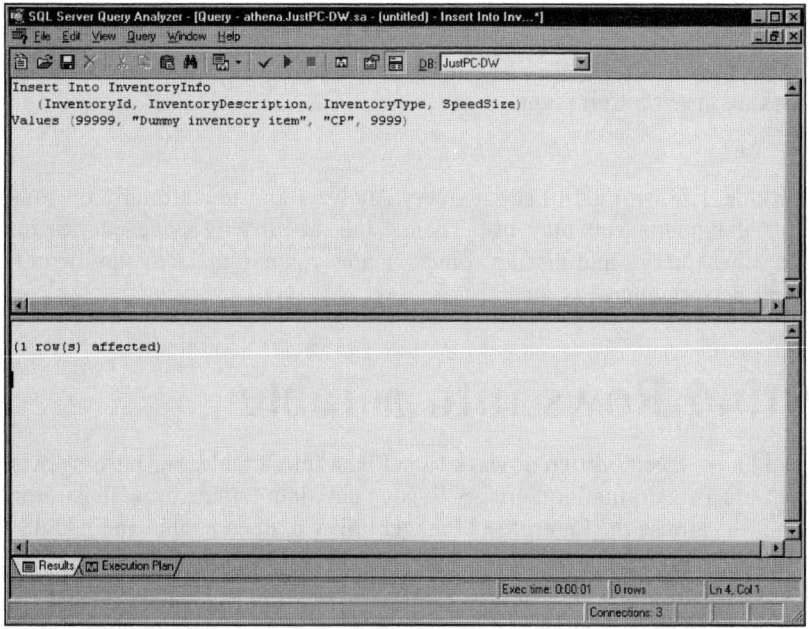

Figure 13-1: Adding a single row to the InventoryInfo table

The following **Insert** statement is identical to the previous one, but it assumes that the order of the columns as defined in the database is the same as the order listed in the **Value** clause.

```
Insert Into InventoryInfo
Values (99999, "Dummy inventory item", "CP", 9999)
```

 Running this statement more than once causes an error. Because the InventoryId field is the primary key for the table and each row must have a unique value, attempting to add another record with the same value causes an error.

Deleting Rows from a Table

Of course, if you can add rows to a table, then deleting rows must be just as easy. The Delete statement removes one or more rows from a table. Its syntax is as follows:

```
Delete From <table>
[Where <expression>]
```

Where

```
<table> is the name of the database table where you want to delete
the records.
<expression> is an expression that is used to determine which
records to delete.
```

 When deleting a specific record from a table, use the primary key in the **Where** clause to identify the specific record you want to delete.

The following **Delete** statement deletes the row I just added (see Figure 13-2). You code the **Where** clause the same way you do for the **Select** statement. In this case, I only want to delete the one record, so I need to code the **Where** clause to select the specific record I want to delete.

```
Delete From Inventoryinfo
Where InventoryId = 99999
```

The **Delete** statement also can be very dangerous. The following statement deletes all of the rows in the InventoryInfo table. Note that the only difference between this statement and the previous one is the **Where** clause.

```
Delete From Inventoryinfo
```

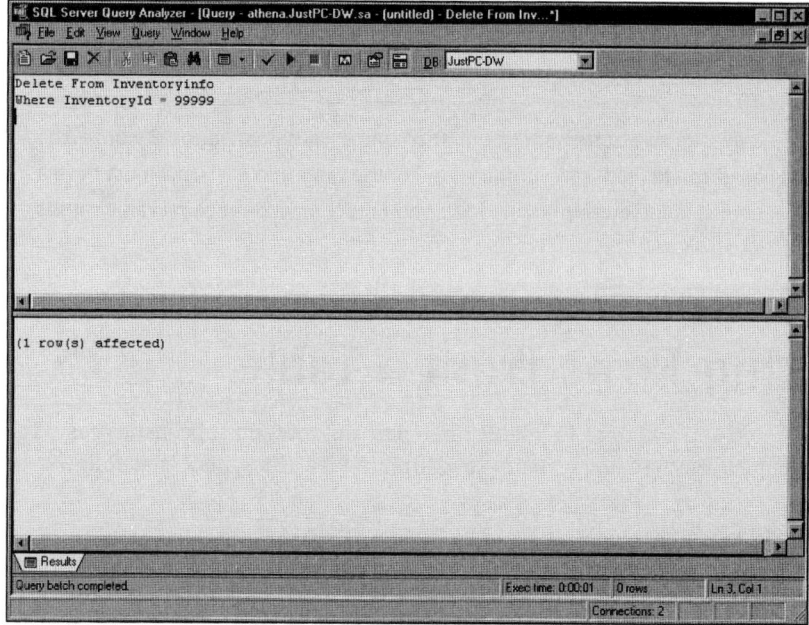

Figure 13-2: Deleting a single row from the InventoryInfo table

 It is very easy to delete everything from a table. For that reason, you should exercise extreme caution whenever you use the **Delete** statement. However, for the most part, only use the **Delete** statement in a data warehouse when you need to delete everything in a table before you reload it.

Updating Rows in a Table

The **Update** statement enables you to change any value in any row in a table. Like the **Delete** statement, you must add a **Where** clause to isolate the effects of this statement to include only the rows you want to update. Otherwise, you apply the change to all of the rows in the table. Its syntax is as follows:

```
Update <table>
Set <column> = <value> [, <column> = <value>] ...
Where <expression>
```

Where

```
<table> is the name of the table you want to update.
<column> is a column name in the table you want to update.
<value> is an expression containing the new value for the column.
<expression> is true for the rows you want to update in the table.
```

Now, let's add the row back that I just deleted (see Figure 13-3). The following **Update** statement increases the value in the SpeedSize field by 10 percent. It uses a **Where** clause to ensure that only the row with an InventoryId value of 99999 is changed.

```
Update InventoryInfo
Set SpeedSize = SpeedSize * 1.1
Where InventoryId = 99999
```

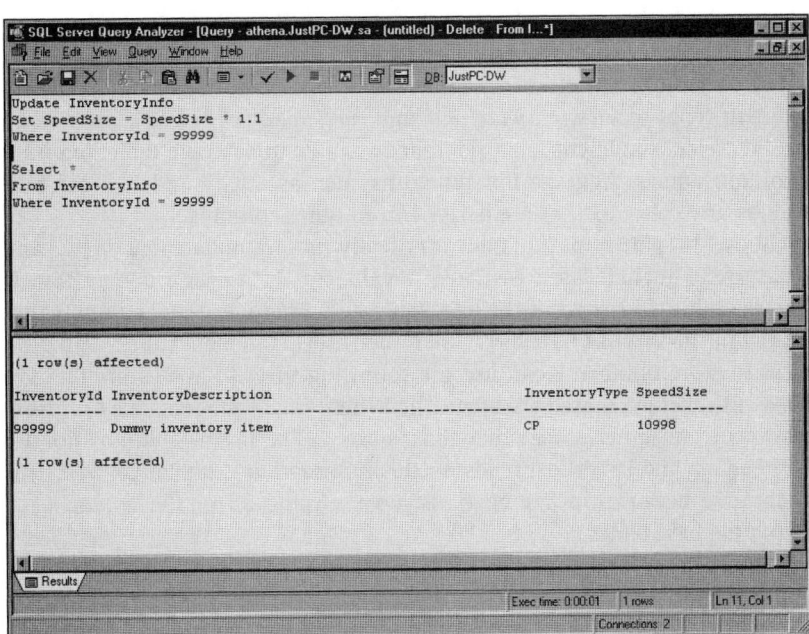

Figure 13-3: Updating a single row from the InventoryInfo table

 **TIP**

If you enter multiple statements into the Query Pane, Query Analyzer runs them in sequence. Hence, you can execute an **Update** statement followed by a **Select** statement to verify that the **Update** statement worked properly.

Creating Views

A *view* represents a virtual table in your database that is created on the fly by using the results of a **Select** statement. Its syntax is as follows:

```
Create View <view> As <selectstatement>
```

Where

```
<view> is the name of the view you are creating.
<selectstatement> is a Select statement that defines the view.
```

The concept of a view is an important one in a relational database. It enables you to define an alternate way of looking at your data. Once a view is defined, you may use it just like any other table in your database.

You can define security on views just as you do with a table. This makes it possible to allow limited access to the data. You can partition the data vertically by hiding some of the columns in a particular table or horizontally by restricting access to only a subset of the rows in a table.

There are two types of views: *updateable* and *non-updateable*. For a view to be updateable, the **Select** statement must reference a single updateable table and only reference column names. Aggregation functions such as COUNT and SUM can't be used, as well as any columns that are derived from other columns.

If you choose to partition the table vertically in an updateable view, any columns that aren't included are assigned a value of Null when a new row is inserted into the table. Of course, if the base table defines any of these columns that aren't included in the view as Not Null, then the **Insert** statement fails.

Employees in store number 1 can use the following view to access information about when a customer purchased a system. The **Where** clause prevents the user from seeing data about any other store other than store 1. The list of columns doesn't include the ItemCost and LaborCost fields, so this information is hidden as well. This view is updateable because no aggregations are used and all of the columns are extracted from the base table.

```
Create View SystemInfo1 As
   Select CustomerId, SystemId, DatePurchased, SalesPrice
   From SystemInfo
   Where StoreId = 1
```

The next view is not updateable, but it provides an easy way for someone to get summary information from the database. Note that I took the time to use aliases for both of the aggregated fields. This makes it easier for the user to understand the results from queries run against the view.

```
Create View SystemSummary As
```

```
Select CustomerId, Sum(SalesPrice) TotalSales,
    Count(SystemId) TotalSystems
From SystemInfo
Group By CustomerId
```

To delete a view from your database, use the **Drop View** statement. It takes only a single parameter – the name of the view. Thus, the following statement deletes the MyView view from the database.

```
Delete View MyView
```

Understanding the Costs of a Query

Up until now, I haven't discussed how a query performs. Many people believe that the database server should process a query and return the data almost instantly. Unfortunately, this is an unrealistic expectation. Many of the queries that you run against your data warehouse take a lot of time to process. Depending on how many tables you access, the size of the tables you access, the exact composition of the **Where** clause, and the speed of your database server, your query can run from less than a second to several hours or more. Obviously, the faster your queries run, the quicker you can find the information you need. For the rest of this chapter, I want to talk about understanding how your query is run and what you can do to improve its performance.

Introducing Indexes

The primary tool in your arsenal is known as an *index*. An index operates much like an index in a book. It contains an ordered list of the index values, with pointers to every row that contains that value. If you know a particular value for an index, then you can locate the list of pointers to the rows very quickly.

You can place indexes on one or any combination of columns in a table. While indexes are not connected to the table, the information inside an index is updated whenever the table is updated. You can add or delete indexes on the fly – depending on your needs – and see the impact on your queries.

In addition to the standard indexes, SQL Server 7 also has a special type of index known as a *clustered index,* which is used to physically order the rows in a table. It can often speed up queries where you retrieve a series of rows based on a range of values. Only one clustered index is available per table. By default, SQL Server creates a clustered index on the primary key of a table; however, you can define a clustered index on any key in the table. You should use the Index Tuning Wizard with a list of typical queries to help you determine the best key for the clustered index.

> ## Database Theory versus Reality
>
> One advantage of a relational database is the use of set theory to describe operations against its data. It allows a high degree of separation between how the data is viewed by the database user and how the data is stored internally. However, just because something makes sense from a theoretical point of view doesn't necessarily mean it is a good idea because this theory doesn't take into consideration the physical limitations of your database server.
>
> Without indexes, every query would have to read every row in a table. On small tables, this wouldn't be a big handicap because it doesn't take very long to read all of the rows. However, this can be a major problem on large tables.

There is one major drawback to using indexes. Keeping an index up-to-date can take a lot of resources. If you have a lot of indexes on a particular table, you may find that you spend more time keeping the index up to date than you would save using the index. However, this may not have a big effect in a data warehouse where you update the data very infrequently.

SQL Server 7 automatically includes an index on the primary key of every table. The index has two purposes. First, it allows the server to find a row quickly based on the primary key. Second, it prevents a row with a duplicate primary key from being added to the table.

In most cases, you want to keep the number of indexes to a minimum. Updating an index each time you add a row to the database is an expensive operation. However, a data warehouse isn't updated very frequently so having a lot of indexes in a data warehouse doesn't cause the same problem.

Creating Indexes

While you can create indexes manually, using the *Index Tuning Wizard* is probably a better idea. This tool analyzes a file containing one or more queries to determine the optimal set of indexes for the database. It can create the indexes as part of the process or it can save information for you to create them later.

TIP You should keep a file with the most commonly executed queries in it. This way, you can run the Index Tuning Wizard each time you update the data warehouse or add a new query to the file to make sure that you are using the optimal set of indexes.

STARTING THE INDEX TUNING WIZARD

In Enterprise Manager, choose the database you want to access and then select Tools → Wizards from the main menu. Then choose Management → Index Tuning Wizard from the dialog box and press OK. This starts the Index Tuning Wizard (see Figure 13-4).

Figure 13-4: Welcome to the Index Tuning Wizard

SELECTING THE DATABASE

The second step of the wizard asks you to specify the name of the database server and the database you want to analyze (see Figure 13-5). One limitation of the Index Tuning Wizard is that it only optimizes queries inside a single database. If the query spans two or more databases, only the references inside the current database are analyzed.

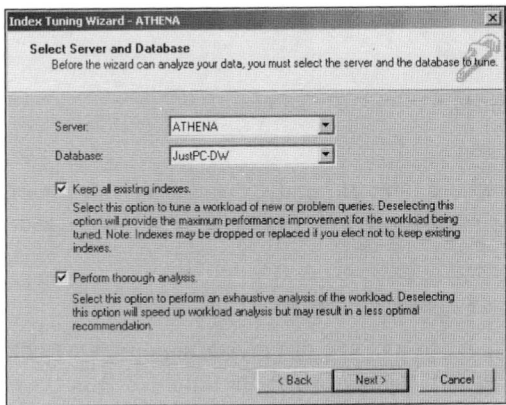

Figure 13-5: Selecting the name of the database and setting analysis options

It also asks you if you want to keep the current indexes. Always keep this value checked, unless you have all of your queries that you want to analyze in a single file. This way you won't lose any indexes that already may be helping you.

In the last checkbox, you can opt to do a thorough analysis. You probably should check this box, especially if you are analyzing a large number of queries all at once. The Tuning Wizard looks at your queries in more depth, including analyzing the data itself to determine which indexes can help you the most.

IDENTIFYING THE WORKLOAD AND TABLES

In the next step, you need to tell the Tuning Wizard the source of the data. You have two choices: give the wizard a file containing one or more SQL statements to analyze or create a real workload file based on capturing a lot of tracing information. Using the file of SQL statements is easier and still effective, so select the *I have a saved workload file* option and press Next. You specify the workload file on the following screen.

In the Specify Workload step (see Figure 13-6), click the *My workload file* field. Then, use a normal Windows Open file dialog box to locate your workload file. Press Next when you're ready to go on to the next step.

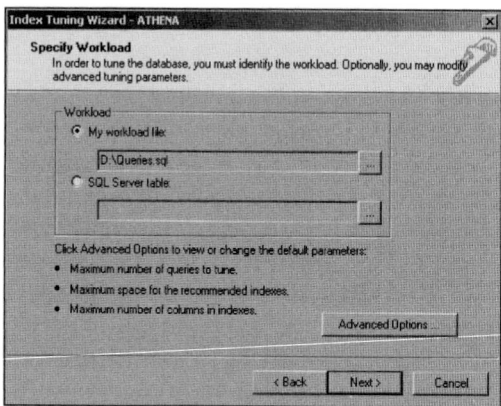

Figure 13-6: Specify the location of the workload file.

In the next step, you can choose which table to analyze and which to ignore (see Figure 13-7). In general, analyze everything unless you have a good reason why you should exclude a table.

RUNNING THE ANALYSIS

Pressing Next after choosing which tables to analyze displays a popup dialog box (see Figure 13-8) that tracks the analysis process. When the analysis process is finished, the Index Recommendations form is displayed (see Figure 13-9).

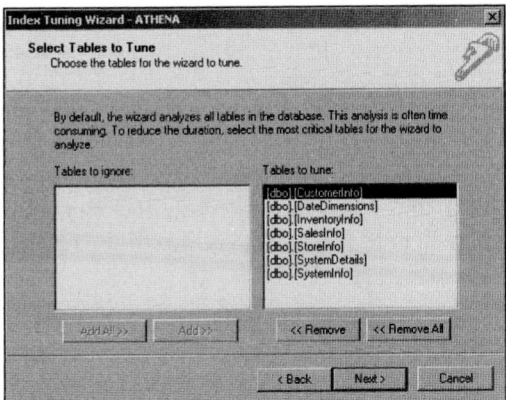

Figure 13-7: Choose the tables you want to analyze.

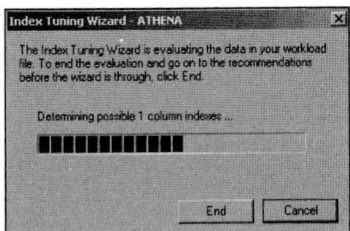

Figure 13-8: Watching the analysis process

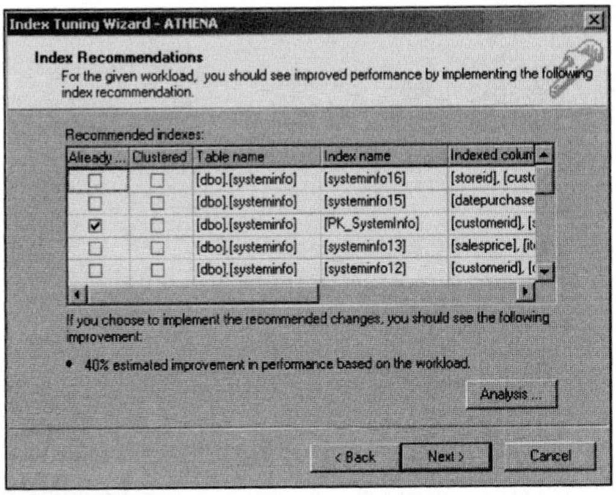

Figure 13-9: Reviewing the Index Tuning Wizard's recommendations

On the recommendations form, you see the list of indexes that it recommends. Each index identifies the table and fields that you should index. It also identifies any existing indexes.

If you press the Analysis button, you can see the information that the Tuning Wizard found in the queries. There are six different reports: the Index Usage Report for the Recommended Configuration, the Index Usage Report for the Current Configuration, the Table Analysis Report, the Query Cost Report, the Workload Analysis Report, and the Tuning Summary Report. Press OK to return to the recommendations form.

APPLYING THE INDEXES

You have three basic options for applying the indexes:

◆ Apply them in the wizard

◆ Schedule them to be created at a specific date and time

◆ Save the indexes as a SQL script file that you can run using Query Analyzer (see Figure 13-10)

Press Next to go to the last step in the wizard.

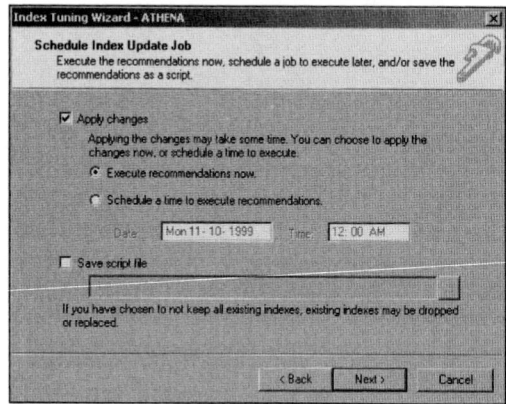

Figure 13-10: Indicating when to build your indexes

Pressing Finish on the last step takes whatever action you choose on the previous step. If you choose to create the indexes now, be prepared for a long wait while the indexes are created. Otherwise, the wizard finishes and you have to wait for the job to finish or use Query Analyzer to create your indexes.

 **TIP** Creating indexes can be a time- and resource-intensive task. If your database server already is overloaded, choose to build them in the middle of the night or over a weekend when the server's workload is lighter.

Studying the Query Execution Plan

When Query Analyzer passes your query to the database server for execution, the first thing the server does is to verify that the query has the correct syntax. If there are any errors, a brief error message is returned to Query Analyzer. If the syntax is correct, SQL Server 7 analyzes the query to find the best way to generate the data. Once its analysis is complete, SQL Server 7 takes this information and incorporates it into an execution plan. This plan is used to execute the query.

VIEWING THE QUERY EXECUTION PLAN

By default, Query Analyzer doesn't display the query plan. However, by selecting Query → Show Execution Plan or by choosing Show Execution Plan from the Execute Mode button the next time you execute a query, the plan is displayed on the Execute Plan tab in the Results Pane.

VIEWING THE PLAN FOR A SIMPLE QUERY

Consider the following query. This query retrieves all of the rows from the CustomerInfo table. The query plan you see in Figure 13-11 shows that it is broken into two parts: the Select part, which is responsible for returning 15,086 rows, and the Table Scan, which is used to scan the database table for all of the rows in the table. Note that 99 percent of the cost in this query is for reading each row in the table, while only 1 percent of the cost is for returning the rows to the Query Analyzer program.

```
Select *
From CustomerInfo
```

SEARCHING FOR A SPECIFIC ROW

The following query looks for a specific value in the table using an index (see Figure 13-12). The estimated cost is almost evenly split between using the index to get the location (more formally called the *bookmark*) of the row (51 percent) and retrieving it from the table (49 percent).

```
Select *
From CustomerInfo
Where CustomerId = 12345
```

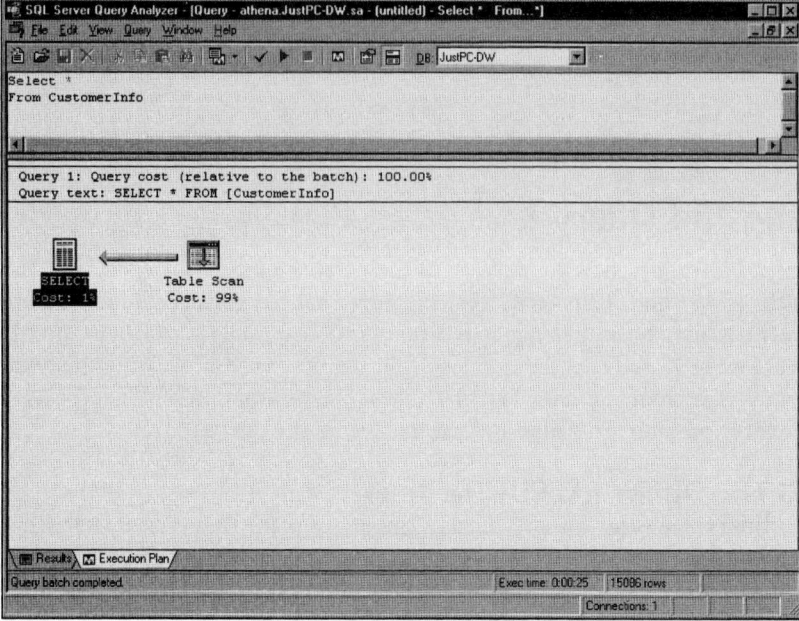

Figure 13-11: Viewing a query plan that retrieves all of the rows in a table

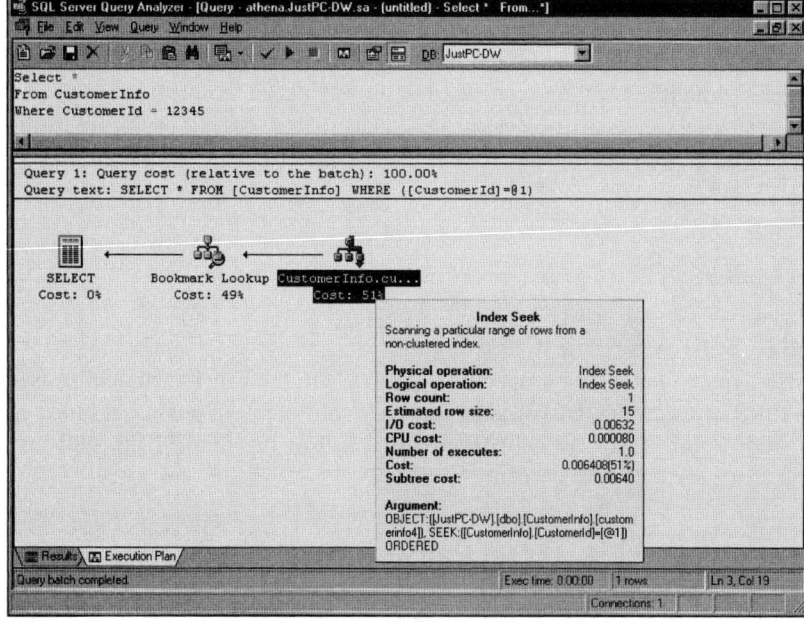

Figure 13-12: Looking for a specific row using an index

If you hold the cursor over an icon on the execution plan, you can see the details of what that phase of the query is performing. This includes information about the estimated number of rows that it expects to retrieve, a breakdown of the relative costs to perform the operation, and the subtree cost totaling the cost of all the steps up to and including the current step.

SEARCHING FOR ROWS WITHOUT AN INDEX

The following query also scans through the entire table; however, this time I'm only looking for specific rows (see Figure 13-13). This can happen when you are searching for a specific value in a column without an index or you are searching for values using a relational operator other than = (such as >, >=, <, <=, or <>).

```
Select *
From CustomerInfo
Where CustomerId <> 12345
```

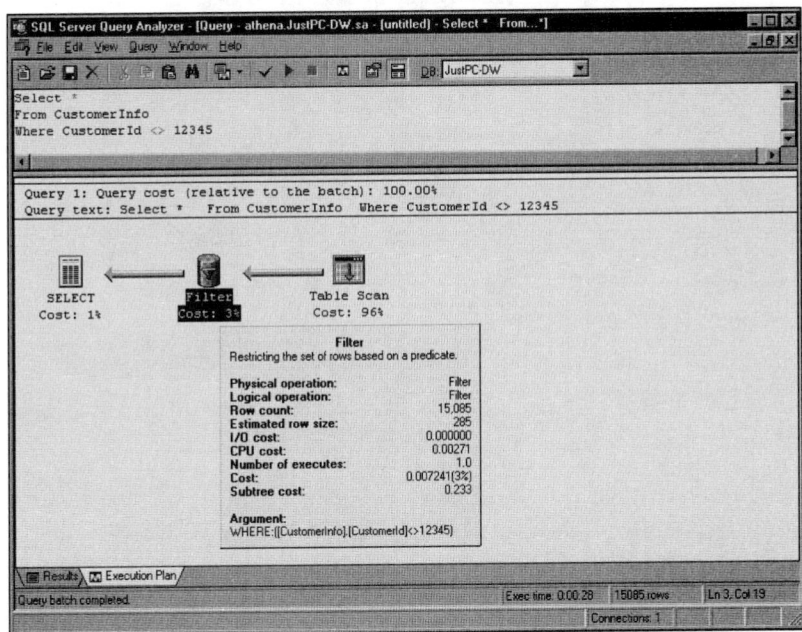

Figure 13-13: Looking for information without using an index

 **TIP** Looking at a query execution plan lets you know if an index is being used. If an index isn't being used and there is an index available, try to rewrite your query in a different way so that an index can be used. This generally improves the performance of your queries.

RUNNING A COMPLEX QUERY

The last query I'm going to talk about is a complex query that includes a nested subquery (see the following query and Figure 13-14). Note that this query includes two different subtrees that are used as input to either a nested loop or hash match. Both of these functions perform an inner join that combines two input sets to produce a single output set.

```
Select Zip, Sum(SalesPrice) SalesPrice, Count(SystemId) SystemCount,
   (Select Count(*)
    From CustomerInfo X
    Where X.Zip = Z.Zip) CustomerCount
From CustomerInfo Z, SystemInfo Y
Where Z.CustomerId = Y.CustomerId
Group By Zip
```

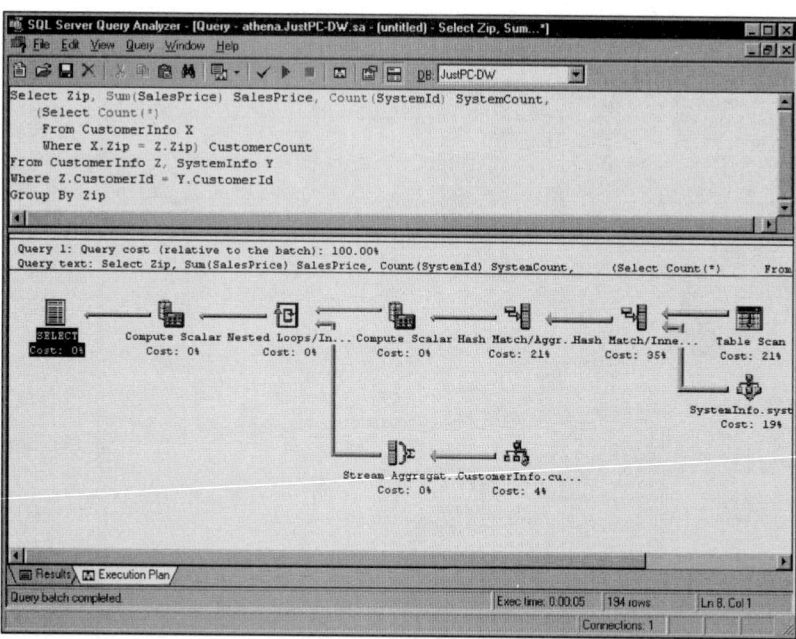

Figure 13-14: Analyzing a complex query

Summary

SQL is a rich language with many different statements – only a few of which I cover in this book. In a data-warehousing environment, you rarely need any statements other than the **Select** statement. However, it is nice to know how to add, delete, and change rows directly from Quer Analyzer using the **Insert**, **Delete**, and **Update** statements. These statements come in handy when you need to fix a corrupted record in your data warehouse. But use these statements with caution, because it is easy to destroy the information in your data warehouse.

Views, on the other hand, can be a very useful tool in your data warehouse. They enable you to define alternate ways to look at your data. You can create views for use as shortcuts for performing common queries or use them to restrict access to some of your data. In many data warehouses, you can find many more views of the data than base tables because of the convenience they offer.

In data warehouses, indexes are critical to making your queries run efficiently. While choosing the best set of indexes to use can be difficult in other database management systems, the Index Tuning Wizard makes it easy for you. Simply keep a list of your most frequently used queries in a file and use the Index Tuning Wizard to optimize the indexes. Unlike most other database applications, it's nearly impossible to have too many indexes.

If you're satisfied with how your query runs, then there is no need to worry about the execution plan – unless of course you're simply curious about how the database server runs your query. By looking at an execution plan, you can determine what part of the query is consuming the most time. This tells you which parts of the query you should focus your attention on if you want to make the query run faster.

This concludes my discussion of the SQL language and Query Analyzer. In Part IV, I'm going to introduce you to a pair of very interesting tools – English Query and MapPoint 2000. English Query allows you to retrieve information from your data warehouse by asking English-like questions. MapPoint 2000 helps you analyze geographic information.

Part IV

Analyzing Data with English Query and MapPoint 2000

Chapter 14

Teaching English Query about Your Database

IN THIS CHAPTER

- ◆ Introducing English Query
- ◆ The Query domain
- ◆ Using the Guided Application Wizard
- ◆ Teaching English Query about your data warehouse

ENGLISH QUERY IS AN alternative to Query Analyzer. In this chapter, I introduce you to Microsoft English Query and discuss how to teach it about your data warehouse.

Introducing English Query

Are there people in your organization who need information from your data warehouse, but aren't up to using Query Analyzer to search for the information they need? English Query may be the solution. Rather than typing in a highly structured SQL Select statement to retrieve information, English Query enables users to ask questions in English (see Figure 14-1).

Of course, you have to teach English Query about your data warehouse before you can use it. First, you must create a knowledge base called a *domain* that contains information about your database and how it should be accessed. This domain translates what the end user enters into a database query. The domain is stored in an English Query project file.

Inside the domain, you need to define the entities and relationships among entities that the user asks during a query. An *entity* typically is a noun that describes an object in the database. Some common entities are customer, employee, address, and so on.

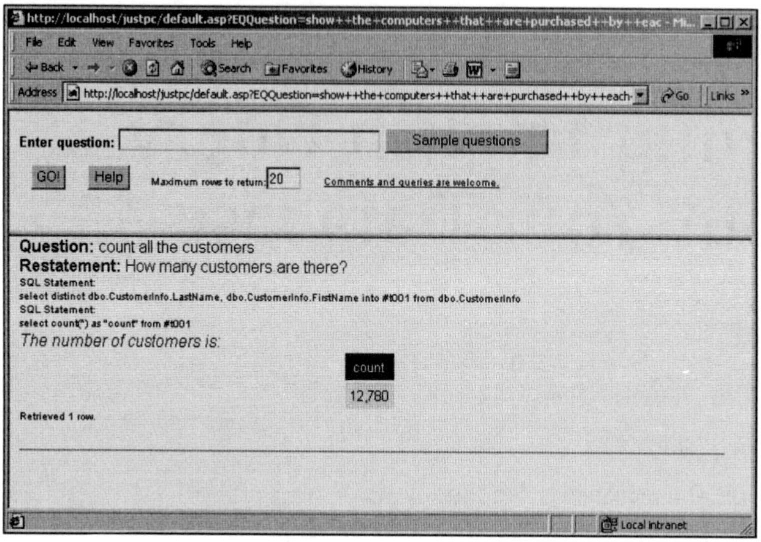

Figure 14-1: Asking English Query a question

A *relationship* describes how two entities are related to each other. For example, the customer and address entities are related by a trait. The best way to determine the relationship between two entities is to describe the two entities in a sentence and look at the word or words that connect them. In the sentence, "A customer has an address", the words "has an" implies that address is a trait of customer. I talk more about the types of relationships supported in English Query later in this chapter.

Once you've built an English Query application, you must develop a program to use it. Typically, you would write a program in Visual Basic or some other programming language and access the English Query application directly. However, Microsoft has included the tools to create a simple web-based tool that allows end users to interact with your English Query application directly. Figure 14-1 is the result of incorporating the English Query application I'm going to build into a simple, web-based program.

Creating an English Query Project

In order for English Query to interact with a user, you must create a project file that connects to the database server and contains the information necessary to translate the English language request into a database request. One of the nice things about English Query is that it includes a wizard called the *Guided Application* that helps you create your English Query application. This is the easiest way to get a working application. Once your application is complete, you can fine-tune it using the rest of the tools in English Query.

Creating a New Project

When you first start English Query, you are prompted to create a new project (see Figure 14-2) or open an existing one. Because you don't have an existing project, you need to create a new one. You then have the choice of creating an empty project, in which you need to add all of the information manually, or loading most of the information directly from your database. I'm going to use the Guided Application Wizard, so an empty project is sufficient. The Guided Application Wizard helps you build an English Query application by asking you questions about your database.

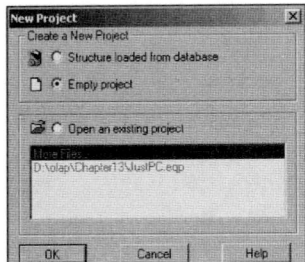

Figure 14-2: Creating a new project

Starting the Guided Application Wizard

To run the Guided Application Wizard, choose Guide → Guided Application from the main menu. This displays the wizard's first screen, as shown in Figure 14-3. Pressing Next takes you to the second step of the wizard, which informs you that you need to select an ODBC data source for your database.

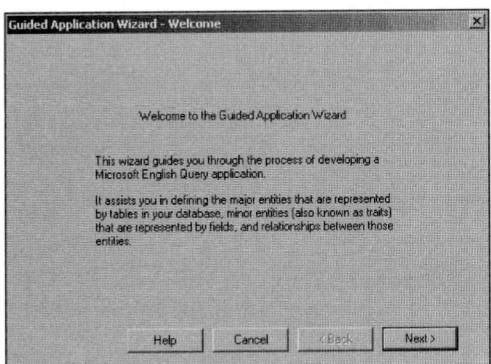

Figure 14-3: Starting the Guided Application Wizard

 Unlike many wizards, the Guided Application Wizard doesn't consist of a handful of fixed steps. It asks questions and chooses different paths based on the responses it gets. It sometimes skips steps and other times it asks for additional information, depending on the information already in its knowledge base. Fortunately, all of the forms are very clear and the wizard is sufficiently smart, so you're not able to proceed if the wizard detects a problem with the information you enter.

Creating an ODBC Data Source

After pressing Next again, you see the Select Data Source window, which prompts you to specify the name of the data source for your database. This is the first time I've created a data source for the JustPC data warehouse, so I pressed the New button to start the Create New Data Source Wizard. The first step of this wizard (see Figure 14-4) asks you to select a driver for the new data source. You want to access the SQL Server database, so choose SQL Server and press Next.

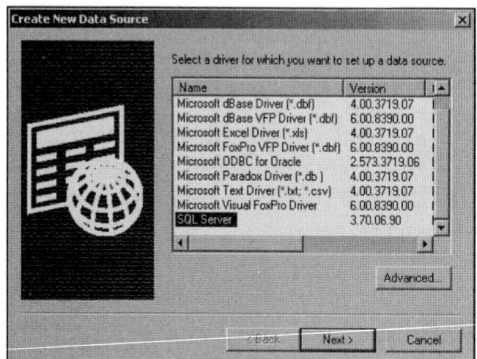

Figure 14-4: Selecting a driver for the data source

 Unlike the rest of the tools I talk about in this book, English Query doesn't support OLE DB.

The wizard then asks you for the name of the new data source (see Figure 14-5). Fill in a value that is meaningful to you. Ideally, it should describe the location of the server and the name of the database you wish to access. Then press Next.

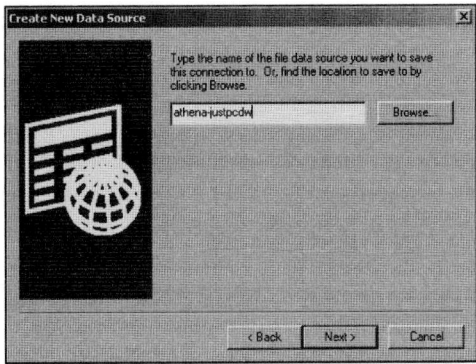

Figure 14-5: Choose a name for your data source.

The final step of the wizard displays the information you entered. You should verify that these entries are correct. If they're not, press the Back button to change them. Otherwise, press Finish. Note that while the wizard finishes, the ODBC driver prompts you for more information.

CREATING A SQL SERVER 7 DATA SOURCE

In order to connect to SQL Server 7, the ODBC driver needs some additional information. It has its own wizard that prompts you for this information. The first step of the wizard asks for the name of the database server and a description of the data source (see Figure 14-6). Fill in the text boxes and press Next.

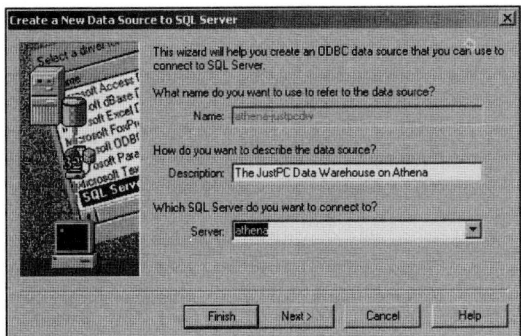

Figure 14-6: Entering information specific to the SQL Server 7 ODBC driver

The next step of the wizard (see Figure 14-7) asks for the information needed to log on to the SQL Server 7 database server. Fill in the appropriate information and press Next.

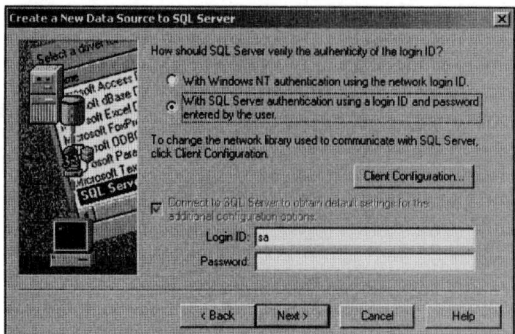

Figure 14-7: Specifying login information for the database server

While this step of the wizard asks for a lot of information (see Figure 14-8), the only piece of information you need to specify is the default database. Place a checkmark in the *Change the default database to:* checkbox and select the name of your data warehouse. In this case, I specify the database JustPC-DW. Then press Next to continue.

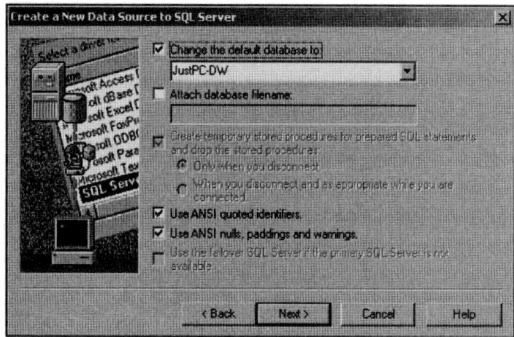

Figure 14-8: Selecting the data warehouse database

The last step of the wizard enables you to change even more options. The default settings are fine. Just press Finish. Another window is displayed verifying the values you entered (see Figure 14-9).

If you press OK, the values are saved to your new data source. However, you may want to press the Test Data Source... button near the bottom of the form to test the connection to the database. The results are displayed in yet another window. Look for the line TESTS COMPLETED SUCCESSFULLY! at the bottom of the new window and press OK to return to the previous window. Press OK again to save the values to your new data source. If you receive any other message, make sure that you correctly entered all of the information.

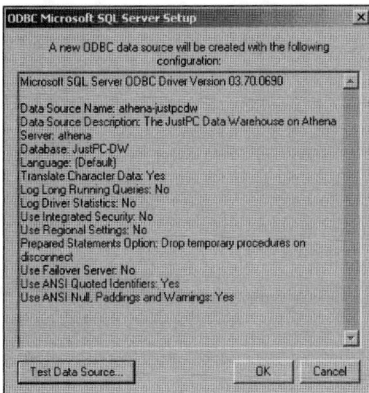

Figure 14-9: Verification of the information entered into the wizard

Once you're finished creating your new data source, select it to continue creating your new English Query application (see Figure 14-10). Pressing OK returns you to the Guided Application Wizard, which attempts to log into the database. A login window may appear asking you for a Login ID and Password for the database. Enter these values and press OK.

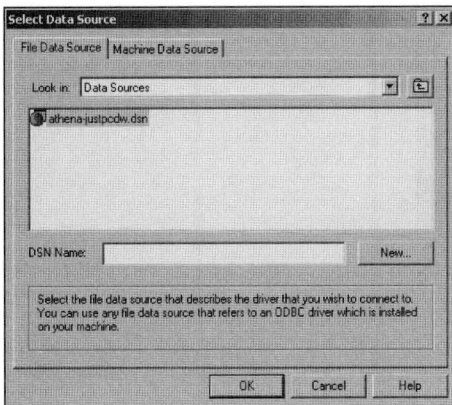

Figure 14-10: Select the data source you just created.

Identifying Your Database Entities

The wizard then queries the database for information about the tables, indexes, and other items stored inside the database (see Figure 14-11). Depending on the complexity of your database, a progress bar may appear while the wizard processes this information.

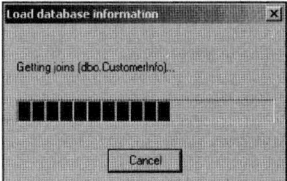

Figure 14-11: Loading database information

IDENTIFYING CORE ENTITIES

Once the wizard processes the information in your database, it asks you to identify the three or four core entities in your database (see Figure 14-12). These words are not necessarily the names of tables, columns, or other physical things in your database (unless you happen to use terms like "salesperson" for a column), but rather words that represent the most important pieces of information contained in your database. In the JustPC database, you might choose customers, computers, and orders. Always use singular nouns because English Query will automatically translate any plural words into singular words when processing a user's query.

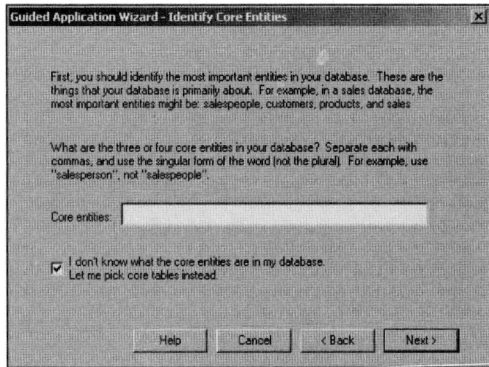

Figure 14-12: Identify the core components of your database.

Most relational databases are designed using the Entity/Relationship model. So refer back to your original database design notes to help you identify the core entities in your database.

To make life easier, the wizard enables you to choose the three or four most important tables from your database rather than try to determine the most important entities. Personally, I think picking the tables is easier for most people, unless they are active participants in the database design process.

After checking the *Let me pick core tables instead* checkbox, you see the window shown in Figure 14-13. You need to pick the three or four most important tables and add them to the Core tables list on the right side of the form.

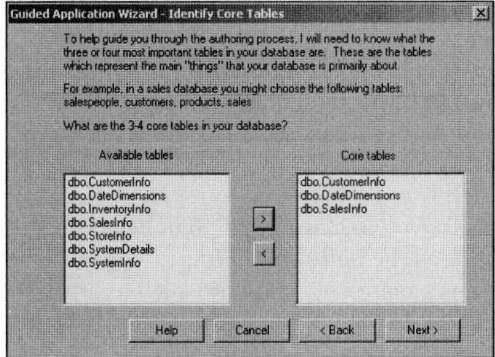

Figure 14–13: Choosing the core tables

 The Guided Application Wizard repeats this process for each of the entities you define. In this chapter, I follow only one table and entity through this process.

After pressing the Next button, you see the window in Figure 14-14. This window asks you to describe the table you just entered with an English noun. This noun is equivalent to the entity name you may have entered earlier. At the bottom of the form, you see a couple of questions that you can ask English Query using this noun.

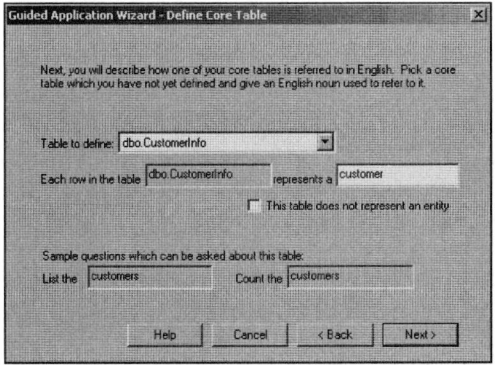

Figure 14–14: Describing the core table with a noun

 By choosing to specify the tables, I have to create an entity name for each of them. Had I chosen to specify the entities, I would have had to relate each entity to a table. Either way, I ended up with the same information.

USING THE ENTITY WIZARD

If the word you enter isn't known to English Query (and it shouldn't be), the Entity Wizard pops up and asks you if the word has a plural form. If it does, you should select *This word has a singular form and a plural form* and enter the word in the appropriate text box.

The second step of the Entity Wizard asks you to classify the noun by how it can be used (see Figure 14-15). This is known as the *entity type*. You can classify the noun by telling English Query that the noun represents an object such as a person or other animate object, a location, or a date or time. If your entity doesn't fit into any of these categories, choose the *None of these* option. If the entity is a type of person, such as a customer or employee, then check the *Entity is a kind of person* box; otherwise leave this box blank.

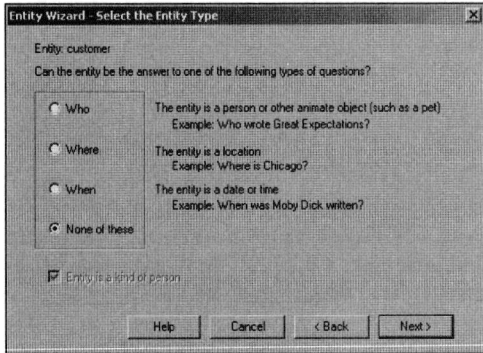

Figure 14–15: Classify the noun

After pressing Next, the Entity Wizard asks you to choose which fields to list when someone asks for a customer. You've already selected the table that is associated with this entity, so you simply have to press the Select fields button to display another window with a list of fields from the table. Select the fields you want to display from this window and press OK to add those values to the previous window.

WORKING WITH NAMES

After working with the Entity Wizard, the Guided Application Wizard resumes and asks for the fields that contain the names of your noun (see Figure 14-16). Select the fields and press Next.

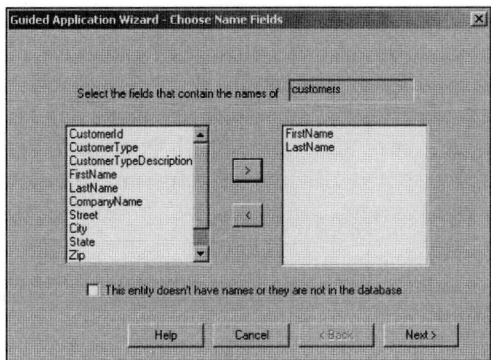

Figure 14-16: Selecting fields that contain the names of your noun

If you choose more than one field, English Query needs to know how these fields are related to the noun (see Figure 14-17). In the JustPC data warehouse example, I'm working with customers and the fields containing the name of a customer are FirstName and LastName. I want to tell English Query that the both FirstName and LastName are part of a person's name.

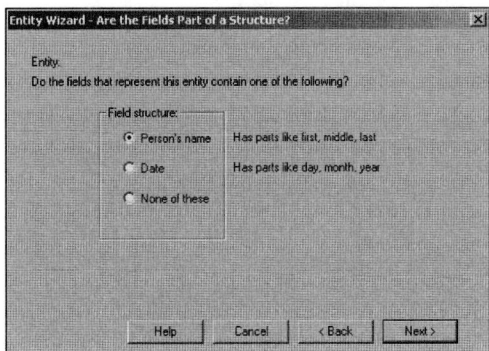

Figure 14-17: Describing the parts of a structure

When you're finished describing the noun, the wizard asks you to relate it to the entity. These questions vary depending on the type of information you provide. Most of the forms are very straightforward, so I do not discuss them here. However, one is worth talking about.

In Figure 14-18, the wizard asks if you want to add the field values from the database to the domain dictionary. In the example I'm using, doing so would enable me to ask questions such as "List Samantha Freeze" rather than "List customer Samantha Freeze" to see information about Samantha Freeze. While the set of quotation marks is the only difference between the two queries, the amount of data that may be needed to load into the dictionary is significant. English Query would have to load every name in your database in order to recognize a name without quotes. However, this shouldn't be your primary consideration. If you expect your users to perform frequent queries using a customer name such as "List sales for Samantha Freeze," then you should add the names. After all, English Query is about making life easier for the user, not being resource efficient. If you want resource efficiency, teach your users SQL and Query Analyzer.

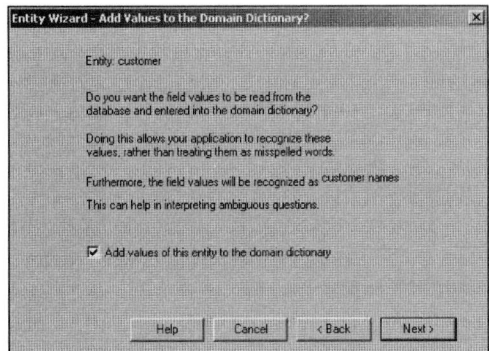

Figure 14-18: Adding values from the database to the domain dictionary

CONNECTING NAMES AND ENTITIES

This phase of the Guided Application Wizard asks questions that describe how the name and entity are related. Again, these questions are straightforward and vary somewhat depending on the type of information entered in the previous steps.

Figure 14-19 asks you how to tie an ID value for an entity to a field in the database table. Typically, the ID value is the primary key of the table (as in the JustPC example in which CustomerId is the primary key for the CustomerInfo table). This enables the user to query information by the customer's name or CustomerId value – as in the following query, "Show customer 42."

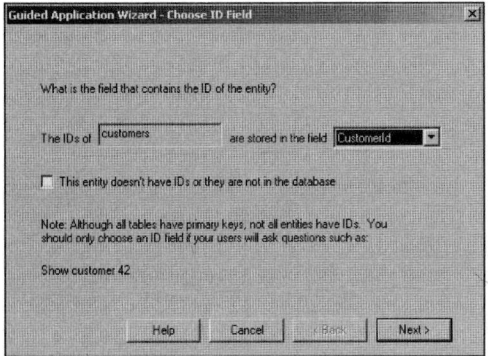

Figure 14-19: Relating primary key to the entity's ID

Defining Traits of an Entity

For each of your entities, you need to describe how it relates to the fields (see Figure 14-20). Select the entity you want to use and the field from the table that is related to the entity. Then press Next. If there are no more fields to be defined, check the *I am done defining traits for this entity* box and press Next.

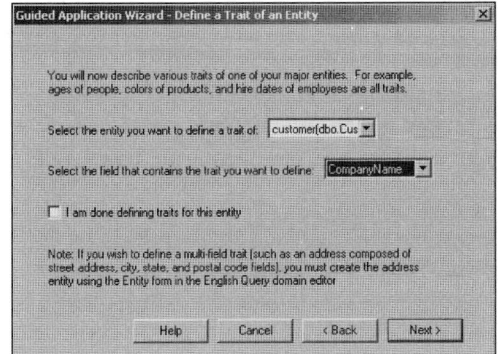

Figure 14–20: Describing traits of an entity

 If you have a trait that consists of multiple fields (such as an address, which is composed of Street, City, State, and Zip), you need to handle that outside the Guided Application Wizard using the Entity form in the domain editor.

In the JustPC example, I defined CompanyName as a trait of customer using the word company as the entity name. The Guided Application Wizard automatically creates a new minor entity for this object and repeats some of the steps I previously described in the "Identifying Your Database Entities" section.

USING THE RELATIONSHIP WIZARD

The next step is to define the relationship between the two relationships. English Query understands six different kinds of relationships. The easiest way to classify a relationship is to use both entities in a sentence and look at the words that join them.

♦ **Name or Identifier** describes a relationship between two entities. The name is used to identify one entity based on another entity. A typical sentence using customers and CustomerIds is "CustomerIds are the IDs of customers". The key phrase here is "are IDs of" – in other words, "are names of".

♦ **Adjective** is used to clarify an entity. For instance, the phrase "Small Business customer" relates a value from the CustomerTypeDescription (Small Business) to clarify the type of customer entity.

◆ **Trait** is a catchall category indicating that one entity possesses another entity. For example, "customers from Samantha's Swingsets" relates the customers entity with the CompanyName entity. Look for keywords like "whose", "of", "for", "from", "with", "have", as well as those that have an "s" at the end of a value from an entity.

◆ **Preposition** uses prepositions other than "of" or "for" to describe a relationship. For example, "customers in Beltsville" describes the collection of customer entities that live in the city of Beltsville. This relates the customer entity with the city entity.

◆ **Verbs** often are used to relate major entities together. Consider the phrase "customers by computers." This relates the entity customers to the entity computers. Generally, any verb except for "be", "is", "are", or "have" falls into this category.

◆ **Subsets** are nouns that describe a subset of a collection of entities, such as "some employees are managers." Subsets typically use a hard-coded SQL query value, such as EmployeeType = "1", to determine the subset.

This information is important because it helps English Query to parse sentences containing the entities. While I understand that you may find a relationship that fits into more than one of these categories, try to pick the one that you believe is best.

The next step in the wizard asks you if any queries may ask for an amount or quantity (see Figure 14-21) from the entity. For instance, the user may ask, "How many systems were purchased in December?". This implies that the sales price from the SystemInfo table needs to be totaled.

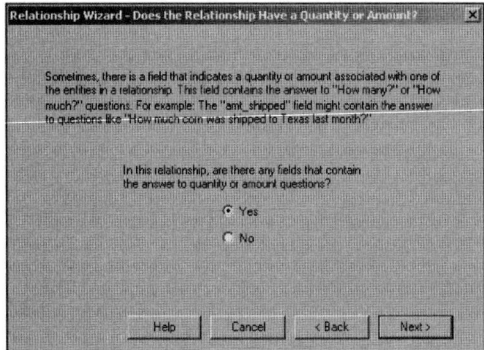

Figure 14-21: Asking for amounts or quantities

If you respond yes to this question, you are asked to specify which fields contain numeric values – which you may add. Remember, just because a field is numeric doesn't mean that you automatically can perform arithmetic with it. Any field that is used as an identifier (such as CustomerId) should not be used. This also applies to any fields (such as Zip) whose values are strictly numeric but whose values don't represent amounts or quantities.

Do It Again and Again

At some point while using the Guided Application Wizard, you will see the display shown in Figure 14-22. This window enables you to repeat the preceding process until you've defined everything you need.

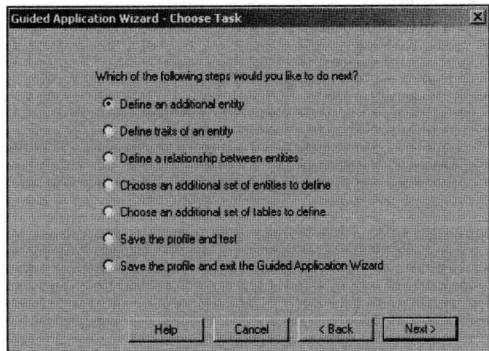

Figure 14-22: Doing it as many times as you want until everything is defined

 Don't worry if you don't complete all of the answers. You can always go back and edit the information directly in English Query.

Testing the Application

When you think you're finished designing your application, it's time to try it out. Return to the screen in Figure 14-22 and choose the option to Save the profile and test. This displays the Test Application window shown in Figure 14-23. You can enter your question at the top of the form and press the Submit button. The question is analyzed and the SQL statement that it generates is displayed in the Answer tab. If you check the Execute SQL checkbox, English Query also executes the SQL statement and returns the results.

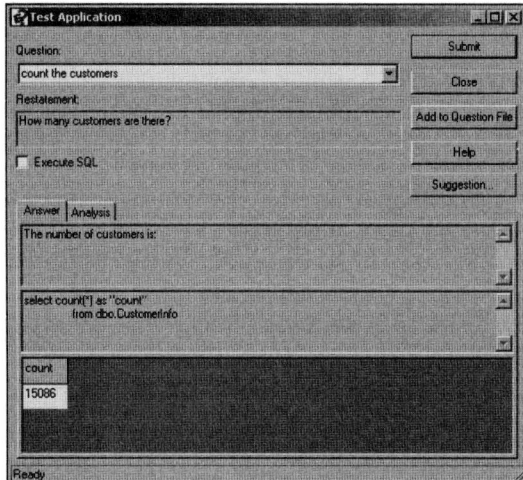

Figure 14-23: Testing the application

Summary

In this chapter, I demonstrated how to use the Guided Application Wizard to begin entering information for your application. The Guided Application Wizard asks you for information about entities, relationships, tables, and fields. It also asks a lot of obvious questions that actually describe how the words you enter can be parsed.

In the next chapter, I show you how to refine this information in order to finish your English Query Application. Once you're finished with the Guided Application Wizard, you'll find that you have enough information to test your applications and let your users work with them.

Chapter 15

Polishing Your English Query Application

IN THIS CHAPTER

- ◆ Editing entities
- ◆ Editing relationships
- ◆ Testing and deployment

EVEN THOUGH YOU MAY have finished teaching English Query about your database, there is still a lot of work left to do in order to make it really useful. As you test your application, you may find that English Query can't understand some of your questions. Maybe you use a different word for an entity that isn't in the domain. Maybe you ask for information about a field that isn't defined. Perhaps you want to tweak the answer to the question by sorting the results before they're displayed. In this chapter, I address these issues and a few others, such as deploying your application.

Entities Revisited

As you saw in Chapter 14, entities are nouns that describe information you want to retrieve from the database. But there is a lot you can do to refine the information stored in an entity to make your user's life easier.

To edit an entity, select the Semantics tab of the English Query main form and expand the Entities icon to show the entity you wish to modify (see Figure 15-1). Then right-click the entity and select Edit from the popup menu. You also can add a new entity by right-clicking the Entities icon and selecting Insert Entity. Additionally, you can access the popup menu, select an entity, and choose Delete to delete any entity.

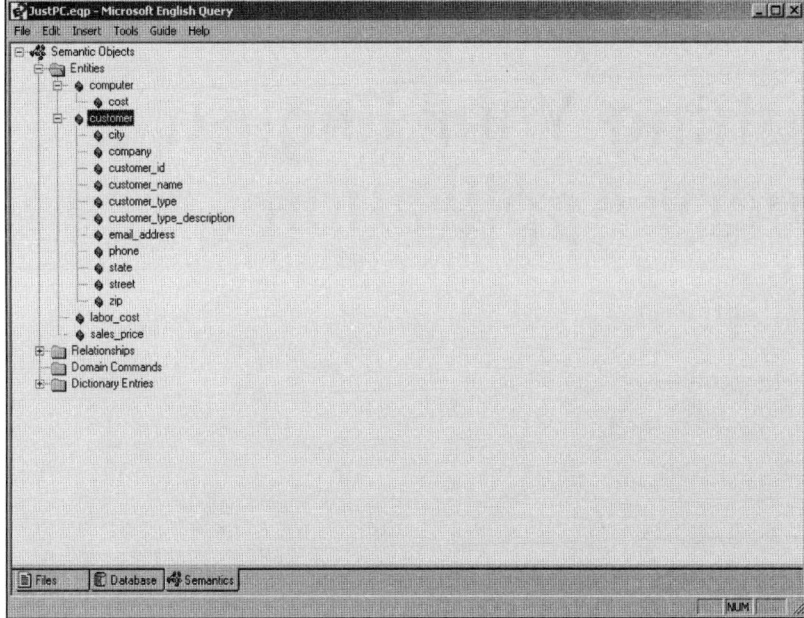

Figure 15-1: Selecting an entity

The Entity form enables you to change a number of different values associated with an entity (see Figure 15-2). Four action buttons are placed near the bottom of the form. The Apply button accepts the changes made to the entity and closes the form. The Cancel button leaves the form without making any changes. The Delete button deletes this entity. And the Help button displays help for English Query.

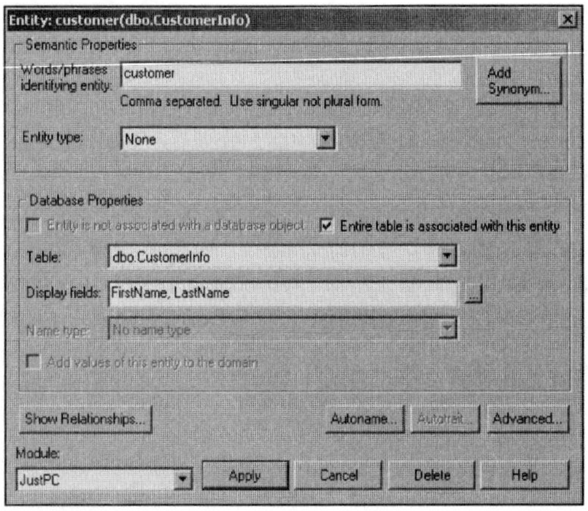

Figure 15-2: Editing an entity

Adding Synonyms

In the JustPC data warehouse, the *entity customer* refers to a person who purchases a computer. However, if someone refers to a customer as a client or buyer, English Query doesn't understand it. To address this problem, you can add synonyms to the entity by pressing the Add Synonym button located in the top right corner of the Entity form. This displays another dialog box that you can use to enter a list of words in place of the entity's name. Be sure to use commas to separate the words because English Query does allow you to enter synonyms that use more than one word.

 Sometimes you may find it difficult to think of synonyms for your entity. Try entering the entity's name into the Microsoft Word Thesaurus. You may be surprised at how many different words it finds.

Clarifying the Entity Type

The Entity type drop-down box on the Entity form enables you to describe the entity in terms of how it will be used. This helps English Query understand how you may use it in a sentence. You can choose from Person, Geographic Location, Animate Object, Physical Object, or Date or Time. If your entity doesn't fall into any of these categories, choose None.

- **Person** allows the entity to be referred to as "who" or as a person, as in "Who bought computers in Beltsville?" or "Which person bought system 12345?"

- **Geographical Location** allows the entity to be referred to as "where" or as a location, as in "Where is Beltsville?" or "Show the location of Beltsville."

- **Animate Object** allows the entity to be referred to as "who", as in "Who bought the most computers?"

- **Physical Object** allows English Query to give more descriptive error messages when the user asks questions about traits that aren't in the database.

- **Date or time** allows the entity to be referred to as "when", as in "When did Samantha Freeze buy a computer?"

- **Address** allows the entity to be treated as an address with multiple values from the database, as in "What is customer 12345's address?"

Choosing Database Properties

Each entity may or may not be associated with a database object. However if it is, then there is a lot of information that you can supply to clarify how the entity is used in the English language and the type of information it might retrieve from the database.

NON-DATABASE ENTITIES

If the entity isn't associated with a database object, then check the *Entity is not associated with a database object* box. Then the rest of the database properties are disabled on the form. This form is useful when you want to allow a noun in a relationship but the noun doesn't refer to a database. For example, consider the relationship "readers like books". Readers doesn't really refer to a database object, but the relationship may enable you to specify a **Where** clause such as `Books.Sales > 10000`.

DATABASE ENTITIES

If an entity is associated with the database, you must choose the table and field or fields that are associated with the entity. Just select the table from the drop-down menu of choices and press the button next to the Fields text box to select the field or fields. You also can choose to classify the name of the object and optionally load the names into the English Query domain. The entity must have a type of name in order to load the values from the database. The different types of names describe how the name is used in a sentence.

- **Proper Name** is used when the name is a proper name. Proper names are capitalized and are not preceded by an article (a, an, or the). Samantha Freeze is a proper name.

- **Common Name** describes a general term for something. Common names are not capitalized and usually are preceded by an article. This name type generally is used when you want to load the name of an item from your database. Examples of a common name include motherboard, video card, and so on.

- **Classifier Name** describes the name of something that includes the entity name as part of a phrase, with an article typically preceding it. Examples of classifier names for the entity CPU are Pentium CPU, AMD CPU, and so on.

- **Model Name** describes a capitalized name, which is preceded by an article, but doesn't include the entity name. For example, if your database holds cars, you may use the follow query, "Count the Porsches". You don't say, "Count the Porsche cars", as you would with a classifier name.

- **Unique ID** describes an object that is represented by a unique value in the database, such as CustomerId. This is useful for queries such as "Show me customer 12345."

ROW-ORIENTED ENTITIES

If the entity is associated with the entire table, check the *Entire table is associated with this entity* checkbox. This is useful when the entity really is related to the entire table, and not just any particular set of fields. Consider the case of the customer in the JustPC example. While you may think that customer is only related to the fields FirstName and LastName in the CustomerInfo table, it is possible to have two different customers named Samantha Freeze. Their addresses would be different and so would their CustomerId.

Even though you checked the *Entire table is associated with this entity* checkbox, you still can select the fields to display for this entity. Press the button next to the Display fields text box to choose the fields.

Checking Relationships

To check the relationships that are associated with the entity, press the Show Relationships button located near the bottom left corner of the Entities form (see Figure 15-2). This displays a dialog box containing each of the relationships in which the entity participates. This is the same dialog box that you can display by right-clicking the entity and choosing Show Relationships. I talk about this more in the next section.

Using Autoname and Autotrait

The Autoname button on the Entity form (see Figure 15-2) enables you to specify the type and name of fields used in a name entity. This button is disabled if the entity already has a name relationship.

The Autotrait button also on the Entity form (see Figure 15-2) enables you to create minor entities for each field in the table that is represented by the entity. This option is disabled if all of the fields in the table are associated with a minor entity.

Advanced Entity Settings

There are several screens of advanced settings that you can use to further customize an entity.

SEMANTIC PROPERTIES

The form shown in Figure 15-3 enables you to refine how the entity is parsed. Checking the *This is a standalone minor entity* checkbox enables you to display data from the entity by itself, without data from the major entity or name entity. This option isn't available if the entity participates in a name relationship or if the entity is not represented by fields.

You also can specify that this entity is a subentity of another entity. However, this entity must be associated with a table.

If you check the *Add values of this entity to the domain* box on the main form, you can specify an alternate location to load the entity's values. This may be a special view of the table that restricts the number of values loaded into the domain.

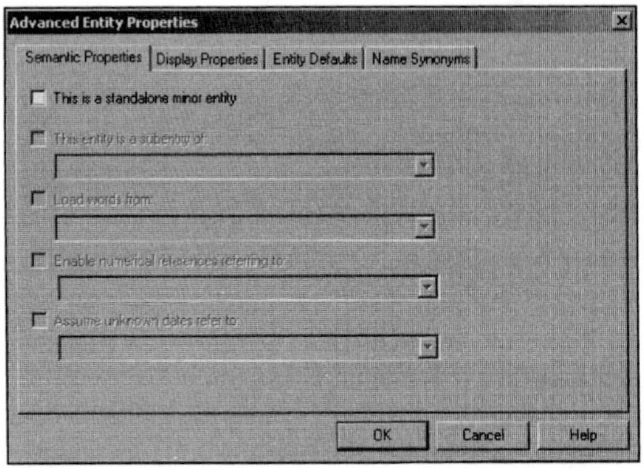

Figure 15-3: Changing semantic properties

The next option (Enable numerical references referring to) allows you to specify a default field in the table when the parser determines that the answer to the query is an amount. It solves the problem when you ask for a numeric value from the entity that is composed of multiple fields.

In the *Assume unknown dates refer to* option, you can specify the relationship that should be used in case the user asks an ambiguous question involving a date (such as "Show last week's sales"). This question can be answered by a list of the individual sales, the total sales prices, or the count of the number of systems sold.

SETTING DISPLAY PROPERTIES

Probably the most useful tab on the Advanced Entity Properties form is Display Properties (see Figure 15-4). This information enables you to specify how the entity is displayed as the result of a query.

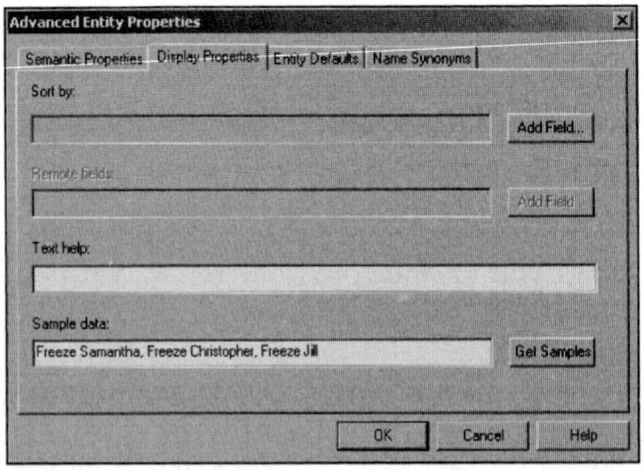

Figure 15-4: Tweaking the default display properties

The first section of this form enables you to specify how the results are sorted. This is really important if the query returns multiple rows of information. By default, the results are displayed in no particular order. This makes it difficult to search through the list to determine a specific value.

The Remote fields section of the form enables you to retrieve values from a second table when the entity is a major entity. The second table must be joined to the referenced table.

The Text help text box enables you to enter information that is displayed about this entity when using the Question Builder feature. Also associated with the Question Builder is the sample data field. The Question Builder uses this data when helping someone to construct a query.

 The Question Builder facility is a part of English Query that helps an end user ask a question by providing answers about the types of information available in the database, the types of relationships and the English phrases that English Query understands. It is automatically incorporated into the standard web-based application that I will cover in "Testing and Deployment" later in this chapter.

ADDING ENTITY DEFAULTS

You use entity defaults to specify a default condition associated with an entity. For instance, you may want the query "List customers" to default to listing individual customers. So you can use the Entity Defaults tab (see Figure 15-5) to specify a relationship that is used as the filter.

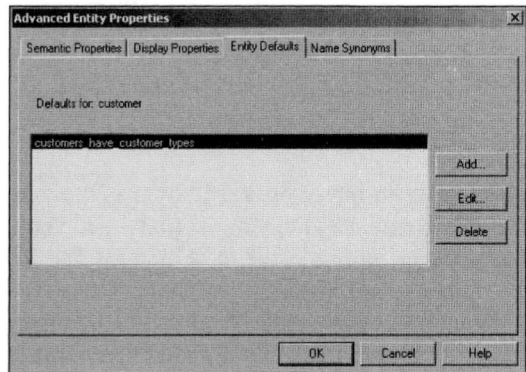

Figure 15-5: Changing semantic properties

To change or add a relationship, press the Add button or select the relationship you want to modify and press the Edit button. This displays the dialog box shown in Figure 15-6. You can select the relationship you wish to use from the Relationship drop-down box.

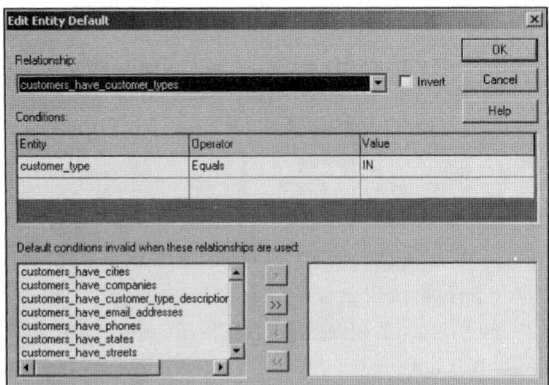

Figure 15-6: Setting the parameters of the relationship filter

Once you select a relationship, you can refine the records selected by specifying a condition on the entity. In Figure 15-6, I specified that the customer_type entity should equal IN. This implies that the customers selected should be individual customers. If you check the Invert checkbox, then the default query for customer returns every row except for those applying to an individual customer.

Just because you specify a default condition doesn't mean that the user can't select a different set of records. Using "all" in the query overrides the default condition and returns all of the rows.

CREATING NAME SYNONYMS

Sometimes you may want to allow your user to query on a synonym of a name value. This is different from working with regular synonyms in that it prevents problems such as the name Bill being confused with bill, the total amount due for an order, and so forth.

You can enter these values on the Name Synonyms tab (see Figure 15-7). Simply enter the synonym in the first column and the original value in the database in the second column.

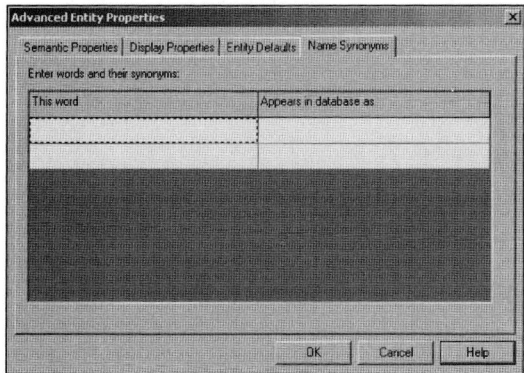

Figure 15-7: Entering synonyms

Tweaking Relationships

The key to making English Query understand what your users enter is adding as many relationships as possible. Each relationship really corresponds to a general type of query that is used to satisfy the user's request for information. You can adjust the details of a relationship by right-clicking a relationship and choosing Edit. You also can insert a new relationship by right-clicking the Relationships icon and choosing Insert Relationship. Either option displays the same dialog box. However, the Edit option displays the current values for the relationship, while the Insert Relationship option gives you a blank form.

The Entities Tab

The Entities tab displays the entities involved in the relationship (see Figure 15-8). You can include help text at the bottom of the form for use in the Question Builder. Pressing the Add Entity button shows you a list of entities in the application and enables you to choose which one you want to add. Pressing Delete Entity removes the currently selected entity from the relationship.

Pressing the Edit Entity button displays the form shown in Figure 15-9, which enables you to refine how the entity is used in this relationship. The Select entity field shows you the current entity you are working with. If you choose another entity from the drop-down list, it automatically adds a new entity to the relation or enables you to browse the existing entity.

Checking the *Always display this entity when this relationship is used* box means that even if this entity is not the last entity in the relationship, its values are included in the result. This is useful for relationships that are constructed from three or more entities.

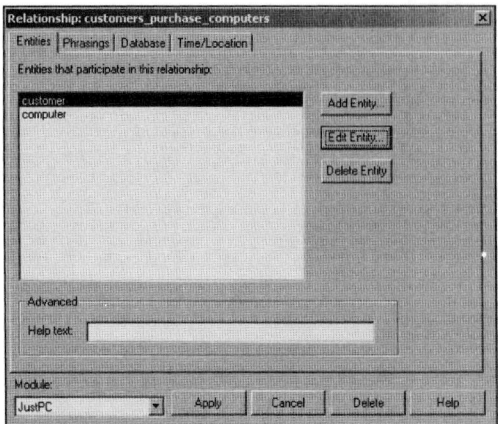

Figure 15-8: Adding help for an entity

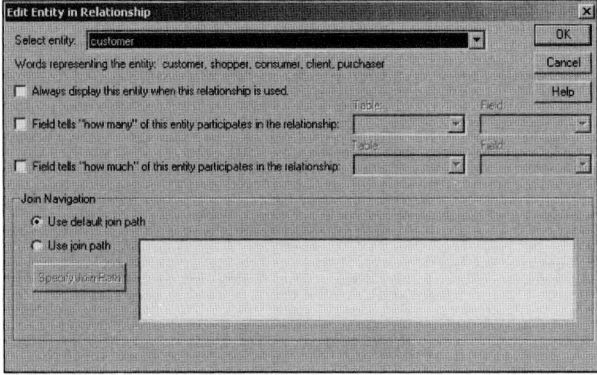

Figure 15-9: Tweaking an entity in a relationship

The "tell how many" and "tell how much" checkboxes help analyze queries that return numeric values. You should check "tell how much" when the numeric value includes units of measures such as pounds, feet, or bottles. You should check "tell how many" when dimensions are not needed. Note that it is appropriate to check both boxes depending on how you phrase the questions and answers.

Join Navigation primarily is used when there are multiple ways to join the same table for the relationship. This enables you to gather the exact information you need. Select Use join path and press the Specify Join Path button to display a list of different ways to retrieve the information.

The Phrasings Tab

The Phrasings tab lists the phrases that describe this relationship (see Figure 15-10). The parser uses these phrases as skeleton sentences to understand queries.

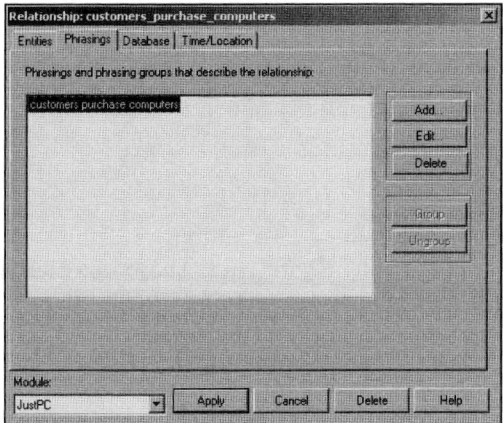

Figure 15-10: Viewing phrasing in a relationship

 Don't underestimate the importance of phrases. The more phrases you enter, the wider range of questions English Query can answer. This is a situation in which more is better and too much is just right.

CHOOSING A PHRASE TYPE

Pressing the Add button displays the dialog box shown in Figure 15-11. You should choose the type of phrase that fits the type of question you expect your users to ask and press OK. You can select from the following list of phrases:

◆ **Name/ID Phrasing** creates phrases such as "customerids are the names of customers."

◆ **Trait Phrasing** creates phrases such as "customers have emailaddresses."

◆ **Preposition Phrasing** creates phrases such as "cities are in states."

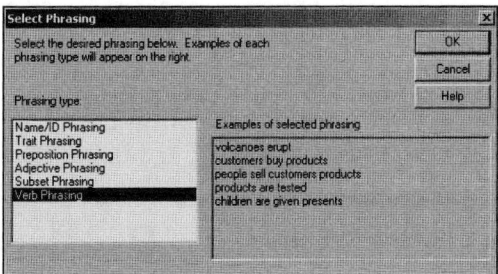

Figure 15-11: Selecting a phrase type

♦ **Adjective Phrasing** creates phrases such as "some computers are fast."

♦ **Subset Phrasing** creates phrases such as "some customers are corporate."

♦ **Verb Phrasing** creates phrases such as "customers purchase computers."

EDITING A PHRASE

After selecting a phrase type by pressing the Add or Edit buttons, a dialog box based on the phrase type is displayed. For example, Figure 15-12 shows the dialog box for Verb Phrasing. In this dialog box, you can choose from several different sentence types. These types provide the prototype for your phrase. In this case, I choose Subject Verb Object, which is a very common form for a verb phrase.

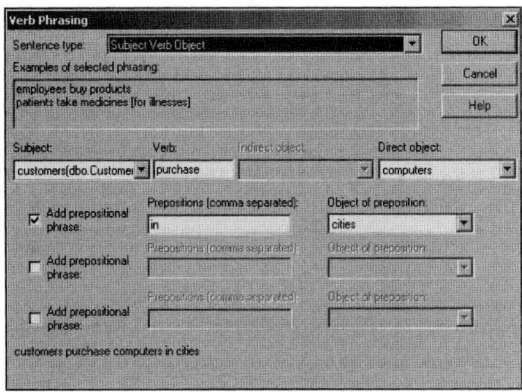

Figure 15-12: Working with phrases

Next, you simply fill in the entities for each of the objects in the phrase. For the subject, I choose customers. For the verb, I choose purchase. And for the direct object, I choose computers. While the subject and object must be entities, the verb can be any value you want.

In addition to the base sentence type, you can add prepositional phrases to qualify queries further. In this example, I add the prepositional phrase "in cities". When combined with the rest of the sentence, English Query can answer queries such as "Count the customers who purchased computers in Beltsville." This returns the number of customers who purchased one or more computers from the city of Beltsville.

The forms for the other phrases are fairly similar. Of course, the exact composition of each form depends on how the phrase is constructed. The key to making this work is to keep adding phrases and to continue trying them with the Test Tool.

The Database Tab

The Database tab enables you to do two things. First, you can specify the database table that contains links to the tables represented by the entities. This is used as the default join table.

The other function on the tab enables you to place a condition on the relationship. This means that the relationship is only valid when the specified condition involving the entities is true. The condition works just like a **Where** clause from a **Select** statement.

The Time/Location Tab

The Time/Location tab enables you to clarify how date, time, and location information can participate in a relationship (see Figure 15-13). You can set five main attributes:

◆ **This relationship occurs at the time specified by this entity:** enables you to answer questions such as "How many computers were purchased this year?"

◆ **This relationship starts at the time specified by this entity:** enables you to answer questions such as "When did Samantha Freeze start purchasing computers?"

◆ **This relationship ends at the time specified by this entity:** enables you to answer questions such as "When did customer 12345 stop buying computers?" Note that you may combine this option with the previous option to specify a date range.

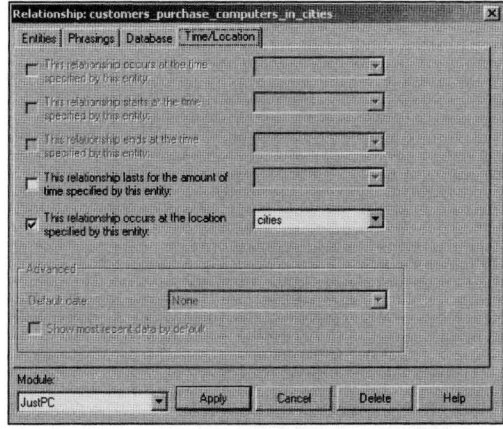

Figure 15-13: Setting time and location attributes

◆ **This relationships lasts for the amount of time specified by this entity:** enables you to answer questions such as "How many computers were purchased in March?"

◆ **This relationship occurs at the location specified by this entity:** enables you to answer questions such as "How many computers were purchased in Beltsville?"

Testing and Deployment

In Chapter 14, I talked about how to test your application (Tools ÿ Test Application from the main menu). Now I want to talk about testing your application in more detail and how to make your application available to users.

Testing Your Application

The Test Application function enables you to do more than simply enter queries and see their results. You can analyze the queries to improve your application and you can collect the questions for use in Regression Testing.

ANALYZING YOUR QUERIES

As you test queries, you'll find a lot of information on the basic Test Application form (see Figure 15-14). The first thing you see below the question is the equivalent question restated by English Query. Below that, you see the Answer and Analysis tabs.

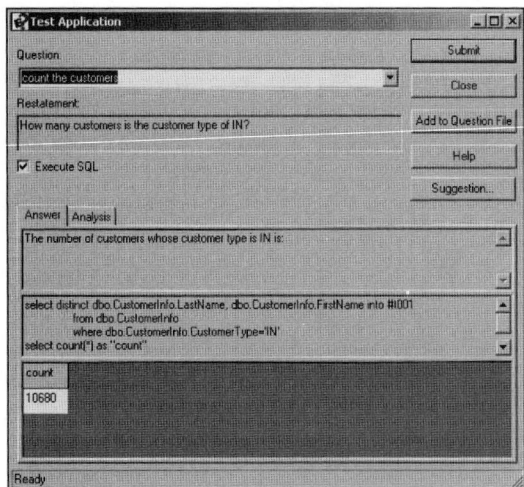

Figure 15-14: Information found while testing your queries

On the Answer tab, you see three sections. The first section contains the restated query reworded in the form of a sentence. This functions as a header for the answer. The second section shows the SQL statements that are used to execute the query, while the bottom section contains the results from the query. You can use this information to determine if the question you asked is translated into the correct query. If it doesn't translate, you may need to review your entities and relationships.

On the Analysis tab (see Figure 15-15), you see a list of entities and phrases that are used to process your query. Double-clicking any of these items automatically takes you to the appropriate dialog box so that you may change its configuration.

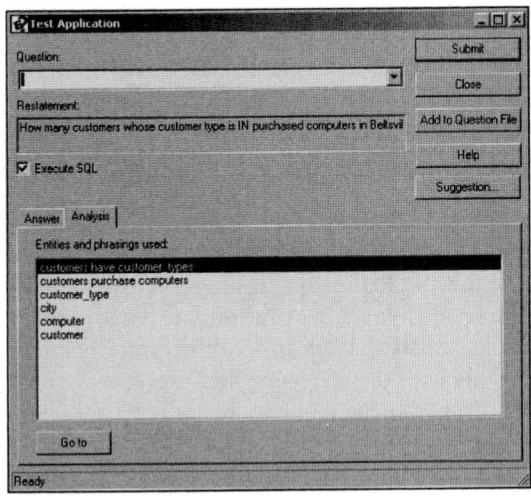

Figure 15-15: Looking at the entities and phrases used in the query

GETTING SUGGESTIONS

Perhaps one of the most useful tools in English Query is the Suggestion button on the Test Application form. Pressing the Suggestion button starts you through a process that asks you to map the various words in the query into the entities that English Query understands (see Figure 15-16). After it maps the entities, English Query offers suggestions for the phrasing or takes you directly to the phrase window if it has only one recommendation. Of course, if English Query understands the phrase and entities, it lets you know that it has no suggestions.

If you're not sure how to define entities and phrases, just try entering some queries and pressing the Suggestion button. This is also helpful if one of your users complains that English Query doesn't understand a particular query.

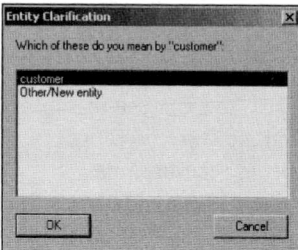

Figure 15-16: Information found while testing your queries

REGRESSION TESTING

As you try various queries, remember them so that you can test your application to ensure that the queries you already tested continue to work properly. This is where Add to Question File and Regression Testing come into play. Each time you press the Add to Question File button, your current query is saved into your current question file.

Regression Testing works by building a list of queries, testing them multiple times, and comparing the differences in the test results. You start by saving one or more questions to your question file and using Regression Testing to create an output file. Once you're satisfied with the results, you save your output file as a reference file. Then the next time you make changes to your application, you can create a new output file and compare the results with the reference file.

You can start Regression Testing from the main menu by selecting Tools → Regression Test. This displays the dialog box shown in Figure 15-17. The current question file is listed in the first text box. Changing this file affects where the questions are stored when you press the Add to Question File button.

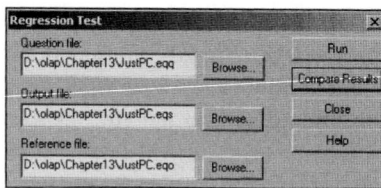

Figure 15-17: Preparing to run a Regression Test

Pressing the Run button runs the test and saves the results in the output file, which has a file type of .EQO. When you are satisfied that this file represents a good test, you can change the file type from .EQO to .EQS, which makes it a reference file. After working with your English Query application some more, you can create a new output file, which has a file type of .EQO again. Then compare this output file (file type .EQOO) with the reference file (file type .EQS) by pressing Compare Results. This displays the Regression Output Differences window shown in Figure 15-18.

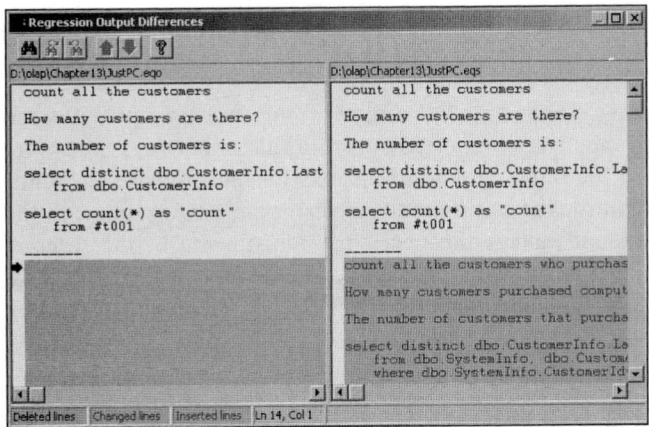

Figure 15-18: Looking at differences

This Regression Output Differences window contains information on each query in the query file. This information includes the name of the query as the first line in each section, the restated query, the response heading, and the SQL statements used to create the query. Any differences between the output file and the reference file are highlighted on the screen to make it easy to spot their differences.

Deployment

Once you're happy with your English Query application, you need to make it available to your users. However, making your English Query application accessible is a little more difficult. English Query is designed to integrate into a custom application developed in a programming language such as Visual Basic. There isn't a general-purpose utility program that enables your users to interact with English Query.

Remember that the English Query program is designed to help you create the knowledge base to answer natural language questions. End users should not use this tool. The user interface is not designed for the novice user and there is nothing to prevent the user from destroying your application.

There are, however, several sample applications that come with English Query. You can use one of these applications to create your own application with almost no effort.

To create this application, you must build the application by choosing Tools → Build Application. In the case of the JustPC application, this creates a file called JustPC.EQD. This file is used as input to the Windows Scripting Host program found in the \Program Files\Microsoft English Query\Samples\ ASP2 directory.

When you run the file, SETUPASP.CMD, (found in the \Program Files\ Microsoft English Query\Samples\ASP2 directory) you are prompted for the name of the English Query application and the directory that holds the application. Then you are prompted for the DSN (Data Source Name) for the database, the database login ID, and its password. The setup program creates a directory to install the English Query application and makes the necessary adjustments in the *Internet Information Server (IIS)* for it to run. Once the application is installed, it provides a much smoother interface to English Query than the Test Application facility (see Figure 15-19).

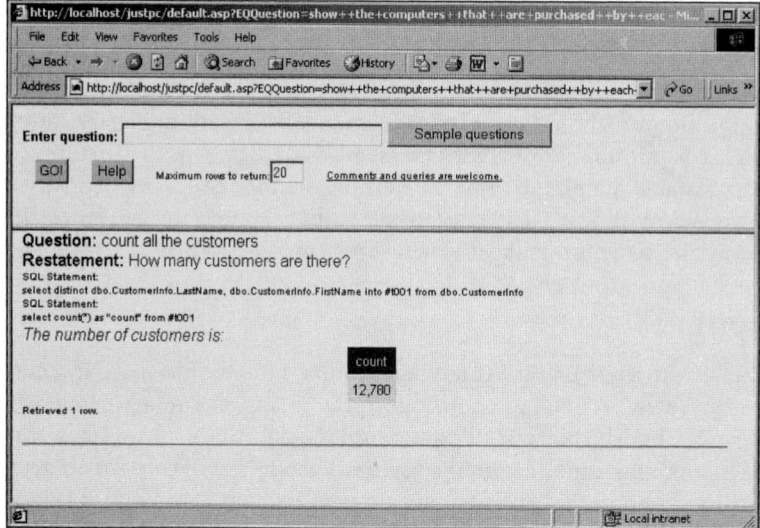

Figure 15-19: Accessing English Query over the Web

 This setup program is very simplistic; you may need to modify it before it works on your Web server. Most of these modifications are limited to the params.inc file used to drive the application. For instance, you may need to modify the virtual directory, which is not properly created in IIS and you may need to create a system DSN (which is different from the file DSN that you created to use English Query). Of course, you should double-check the security of your application before allowing access to it through your Web site.

Summary

English Query is a powerful tool that enables nontechnical users to search for information using queries written in English. While the tool itself doesn't really understand English, it does understand sentence structure. If you give it enough information about your application, it can translate the words and phrases into a standard SQL query, which then can be executed.

While English Query doesn't supply a basic user interface, it is designed to easily integrate into any application program. However, English Query does come with a number of sample applications. One of these applications enables you to build a simple Web page that runs on IIS 4.0 or later Web servers.

In the next chapter, I present one more data analysis tool before diving into a discussion on OLAP cubes. This tool, known as Microsoft MapPoint 2000, enables you to look at data in your database from a geographic point of view. It addresses the problem of how to identify trends in geographic data where it is impossible to tell, just by looking at them, what states and zip codes are next to each other.

Chapter 16

Mapping Data with MapPoint 2000

IN THIS CHAPTER

- ◆ Introducing MapPoint 2000
- ◆ Using MapPoint 2000
- ◆ MapPoint 2000 and your database
- ◆ Publishing the maps

MAPPOINT 2000 IS A member of the Microsoft Office family of products. It is designed to do three main things: analyze statistics by geographic location, compare and contrast your data with its own demographic data, and create maps with driving instructions. MapPoint can plot an area that is as small as your local neighborhood or as large as the entire world.

Introducing MapPoint 2000

With the tools I talked about so far, it is easy to build a table and sort the data. You can identify values that are close to each other by their relative closeness in the table. Analyzing tabular data is easy when compared with geographic data related to cities, states, and zip codes, which does not have any bearing on their relative location. Just because Massachusetts immediately follows Maryland in the list of states doesn't mean that Massachusetts borders Maryland.

Using MapPoint

You can start MapPoint 2000 by choosing Start → Programs → Microsoft MapPoint. This displays the window you see in Figure 16-1. This window is broken into three main parts: the overview (in the upper-left corner), the legend (in the lower-left corner), and the map view (on the right). By choosing View → Legend and Overview, you can toggle the display of the legend and overview sections of the display.

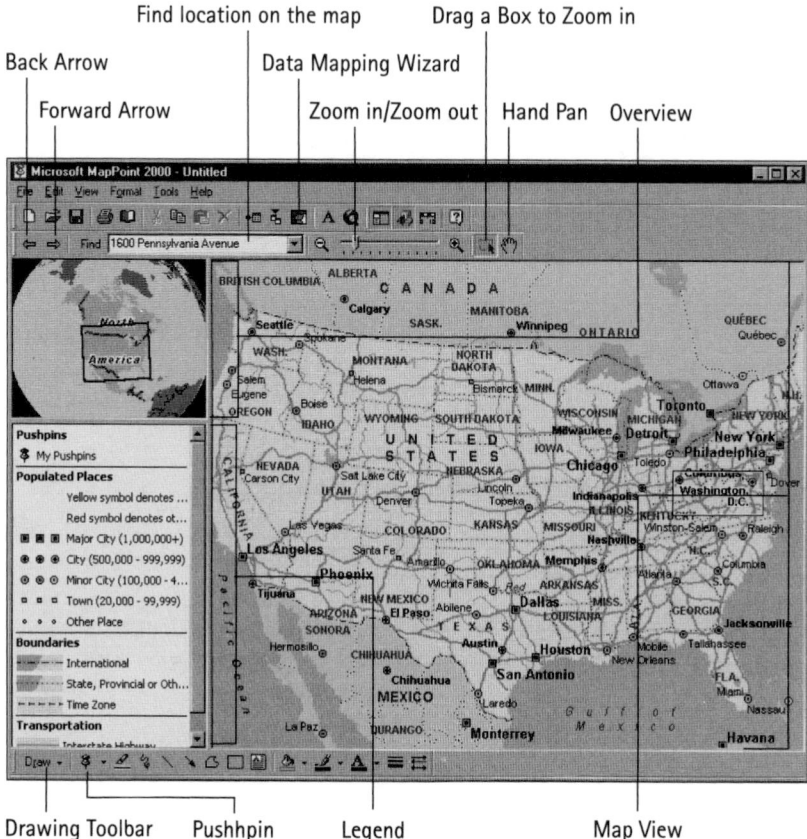

Figure 16-1: Starting Microsoft MapPoint 2000

Zooming Around

There are several different ways to find places in MapPoint. You can use the zoom functions to see more details about a smaller part of the map or you can use the Find dialog box if you know an exact location such as a state, city, or street address.

USING CURSORS

There are two cursors that you can use to move around the map. The default icon is a small box attached to an arrow; it is located to the left of the Hand Pan cursor. The default cursor enables you to draw a box on the map. Then if you click inside the box, MapPoint zooms to the indicated area.

The other cursor is called *Hand Pan*. Using this cursor, you can point to a location on the map and double-click to zoom to it. You also can use the cursor to drag the map to see the parts of the map that aren't visible, without changing the level of detail.

The Zoom in and Zoom out buttons, plus the slider between them, zoom in closer to the area at the center of the map. You also can use the back arrow to display the previous view of the map. If you are not at the last map, you can use the forward arrow to move toward the most recently displayed map.

 At the higher levels of magnification, things may not be placed exactly where they are located in real life. This can happen if the buildings in a particular area have a different size or shape than MapPoint expects. It is also possible that the information in MapPoint's databases is wrong. In this case, Microsoft urges you to file a report that corrects the information. In either case, the information is very close. For example, the exact location of my house is off by about a half a block, but you only notice this when you are using a very high magnification. With most views of the map, you can't notice that the house wasn't in the exact location.

USING THE FIND FUNCTION

The Find location on the map drop-down box enables you to specify the location you want to find. This can be a street address, city, state, zip code, place name, or latitudinal and longitudinal coordinates. Simply enter the text and press Enter. MapPoint 2000 automatically searches for the location and displays a list of choices in the Find dialog box.

Entering 1600 Pennsylvania Avenue into the Find location drop-down box in the toolbar finds a number of different locations from which you can choose. Choose DC-District of Columbia from the State drop-down menu and press the Find button again to locate the White House on the map (see Figure 16-2). Pressing OK leaves the map zoomed to your new location, while pressing Cancel returns the map to the previous location.

Marking Locations with Pushpins

Once you find a location on the map, you probably want to mark it. Maybe you want to mark the locations of your customers or supporters. Maybe you want to mark the locations on a delivery route. Perhaps you just want to mark interesting locations on your map.

MapPoint 2000 includes a feature called *pushpins*, which enable you to mark various locations on the map. Associated with each pushpin is an icon used to mark the location on the map and a balloon containing the name and description of the pushpin. This works just like a map that you can put on a bulletin board and use pushpins to mark locations.

To add a pushpin to the map, click the pushpin icon. The cursor then turns into a pushpin. Move the cursor to the location on the map where you want to place the pushpin and click once. A pushpin appears with a balloon for you to enter information (see Figure 16-3).

Figure 16-2: Finding the White House

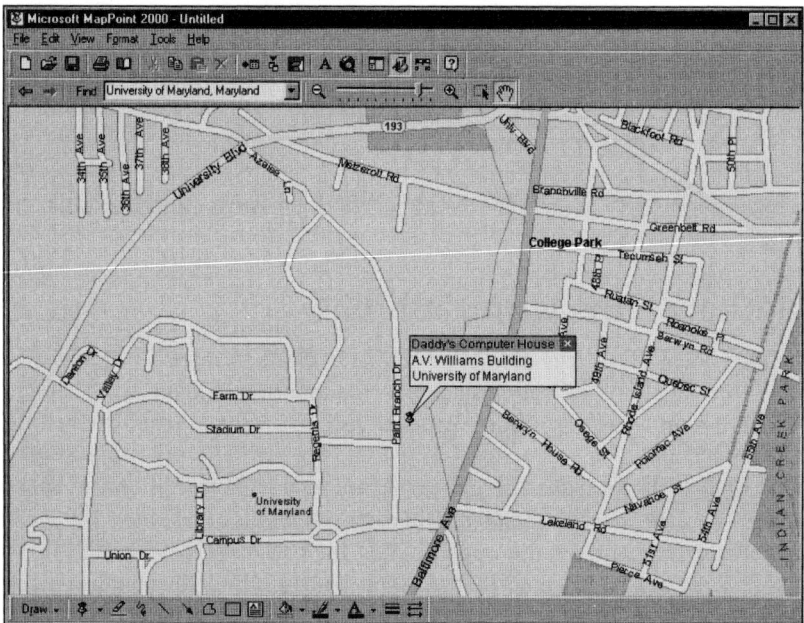

Figure 16-3: Locating my old office at the University of Maryland

 **TIP** Clicking the down arrow next to the pushpin icon displays over 200 push-pin icons from which to choose.

Marking Up Your Map

The drawing toolbar enables you to highlight features on your map. You can add text annotations and mark map highlights. You also can draw lines, arrows, and other shapes in multiple colors. This enables you to draw attention to various parts of map, such as marking districts and territories, identifying various regions, or pointing out interesting locations without using a pushpin.

Saving Your Map

After adding a bunch of pushpins to your map, you may want to save it. MapPoint 2000 doesn't save the map itself, but rather it saves the information it needs to re-create the map (for example, the location of the pushpins and drawings you make on the map). Like all Office applications, simply choose File → Save or File → Save As or press the appropriate icon to save your map. Likewise, you can open an existing map by selecting it from the list of files at the bottom of the File menu option or choosing File → Open from the main menu.

MapPoint 2000 and Your Database

Now you have a brief overview of what you can do with MapPoint. While these features are interesting, using a database with MapPoint brings the product to a much higher level. MapPoint has the ability to import data from a variety of sources, including your SQL Server 7 database. You can turn this data into a series of pushpins or analyze it directly at several different levels. MapPoint includes a powerful tool called the Data Mapping Wizard, which helps you load the data from your database in MapPoint into one of four different styles.

Before You Start

As with most projects, you should decide what information you want to include on the chart. MapPoint is limited to reading information from only a table or a view. It can't execute SQL statements directly. Therefore, if the information you want to map isn't in an existing table or view, you may have to create a new one.

In the rest of this chapter, I use the JustPC data warehouse as an example of some data I want to analyze. In this case, I want to understand how JustPC's sales are spread geographically by zip code. This can help me determine where to place new stores and where to place local advertising.

Because I want to organize my data by zip code, I create the following view that returns the number of customers, the number of systems sold, and the total retail sales by zip code. Then I can compare this information with the information in MapPoint's demographic database.

```
Create View CustomerStatsByZip As
    Select Zip,
           Sum(SalesPrice) SalesPrice,
           Count(SystemId) SystemCount,
           (Select Count(*)
              From CustomerInfo as X
              Where X.Zip = Z.Zip) CustomerCount

    From CustomerInfo As Z, SystemInfo Y
    Where Z.CustomerId = Y.CustomerId
    Group By Zip
```

 When dealing with complex views such as the preceding one, you need to be concerned with performance. If the view takes more than 60 seconds to open, MapPoint is unable to read the data.

Starting the Data Mapping Wizard

Now that I know the kind of data I'll be viewing, I can start the Data Mapping Wizard (for a new map) by choosing File → New and selecting Data Format Wizard from the dialog box. Or I can choose Form → Data Mapping Wizard to add data to an existing map. When the wizard starts, you're offered a choice of four different map styles (see Figure 16-4).

The *Shaded Area Map* breaks up a map into different areas — such as states, counties, or zip codes — and then shades each based on a value you specify. This map is very useful when analyzing statistical data that spans larger areas such as counties or states. It's also good for analyzing non-numeric data.

The *Sized Circle Map* draws circles on the map at specified locations where the size of the circle is dictated by the relative size of the data value. This map is also useful for analyzing statistical data over larger areas such as cities or states.

The *Shaded Circle Map* is similar to the Sized Circle Map, but the relative size of the data value dictates how dark the circle is shaded.

The *Pushpin Map* uses data from your database to create a series of pushpins on your map. This is ideal when you want to graphically see the location of customers or other address-oriented data values.

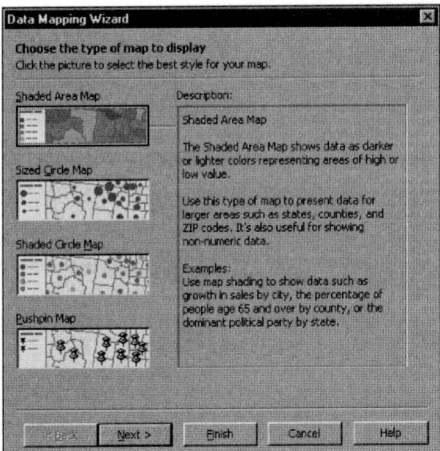

Figure 16-4: Choosing the type of map you want to create

It is possible to combine multiple types of maps together. For instance, you may want to use the Shaded Area Map to show potential customers for your product, and then add a Shaded Circle Map to show the distribution of your current customers. By combining multiple maps this way, you easily can identify areas where you have a lot of potential customers and few current customers.

In the following example, I try each of these styles — except the last one using zip code information. This is because the street addresses in the JustPC database are invalid. This was done deliberately to ensure that no one mistook the data for live data. See the appendix for comments about the JustPC database and data warehouse.

Linking to Your Data

The next step of the wizard asks you to identify the source of your data (see Figure 16-5). While there are four buttons, only the Import and Link buttons load data into your application. Both buttons enable you to get data from a database or from regular files such as Excel worksheets, Outlook Contact Lists, or comma-separated value files. The Import button loads a copy of the data into the MapPoint document, while the Link button creates a link to the data source.

IMPORTING VERSUS LINKING

Each approach has its advantages and disadvantages. By linking to a copy of your data, you easily can update the values in your map. However, this can be a time-consuming operation if you have to do it frequently. It also can be difficult to analyze data if it is changing constantly. You may create multiple maps based on what you think is the same data, but find that the values among the maps are not consistent because the data changed while you were analyzing it.

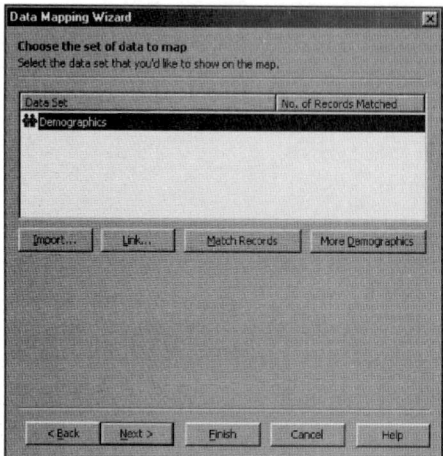

Figure 16–5: Choosing the source of the data

By importing a copy of your data, you ensure that all of the data is included in the MapPoint document. Also, changes in the database aren't reflected in the map. The primary downside to this approach is that the data takes up a lot more disk space on your local computer. Also, it is more difficult to get current data if you need it. In general, I prefer to import data because I can work with a consistent set of data. However, if your data warehouse is updated only once a month, and you're sure the data isn't going to change, then linking to your database is also a good solution.

Sometimes you don't have a choice. Linking to your data requires that your data reside in a table or come from an updateable view. If your data is the result of a view created by summarizing information or joining multiple tables, you can only import the data into MapPoint 2000.

CREATING A DATA LINK FILE

Once you decide to import or link to your data, press the appropriate button. A list of files will be displayed (see Figure 16-6). If you have an existing data link file, select it and press Open. If you don't, right-click the area inside the File open dialog box and select New → Microsoft Data Link from the popup menu to create a new, empty data link file with the name `New Microsoft Data Link`.

Rename the file to a more meaningful name, then right-click it and select Properties from the popup menu. This displays the Properties window for the data link file. Click the Provider tab to begin configuring the data link (see Figure 16-7). Choose *Microsoft OLE DB Provider for SQL Server* and press the Next button.

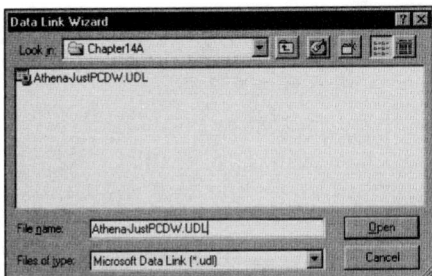

Figure 16-6: Selecting a Microsoft Data Link file

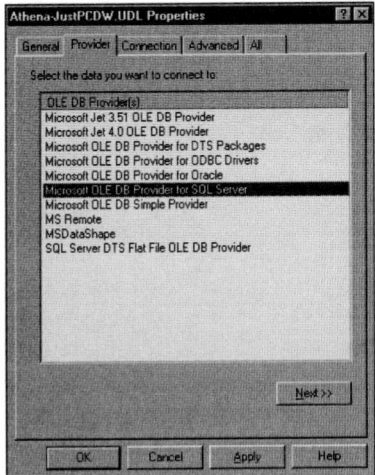

Figure 16-7: Choose OLE DB Provider for SQL Server.

The next window captures the specific information needed to connect to your SQL Server (see Figure 16-8). Choose the name of the server under item 1, enter your logon information under item 2, and choose your default database under item 3. Press the Test Connection button to verify that the information you entered is correct. If it is, press OK to close the data link properties window and press Open on the File open dialog box to select the file you just created.

CHOOSING THE DATA TO MAP
The next step of the wizard asks you to choose a table or view from the database you want to include in your map (see Figure 16-9). In the case of the JustPC data warehouse, I want to use the CustomerStatsByZip view I created earlier in this chapter in the "Before You Start" section. Remember that unless the data has geographic information – such as country, state, city, or zip code – MapPoint is not able to use it.

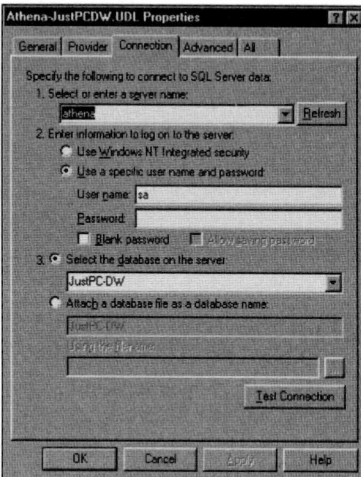

Figure 16-8: Specifying your database server and logon information

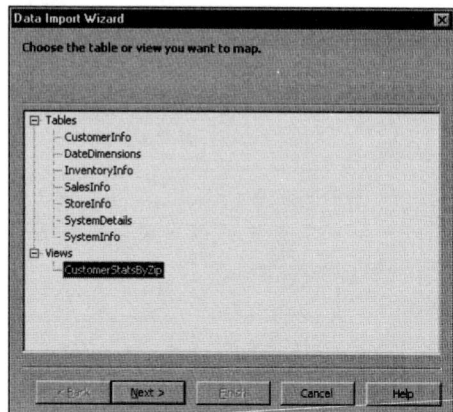

Figure 16-9: Selecting the CustomerStatsByZip view from the database

TIP   While MapPoint can perform some data aggregation, it runs considerably slower than most other tools. This is because MapPoint looks up the geographic location for every record. You are better off creating a view for small volumes of data. For large volumes, you may want to create a summary table using the **Into** clause of the **Select** statement and use the Data Transformation Services (discussed in Chapter 5) to export the data to a comma-separated value text file.

IDENTIFYING COLUMNS OF INFORMATION

After a few minutes of processing, the next step of the wizard shows you some sample information from the database. You should review the column headings at the top of each column and choose new headings if appropriate (see Figure 16-10). If you choose to import data, rather than link to it, you can select a heading of <Skip Column> to ignore the data in that column.

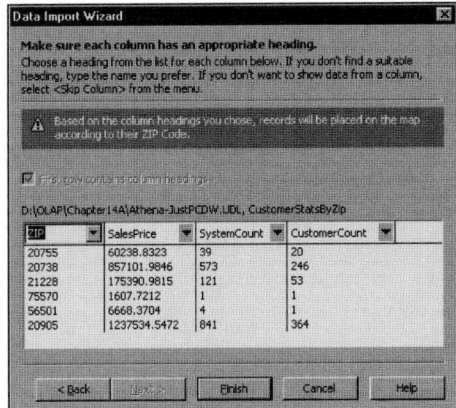

Figure 16-10: Editing the column headers

If you choose to link to your data, you are prompted to identify the primary key for the table or view when you leave this form. This allows MapPoint to store only the primary key value in its document. Each time it needs a value from the database, it uses the primary key value to fetch it.

LOADING THE DATA

Once you're satisfied with the definitions for your data, press Finish. This loads your data into MapPoint (see Figure 16-11). Be prepared to wait for a while as this process runs. Depending on the number of rows in your database and the level of detail (for example, street address versus zip code versus state), the load process can take an extremely long time.

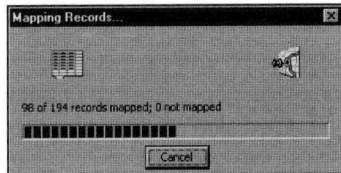

Figure 16-11: Loading the data into MapPoint

When the loading process is complete, you are returned to the step of the Data Mapping Wizard you saw in Figure 16-5. Select the set of data you just created and press Next.

Selecting the Data Column

The next step in the Data Mapping Wizard is to choose the field you want to get the data from and how you want to display it on the map (See Figure 16-12). By default, the data is shown at the lowest geographic level available. However, you can aggregate the data over larger areas. In this case, the data is at the zip code level, so the options to display data at the address or census tract level aren't available. However, I can choose to aggregate the data to a higher level including county or state. By selecting ZIP Code, each zip code will be shaded to represent the total number of customers located in that particular zip code. When you view the entire map, you'll see the relative density of customers in each zip code.

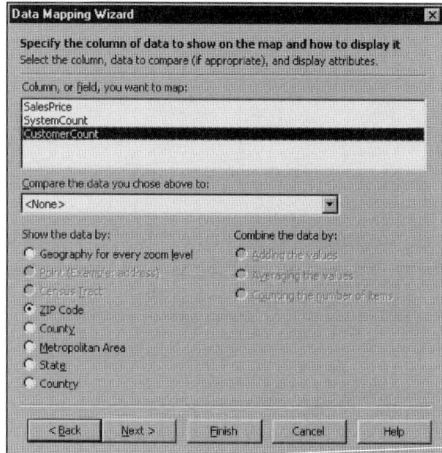

Figure 16-12: Selecting the data column

 **TIP**   When aggregating data, beware of averaging averages. Assume that you are tracking average sales, in dollars, for each zip code. In one zip code, you have 10 customers who spend a total of $20,000, for an average of $2,000 per customer. In another zip code, assume that you have only one customer, who spends $10,000, for an average of $10,000 per customer. If you average those two values, you have a total of $12,000 for two areas with an average of $6,000. The real average should be $2,727 based on sales of $30,000 and 11 customers. The moral of the story is never average an average.

If I choose to chart the data at a level above a zip code, I need to instruct MapPoint on how to aggregate the data. I can add the values from the various areas together, averaging their values or counting the number of items charted.

Specifying Data Attributes

In the last step of the wizard, you need to specify how the data should appear on the map (see Figure 16-13). The data attributes form varies depending on the options you select; however, all forms contain these elements:

◆ **Map Title** holds the title of the map.

◆ **Range Type** describes how the information is drawn on the map. You can choose from any of six different ranges or you can create your own custom range.

◆ **Order** enables you to choose whether the highest values or the lowest values are displayed with the darkest color.

◆ **Colors** enables you to choose from one of 16 different color schemes. Eight are from a single color to white. Five are from a single color to yellow. Of the remaining three, one is red to white to blue, one is gold to green, and the last is rainbow.

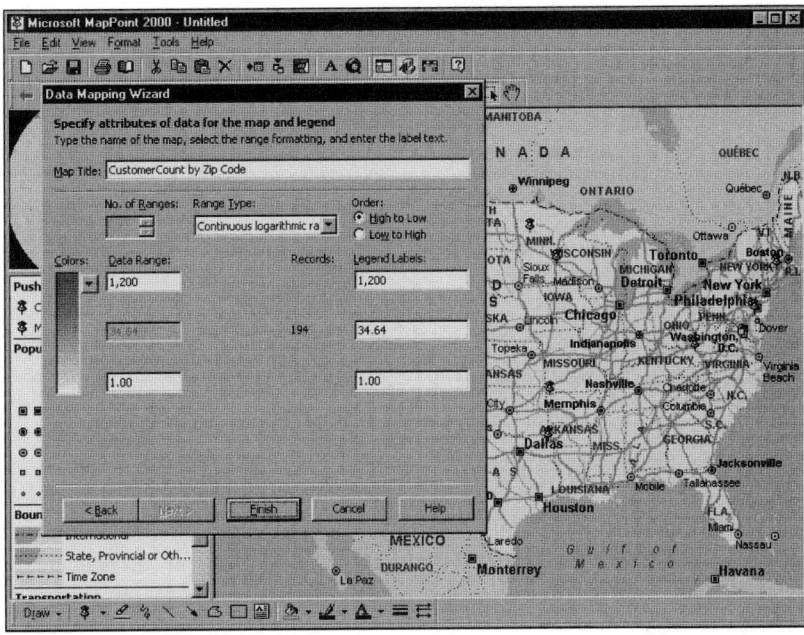

Figure 16-13: Setting data attributes

MapPoint includes two continuous ranges, four discrete ranges, and a custom range that you define for yourself:

- ◆ **Continuous range** selects the largest and smallest data values you want to chart and distributes the values evenly throughout the range. This range is great if your data is distributed evenly.

- ◆ **Continuous logarithmic range** selects the largest and smallest data values you want to chart and distributes the values using a logarithmic curve. This approach is ideal if you want to see more detail at one end of your data range or the other.

- ◆ **Discrete equal ranges** examines your data to determine the size difference between the largest and smallest data values. Then it breaks this size value evenly into the specified number of individual ranges.

- ◆ **Equal data points (quantiles)** examines your data and creates ranges so that an equal number of data points are in each range.

- ◆ **Discrete logarithmic ranges** is similar to the continuous logarithmic range, but it groups the data in up to eight discrete ranges.

- ◆ **Unique values** enables you to assign a color for each unique data value. You should use this range if you have non-numeric values you want to chart. Note that you can chart more than eight values.

- ◆ **Custom** is a variation of the discrete range options. It enables you to specify a starting and stopping value for each range rather than using equal or logarithmic ranges. If none of the standard distributions meet your needs, simply change the range value to whatever you need. MapPoint will convert the range to Custom.

Continuous ranges use all possible colors to represent your data, while discrete and custom ranges map your data values into different categories depending on the data value.

In addition to setting the ranges, you can adjust the text that is displayed in the legend for each data range. By default, the numeric value is displayed; but you are free to change that as you wish. The legend is displayed in place of the default legend supplied by MapPoint.

Looking for Information Geographically

After you finish making your definitions, press Finish. You should see a map that looks something like the one in Figure 16-14. As you scroll around the map, you can see heavy concentrations of customers in some zip codes and other zip codes with few or no customers.

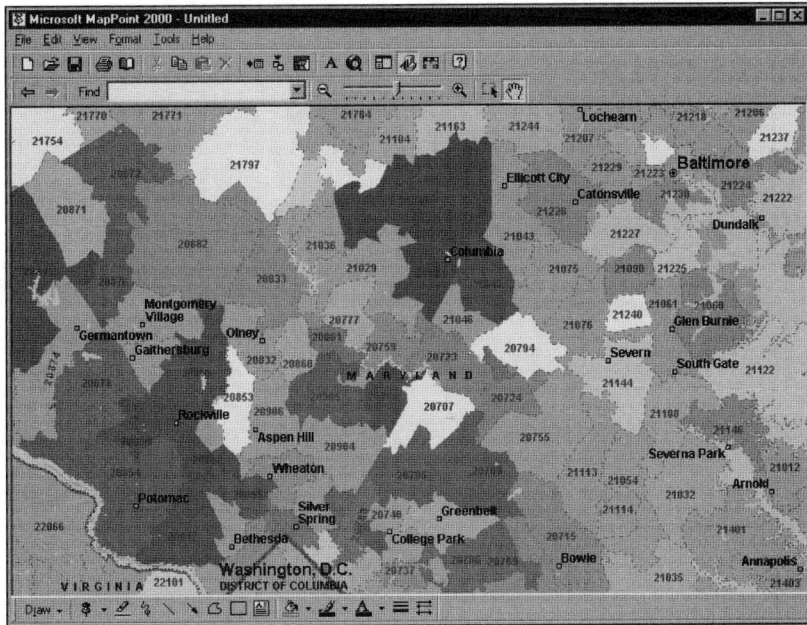

Figure 16-14: Seeing the final product

Changing Your Mind

If you decide you want to change the colors on the map or the type of range used, you can restart the Data Mapping Wizard by choosing Format → Map Type. This enables you to select the type of map you wish to see (Shaded Area, Sized Circle, Shaded Circle, or Pushpin), the data element you wish to chart, and the data attributes. Selecting Format → Data Fields skips the type of map form and enables you to change values on the last two forms, while selecting Format → Legend skips the first two forms and jumps you directly to the data attributes form.

By default, MapPoint 2000 displays roads on your map. However, you can choose not to display roads by selecting Format → Map Style → Data Map. You can include the roads again by choosing Format → Map Style → Road and Data Map.

Adding More Information

Now that I have JustPC statistics on my map, I want to compare it to the population base. To do this, I simply need to use the Data Mapping Wizard again. This time, it adds the data to my current map. Note that I need to use a different map type than I'm using already or I would replace the current map with the revised map.

When I start the Data Mapping Wizard, I select the Sized Circle Map on the first step and the Demographics data set on the second step. On the third step, I select the 1998 Population data and I choose a continuous range to display the results (see Figure 16-15).

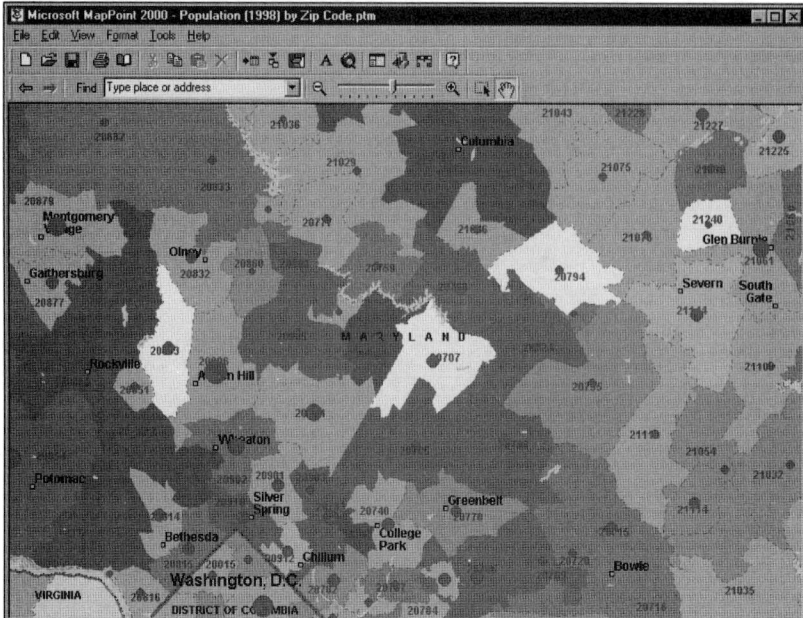

Figure 16-15: Adding a second set of data

Publishing Your Maps

Once you've created a map, you have a number of options available to you to make your map available to others. Which option you choose depends on how you plan to use the map.

◆ You may use File → Save As command from the main menu to save your map as a MapPoint file. You can then make the file available to anyone who wants it. To read this file, the person will need a copy of MapPoint 2000 on their system.

◆ You can use File → Save as Web Page command from the main menu to save your MapPoint file as a web page. This will save your current view of the map as a .GIF file and create a simple web page to display it. You can then easily modify the web page to include it on your Web server.

◆ You may copy some or all of the visual part of the map to another application, such as Word or Excel, by using the Drag a box button to select the part of the map you want to copy. The just right-click inside the selected area and select Copy from the popup menu to copy the map to the clipboard. You can then use the Paste function in the other application to create a static copy of your map.

◆ You may export some or all of the visual part of the map to Excel by using the Drag a box button to select the part of the map you want to export, right-click inside the selected area, and select Export to Excel from the popup menu. This will automatically start Excel and create a worksheet with all of the raw data from the selected area.

You should read the license and its copyright notices carefully before publishing maps. Microsoft has some specific language that covers how you may use the maps. For internal data analysis, this isn't a problem. But before you include the maps in your next ad campaign or make the map available on your Web site, make sure that you aren't violating the license agreement.

Summary

MapPoint 2000 is the sleeper product in Microsoft's Office product line. It is a powerful data analysis tool that easily is dismissed at first glance as a tool that lets people put comments and icons on a map. There are many more features in the program that go beyond the realm of this book, such as the ability to save your map as a Web page and to measure distances between points. If you have a need to analyze geographic data, I highly recommend MapPoint.

While I didn't discuss this, MapPoint is equipped to deal with international locations. Thus, you can build maps that chart international sales or track pushpins for international visitors. The same techniques I use to get the data from the database into MapPoint and to display the data still apply.

When dealing with geographic data, you shouldn't expect perfect data. In fact, you should plan on having problems. Most application systems check for a valid state and numeric zip code, but how many verify that the city is correct for the zip code? A more extreme case is to verify that the street address is correct. In the real world, you may be surprised how incorrect this information can be.

If MapPoint can't verify that the address is correct when you load it, MapPoint sets it aside for later processing. This is known as an *unmatched record*. MapPoint asks you to select the best match for the record based on its databases. You can fix the problem there or instruct MapPoint to skip the record. If you skip it, MapPoint saves the record for processing later. Once you fix the problem with the record's geographic location, you easily can load the corrected record by selecting the data source of Match Records.

This chapter concludes Part IV, Analyzing Data with English Query and MapPoint 2000. In the next Part, I'm going to cover OLAP databases, from the fundamental concepts to the extensions to SQL that allow you to manipulate an OLAP database.

Part V

Understanding OLAP Databases

Chapter 17

The OLAP Data Model

IN THIS CHAPTER

♦ OLAP cubes

♦ Dimensions of a cube

♦ Measures of a cube

♦ OLAP data storage models

♦ Designing OLAP cubes

WHILE TOOLS SUCH AS Query Analyzer or English Query can help you answer many business questions using information from the data warehouse, sometimes you don't know which questions to ask. This is why many organizations are using analytical tools to look at their data. Until recently, most of the tools were cost-prohibitive for many organizations. Now that Microsoft includes OLAP Services with SQL Server 7, many companies can take advantage of these strategic tools.

Introducing OLAP Services

OLAP Services is designed to meet the needs of people who want more out of their data analysis tools than merely responding to a specific request for data. The reason most organizations need to perform analytical processing is that they are looking for hidden information in their data. If these organizations knew the exact questions they wanted to ask, then they easily could solve them with regular queries.

Analyzing data with OLAP is a lot like playing with a Rubik's' Cube. You twist the sides around and around until you see a pattern you understand. From there, hopefully you see the answer in plain sight.

Seeing a pattern in data is not very easy to do, especially if you're dealing with thousands of data points. However, by building an OLAP cube, you can manipulate the data and look at it from many different directions. While doing this, you may notice a pattern start to form.

Suppose you see a gradual change in the data over time. Maybe you need to look for other factors that are behaving the same way. Perhaps all of the data in your cube looks the same, except for a few cells. And maybe you want to find out why those cells are different. No matter what you see in the data, looking at it interactively using OLAP tools takes less time than other methods.

Inside OLAP Services

OLAP Services is a general term that describes a number of things working together to help you analyze your data. Figure 17-1 shows a simple block diagram of the OLAP Services.

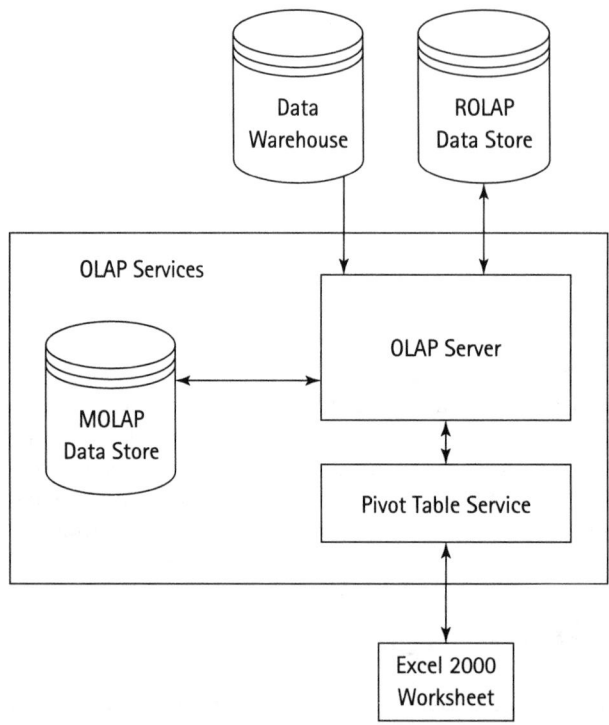

Figure 17-1: The key components used by OLAP Services

Information from your data warehouse is extracted periodically and used to update the objects in OLAP Services. The OLAP Server takes the data from the data warehouse and updates the information it maintains in the *Relational OLAP (ROLAP)* and *Multidimensional OLAP (MOLAP)* data stores. (I discuss both of these topics later in this chapter.) The ROLAP data store is nothing but a regular relational database that supports OLE DB – meaning that you can use Access 2000/97 databases as well as Oracle version 7.3 and newer databases. The MOLAP data store, a special storage mechanism that is a part of OLAP Services, is designed to provide high-performance access to the information in your cube. (Cubes are discussed in the next section.)

Once the information is accumulated, the PivotTable Service works with an Excel 2000 Pivot Table or any other tool that supports OLE DB with OLAP extensions. Thus, you can use Microsoft Access, Visual Basic, and several different third-party tools. The PivotTable Service allows these tools to access and manipulate much larger Pivot Tables than the client can by itself. And after all, isn't a Pivot Table just another way to view multidimensional data?

Just like in SQL Server, your OLAP cubes are stored in databases. Unlike SQL Server, an OLAP database doesn't specify where the data is stored. Instead, the location where the files are stored is specified in the OLAP Services configuration parameters. Each database is stored in a separate subdirectory under the OLAP Services' data directory.

About NTFS. When installing OLAP Services on a Windows 2000/NT system, you should choose an NTFS-formatted disk drive. NTFS is both more reliable and more secure than regular FAT or FAT-32 formatted disk drives.

OLAP Cubes

The primary object stored in an OLAP database is the *cube*. A cube is a multidimensional representation of a set of data, containing both detail and summary data. An OLAP database can have as many cubes as necessary, with each cube drawing data from the data warehouse. A cube is built using two main components: *measures* and *dimensions*. A measure is a numerical value from a fact table in your data warehouse, such as the price of a computer or the quantity of an inventory item, while a dimension categorizes a measure, such as how the measure changes over time.

Measures

A *measure* is the fundamental unit of analysis in a cube. If you look at an Excel Pivot Table, the information that is stored inside the table is generated from a measure.

A measure can contain a single column from the fact table or it can be computed using an expression involving one or more columns from the fact table. While a cube can reference only one fact table, you can include up to 127 measures in your cube. If you want to create calculated members (see the "Virtual Dimensions and Calculated Members" section later in this chapter), you can have up to 65,535 calculated members in your cube.

A measure can be *additive* or *nonadditive*. Additive implies that the measure's values can be added together when summarized. A good example of an additive measure is a sales price. Nonadditive measures can't be added together, but you can use them with a function such as COUNT, whose results can be added.

About numeric values. Just because a value is numeric doesn't mean that you can add it. For instance, CustomerId contains a numeric value, but adding two CustomerIds together doesn't return a meaningful result.

Dimensions

A *dimension* is a way of categorizing a measure, such as how many computers were sold over time or the type of inventory item that was sold. Within a dimension, you can define multiple *levels*. A level merely specifies the degree of aggregation. In an Excel Pivot Table, the dimensions supply the column and row headers for the table in addition to the page area on the worksheet. You are limited to a maximum of 63 dimensions in a cube. You also can create virtual dimensions (see the "Virtual Dimensions and Calculated Members" section that follows) that are derived from existing dimensions.

While all this sounds complex, it really isn't. Consider how many computers were sold over time. The number of computers sold is the measure; time is the dimension. Using the time dimension, you can specify a level of "All", which totals all of the computers sold; "Year", which totals the computers sold each year; and "Month", which totals the computers sold by month and year. The same concept easily applies to other dimensions, such as `InventoryType` value and `InventoryId` value or `State` and `ZipCode` values.

Levels are arranged as a hierarchy; the highest level is the most aggregated and the lowest level is the least aggregated. The only requirement for levels is that the number of members in each level must be as large as the number of members in the previous level. You can have up to 64 levels in a single dimension and up to 128 levels in a cube.

Information about when the computers were sold presents a good example of a dimension and a set of levels. The top level of the dimension is "All", encompassing all of the computers sold by the company. The next level is "Year", followed by "Quarter" and "Month".

Virtual Dimensions and Calculated Members

You create a *virtual dimension* by mapping the properties from another dimension into a new dimension. Because the dimension with the properties already exists in the database, only the mapping information is stored. For instance, consider the Time dimension. If you physically store `Date`, you can perform a simple calculation to change the `Date` value into a `Weekday` value. Virtual dimensions are computed only as needed, but you should expect a query using virtual dimensions to be significantly slower than real dimensions. Also, a virtual dimension is limited to two levels – the All level and the level that is created dynamically.

Similar to virtual levels are *calculated members*. While a virtual dimension is made up of values from a different dimension, a calculated member is a member whose value is calculated at run-time using data from a variety of places within the cube. Like the virtual dimension, using calculated members can impact your query's performance significantly. Unlike virtual dimensions, a calculated member also can be used as a measure.

You can have over 65,000 calculated members in your cube. While this number is much higher than the number of real measures, you'll run out of resources to process queries long before you reach this value. Essentially, you can have an unlimited number of calculated members.

Virtual Cubes

Virtual cubes are defined in terms of other existing cubes. Think of it like a view in a relational database. You can create a virtual cube to show a subset of the data from a real cube or you can combine portions of several other cubes to create a virtual cube. Like virtual dimensions, a virtual cube doesn't really exist until you access it. Then you have to wait while the OLAP Services engine assembles the data in the cube.

OLAP Services limits you to a maximum of 32 cubes in a virtual cube. Considering the resources needed to load the data into a virtual cube, this should not be a big limitation.

OLAP Data Storage Models

OLAP is used to process information and display it in the form of a multidimensional report. However, just because you view data in one form doesn't necessarily mean that the data is stored that way. There are three basic techniques for storing OLAP data:

◆ Multidimensional OLAP (MOLAP)

◆ Relational OLAP (ROLAP)

◆ Hybrid OLAP (HOLAP)

Each approach, with its advantages and disadvantages, actually refers to the underlying database technology that is used to store the information.

MOLAP

One common way of storing the data is in a multidimensional database. Unlike a relational database that stores information as a series of rows in a table, a multidimensional database stores its information as a series of multidimensional arrays. Because the dimensions are easily accessible, you can perform queries against a MOLAP database very quickly. Besides holding the raw data, a MOLAP database also aggregates the data so that it can respond faster to queries. OLAP Services contains an internal MOLAP database that can hold both summary and detail data.

ROLAP

Many people argue that using a special purpose database isn't necessary. Today's high-performance relational databases are fast enough to perform the processing necessary to display OLAP information. This is only true to a certain degree. Under many conditions, you may end up retrieving thousands or hundreds of thousands of records. To get around this problem, most ROLAP implementations create additional summary tables to help improve performance. OLAP Services can access a SQL Server 7 database for ROLAP storage. It also can access relational databases in Access 2000/97 database or Oracle 8.

HOLAP

Probably the most sensible solution to the problem of storing data is to use a hybrid approach or HOLAP. Detail data is kept in a ROLAP database, while summary data is kept in a MOLAP database. OLAP Services is capable of using MOLAP and ROLAP data simultaneously to solve a query.

Physical Considerations

A cube is a logical object. It is created dynamically from data stored in the database. OLAP Services enables you to specify how the data for the cube is stored. You can store the cube in a MOLAP database, a ROLAP database, or HOLAP database. However, OLAP Services completely controls what is stored. This means that you don't need to specify summary tables, or any other tables for that matter.

OLAP Services determines what data to store and how to store it. It summarizes some of the data to speed responses. For instance, if you need to analyze data by both month and year, OLAP Services may choose to precalculate the monthly values and not the yearly values. Thus, if you request information for a particular year, it is a simple matter to aggregate the monthly values for that particular year. This saves space in the database, while not adding a lot of extra overhead to solve a query.

You also can break a cube into multiple partitions. Each partition represents a separate storage container. In each partition, you can specify how much summarization to take place. This enables you to specify low levels of summarization for less frequently used information, while increasing the summarization level for frequently used pieces of data. Even though a cube may span multiple partitions, The cube appears to the user as a simple cube. The query user doesn't know if the cube is stored in one partition or in a dozen.

 **About multiple partitions.** Multiple partitions are only available with Microsoft SQL Server 7, OLAP Services, Enterprise Edition.

Cube Operations

As you saw in Chapter 1, OLAP displays your information in the form of a multidimensional report. You can perform a number of basic operations against this report. These include processing, slicing and dicing, and drilling down.

Processing

Processing a cube involves loading or refreshing the data in the cube by the OLAP Services engine. The dimensional tables are read first to populate the levels with members from the actual data. The fact table is read next, followed by calculating the specified aggregations. Finally, the results are stored in the cube for processing by users. You only need to process a cube if either the cube's structure has changed or the data in the data warehouse has changed.

When processing a cube, you have two choices. You can refresh the cube completely, which means that the cube is erased and all of the steps described above are performed. You also can update the cube incrementally by loading the data that has been added since the last time the cube was processed. Obviously, an incremental update is faster than a refresh, but you cannot use an incremental update if the structure of the cube has changed since the last time the cube was refreshed.

Slice and Dice

Slice and dice enables you to view the cube from different perspectives. You can choose which dimensions to display and how they are displayed. This is why you want to use OLAP. By twisting and turning the cube in different ways, you can learn a lot about your data.

Drill-Down

Most information displayed in a single OLAP view represents the consolidation of more detailed information. *Drilling down* is the technique used to break a single piece of information into smaller parts so you can see the details behind the value. For instance, when you drill-down on a value that summarizes information into a year, you may see the information displayed over four quarters. Drilling down again displays the information for the three months of data in a single quarter.

OLAP Tools

In order to create and use OLAP cubes, you need to become familiar with some of the tools supplied with OLAP Services. These are the OLAP Manager, the OLAP Cube Editor, and the OLAP Cube Browser. As you may expect, these tools enable you to define OLAP cubes, perform various operations, and display the results.

The OLAP Manager

One tool that you will get very familiar with while creating and maintaining your OLAP database is the *OLAP Manager* (see Figure 17-2). This tool uses the same Microsoft Management Console that the SQL Server Enterprise Manager uses, so there is a great deal of similarity between how the two tools work.

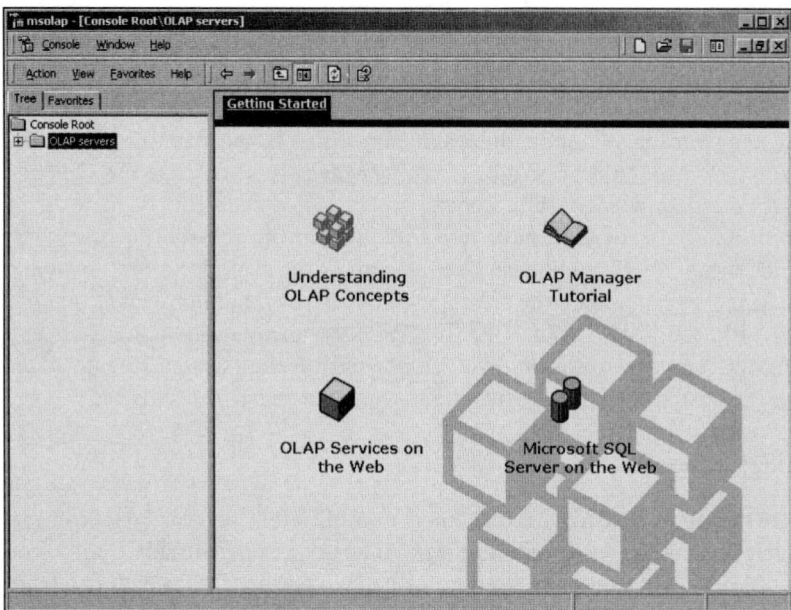

Figure 17-2: The OLAP Manager is similar to the SQL Server Enterprise Manager.

The OLAP Manager window is divided into two main subwindows. The subwindow on the right contains details about the selected item in the OLAP Manager tree view. At the top of this window are two choices: Getting Started and Metadata. Select Getting Started to display the four icons that you see in Figure 17-2, which help you find information about the topics that they describe. Selecting Metadata displays information about the item selected on the left subwindow.

The left subwindow contains the OLAP Manager tree view. The tree begins with the Console Root icon followed by the OLAP servers icon. Beneath this icon, you can see each of the servers on the network that has a registered OLAP server. If you want to access an OLAP server that isn't listed, right-click the OLAP servers icon and select Register Server from the popup menu. This displays the dialog box shown in Figure 17-3. Then enter the name of the server you wish to access in the dialog box and press OK.

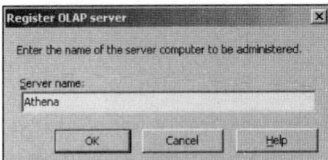

Figure 17-3: Adding a new server to OLAP Manager

Clicking a particular OLAP server icon displays a list of databases beneath it. To create a new database, simply right-click the server name and select New Database. This displays the dialog box shown in Figure 17-4. Enter the name of the database and its description and press OK.

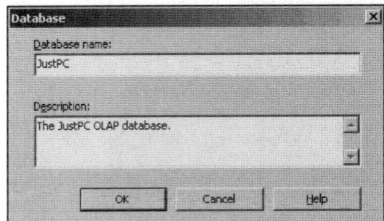

Figure 17-4: Creating a new database on a server

Expanding a database icon displays three major sections beneath the database in the tree view: Cubes, Virtual Cubes, and Library.

The OLAP Cube Editor

You use various tools in the SQL Server Enterprise Manager to create and edit tables in your database. Likewise, in the OLAP Manager, you can use a special tool to help create your own cubes. This tool is known as the *Cube Editor*. Invoke the Cube Editor by right-clicking a cube in the tree view and selecting Edit from the popup menu. This graphically displays the structure of the cube and enables you to make changes to it (see Figure 17-5).

The OLAP Cube Browser

The *OLAP Cube Browser* is a simple tool that enables you to view the contents of a cube. While not as powerful as Excel's Pivot Tables, it enables you to examine the data in a cube once it is processed. To use the Cube Browser, right-click the cube you want to view and select Browse from the popup menu. This displays the cube's data (as shown in Figure 17-6).

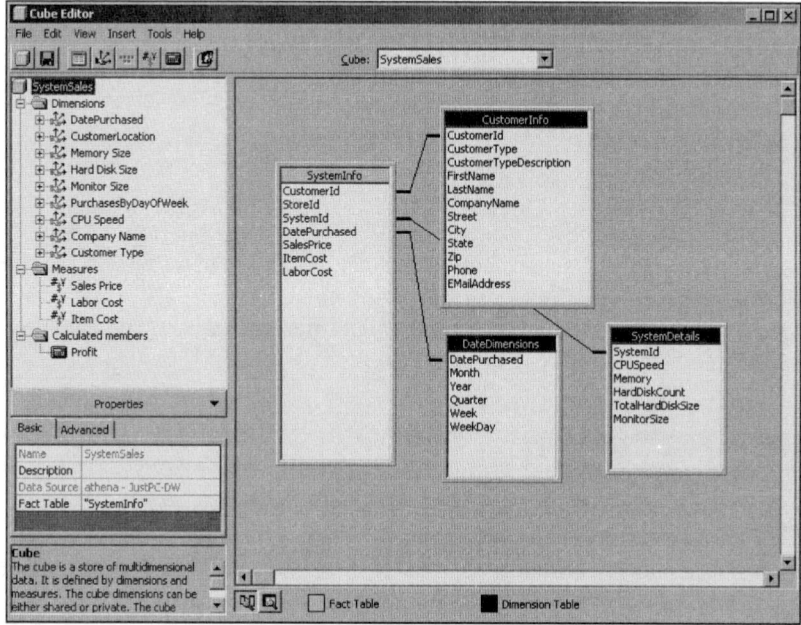

Figure 17-5: Editing a cube's structure with the OLAP Cube Editor

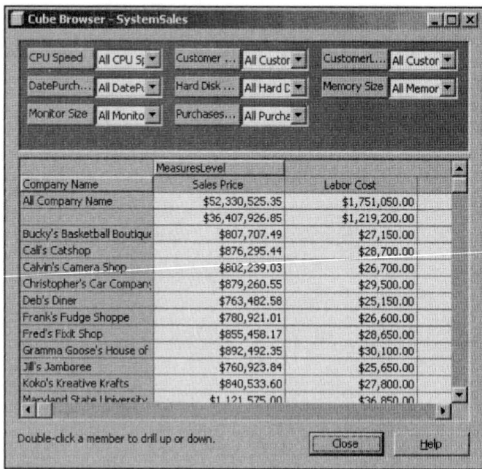

Figure 17-6: Viewing a cube's data with the OLAP Cube Browser

Guidelines for Cube Design

Designing an OLAP cube isn't difficult. You did much of the hard work already when you designed your data warehouse. You determined which values you wanted to include in your fact table and your dimensional tables. You already made the decision whether to organize your data warehouse by using a Star or Snowflake Schema. For the most part, these decisions dictate how you design your cube.

Here are a few things you should think about when designing your cube.

◆ **Star versus Snowflake:** A Star Schema is more efficient than a Snowflake Schema. If you must use a Snowflake Schema, try to keep the number of dimensional tables to a minimum beyond the first level.

◆ **Meaningful dimensional tables:** Dimensional tables should include meaningful information for the users. Include any items that you believe the user may want to query.

◆ **Unrelated information:** Don't try to group unrelated information into a dimensional table. Also, don't duplicate information in multiple dimensions; create a new dimension instead.

◆ **Don't over-summarize:** Try not to over-summarize the information in the fact table. OLAP Services automatically keeps the summary information it needs to best satisfy your queries.

◆ **Use common fact tables:** Try to use a common fact table whenever possible. You can combine multiple fact tables together as long as the dimensional tables are compatible. This makes it easier to analyze data.

◆ **Avoid auxiliary tables:** Don't create auxiliary tables with summary data; OLAP Services won't use them.

◆ **Use indexes for primary keys:** Make sure that all fields used as keys have an index. It is especially important to have a single index on the combination of foreign key fields in the fact table. These indexes make a big difference in how quickly OLAP Services can process a query.

◆ **Foreign keys need indexes, too:** Make sure that each foreign key value in a fact table has a corresponding value in the dimensional table. If the value in a fact table can't be found in a dimensional table, the row may be ignored. Likewise, having a value in the dimensional table with a corresponding value in the fact table may cause empty cells to appear in your cube.

◆ **Don't update, add instead:** If possible, try not to update data in the data warehouse. Instead add new rows to the tables. Updated values in the data warehouse force the cube to be refreshed, while additional rows only require that the cube be updated incrementally.

Summary

OLAP Services offers a middle tier between the data warehouse and Excel. This tier speeds up processing while preventing Excel from being overwhelmed by data. In essence, the user can use an off-the-shelf tool, such as Excel, for analyzing rather large volumes of data even though the spreadsheet program is limited to about 16,000 rows of data.

You create your cubes by using the OLAP Manager. While the OLAP Manager includes wizards to help you perform most common tasks, you also can perform those tasks directly using tools such as the OLAP Cube Editor and the OLAP Cube Browser, which are launched from within the OLAP Manager.

When building your cube, you have a choice of three different ways to allocate space. However, choosing MOLAP versus ROLAP is similar to choosing a religion. Both sides have their believers and neither side believes in a compromise like HOLAP. However, I believe that this is a moot point. Most people don't really care about the underlying technology as long as they get the results they need in the timeframe they need them.

Once the cube is built, you still have a lot of work to do. One of the things that is critical to your success is developing a process to refresh the contents of your cube with new data from your data warehouse. This process should run automatically on a regular schedule and your users should know the schedule. This helps your users know how current the data is that they're using.

In the next chapter, I'll discuss some extensions to the SQL language that allow you to work with cubes. These extensions are known collectively as MultiDimensional eXtensions (MDX). Understanding these extensions will give you some more insight into how multidimensional cubes work.

Chapter 18

The Language of OLAP: Creating Cubes

IN THIS CHAPTER

- ◆ The Create Cube statement
- ◆ The Create Member statement
- ◆ The Drop Member statement
- ◆ The Insert Into statement
- ◆ The Refresh Cube statement

IF SQL IS THE LANGUAGE of SQL Server, MDX is the language of OLAP Services. *MDX* is short for *MultiDimensional eXtensions*. MDX is a set of enhancements to SQL that enables you to define and query OLAP cubes. In this chapter, I discuss the statements used to create and maintain your cubes. In Chapter 19, I continue this discussion by talking about the statements you use to access the information in the cube.

Dimensions, Measures, and Other Parts of a Cube

Every OLAP cube is made up of *dimensions* and *measures*. A dimension corresponds to an axis on a cube, while a measure refers to the values inside each cube (see Figure 18-1). Note that an OLAP cube is not a square. Each edge of the cube typically has a different number of elements depending on how your data looks.

Slices

If you look at the cube long enough, you can see that it is made up of a series of two-dimensional grids. Each grid is known as a *slice*. In Figure 18-2, you see a two-dimensional slice of the cube shown in Figure 18-1. Assume that you select the first quarter, you can view the same slice of information that shows the Salesperson and Product dimensions.

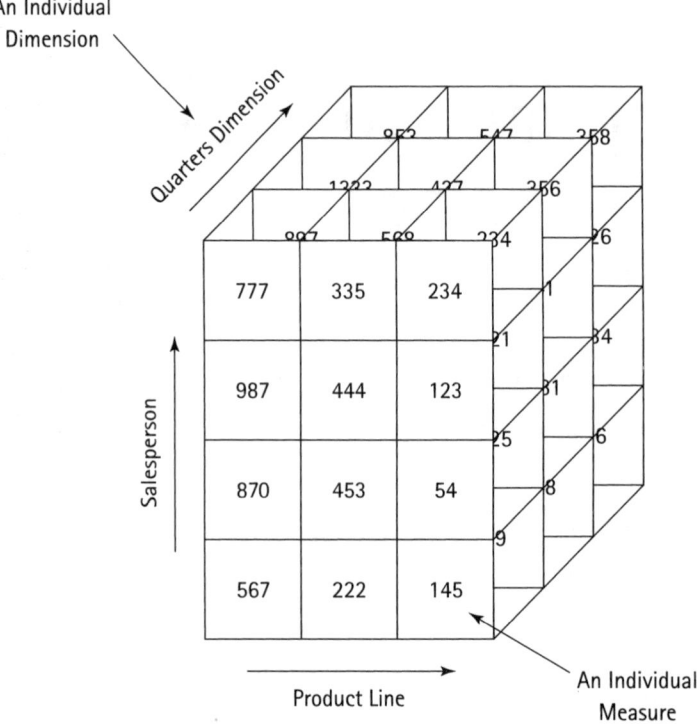

Figure 18-1: A cube has dimensions and measures.

Sum of Total Sales	Product			
Salesperson	Computers	Networks	Printers	Grand Total
Chris	777	335	234	1346
Jill	987	444	123	1554
Samantha	870	453	54	1377
Terry	567	222	145	934
Grand Total	3201	1454	556	5211

Figure 18-2: A two-dimensional representation of a cube

Unlike the cube of data in Figure 18-1, this slice contains a lot more information. To the right and below the individual measures are a series of totals. These totals are merely the sum of the individual measures that appear to the left or above the total box. Also, a grand total is shown at the lower right of the display. This is the summation of all the individual measures.

Associated with each measure is a function used to combine multiple individual measures into a single value. Typically, this function is SUM, but other functions — such as COUNT, MIN, and MAX — may be used.

Levels

To the left and top of the individual measures is a series of labels. Each label corresponds to the value along the dimension. For instance, on the Salesperson dimension, the values are Chris, Jill, Samantha, and Terry; along the Product dimension are Computers, Networks, and Printers. Each series of label values corresponds to a *level*.

In this example, each dimension has two levels: the low-level dimension, such as the quarter number or the salesperson's name, plus a dimension called All that corresponds to the Grand Totals shown in Figure 18-2. The totals are computed automatically based on the rules established when the cube was defined. The collection of levels is known as a *hierarchy*.

Hierarchies

The previous examples showed a dimension with two levels. The first level is an All level that encompasses all measures along that particular dimension. The second is a lower level that has a one-to-one mapping between each value in the dimension and each measure along that dimension.

It is important to note that you are not limited to two levels. Some dimensions, such as Time, have a number of natural levels. If the dimension spans several years, consider using Year, Quarter, Month, and even Date as possible levels. This provides an easy way to analyze your data. You can look at a range of years and work your way down to looking at the days within a month.

You can even break a dimension down into overlapping hierarchies. For instance, if your fiscal year is not the same as the calendar year, you may want to define a different hierarchy that groups measures by fiscal year, fiscal quarter, and so on.

Combining Dimensions

The two-dimensional slice of the cube is just one way to look at information in a cube. A tool such as the Excel PivotTable enables you to perform a number of different operations on a cube. You can look at various slices of the cube, drag dimensions from one axis to another, and even combine dimensions (as shown in Figure 18-3). Chapter 25 covers PivotTables in more depth.

Sum of Total Sales		Quarter				
Product	Salesperson	1	2	3	4	Grand Total
Computers	Chris	777	897	1323	952	3949
	Jill	987	987	890	852	3716
	Samantha	870	774	870	752	3266
	Terry	567	587	541	580	2275
Computers Total		3201	3245	3624	3136	13206
Networks	Chris	335	568	437	547	1887
	Jill	444	645	321	598	2008
	Samantha	453	127	439	685	1704
	Terry	222	87	129	256	694
Networks Total		1454	1427	1326	2086	6293
Printers	Chris	234	234	256	258	982
	Jill	123	321	111	126	681
	Samantha	54	125	231	314	724
	Terry	145	89	88	96	418
Printers Total		556	769	686	794	2805
Grand Total		5211	5441	5636	6016	22304

Figure 18-3: Combining dimensions

Tuples

While the preceding discussion is interesting, there is an alternate way to think about cubes. In order to identify a square on a grid, you need to supply two values – one for each dimension. These values can be an *x* and *y* coordinate in a *x-y* graph, row and column names in an Excel worksheet, or even a category title and dollar amount in a *Jeopardy* game.

One way of describing each position is to enclose the values in parentheses like (50, 100), (B, 6), or (History, $300). This is known as a *tuple*. Going back to Figure 18-1, you can express the location of a cell in the cube as (Quarter, Product, Salesperson). Thus, the first cell in the cube is (1, Computers, Chris); the last cell in the last cube is (4, Printers, Terry). These tuples point to the values 777 and 96.

The concept of tuples becomes useful when you have more than three dimensions in a cube. Rather than trying to picture what a four-dimensional cube would look like, you simply can write the four dimensions as a tuple. For instance, suppose that I add a geographic dimension to the example in Figure 18-1. A tuple then looks like (1, Computers, Chris, Maryland).

The beauty of tuples. Some of the concepts used in mathematics are useful in describing database concepts. The concept of a tuple comes directly from set theory. When dealing with complex sets, don't try to picture how an object looks in your mind; try to express the concept mathematically. In this case, using tuples makes it possible to think about n-dimensional objects without becoming lost in space.

The Create Cube Statement

The **Create Cube** statement is similar to the **Create Table** statement. Both statements create an empty structure that will hold your data eventually. However, the **Create Table** statement creates two-dimensional objects, while the **Create Cube** statement defines objects with three or more dimensions. Its syntax appears as follows:

```
Create Cube <cname> (
   {Dimension <dname> [Type Time], <hierarchy> [, <hierarchy>]...}
   {Measure <mname> <mfunction> [<mformat>] [<mtype>]}
   {Command <mdxstatement>}
   )
```

Where

```
<hierarchy> ::= [Hierarchy <hname>,] <level> [, <level>] ...
<level> ::= Level <lname> [Type <ltype>] [<lformat>] [<loptions>
<ltype> ::= All | Year | Quarter | Month | Week | Day | DayOfWeek |
Date | Hour | Minute | Second
<lformat> ::= Format_Name <expression> [Format_Key <expression>
<loptions> ::= Options ( <loption> [, <loption>]...)
<loption> ::= Unique | SortByName | SortByKey

<mfunction> ::= Function <functionname>
<functionname> ::= Sum | Min | Max | Count
<mformat> ::= Format <expression>
<mtype> ::= Type <oledbtype>
<oledbtype> ::= DBType_I1 | DBType_I2 | DBType_I4 | DBType_I8 |
DBType_UI1| DBType_UI2 | DBType_UI4 | DBType_UI8 | DBType_R4 |
DBType_R8 | DBType_CY | DBType_Decimal | DBType_Numeric |
DBType_Date
```

And

```
<cname> is the name of your cube.
<dname> is the name of a dimension.
<hname> is the name of a hierarchy.
<lname> is the name of a level.
<mname> is the name of a measure.
<mxdstatement> is a legal MDX statement such as Create Member or
Create Set.
```

The **Create Cube** statement performs three major tasks: defining dimensions, defining measures, and executing a series of commands. I discuss each of these tasks next.

DIMENSIONS

When you define a dimension using the **Dimension** clause, you need to provide the values that are used to locate a particular measure in the cube and to group the measures in the cube. Each dimension can have a hierarchy, which is just one or more independent sets of levels If your level only has one hierarchy, then you may omit the **Hierarchy** clause. Otherwise, you must precede each set of levels with a **Hierarchy** clause as well as a unique name for the hierarchy.

Within a hierarchy, you identify each of your levels. The level with the fewest entries is listed first; this is followed by entries that break down each entry in the first level into one or more elements. For example, in the JustPC database, a customer has a hierarchical geographic location. Customers are located in a state. Those customers can be broken into cities within the state and zip codes within a city.

Time dimensions are handled a little differently than other dimensions. Declaring a dimension of type time enables you to use data containing a date/time value such as a SQL `DateTime` or `SmallDateTime` value. Then, on the **Level** clause, you can specify **Type Year, Type Quarter, Type Month, Type Week, Type Day, Type Day-of-Week, Type Date, Type Hour, Type Minute,** or **Type Second** and the appropriate calculations automatically are done to map the date/time value into the appropriate level value.

The **Type** clause also can be used to identify a level for all of the items in a particular level. This is known as **Type All.** If you don't specifically include a **Type All** level, one is created for you automatically.

MEASURES

The **Measure** clause identifies a measure that can be included in a cube. Note that unlike the previous examples in this chapter, a cube can have more than one measure. Associated with each measure is the function used to combine measures (via the **Function** clause), the format used to display the measure (via the **Format** clause), and the data type of the measure (via the **Type** clause).

You have a choice of four different functions for a measure: SUM, COUNT, MIN, and MAX. These functions work just like you may expect. The SUM function adds all of the measures to be combined, while the COUNT function counts the number of cells. The MIN and MAX functions return the smallest and largest values within the group of measures.

By using the **Format** clause, you can specify how a measure is displayed. You may use any legal Visual Basic format string. Table 18-1 lists some common format names. In addition, you can develop your own format string using the standard formatting symbols.

TABLE **18-1 COMMONLY NAMED FORMATS**

Name	Description
Currency	Displays the number with a leading dollar sign, thousands separator, and two decimal digit (for example, $123,456.79).
Fixed	Displays the number with at least one digit to the left of the decimal point and two digits to the right. Do not use the thousands separator (for example, 123456.79).
General Date	If date information is included in the expression, this format displays the date as mm/dd/yy. If time information is included in the expression, it displays the time as hh:mm XM (for example, 5/15/97 2:37:00 PM).
General Number	Displays the number without a thousands separator (for example, 123456.789).
Long Date	Displays the date in your system's long date format (for example, Thursday, May 15, 1997).
Medium Date	Displays the date in your system's medium date format (for example, 15-May-97).
Short Date	Displays the date in your system's short date format (for example, 5/15/97).
Long Time	Displays the time in your system's long time format (for example, 2:37:00 PM).
Medium Time	Displays the time in your system's medium time format (for example, 02:37 PM).
Percent	Displays the number multiplied by 100 and with two decimal places (for example, 12345678.90%).

Continued

TABLE 18-1 COMMONLY NAMED FORMATS *(Continued)*

Name	Description
Scientific	Displays the number as a leading digit, with two decimal places times 10 to the nth power (for example, 1.23E+05).
Short Time	Displays the time in your system's short time format (for example, 14:37).
Standard	Displays the number with at least one digit to the left of the decimal point and two digits to the right. Use the thousands separator if needed (for example, 123,456.79).

The **Type** clause enables you to specify the data type of the measure (see Table 18-2). For the most part, you should use either an integer format such as **DBType_I4** or **DBType_I8** or an exact numeric format such as **DBType_CY** or **DBType_Numeric**. If you are unsure, choose a type compatible with the data type from the source field in your data warehouse.

TABLE 18-2 DATA TYPES

Name	Size in Bytes	Description
DBType_I1	1	An 8-bit integer value
DBType_I2	2	A 16-bit integer value
DBType_I4	4	A 32-bit integer value
DBType_I8	8	A 64-bit integer value
DBType_U1	1	An unsigned, 8-bit integer value
DBType_U2	2	An unsigned, 16-bit integer value
DBType_UI4	4	An unsigned, 32-bit integer value
DBType_UI8	8	An unsigned, 64-bit integer value
DBType_R4	4	A 32-bit floating-point value (Single)
DBType_R8	8	A 64-bit floating-point value (Double)
DBType_CY	8	A 64-bit integer value divided by 10,000 (money)
DBType_Decimal	varies	A packed decimal value (Money)

Name	Size in Bytes	Description
DBType_Numeric	16	A general-purpose numeric value that may contain up to 32 digits of accuracy
DBType_Date	8	A date/time value (DateTime)

COMMAND

In the **Command** clause, you can execute another MDX statement once the **Create Cube** is created. Typically, this is a series of **Create Member** statements used to define new calculated members associated with the cube. However, you also may want to use an **Insert Into** statement to load data from your data warehouse into the cube. You can use as many **Command** clauses as you want, but you are limited to executing a single MDX statement in each one.

If your command contains spaces, you must enclose the command with square brackets ([ ]). (You get an error if your command contains quotes.) Square brackets aren't affected because the OLAP statement parser supports nested square brackets.

In the following example, I build an OLAP cube using information from the JustPC data warehouse. The cube has a time dimension in addition to other dimensions such as the store where the computer was sold, the speed of the CPU, and the location of the customer. There are four measures: the number of computers sold, the total sales price, the total cost of the computers, and the cost of the labor to assemble them.

```
Create Cube ComputersSold (
   Dimension Time Type Time,
      Hierarchy [Annual],
         Level [Year] Type Year,
         Level [Month] Type Month,
      Hierarchy [WeekDay] Type Time,
         Level [WeekDay] Type DayOfWeek,
   Dimension [Store],
      Hierarchy [Stores],
         Level [AllStores] Type All,
         Level [StoreId],
   Dimension [SystemDetails],
      Hierarchy [CPUSpeed],
         Level [AllCPUs] Type All,
         Level [CPUSpeed],
   Dimension [Customer],
      Hierarchy [AllCustomers] Type All,
         Level [State],
         Level [City],
```

```
        Level [Zip],
    Measure [Computers],
        Function Count,
    Measure [SalesPrice],
        Function Sum,
    Measure [ItemCost],
        Function Sum,
    Measure [LaborCost],
        Function Sum)
```

The Create Member Statement

The **Create Member** statement defines calculated members. You may include this statement as part of the **Create Cube** statement or in the **Command** clause. It also can stand alone as part of a query session to create temporary values that are useful when solving a query. Its syntax appears is as follows:

```
Create [ Session ] Member <cname>.<qmname> As ' <expression> '
```

Where

```
<cname> is the name of a cube.
<qmname> is the fully qualified member name.
<expression> is a formula to compute the value of the new member.
```

The **Create Member** statement simply defines a new member that can be analyzed as part of a cube. If you specify **Session**, the definition exists only for the current session with the cube. Otherwise, the new member is deleted when the query finishes (if it was specified as part of a query). The new member remains with the cube if the statement is included in the **Command** clause of the **Create Cube** statement.

A fully qualified name consists of three parts: the name of the cube, followed by the name of the dimension or hierarchy or **Measures**, followed by the name of the new member.

The expression must be enclosed in single quotes; you can use any legal MDX expression, including many Visual Basic for Applications functions.

 **A word about functions.** For a complete list of functions, see the OLAP help files. But in general, if a function doesn't perform a mathematical calculation, it can't be used. Thus, such functions as GETOBJECT and RANDOMIZE aren't legal, while functions such as LOG, PMT, and NOW are legal.

In the following example, I create a measure called Profit that is computed by taking the SalePrice measure and subtracting the ItemCost and LaborCost measures.

```
Create Member ComputersSold.Measures.Profit As
    'Measures.SalesPrice - Measures.ItemCost - Measures.LaborCost '
```

The Drop Member Statement

The **Drop Member** statement removes a calculated member from a cube. Its syntax appears as follows:

```
Drop Member <cname>.<qmname>
```

Where

```
<cname> is the name of a cube.
<qmname> is the fully qualified member name.
```

The **Drop Member** statement deletes a member that is defined using the **Create Member** statement.

In the following example, I delete the ComputersSold.Measures.Profit calculated member.

```
Drop Member ComputersSold.Measures.Profit
```

The Insert Into Statement

The **Insert Into** statement loads data into a cube — created with the **Create Cube** statement — from an outside data source. Its syntax looks like this:

```
Insert Into <cname> ( <targets> ) <options> <binds> <source>

<targets> ::= <target> [,<target>]...

<target> ::= [<dname>.[<hname>.]]<lname>[.Name | .Key]
             <tdname>[.Name | .Key]
             [Measures.]<mname>
             SkipOneColumn

<options> ::= Defer_Data | Attempt_Defer | PassThrough |
Attempt_Analysis
<binds> ::= <colname> [,<colname>] ...
```

```
<source> ::= Select <cols> From <tables> [Where <where>] [
DirectlyFromCachedRowSet <hexnumber>
```

And

```
<cname> is the name of your cube
<colname> is the name of a column
<dname> is the name of a dimension
<hname> is the name of a hierarchy
<lname> is the name of a level
<mname> is the name of a measure
```

The **Insert Into** statement populates a cube, created with the **Create Cube** statement, with data. To use it, you must list the elements in the cube you wish to populate – including both dimensions and measures. Of course, you shouldn't include calculated measures because they are logical values that are derived from the physical values you are loading.

When writing an **Insert Into** statement, you need to identify each of the members you want to load information into and how to retrieve the data from your data warehouse. Then, you need to build a regular SQL **Select** statement to retrieve this information. A one-to-one correspondence must exist between each of the listed elements of the cube and the fields retrieved from the database.

To avoid confusion between fields with the same name, qualify levels with the appropriate dimension name and measures with **Measures**. The `SkipOneColumn` keyword enables you to ignore a column returned by the **Select** statement. You can use this keyword each time you want to skip over a retrieved value.

If you are retrieving a value into a dimension of **Type Time**, you need only specify a date/time field in the **Select** statement. OLAP automatically extracts the information necessary for all the specified levels in that dimension.

One advantage of OLAP is the ability to defer retrieving data from your data warehouse until you need it. You can specify this by using the `Defer_Data` keyword. This instructs OLAP to load only the data necessary to solve the current query. If OLAP can't process the query locally, an error message is returned. The `Attempt_Defer` keyword instructs OLAP to parse the query, and if it can't be parsed, then to pass the query onto the database server for processing.

You can specify how you want your query to be processed. `PassThrough` indicates that the **Select** statement should be sent directly to the database engine without modification by OLAP. The opposite of `PassThrough` is `Attempt_Analysis`, which instructs OLAP to analyze the query and break it into multiple queries that are often more efficient than the original query. If you don't specify either, OLAP assumes `Attempt_Analysis`.

In the following example, I populate the various elements in the ComputersSold cube with values from the SystemInfo, CustomerInfo, and SystemDetails tables in the data warehouse.

```
Insert Into ComputersSold (Time, Store, SystemDetails, State,
   City, Zip, Computers, SalesPrice, Item Cost, LaborCost),
Options Defer_Data,
Select SystemInfo.DatePurchased, SystemInfo.StoreId,
   SystemDetails.CPUSpeed, CustomerInfo.State,
   CustomerInfo.City, CustomerInfo.Zip, 1,
   SystemInfo.SalesPrice, SystemInfo.ItemCost,
   SystemInfo.LaborCost
From SystemInfo, CustomerInfo, SystemDetails
Where SystemInfo.CustomerId = CustomerInfo.CustomerId
   And SystemInfo.SystemId = SystemDetails.SystemId
```

The Refresh Cube Statement

The **Refresh Cube** statement ensures that the current cube is up to date. Here is its syntax:

```
Refresh Cube <cname>
```

  Where

```
<cname> is the name of a cube
```

The **Refresh Cube** statement synchronizes the contents of the cube with the OLAP server.

In the following example, I get an up-to-date copy of the ComputersSold cube.

```
Refresh Cube ComputersSold
```

Summary

Creating cubes using MDX statements can be a bit of a challenge, so it is highly unlikely that you will build your cubes this way. In Chapter 19, I show you how to use the wizards in the OLAP Manager to build your cube. However, understanding these statements helps you understand query statements, which I cover in the next chapter.

Chapter 19

The Language of OLAP: Querying Cubes

IN THIS CHAPTER

♦ The Create Cache statement

♦ The Create Set statement

♦ The Drop Set statement

♦ The Select statement

UNDERSTANDING HOW TO define cubes is important, but you're far more likely to spend your time building queries. This is where MDX expressions come into play.

Set Expressions

When describing data in a cube, it is useful to use *set notation*. To denote a set, you list all of the elements inside the set and enclose them in a set of braces ({}). For example, this set {Wayne, Jill, Christopher, Samantha} contains the set of people in my family.

MDX uses set notation to describe the dimensions in a cube. Thus, for a Time dimension, the set {1997, 1998) describes slices of the cube in which the year is either 1997 or 1998. You can express the entire life of the JustPC organization as the set {Time.[All]}. Because this set returns the entire cube, it is equivalent to the set {[All]}.While a set can consist of objects from one dimension, this isn't a requirement. For instance, you easily can have a set {1999, store 1} that describes JustPC's sales from store 1 for 1999.

The CROSSJOIN function combines multiple sets. Basically, this function returns a new set of sets in which each individual set in the returned set consists of one member from each of the sets passed to it. For example, CROSSJOIN({store 1, store 2}, {1998, 1999}) results in the set {{store 1, 1998}, {store 2, 1998}, {store 1, 1999}, {store 2, 1999}.

Dimension Expressions

You can describe the contents of a dimension as a set expression {1996, 1997, 1998, 1999} or you can use the function CHILDREN as in Year.CHILDREN in which Year refers to the Year member of a cube. This shortcut is often useful when you want to refer to an entire dimension in your cube without knowing all of the levels beneath it.

Running Queries

A query divides the dimensions of a cube into two groups: *slicer dimensions* and *axis dimensions*. Slicer dimensions retrieve data for a single member, while *axis* dimensions retrieve data from multiple members. In the classic situation, you have two axis dimensions called columns and rows that looks like a regular Excel worksheet.

The rest of the dimensions are assigned to the slicer dimension. This information doesn't appear with the rows and columns, but may appear elsewhere depending on the tool used to display the results of the query.

The Create Cache Statement

The **Create Cache** statement populates a cache with a series of cube slices. The cache helps to improve performance of subsequent queries. You can use this statement as a standalone, or you can include it with other statements as part of a **With** clause. Its syntax appears as follows:

```
Create [ Session ] Cache For <cname> As ( <setexpression> [,
<setexpression>] ... )
```

Where

```
<cname> is the name of a cube.
<setexpression> is a valid set expression.
```

While each <setexpression> must contain only distinct members from a single dimension, you can use a different <setexpression> for each dimension you want. Note that <setexpression> can't include a reference to a measure.

Specifying Session means that the data is kept in cache for the duration of the current query session. For standalone **Create Cache** statements, Session is specified by default. If Session is not included when the **Create Cache** statement is added as part of a query, then the data is deleted from the cache as soon as the query is finished.

When the `Create Cache` statement is used as part of a **With** clause in a **Select** statement, the `Create` keyword must be omitted and the `Session` keyword is illegal.

In the following example, I load all of the information from the ComputersSold cube into cache memory for the year 1999.

```
Create Cache For ComputersSold As ( {Time.Year = 1999} )
```

The Create Set Statement

The **Create Set** statement defines a set of data. You can use this statement as a standalone in the **Command** clause of a **Create Cube** statement, or you can include it with other statements as part of a **With** clause. Its syntax appears as follows:

```
Create [ Session ] Set <cname>.<setname> As ' <expression> '
```

Where

```
<cname> is the name of a cube.
<setname> is the name of the set being created.
<expression> is a valid MDX expression.
```

Specifying `Session` means that the set is deleted automatically at the end of your current session. If you don't specify `Session` and the **Create Set** statement is included in a **With** clause, your set definition is lost when the query is completed. Otherwise, the definition is kept around as long as the cube exists or until you explicitly delete it with the **Drop Set** statement.

When the `Create Set` statement is used as part of a **With** clause in a **Select** statement, the `Create` keyword must be omitted and the **Session** keyword is illegal.

In the following example, I load a slice of the ComputersSold cube into a set that you can include in other cubes.

```
Create Set ComputersSold.LocalSet As ' {Time.Year = 1999} '
```

The Drop Set Statement

The **Drop Set** statement removes a set definition from a cube. Its syntax appears as follows:

```
Drop Set <cname>.<setname>
```

Where

```
<cname> is the name of a cube.
<setname> is the name of the set being created.
```

While a set automatically is dropped at the end of a session or when it goes out of scope, using the **Drop Set** statement enables you to explicitly delete the set.

In the following example, I delete the set called ComputersSold.LocalSet.

```
Drop Set ComputersSold.LocalSet
```

The Select Statement

The **Select** statement extracts information from a cube. Running a **Select** statement is also known as performing a *multidimensional query*. Its syntax appears as follows:

```
[ With <withstatement> [ <withstatement> ] ... ]
Select [ Distinct ] <selectitemlist>
From <cname>
[ Where [ <searchexpression> ] ]
[ Group By  ( <columnref> ) [, ( <columnref> ) ] ... ]
```

Where

```
<withstatement> ::= <cachestatement> | <memberstatement> |
<setstatement>

<cachestatement> is a Create Cache statement
<memberstatement> is a Create Member statement
<setstatement> is a Create Set statement
```

When a **Create Cache**, **Create Member**, or **Create Set** statement is used in the **With** clause, the Create keyword must be omitted and the Session keyword is illegal.

```
<selectitemlist> ::= * | <selectitem> [, <selectitem> ] ...
<selectitem> ::= <axisspecification> | <columnref> | <aggregate> | (
<columnref> ) As Identifier

<axisspecification> ::= <set> On <axisname>
<set>   ::= { <value> [, <value> ] ... }
<axisname> ::= Columns | Rows | Pages | Sections | Chapters | Axis (
<axisindex> )

<columnref> ::= <measureref> | <levelref>
<aggregate> ::= Count(<measureref>) | Min(<measureref>) |
Max(<measureref>) | Sum(<measureref>)

<searchexpression> ::= <searchexpression> And <searchexpression> |
                       <searchexpression> Or <searchexpression> |
                       ( <searchexpression ) |
                       ( <levelref> ) = <value> |
                       <value> = ( <levelref> )

<value> ::= <string> | <number> | <date>

<axisindex> is a number that corresponds to an axis.
<cname> is the name of the cube to be queried.
<date> is a properly formatted date value.
<levelref> is the name of a level in the cube.
<measureref> is the name of a measure in the cube.
<number> is a legal numeric value.
<set>
<string> is a text value enclosed in quotes.
```

A **Select** statement returns a subset of a cube. You can return either a single cell from the cube or another cube made up of some or all of the dimensions in the cube. You must explicitly identify the dimensions you want to manipulate using the **On Axis** clause. The rest of the dimensions are used as the slicer dimensions.

The keywords Columns, Rows, Pages, Sections, and Chapters are merely shortcuts for **Axis**(0), **Axis**(1), **Axis**(2), **Axis**(3), and **Axis**(4) respectively. Thus, you can assign a dimension as **On Columns** instead of **On Axis**(0).

 In order to have an **Axis**(2), you must have an **Axis**(0) and **Axis**(1).

When selecting a single cell from the cube, you must choose a value from one of the measures defined in the cube. This means you must specify which member you want to use for all of the dimensions in the cube. For those dimensions that don't have a default member, you must explicitly specify the member in the **Where** clause.

In the following example, I return a cube in which the Time dimension is expanded to show the Year values and is arranged across the columns. The StoreId dimension is arranged across the rows.

```
Select Time.Year On Columns, StoreId On Rows
From ComputersSold
```

Summary

This chapter brings to a close my discussions on MDX theory. Understanding MDX expressions is important when working with cubes. While you may not use these statements directly, knowing how to form expressions is important when you choose the part of the cube you really want to analyze.

In the next part of this book, I introduce you to the OLAP Manager. You'll learn how to use it to create an OLAP database and create and populate cubes in the database. The OLAP Manager provides simpler tools to perform the same functions that the MDX statements do in this chapter. However, like the SQL statements I discussed in Part 3 of this book, I believe that understanding the underlying MDX helps you understand what OLAP Manager and Excel are doing with your data.

Part VI

Creating an OLAP Database

Chapter 20

Using OLAP Manager to Build Cubes

IN THIS CHAPTER

- ◆ Preparing to build a cube

- ◆ Building a cube with the wizards

- ◆ Changing the cube's structure with the Cube Editor

IN THIS CHAPTER, I discuss how to build a cube and populate it with data from your data warehouse. The easiest way to build a cube is to use the wizards available in the OLAP Manager. Once you build your cube, you can use the Cube Editor – which is included with the OLAP Manager – to change its structure.

Introducing the OLAP Manager

In Chapter 6, I introduced you to the Enterprise Manager utility for SQL Server 7. With this tool, you can design and create relational databases and perform various management functions against them. OLAP Services includes a tool that is similar to Enterprise Manager – it is called OLAP Manager.

You can start the OLAP Manager by choosing Start → Program Files → Microsoft SQL Server 7.0 → OLAP Services → OLAP Manager. Like the Enterprise Manager, the OLAP Manager includes a variety of tools that enable you to perform the following functions:

- ◆ Create OLAP databases

- ◆ Create cubes and virtual cubes

- ◆ Process and refresh cube data

- ◆ Design cube storage

- ◆ Manage cube data sources

◆ Perform usage-based optimization

◆ Browse data using the Cube Editor

◆ Manage cube security

The OLAP Manager's main window is divided into two pieces. The left side holds a tree view of the objects that the OLAP Manager controls, while the right side displays information about the selected item in the tree view. This information is arranged as a series of subwindows, which you can view by choosing the appropriate tab at the top of the window.

In Figure 20-1, you see the initial startup screen for OLAP Manager. Notice that two tabs are displayed on the right side of the screen, while on the left side is the Console Root icon, followed by OLAP servers and ATHENA (the name of my server). The Metadata tab displays information about the databases and cubes stored on the server. The Getting Started tab provides links to useful references.

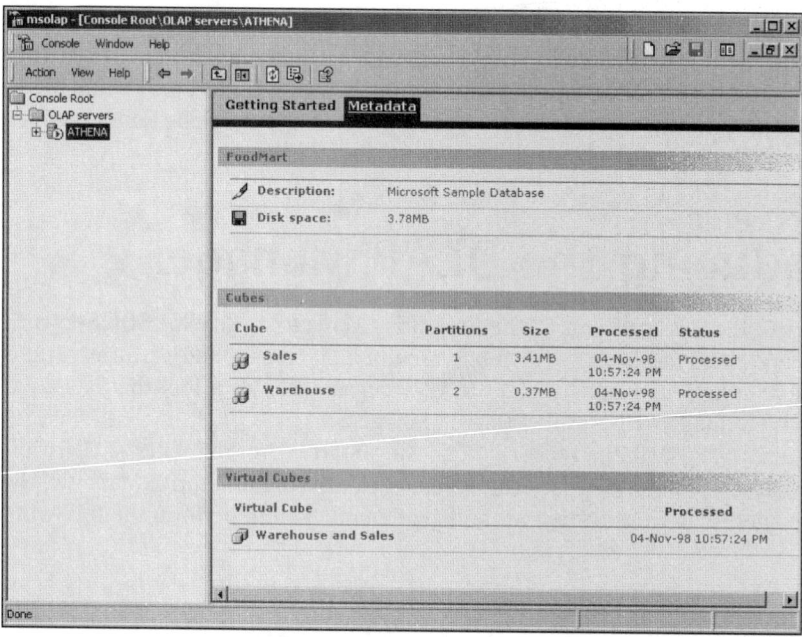

Figure 20-1: The OLAP Manager's main form

OLAP Database and Server Functions

An OLAP database holds cubes and the information associated with them. You must create it on a Windows 2000 Server system that has OLAP Services installed on it.

Registering a Server

Using OLAP Manager, you can manage multiple OLAP servers on your network. Right-click the OLAP servers icon and select Register Server from the popup menu. A dialog box appears asking for the name of the server computer. Simply enter the name of the server you want to register and press OK. OLAP Manager contacts the OLAP server for information and adds it to the list of servers shown below the OLAP servers icon.

Modifying a Server's Properties

Once the server is created, you can right-click the server's name to display a tabbed dialog box that contains its properties (see Figure 20-2). The General tab enables you to change the location of the Data folder, which holds information about your cubes, as well as the temporary file folder, which is used when the OLAP server needs temporary disk space. The information on the rest of the tabs deals with performance and tuning parameters, which I cover in Chapter 22.

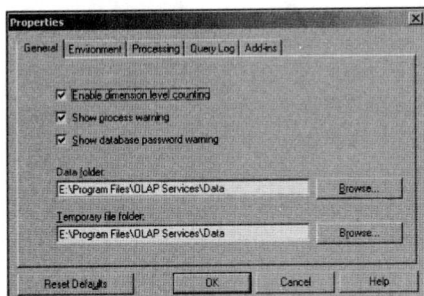

Figure 20-2: Displaying the properties of the OLAP server

Creating a Database

An OLAP database is a place where OLAP Services stores metadata about your cubes in addition to the cube's data, shared dimensions, and security information. The database is stored as a series of normal disk files on your server's hard drive. SQL Server 7 storage space isn't used unless you specifically request it.

You can't directly choose where the database file you create is stored. However, you can choose where you want to store OLAP data when you install OLAP Services. You also can change the location of the data directory by changing the server's properties using OLAP Manager. You should make sure that you have sufficient storage space for your cubes before you build them.

To create a database, right-click the Database server icon in the tree view and select New Database from the popup menu. This displays the dialog box shown in Figure 20-3. Enter the name and a short description of your database and press OK.

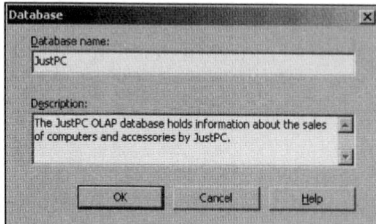

Figure 20-3: Creating a database using the Database dialog box

Once you create a database, you can't rename it. Your only options are to delete it by right-clicking the Database icon in the tree view and selecting Delete, or to change its description by right-clicking the Database icon and selecting Edit.

Building a Cube with the Cube Wizard

The mechanics of building your cube aren't difficult; you simply input a series of values in response to dialog boxes presented by a wizard and OLAP Services takes it from there. The hard part is designing a cube that is complex enough to answer your "what if" questions, but not so large that you can't process your data in a reasonable amount of time. The preparation you do before you start can make it much easier to design your cube, as well as make it more comprehensive when you go to use it.

Before you build your cube, you need to identify the facts and dimensions you want to use with it. Because you get the data for the cube from the data warehouse, the structure of your cube will resemble your data warehouse. The measures for your cube will come directly from your fact tables in the data warehouse. Likewise, the dimensions for your cube will come directly from the dimension tables

Once you define at least one data source, you also can use the Cube Editor to define your cube. I talk about the Cube Editor in more detail in Chapter 21.

Starting the Wizard

To create a new cube, expand the icons in the tree view and select the server and database you want to use. When you see the Cubes icon, right-click it and select New Cube → Wizard from the popup menu. This displays the first step of the wizard shown in Figure 20-4.

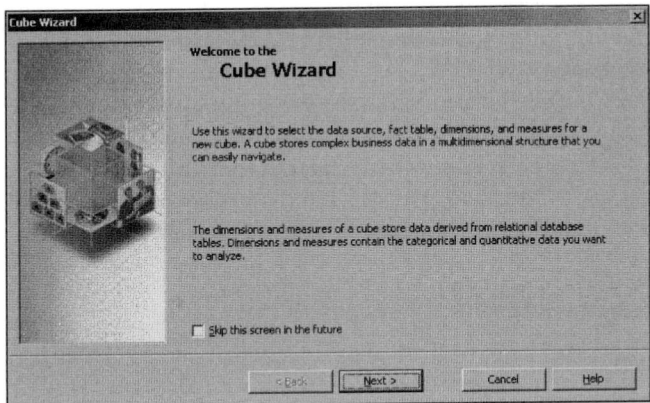

Figure 20-4: Creating a cube with the Cube Wizard

Defining the Fact Table

The first step in defining your cube is defining a data source for the fact table. Typically, your data source is your data warehouse. To define a new data source, push the New Data Source button found beneath the Data sources and tables section of the form (see Figure 20-5) and follow the instructions in the "Creating a New Data Link" section that follows this one.

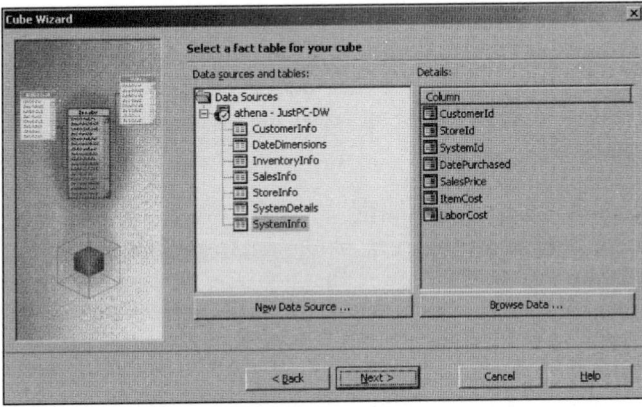

Figure 20-5: Choosing your data source

Once you have a single data source, you can see the data source name listed beneath the Data Sources icon. Expanding that data source name (in this case, athena - JustPC-DW), you see a list of the tables available in the database. Select one of the tables to display the list of columns it contains in the Details section of the form.

If you press the Browse Data button, you see the first thousand rows for the currently selected table in a grid. Because I want to analyze information about the systems sold by JustPC, I select the SystemInfo table.

If you expect to use data from multiple databases in your first cube, you may want to take a minute and define them here. It can save you work in the long run. In the case of the JustPC example, all of the data I need is in the JustPC data warehouse so I only need the one data source. If I need additional data sources, I can add them directly by right-clicking the Data Sources icon in the OLAP Manager tree view (found by expanding your Database icon and the Library icon below it) and choosing New Data Source from the popup menu.

Creating a New Data Link

OLAP Services takes advantage of the OLE DB data-link facility to communicate with your data source. You can choose a number of different providers that can talk to different types of data sources. There are OLE DB providers for SQL Server, Oracle, Excel, Access, and ODBC just to name a few.

 **TIP** Always choose the OLE DB provider that corresponds to your data source because that provider is much more efficient than the default OLE DB provider for ODBC Drivers.

CHOOSING A PROVIDER

The New Data Source button shows the Provider tab of the Data Link Properties dialog box in Figure 20-6. Because I'm talking to a SQL Server 7 database, I can use the OLE DB provider for SQL Server rather than the default OLE DB Provider for ODBC Drivers. Then I can press the Next button or select the Connection tab to finish choosing a provider.

CONNECTING TO THE DATABASE SERVER

On the Connection tab of the Data Link Properties dialog box (see Figure 20-7), you can specify the name of the database server in the first box and the security information needed to access the database server in the second box. Then press the Test Connection button. If everything is all right, you get a message saying the test connection succeeded; otherwise, you may want to check the information you provided and try it again.

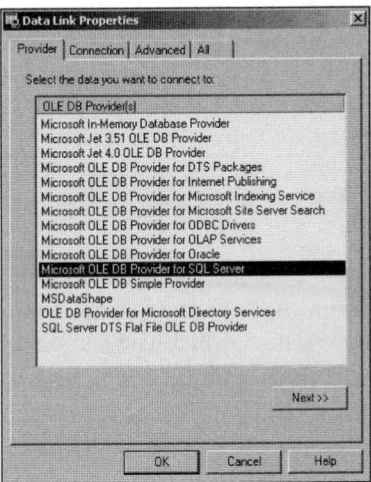

Figure 20-6: Choosing a provider

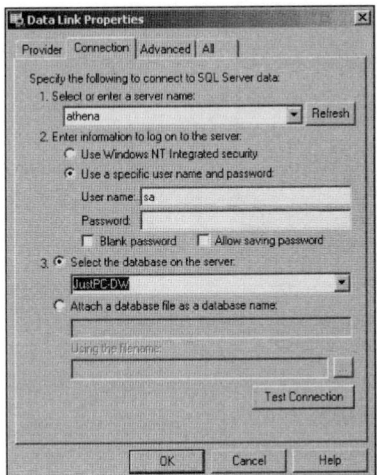

Figure 20-7: Specifying the database server and
database for the data link

After you verify the connection, you should choose the database from the relational database server you want to access. In my case, it is the JustPC-DW database
that holds the data warehouse information for JustPC. You also may need to specify the JustPC-DB database if you want to access the information in the production
database directly.

The rest of the tabs on the Data Link Properties dialog box are rarely used so you
can ignore them. Once you define your database connection, press OK to accept it
and return to the Cube Wizard.

 This process creates an entry under the Data Sources icon found under the Database and Library icons. You can use this source to access multiple tables in your data warehouse.

Selecting Your Measures

After choosing the fact table, you need to determine which fields, or numeric columns, you want to use as measures. You do this in the next step of the wizard (shown in Figure 20-8). Choose fields that have numeric data, which you can use in calculations.

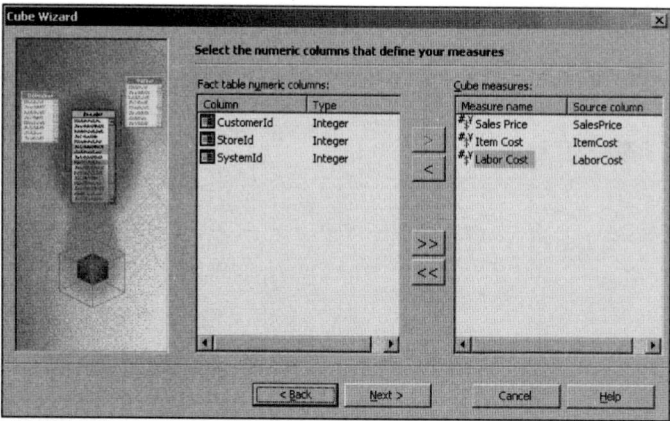

Figure 20-8: Choosing your measures

I decided to use the SystemInfo table as my fact table, so I can choose only SalesPrice, ItemCost, and LaborCost for my measures. While CustomerId, StoreId, and SystemId are numeric, they are not values that I can use as part of a calculation.

 If you aren't sure if you can select a field as a measure, try multiplying the field by two. If you get a meaningful result, then you should be able to use the field in a calculation.

Choosing Dimensions for Your Cube

In the wizard's next step, you are asked to choose the dimensions for your new cube. If you have any shared dimensions, they are listed in the Shared dimensions section of the wizard's dialog box (see Figure 20-9). You can choose one or more of these dimensions or press the New Dimension button at the bottom of the Shared dimensions list to launch the Dimension Wizard. After you create a dimension, you can add it to the list of Cube dimensions and continue onto the next step of the Cube Wizard.

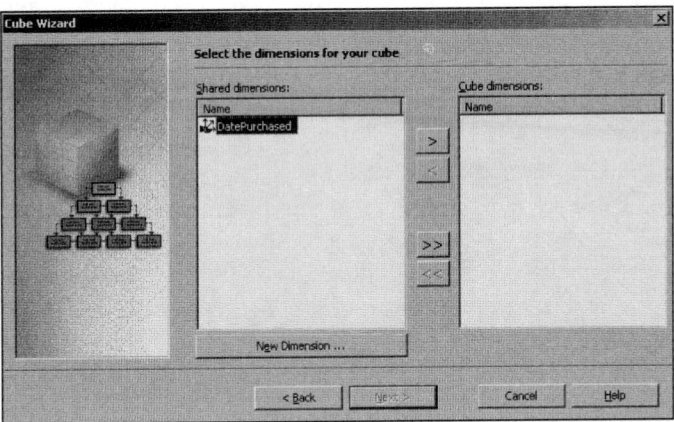

Figure 20-9: Choosing your dimensions

CREATING A NEW DIMENSION

Pressing the New Dimension button displays the Dimension Wizard (see Figure 20-10), which guides you through the selection process. The first step asks you to choose between a single dimension table that is used in a Star Schema and multiple dimension tables that are used in a Snowflake Schema. In the case of the JustPC example, I select a single dimension table.

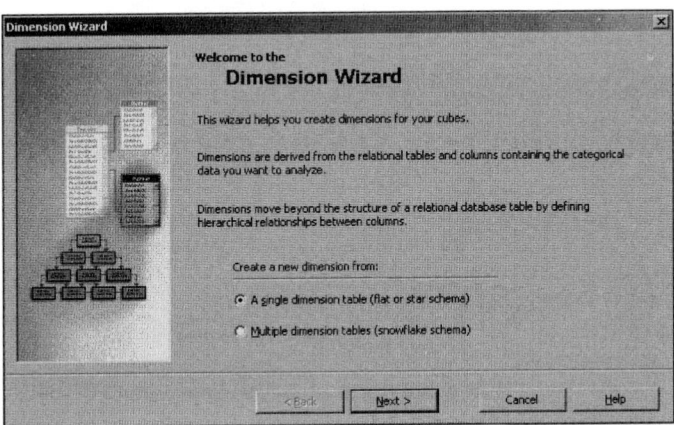

Figure 20-10: Starting the dimension wizard

SELECTING THE DIMENSION TABLE

The wizard next shows you a dialog box similar to one that you used to select the measures table (see Figure 20-11). All of the data sources you previously defined are available for you to choose. Select the table you want to use as a dimension table. As before, you can view the first thousand rows. In the case of the JustPC example, I use the DateDimensions as my first dimension table. Later, I'll go in and add CustomerInfo and SystemDetails as other dimension tables.

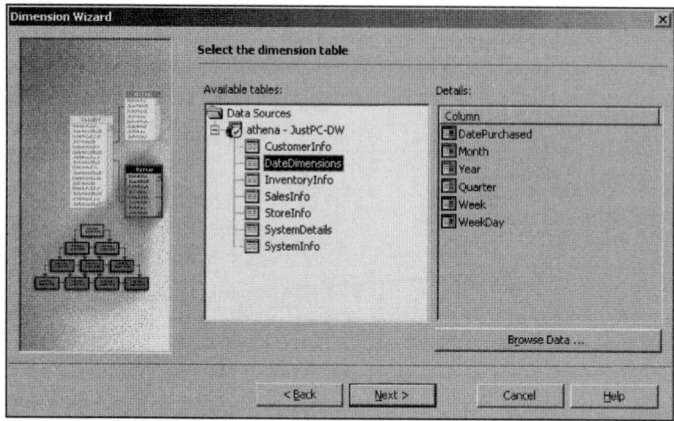

Figure 20-11: Choosing your dimension table

SELECTING A TIME DIMENSION

When a dimension table contains a Date column, the wizard asks you if this dimension is a Standard dimension or a Time dimension (see Figure 20-12). If it is a Time dimension, you also need to specify the name of the column containing the date value.

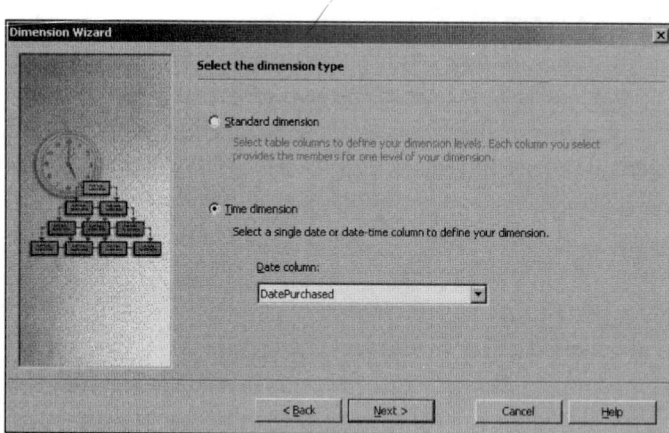

Figure 20-12: Identifying a time dimension

The next form (see Figure 20-13) enables you to choose the hierarchy you want for this dimension as well as specify the starting day of the year. This makes it easy to build a Time dimension based on a fiscal year that doesn't coincide with the calendar year.

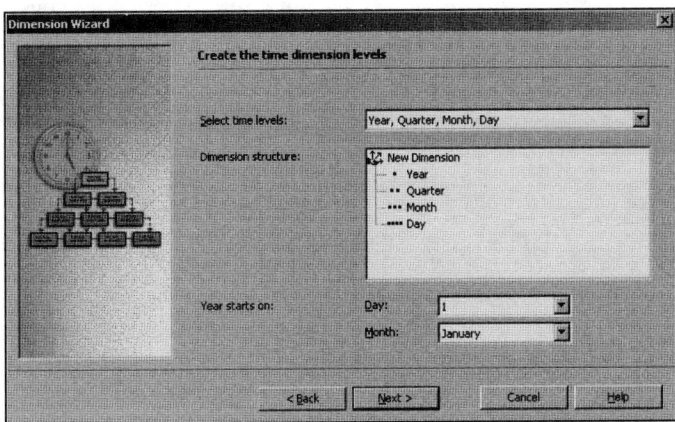

Figure 20-13: Defining the Time hierarchy

SELECTING A STANDARD DIMENSION

If there are no Date columns, or you specify that the dimension is a standard dimension, you see the window shown in Figure 20-14. You need to choose the columns that make up the levels of the dimension. Remember that each level must have more members than the previous level. The wizard automatically scans the data and verifies that the columns you select are proper.

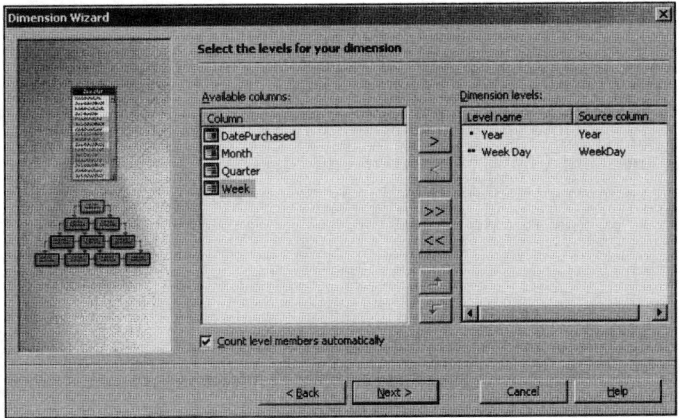

Figure 20-14: Defining the levels for a time dimension

FINISHING THE DIMENSION

In the final step of the Dimension Wizard, you see the window shown in Figure 20-15. You must give the dimension a name. In this example, I call it the DatePurchased dimension. You also can mark the dimension as shared, which means that it can be used in any other cubes you create in this database. This is a good idea because reusing a dimension minimizes the amount of storage needed.

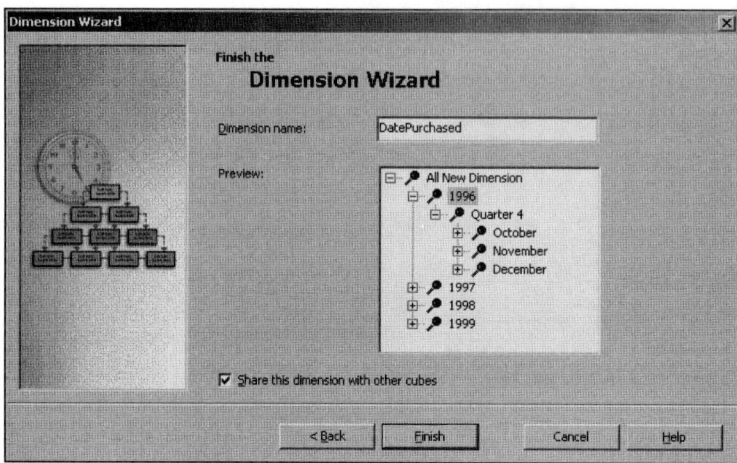

Figure 20-15: Naming the new dimension

As part of the definition process, the wizard scans the dimension table and builds the hierarchy that is used in the cube. You can examine the hierarchy in the preview window to verify that the levels in the dimension are what you want.

Finishing the Cube Wizard

In the last step of the Cube Wizard, you simply give your cube a name and press the Finish button (see Figure 20-16). You can even use the Cube Browser to look at some of the data in the cube by pressing the Browse Sample Data button. I talk about the Cube Browser in more detail in Chapter 21. After you press the Finish button, the Cube Editor is started. It enables you to graphically see the structure of your cube and make changes to it. For now, just exit the Cube Editor to return to OLAP Manager.

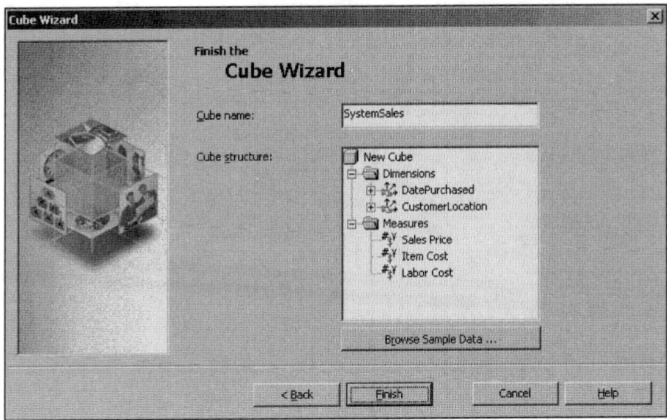

Figure 20-16: Naming your cube

Using the Cube Editor

The Cube Editor is a general-purpose tool that enables you to examine and change the structure of a cube (see Figure 20-17). You also can use the Cube Editor to examine the data in your cube (see Figure 20-18). These two modes are known as the *schema view* and the *data view,* respectively.

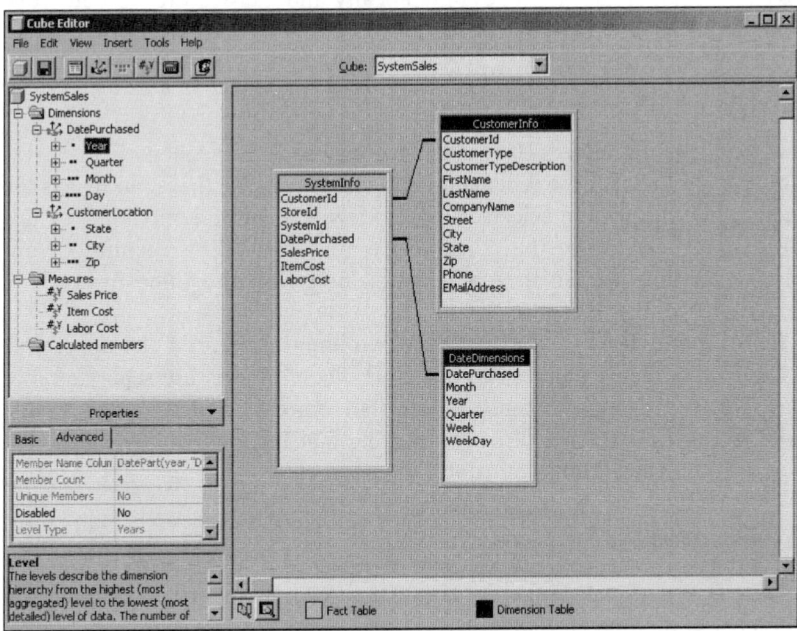

Figure 20-17: Looking at the schema view of your cube

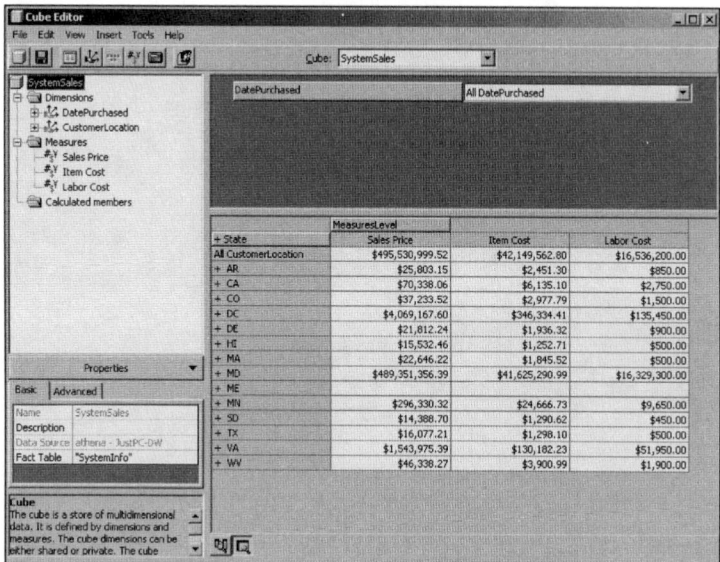

Figure 20-18: Looking at the data view of your cube

You can start the Cube Editor by selecting a cube in the OLAP Manager tree view, right-clicking it, and choosing Edit from the popup menu. Once you are in the Cube Editor, you can change any aspect of the cube you define using the Cube Wizard. Also, you can create new cubes graphically and add features to your cube that the wizard doesn't even approach.

Changing Views

Select View → Schema or View → Data to change views using the menu bar or press the icons on the left beneath the schema or data view area. The first icon selects the schema view, while the second selects the data view. I spend the remainder of this chapter describing how to use the schema view to change the structure of your cube. I also cover how to use the data view, along with the Cube Browser, in Chapter 21.

To the left of these views of your cube are two important areas. The upper area provides a tree view of the objects in your cube. These objects are separated into Dimensions (which lists each dimension with its hierarchy) and Measures (which includes the measures extracted directly from the fact table as well as calculated members based on a calculation you supply).

Listing Property Values

Below the tree view is a small properties area. This area lists any property values for the item selected in the tree view area. The properties for the object are listed under two tabs: Basic and Advanced. Basic properties include such things as the object's name and description. Advanced properties may include such items as the object's data type and the format that should be used when displaying its value.

Some properties can't be changed. In that case, the property name and value are displayed in gray – as opposed to the normal black used to display properties that can be changed. To help you understand what the selected property means, a description of the property appears at the bottom of the Properties section.

 **TIP** You can hide the Properties section by clicking the bar labeled Properties that separates the tree view area from the property area. This bar moves to the bottom of the main window and the tree view area expands. To restore the Properties section, simply click the bar a second time.

The Schema View

In the schema view (see Figure 20-17), you see a diagram of the tables used to construct your cube. The fact tables have a yellow header, while the dimension tables have a blue header. Lines are drawn between the columns that link the fact table to the dimension tables.

While in the schema view, you can change the fact table and insert and delete dimension tables. You also can insert new measures from the current fact table and create calculated members based on the information already in the cube. You can even process the cube to see the results of your changes immediately when you switch to the data view.

Replacing the Current Fact Table

Because every cube must have a fact table, you can't delete the fact table. However, you may substitute a new fact table in place of the current fact table. To do this, right-click anywhere on the schema view and choose Replace Fact Table from the popup menu. This displays a list of tables from your current data sources (see Figure 20-19). You can browse the columns in each of the tables shown by selecting the table name on the left side of the form.

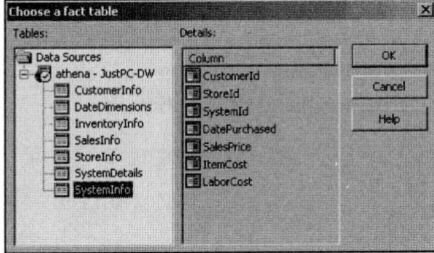

Figure 20-19: Choosing a new fact table

Managing Measures in Your Cube

In a cube, all you really need is a single measure. However, sometimes it is useful to include multiple measures. The measures for your cube are listed under the Measures icon on the left side of the Cube Editor's tree view window.

ADDING A NEW MEASURE

There are two ways to add a measure to your cube. First, you can select a column in the fact table and then right-click to display a popup menu. Choosing Insert As Measure automatically adds the column as a measure in your cube.

You also can right-click the Measures icon, or any of the measures below it, and choose New Measure. This displays the columns in your fact table (see Figure 20-20). You can choose which columns you wish to see based on their data type by checking and unchecking the boxes in the lower right part of the dialog box. Then simply select the column and press OK to add the measure to your cube.

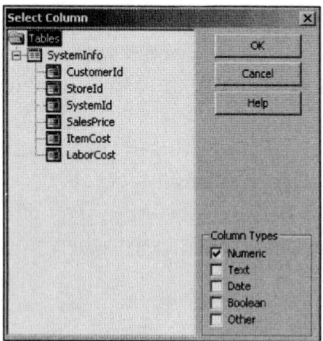

Figure 20-20: Choosing a new measure for your cube

 You can include the same column from your fact table more than once. Each new copy of the column will be mapped into a new measure. Each new measure automatically is renamed to ensure that its name is unique.

DELETING A MEASURE

To delete a measure, right-click the measure you want to delete and select Delete. The measure disappears without any confirmation messages, so make sure that you select the measure you want to delete before pressing the Delete option.

RENAMING A MEASURE

When you create a new measure, the Cube Editor creates a name based on the column name from the fact table. However, you need not use this name. You can rename a measure in two different ways. Select the measure in the tree view and change its name in the property area by changing the name property, or right-click the measure and select Rename from the popup menu to directly change the measure's name.

Managing Dimension Tables

While your cube can have only one fact table, you can have as many dimension tables as you want. These tables are drawn from the same data sources you already defined for your cube.

ADDING A DIMENSION TABLE

To add another dimension table, right-click anywhere on the schema view and select Insert Tables. This displays a dialog box similar to the one shown in Figure 20-19. Simply choose the table you want to add.

If you select a table that is already in the schema, then an error message is displayed instructing you to select a different table. The new table automatically is linked to the fact table or one of the dimension tables based on a common column name.

 **TIP** You easily can create a snowflake cube by linking one dimension table to another.

REMOVING A DIMENSION TABLE

To remove a dimension table, simply right-click the table you want to remove and select Remove from the popup menu. This deletes the dimension table from the cube.

Managing Calculated Members

Calculated members can add value to your cube because they often help you simplify your data from the cube. Consider the JustPC cube example. I have measures for SalesPrice, LaborCost, and ItemCost. It may be useful to define a new member called Profit that is computed by subtracting LaborCost and ItemCost from SalesPrice. This can help me to understand how JustPC's profit changed over time.

ADDING A CALCULATED MEMBER

To add a calculated member, right-click the Calculated members icon in the tree view section of the Cube Editor and choose New Calculated Member. This displays the Calculated Member Builder form shown in Figure 20-21. You also can change the calculation for a calculated member by right-clicking the member and choosing Edit from the popup menu.

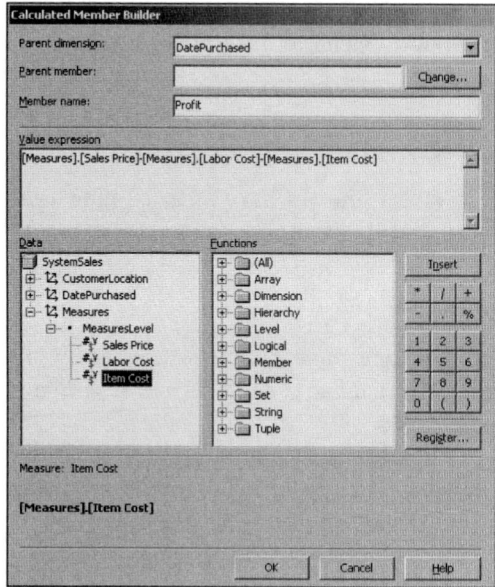

Figure 20-21: Creating a calculated member

IDENTIFYING THE MEMBER

The Calculated Member Builder form contains a number of different pieces of information. At the top of the form, you need to specify the parent dimension of the new member. If the member is to be treated as a measure, select Measure; otherwise, select the desired dimension.

If you add the member to a dimension, you may want to select where in the dimension's hierarchy the member belongs. You can do this by specifying the parent of the member. The easiest way to do this is to press the Change button at the end of the field. This causes another window to appear with the dimension's tree structure. Select the appropriate position in the hierarchy and press OK to add it to the dimension.

The last field in the top section of the Calculated Member Builder form is the name of the new member. By default, the name New Calculated Member is displayed. Change this value to the name you wish to use.

CALCULATING THE MEMBER'S VALUE

The Value expression text box holds the calculation used to compute the member's value. You can enter any formula into this box by directly typing the characters. You can dragand-drop other members from the Data box or functions from the Functions box. You can even use the keypad to enter numeric values and arithmetic operators.

The Register button enables you to register additional function libraries that provide new functions for your calculations. This feature typically is not used because you already have access to the rich set of functions available in OLAP and Visual Basic for Applications. However, it does enable you to create functions in Visual Basic for complex calculations.

Other Cube Editor Functions

Some other functions available in the Cube Editor are worth knowing and are pretty simple to use. Most of these functions duplicate functions that you can perform directly from the OLAP Manager, but a few are unique to the Cube Editor.

The first thing you should know is that you can save your work-in-progress by using File → Save or pressing the Save button in the toolbar. If you make changes to the cube in your editing session, the changes aren't saved until you explicitly save it or exit the Cube Editor and respond Yes to the Save changes message.

You can validate the cube's structure by choosing Tools → Validate Cube Structure from the main menu. If there is a problem with the cube, an error message is displayed. Otherwise, a message saying *Structure successfully validated* is displayed.

The Optimize Schema utility (choose Tools → Optimize Schema) offers suggestions on how to improve your cube.

Summary

In this chapter, I tried to give you a brief overview of how to build an OLAP cube using the Cube Wizard and Cube Editor. These tools are much easier to use than the MultiDimensional eXtensions to SQL. In the next chapter, I discuss how to perform some common operations against your cube and how to view it using the Cube Browser.

Chapter 21

Using OLAP Manager to Browse Cubes

IN THIS CHAPTER

- ◆ Processing a cube

- ◆ Creating new data sources

- ◆ Editing dimensions

- ◆ Browsing your cube with the Cube Browser

- ◆ Filtering data in your cube

- ◆ Drilling down to see the details

IN THIS CHAPTER, I continue my discussion of the OLAP Manager. I show you how to perform common tasks with OLAP Manager and how to examine your data using the Cube Browser.

Performing Common Functions

Besides building a cube and browsing a cube, the OLAP Manager includes facilities that enable you to perform a number of other tasks. Some of these tasks involve optimization and security, which I talk about in the next two chapters. However, there are a few other common functions that you should know about before you start to browse your cube.

Processing a Cube

One of the most important functions you can do with a cube is to process it. This function gets a fresh copy of the data from your data source and loads it into the cube. This, in turn, ensures that you are working with the latest available copy of the data and helps you make better decisions.

When you right-click the cube and select Process from the popup menu, the Process a Cube Wizard is displayed (see Figure 21-1). The wizard gives you three options for processing a cube: Incremental update, Refresh data, and Process. The

Process option is always available. The first two options are available only after the cube is processed at least once after the cube's structure has changed.

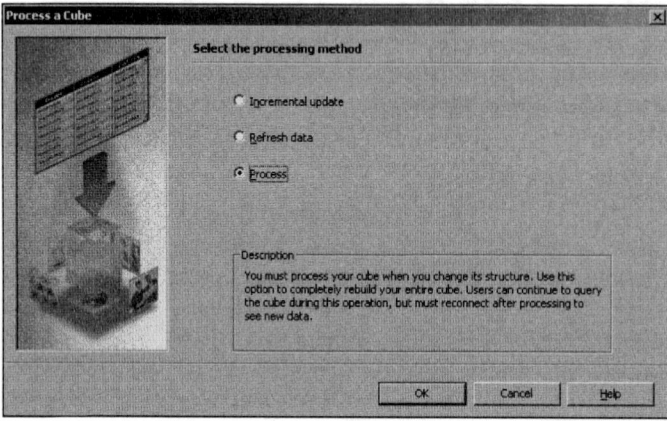

Figure 21-1: Running the Process a Cube Wizard

THE PROCESS OPTION

The Process option rebuilds the cube's structure and then loads it from the cube's data source. This option always works; however, it is the longest running of the three options. The window shown in Figure 21-2 tracks each individual task within the Process activity and lets you know when the process is complete. Processing a cube can run anywhere from a few seconds to a few hours, depending on the size and complexity of your cube.

 In the JustPC cube, a process runs for less than a minute. Considering that I am accessing over 35,000 records in the fact table, the speed is more than acceptable to process the cube, and there isn't much of a need to look at the other options. However, with other data warehouses and other cubes, this task may take considerably longer.

THE INCREMENTAL UPDATE OPTION

The Incremental Update option examines the database for new records that have been added since the last Process or Refresh was run. Performing an Incremental Update launches the Incremental Update Wizard. This wizard asks you to specify the source of the data. Typically, you do not change these values because you want to pull the data from the data warehouse. However, if you have a separate database for data that will be added to the data warehouse, you can point to those tables to update the cube as well.

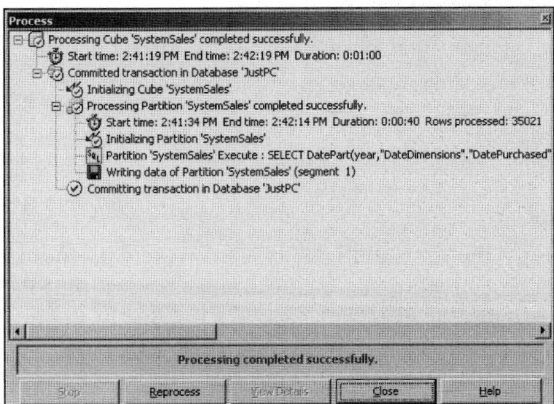

Figure 21-2: Processing a cube

The next step of the wizard asks you for a *filter expression* (see Figure 21-3). This is what makes the Incremental Update different from the other options. The filter expression is passed to the OLAP server to determine which records are new. Basically, the filter expression is the **Where** clause from a **Select** statement without the **Where**.

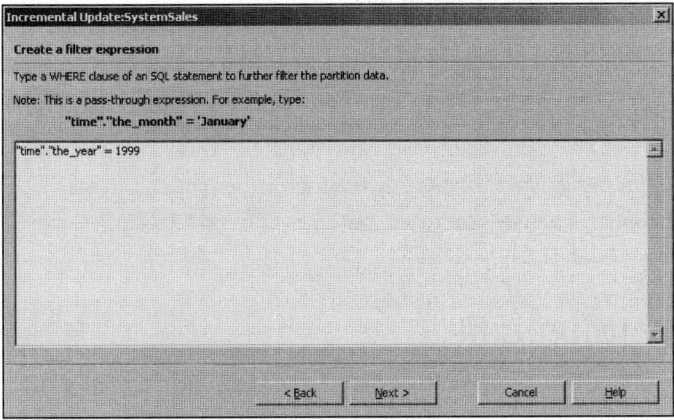

Figure 21-3: Entering a filter expression

The ideal filter expression involves a Time dimension such as this one:

```
"time"."the_year" = 1999
```

This expression selects all elements from the fact table that have 1999 as the year. When you finish the wizard, you see the same status window shown in Figure 21-2 that tracks the progress of the Process.

 If you don't enter a value for the filter expression, the Incremental Update ends up processing all of the data in your cube — which makes it no different than a Refresh.

THE REFRESH DATA OPTION

The Refresh option erases the data in the cube and reloads it from the data source. This option works as long as the cube's structure has changed since the last time the cube was processed. While it is running, it displays a window similar to the one shown in Figure 21-2. A Refresh does nearly as much work as a Process, so you can expect it to run nearly as long.

Defining Data Sources

Defining a new data source involves nothing more than creating a new data link. (I discussed this process in Chapter 18 as part of the Cube Wizard.) Basically, you simply define the database access provider, database server name, user name, password, and database you wish to access. Then OLAP uses this information to provide a list of available tables for you to use as part of your cube.

To define a data source outside the Cube Wizard, right-click the Data Sources icon found below the Library icon in your OLAP database. Then select New Data Source. The same dialog boxes you saw in the "Creating a New Data Link" section in Chapter 20 are used to define a new data link.

 If you want to use the Cube Editor to design your cube (instead of the Cube Wizard), first you must create at least one data source. Then you can access the Cube Editor option when you right-click the Cubes icon and select New Cube.

Using the Dimension Editor

Just as the Cube Editor is a general-purpose tool that changes the structure of a cube, the Dimension Editor is used to create new dimensions and change the structure of an existing dimension (see Figure 21-4). You can browse the data in a dimension and see its hierarchical relationships and you can add and delete members of a dimension's hierarchy. You can even switch to a different dimension inside the cube.

VIEWING THE MEMBERS OF A DIMENSION

Just as the Cube Editor has two main displays — the schema and the data view — so does the Dimension Editor. To view the members of a dimension, simply choose View → Data or press the Preview Dimension Data button beneath the Details window. To see the source table for the dimension, press the View Source Table button or choose View → Schema from the main menu.

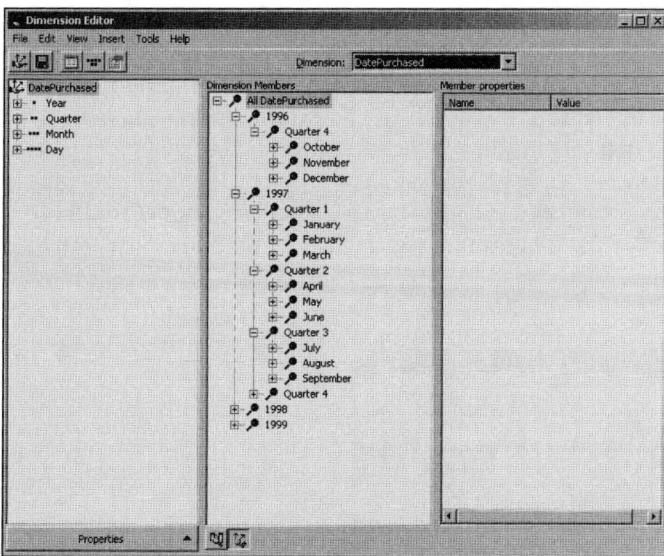

Figure 21-4: Using the Dimension Editor

ADDING A NEW DIMENSION

You can add a new dimension by choosing File → New Dimension → Editor, right-clicking the name of the dimension in the tree view area of the editor, or choosing <New> in the Dimension selection box above the dimension Details area of the form.

When creating a new dimension, you are prompted to choose a dimension table from one of your existing data sources (see Figure 21-5). When you choose a specific table, its columns automatically are displayed. When you find the table you want to use, press OK.

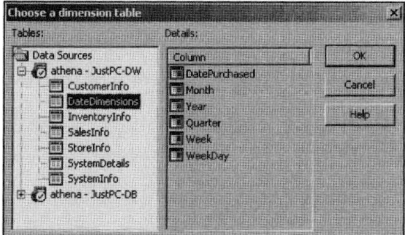

Figure 21-5: Choosing a new dimension table

When you return to the Editor, you see the table you just selected in the Details area. The next step is to choose the levels of the dimension. If you right-click the dimension name (in this case, <New>) in the Details level, you are prompted to choose the name of a column. This is used as the topmost level. You then repeat the process until you reach the bottommost level in the dimension.

After you choose all of the levels, you need to process the dimension. This step is similar to processing the cube in that the data source is scanned for the particular values in each of the levels. To do this, right-click the dimension in the tree view area and select Process dimension. If you haven't saved the dimension, a message box is displayed saying that you must save the dimension before you can proceed. Pressing Yes displays another message box asking you for the name of the dimension. Enter the name you want to use and press OK. Another window is displayed that tracks the activities of the process task (see Figure 21-6). Press Close to return to the Dimension Editor.

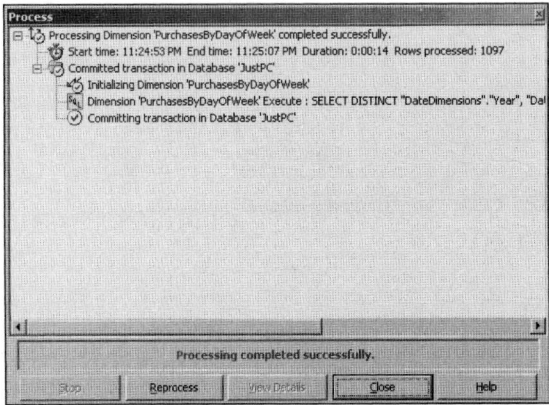

Figure 21–6: Processing a dimension

Browsing a Cube

Browsing a cube with the Cube Browser is just like using the Data View of the Cube Editor. In fact, the same program provides both functions. The only difference between the two is that the Cube Browser doesn't drag along all of the cube definitions. To start the browser, right-click the cube you want to view and select Browse Data from the popup menu.

Using the Browser

The Cube Browser (shown in Figure 21-7) displays your cube in a flattened form. The *slicer pane* at the top of the form contains a list of dimensions whose values are constant for the cells displayed below in the data grid. The *data grid* contains two or more dimensions whose individual members are used to determine the values in each cell.

Dimension   Measures   Level Box   Slicer Pane

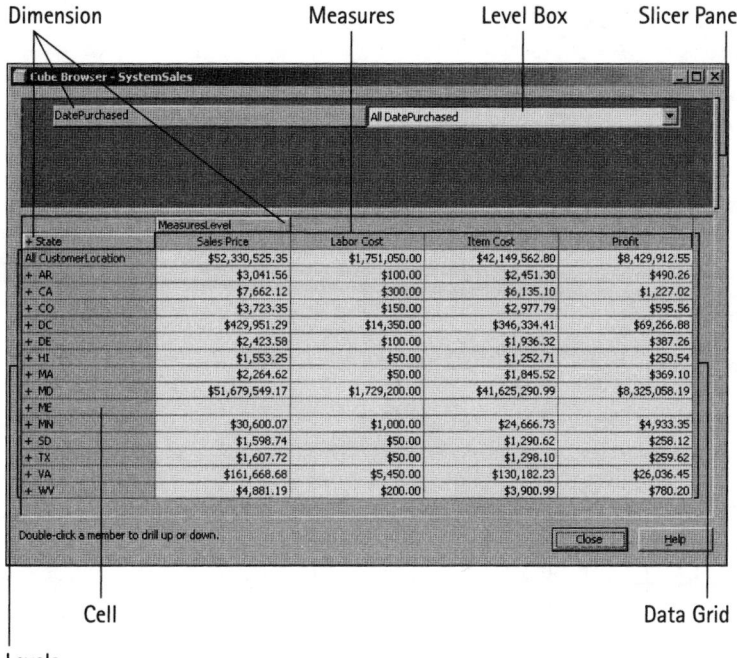

Cell   Data Grid

Levels

Figure 21-7: Browsing a cube

 The Cube Browser has a limited amount of memory and may not be able to display some cubes depending on the number of dimensions, levels, and members displayed. The more detail you display, the more memory you need. If you receive an error message such as "Unable to display current view of the cube" or "Unable to allocate memory for flexgrid," you should use Excel 2000 (which I discuss in more detail starting in Chapter 24).

SLICING THE CUBE

At least two dimensions are always displayed in the data grid area of the form, while the rest of the dimensions are listed in the slicer pane. You can drag a dimension from the slicer pane to the data grid to add that dimension to the cell grid. The browser automatically expands the data to show the highest level of information.

This operation is known as *slicing the cube*. The concept is simple. If you think of your data organized into a three-dimensional cube and hold one value constant, then you are literally taking a single slice from the cube (see Figure 21-8). This same example looks like Figure 21-9 in the Cube Browser.

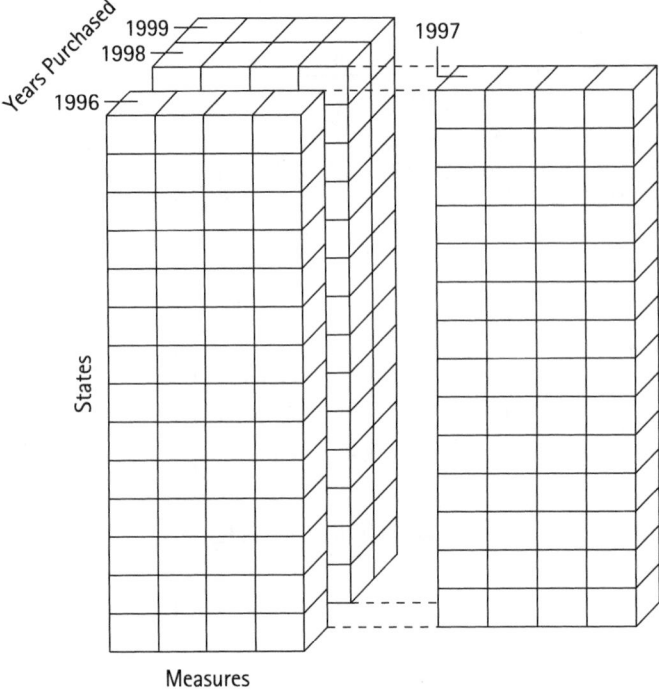

Figure 21-8: Logically slicing a cube

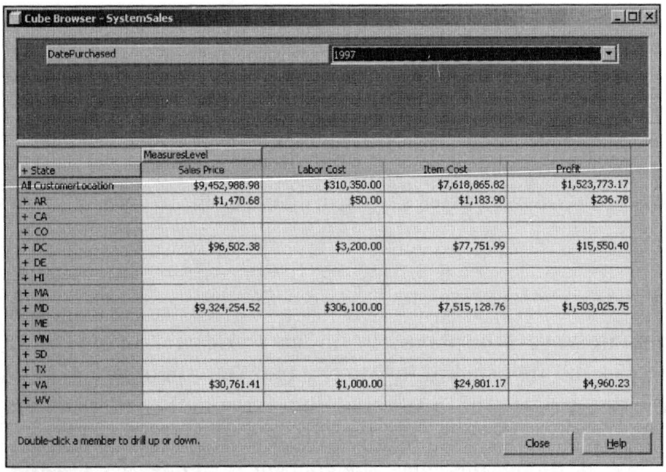

Figure 21-9: The cube slice as seen in the Cube Browser

To slice a cube, you need to select the dimensions that the data grid displays. You should drag them from the slicer pane to the data grid. Drag any dimensions that you don't want to see from the data grid to the slicer pane.

When dealing with the Cube Browser (and PivotTables in Excel), the line between dimensions and measures can start to blur. Measures and dimensions appear to be interchangeable. But you should remember that no matter where the "measures" dimension is located, all of the data values shown in the cells in the data grid come from a field or the sum of all fields in a measure.

Once you arrange the dimensions the way you want them, you should select the values in the slicer pane that you wish to display. You can select these values easily by pressing the drop-down arrow. A tree view list of the values in the dimension is displayed (see Figure 21-10). You can choose any single value for any particular level in the dimension.

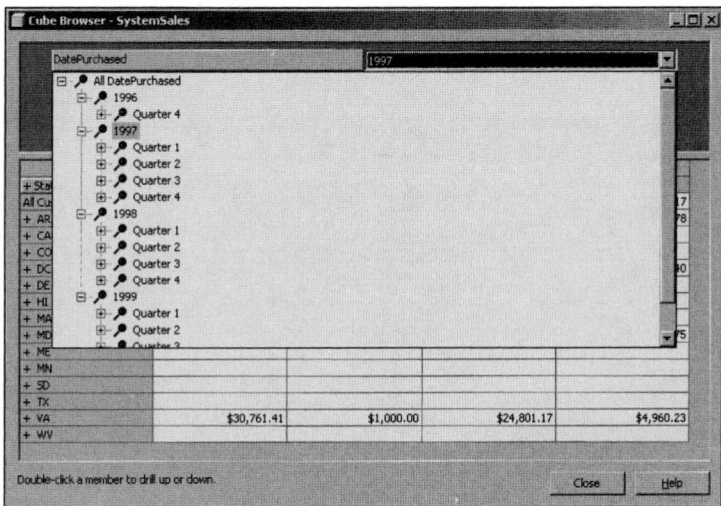

Figure 21-10: Choosing a particular value from a dimension

In the JustPC example, I restrict the cube to the data for 1997 in Figure 21-10 by selecting the year 1997. I can restrict the slice even further by choosing a member lower in the dimension's hierarchy, such as the fourth quarter, December, or the thirty-first of December.

You can select only a single value when slicing the cube. So while I can select the fourth quarter for a particular year, I can't select only the months November and December for that year.

DRILLING FOR DETAILS

When looking at the data in the cube, sometimes you may see something that doesn't make a lot of sense. Perhaps one salesperson sold significantly more goods than the rest. This can be the result of a single large order or a consistently good sales strategy. Unless you go digging for the details, you may never know.

To dig deeper in the cube, you have a couple of options. The first option is to try looking at a finer slice of data. You do this by choosing a finer set of values for the dimensions located in the slicer pane. While this can be useful, it's difficult to find trends involving that dimension. A better approach is to expand the dimensions in the data grid.

You can expand a dimension by double-clicking the Dimension button or a level button with the plus (+) sign. This displays the next lower level in the hierarchy. You can continue this process until you reach the bottommost level in the hierarchy.

For example, you can see in Figure 21-11 that most of the sales were made to customers in Maryland. This is entirely reasonable because all of the JustPC stores are in Maryland. So this information doesn't tell me exactly where the customer base is located.

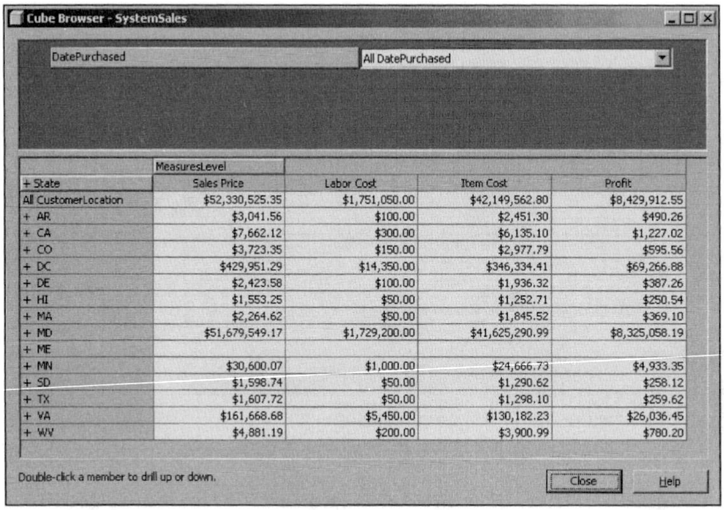

Figure 21-11: Discovering where the customers are located

If I expand the MD entry by double-clicking it, I see the display in Figure 21-12. This figure shows the sales by city. Note that the plus sign on the State button becomes a minus (-) sign and the same thing happens to the MD button. Pressing either button collapses the City column.

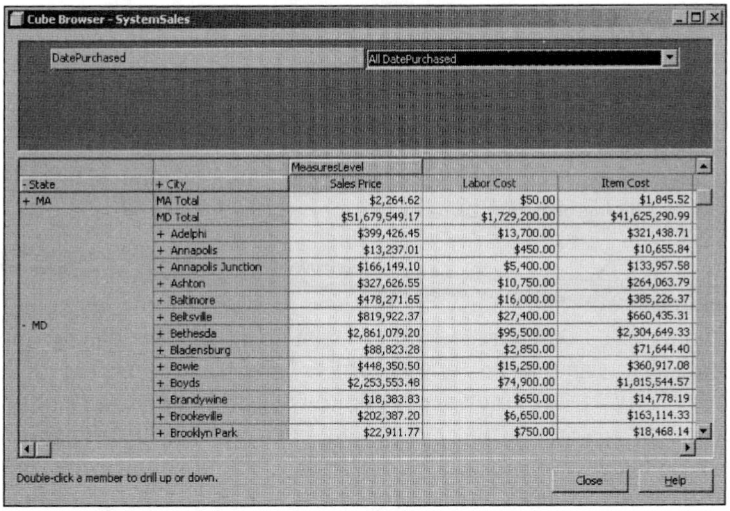

Figure 21-12: Seeing where in Maryland the customers are located

Notice that the plus sign on MA remains unchanged and the MD Total line is also present. Above the column of cities is the City button, which has another plus sign. Also, each of the entries in the City column has a plus sign preceding the city name. This means that you can expand these fields.

Expanding the Beltsville and Bethesda City buttons creates the even more detailed view of the data shown in Figure 21-13. This shows a breakdown by zip code in each city. Notice that Beltsville has only one zip code, while Bethesda has two. Even though Beltsville has only one zip code, a separate total line remains present.

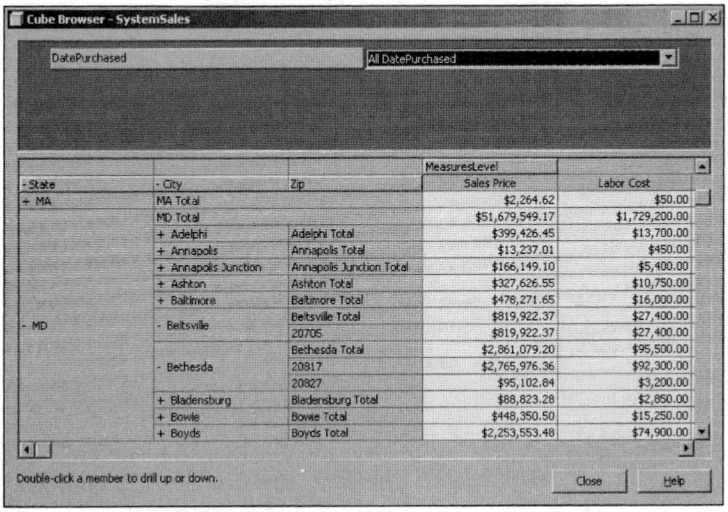

Figure 21-13: Looking at the details pertaining to Beltsville and Bethesda

Unlike the previous drill-downs, the Zip button and the zip code values are not preceded by a plus sign. Essentially, this is as far as you can drill-down in this dimension.

In this example, I use the CustomerLocation dimension down the side of the data grid and the measures across the top. If there was a real dimension across the top, I could drill-down the dimension the same way. The only difference is that additional columns would appear rather than additional rows.

MERGING DIMENSIONS

Another useful way to look at your cube with the Cube Browser is to merge multiple dimensions. Dragging the DatePurchased dimension down the line containing the MeasuresLevel results in an analysis of Sales Price, Labor Cost, Item Cost, and Profit each year (see Figure 21-14). Underneath each field in the measures, the values for each of the four years (1996, 1997, 1998, and 1999) in the dimension, plus the All value for the dimension are displayed. While Figure 21-14 shows only the first four columns, scrolling to the right displays the rest.

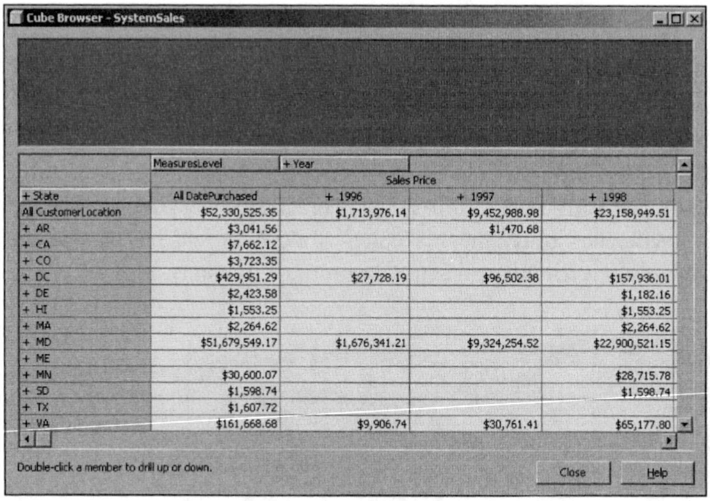

Figure 21-14: Merging columns to see even more data

In this case, merging dimensions clearly shows that the customer base for JustPC is primarily in Maryland, Washington D.C., and Virginia. Customers from the other states never ordered systems with any consistency over time.

Handling Errors

One of the most common errors you'll see is shown in Figure 21-15. Notice that all of the individual cells contain the value #ERR. This indicates that there is a problem with the cube's structure. This problem most likely is caused by a mistake in a calculated member.

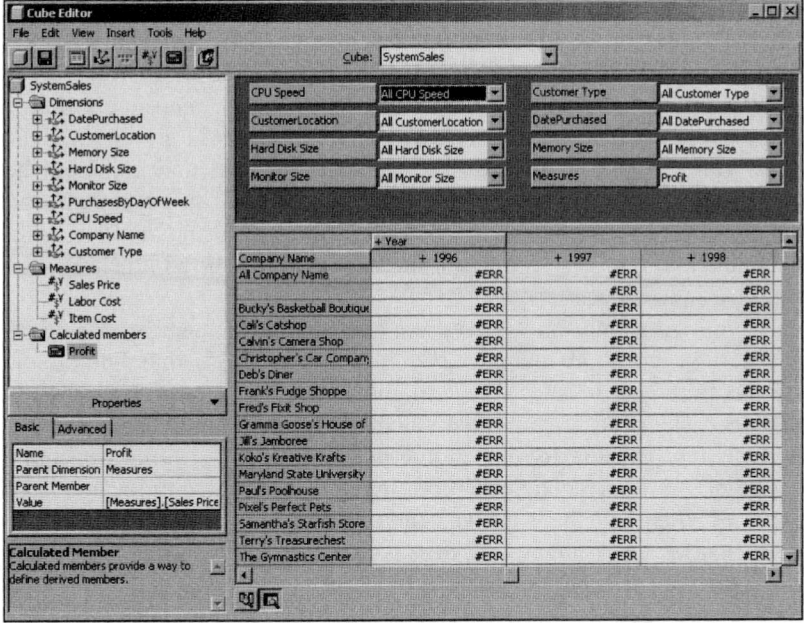

Figure 21-15: Analyzing an error

If you added a dimension or a calculated member and you don't see the members in your cube when you go to browse it, then you forgot to process it. The browser does not display an error message about an unprocessed cube. It happily displays the old information even though it is out of date.

TIP   If you try to browse your data while in the Cube Editor after making a structure change, the Cube Editor lets you know that you need to process the cube before you can see the correct values.

Summary

Building a cube with the Cube Editor is much easier than trying to figure out the corresponding MDX statements. While it isn't as simple as using the Cube Wizard you learned about in Chapter 20, I feel it is a more friendly environment (okay, I admit it ... I hate wizards).

The Cube Browser is not a substitute for a more powerful tool such as Excel. However, it is a good tool to know because it is easy to use and doesn't require setting up any special structures prior to using it. I use it to verify my structure changes while still in the Cube Editor.

If you spend any time with the OLAP Manager and the Dimension Editor, you probably will see something about virtual dimensions or member properties. This is an advanced feature of OLAP that enables you to create a dimension based on other values in selected tables. The primary advantage of a virtual dimension is that it doesn't occupy space. Its levels are derived from the members in another dimension. For most cubes, virtual dimensions aren't necessary and may not even be worthwhile. For this reason, I suggest you avoid using them. If you feel you need another dimension, then go ahead and create a real dimension using the Dimension Editor or the Cube Editor, or as part of the Cube Wizard. You'll be a lot better off in the long run.

However, if you learn only one thing from this chapter, remember to process your cubes after you make any changes. If you add data to the underlying databases where the cube gets it data, reprocess the cube. If you change the cube's structure, reprocess the cube. If you add a calculated member, reprocess the cube. Most of the tools that you use to analyze the data in the cube cannot determine when a change occurs that requires reprocessing the data. The bottom line is, if you're not sure whether the cube is current, then reprocess it.

In the next chapter, I talk about how to make your cube run faster. Until now, I've focused on getting the cube's structure correct, or at least getting it to the point where you can begin playing with it. Once you're satisfied that the cube's structure is where you want it, you can begin making it more efficient by pre-aggregating your data and breaking it into partitions. But in order to use these features, you need to have a relatively stable structure for your cube.

Chapter 22

Performance Considerations

IN THIS CHAPTER

- ◆ Optimizing your cube's performance
- ◆ Allocating storage for your cube
- ◆ Partitioning your cube for speed
- ◆ Analyzing usage information
- ◆ Usage-based optimization

THIS CHAPTER FOCUSES on factors that affect the size and performance of your cube. As with most optimization techniques, you have to decide what the most important aspect about what you're trying to do is and focus on that. For instance, if you want queries against your cube to run faster, then you probably have to perform a little extra work when you update the data in the cube. If you want the cube to occupy less space, your queries may run longer.

Optimizing Your Cube's Performance

Optimization is the process of trying to find the best set of tradeoffs that enable you to live within your resource limits. Every computer system ever built has a fixed amount of each of these resources. In many cases, you can trade one resource for another – but not always. Optimizing a cube is similar to optimizing a relational database.

Optimizing Resources

There are four factors that affect performance:

- ◆ CPU speed
- ◆ Main memory size
- ◆ Disk space
- ◆ Disk input/output (I/O) rate

For instance, Windows enables you to run more programs at the same time than can fit in main memory by trading disk space for main memory. The disk space is called *virtual memory* and it holds programs and their data that haven't been used recently. A disk cache works by using main memory to create a copy of information that is stored on disk. Each time you access something in the disk cache, you save one disk I/O.

Allowing the OLAP server to keep more information in memory, by using faster disk drives and by adding aggregations to solve queries more quickly, will minimize the time spent performing disk I/O. This will help to maximize query performance.

The easiest way (and often the cheapest) to fix a performance problem is to throw additional hardware at it. Unless you're running a very large server, $1,000 easily can buy you 10 gigabytes of fast disk storage, a gigabyte of memory, or a faster (or another) CPU.

Optimizing a Cube

While it is obvious that a larger cube takes up more disk space, you may not realize that it also consumes a lot of other resources. In addition, the larger cube takes more disk I/Os to read, requires more memory to hold the data, and takes more CPU cycles to analyze the data.

The first step in optimizing this cube is to study how it is used. There are only two basic types of operations performed against a cube: updating it and querying it. When you *update* a cube, you append the new data to the cube and then you process the cube to bring it up to date. The keyword here is update. These operations update the values in the cube. A *query,* on the other hand, reads the data from the cube. The data in the cube never changes.

Once you understand how the data is used, you also need to know how frequently it's used. In the case of a cube, it is quite likely that you will query the cube hundreds or thousands of times for every time you update it. Of course, this assumes that you have a stable cube whose structure doesn't change frequently.

Given that the cube is queried more often than it is updated means that you can optimize the query process at the expense of the update process. Even if the update runs a lot longer, it is still worthwhile for queries that run only slightly faster.

One way to improve the speed of the query is to find a way for the query to read fewer records while still returning the same answer. You can do this by precomputing the more frequently used data and keeping a copy of it. These precomputed data values are known as *aggregations*. While the aggregations need to be updated each time the cube is processed, the time it takes to create the copy is insignificant in comparison to how much time you save in queries. (I discuss aggregation in the next section.)

TIP

Don't bother optimizing a cube until its design is stable. Otherwise, you'll spend more time running processes than you will gain running queries.

NOTE

Optimizing is not an exact science. It is a game whereby you try to reduce resource consumption of one activity by allowing another activity to use more resources. Sometimes you win, sometimes you lose. You can never know for sure until you try.

Aggregating Your Data

While it is possible for you to create your own aggregate for use in your cubes, OLAP Services has a mathematical model that it uses to determine which aggregations have the most impact on your cube. In general, you should summarize the information in your fact table so that each row matches the lowest level of your cube and leave any other aggregations to OLAP Services.

The degree of usefulness of the aggregations depends on exactly what is aggregated and the number of different aggregations that are kept. Obviously, the more aggregations you keep, the more choices the OLAP Server has when solving a query. However, too many aggregations may consume so many resources that it is impossible to process the cube in a reasonable amount of time. You may also quickly run out of disk space if you try to keep too many aggregations.

OLAP Services includes a mathematical model that analyzes your cube's structure to determine what data should be aggregated. While the model isn't perfect, it does serve as a starting point. This model enables the server to achieve about an 80 percent improvement in query performance without spending an unrealistic amount of time processing the cube. You can do this by precomputing many values that can be combined in different fashions to solve any given query. The mathematical model also takes into account any available usage information. Based on this data, it can choose better aggregations to help improve specific types of queries.

However, there is a downside to keeping a lot of aggregations. Each time you need to update or process a cube, the aggregations need to be updated. The more aggregations you have, the longer it takes to process your cube. Also, aggregations take up space so you better have sufficient space to handle them.

If your cube is updated frequently, the downsides may outweigh the benefits. Only by trying different amounts of aggregation on your specific cubes can you determine how many, if any, you should use.

Designing Cube Storage

The *Storage Design Wizard* helps you define how you should store the data and what aggregations you should perform. Use this wizard when you are finished designing the cube's structure. Then, after a while, use the *Usage Analysis Wizard* and the *Usage-Based Optimization Wizard* to improve the cube performance.

The Storage Design Wizard

Right-click the name of the cube in the tree view and select Design Storage from the popup menu. The wizard responds by displaying the screen shown in Figure 22-1.

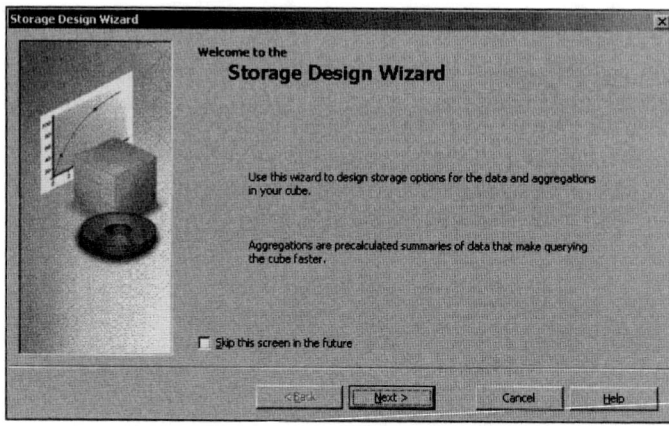

Figure 22-1: Running the Storage Design Wizard

CHOOSING YOUR STORAGE TYPE

The next step of the wizard asks you to decide what type of storage you want to use (see Figure 22-2). You can choose from MOLAP, ROLAP, or HOLAP. Each type of storage has its strengths and weaknesses. (Refer back to Chapter 17 for more information about the various OLAP Data Storage Models available in SQL Server 7).

You should use MOLAP storage when you frequently run queries against the cube and need quick responses. However, MOLAP storage takes a long time to load compared with ROLAP storage.

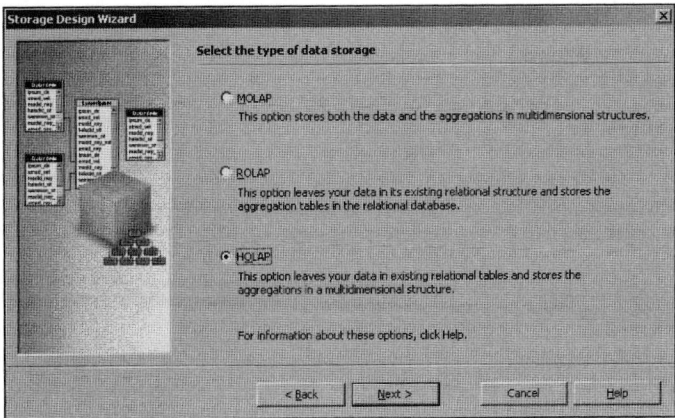

Figure 22-2: Choosing the type of storage

Retrieving information from ROLAP storage is considerably slower than it is with MOLAP storage. However, ROLAP storage is more space efficient and is easier to update. You may want to use ROLAP to hold data that may not be queried frequently, such as older historical data.

 ROLAP information is stored in the same data source used to create your cube.

HOLAP storage, on the other hand, uses ROLAP storage to hold the base data and uses MOLAP storage to hold aggregations. Thus, for most queries, you have the speed advantage of MOLAP combined with the space savings and faster processing time of ROLAP.

I like HOLAP storage. It offers a good compromise between ROLAP and MOLAP. Unless you have an overwhelming reason to choose ROLAP or MOLAP, I recommend you stick with HOLAP.

SETTING AGGREGATION OPTIONS

After you choose your storage type, the wizard asks you to decide how much of the cube's data you want aggregated (see Figure 22-3). By keeping precalculated subtotals of the data, the OLAP server can respond more quickly to most queries.

Aggregating data falls into the law of diminishing returns. Creating one aggregation can make a big difference in how fast the OLAP server responds to queries. A second aggregation also improves the response time. However, by the time you reach five or six aggregations, each new aggregation offers very little improvement.

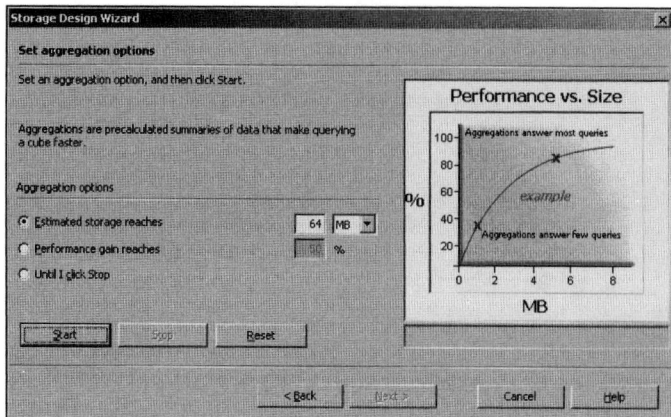

Figure 22-3: Setting the level of aggregation

Microsoft's approach to this is to enable you to determine how many aggregations to create by choosing one of three different methods. The first method sets a limit on the amount of storage that the collection of aggregations is allowed to use. You can specify any number of megabytes or gigabytes of storage. This is a good approach if you are limited on space.

The second method instructs the wizard to keep adding aggregations until the performance gain reaches a specified percentage. The wizard supplies a value of 50 percent as the default value; however, you may find using 75 or 80 percent worth the extra effort.

The last method keeps adding new aggregations until you press the Stop button. This is a good way to experiment with different aggregation levels.

The Reset button on the form enables you to reset the number of aggregations to zero so that you can try different methods. As you try various methods, the performance gain versus the amount of space required is displayed in a graph on the right side of the form. This chart is updated each time a new aggregation is added (see Figure 22-4). Watching this graph change is important for the option that adds aggregations until the Stop button is clicked because it will help you determine when to click the Stop button.

FINISHING THE AGGREGATIONS
Now that I've changed the structure of the cube, I need to process it again (see Figure 22-5). Selecting Process now and pressing the Finish button starts the process activity.

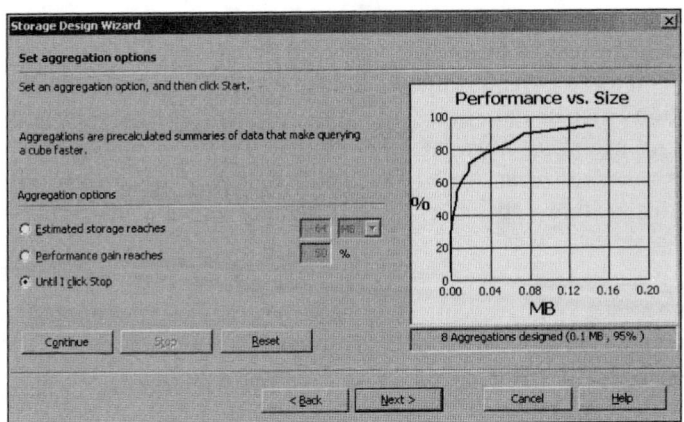

Figure 22-4: Seeing the effect of adding eight aggregations

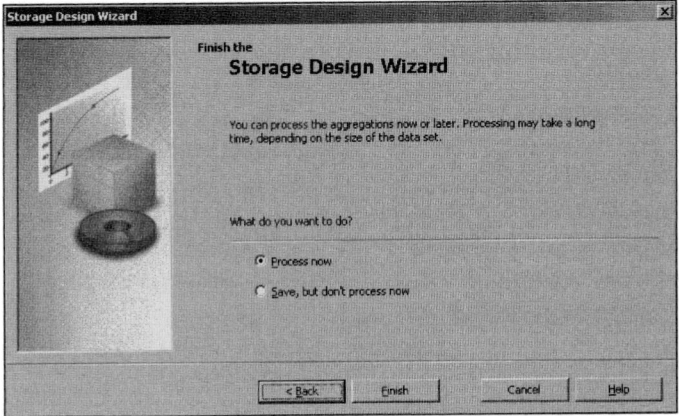

Figure 22-5: Processing the cube to populate the aggregations

Partitioning a Cube

The data for a cube is stored in a partition. *Partitioning a cube* is a feature that enables you to spread your data over several different locations on disk. The cubes I've talked about so far have had only one partition. However, if you are using the SQL Server Enterprise Edition, you can break your cubes into more than one partition.

The multiple partition feature enables you to set different rules for how data is stored. Data that you don't use very often can be stored in ROLAP storage, while data that you access often can be stored in MOLAP storage. You can even choose different aggregation rules for the different partitions.

Using multiple partitions can cause problems if you're not careful. The data within a partition always is correct. However, if you need to access data from multiple partitions whose boundaries aren't properly defined, then you may find yourself counting information twice or not at all.

Multiple partitions are useful for only the largest cubes. This is something that most people will never need. However, if you have cubes that measure in the hundreds of megabytes, this feature can make a big difference in how your cubes perform.

TIP For more information about this advanced feature, read *The SQL Server 7 OLAP Developer's Guide* by William Amo (IDG Books Worldwide, 1999).

Usage Analysis

The OLAP server records information about the queries that are run against your cube. This information is extremely useful when you want to optimize your cube. The *Usage Analysis Wizard* (see Figure 22-6) displays a series of reports that detail when and how the cube was accessed. You start the Usage Analysis Wizard by right-clicking the name of the cube in the tree view and selecting Usage Analysis from the popup menu. Table 22-1 contains a list of the various reports.

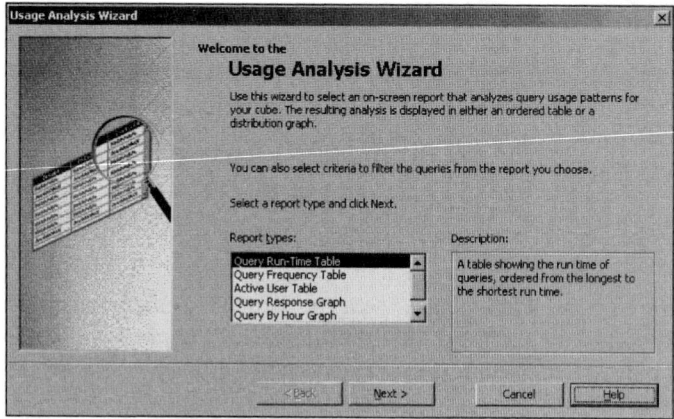

Figure 22-6: Running the Usage Analysis Wizard

TABLE **22-1** USAGE ANALYSIS REPORTS

Report	Description
Query Run TimeTable	Shows the requested data sets listed and the average run time.
Query Frequency Table	Shows the requested data sets and the number of times they were executed.
Active User Table	Lists each user and how many times he or she accessed the cube.
Query Response Graph	Shows the number of times the cube was accessed (grouped by the average duration).
Query By Hour Graph	Shows the number of queries (grouped by the time of day).
Query By Date Graph	Shows the number of queries in terms of the grouped by date.

Filtering the Report's Data

Once you select the report you want to see, the next step is to choose which data to use (see Figure 22-7). You can choose any combination of the following filters:

- Before or after a specified date and time, or between a start and end time
- Included in a list of user names
- Queries that run more than a specified amount of time
- Queries that run more than a specified number of times

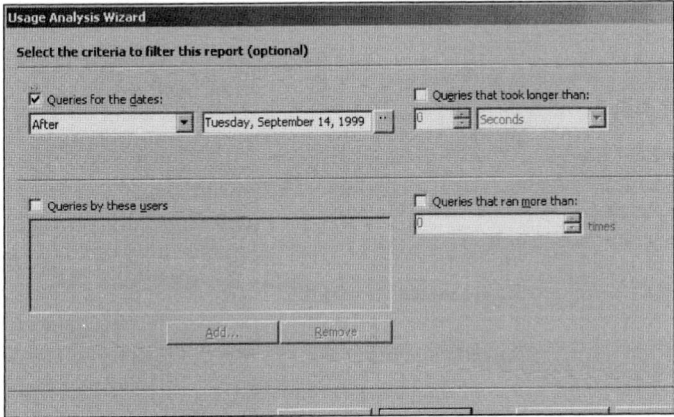

Figure 22-7: Filtering the report's data

Displaying the Report

As the last step of the wizard, the report is displayed. The report can be either a tabular report (see Figure 22-8) or a graphical report (see Figure 22-9). Pressing the Finish button ends the wizard. Note that while the reports aren't saved, you can rerun the wizard to see them again.

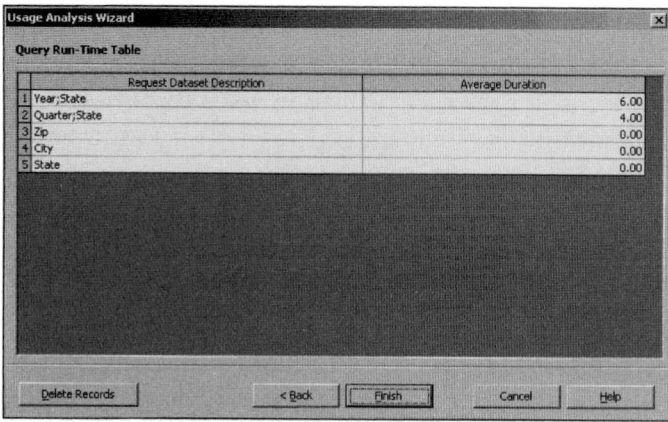

Figure 22-8: Displaying a tabular report

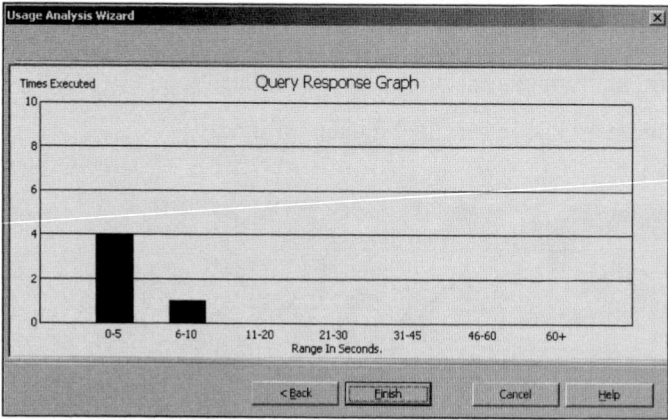

Figure 22-9: Displaying a graphical report

If you want to see multiple reports, simply press the Back button twice to return to the screen where you select the report.

Usage-Based Optimization

Usage-based optimization takes the information generated by the usage analysis reports to create aggregations in your cube. If your cube already has aggregations, it can add new aggregations to help improve performance or replace existing aggregations with different ones that address the types of queries actually executed. To start the Usage-Based Optimization Wizard, right-click the cube in the OLAP Manager's tree view and select Usage-Based Optimization from the popup menu (see Figure 22-10).

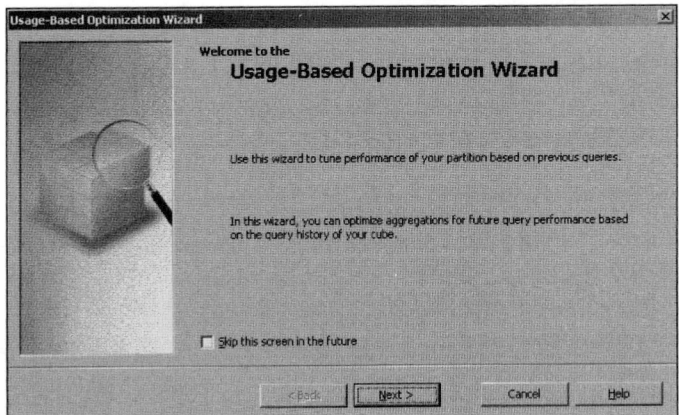

Figure 22-10: Starting the Usage-Based Optimization Wizard

Optimizing for Specific Queries

The next step of the wizard asks you to select the queries you want to optimize. The more information you feed into the mathematical model that OLAP Services uses to choose which aggregations to create, the better job it can do. For instance, if most of your queries are date-oriented, then the optimizer selects more aggregations that help date-oriented queries.

If most of your queries run very fast, but a few run for a long time, you may want the optimizer to work on the long-running queries. You may consider optimizing the cube for a particular group of people, such as your organization's president and vice presidents. After all, they are the ones that are paying for the service.

The form that the wizard uses to select which queries to optimize is the same form used by the Usage Analysis Wizard (see Figure 22-11) with one exception. You also can select queries by storage type.

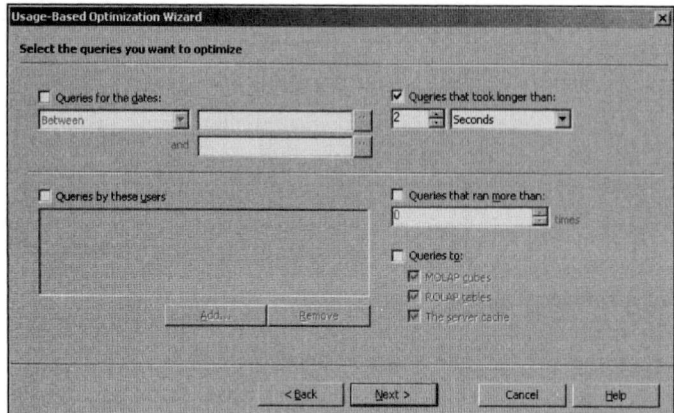

Figure 22-11: Selecting the queries to optimize

 **TIP**   Probably the best set of queries to choose is one that runs very frequently and takes more than a couple of seconds to complete. If the queries run less than a couple of seconds, the average user doesn't notice the difference; if the queries are run infrequently, the time savings isn't that noticeable either.

After you select the queries, the wizard displays a usage report for you to review (see Figure 22-12). Take a few moments to examine the results. If they aren't what you expect, go back to the previous form and select a different set of queries. Also, if your selection criteria is so restrictive that you haven't selected any queries, the wizard refuses to continue and you have to go back and choose less restrictive criteria.

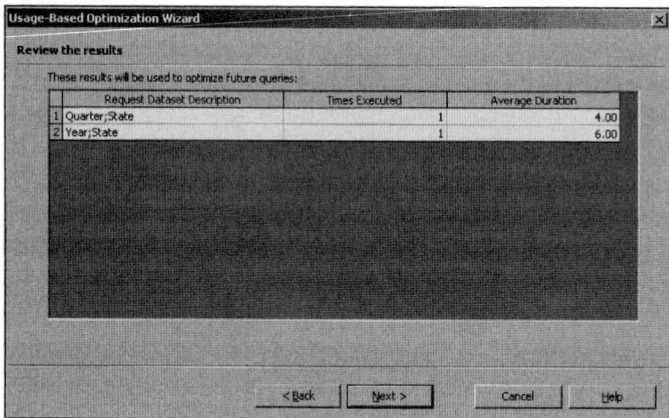

Figure 22-12: Reviewing the selected queries

Replacing the Existing Aggregations

If you already defined aggregations for your cube, the form shown in Figure 22-13 is displayed. This form describes your current aggregations in terms of type of data storage used, the total space they occupy, and the number of aggregations. You can opt to replace the existing aggregations with the new optimal ones, or you can choose to add any new aggregations recommended by the wizard.

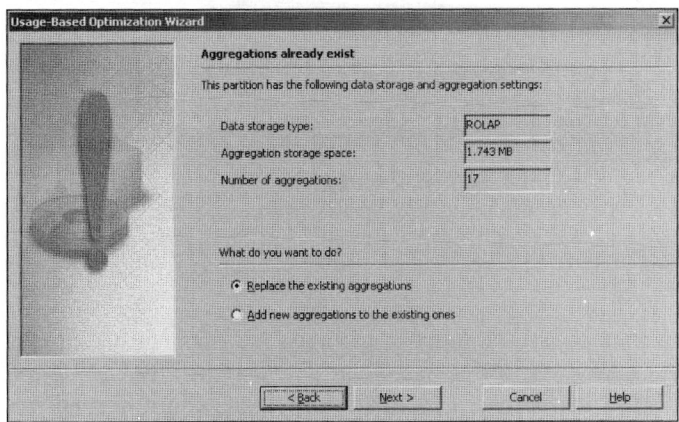

Figure 22-13: Choosing to keep or replace your current aggregations

 **TIP** If you're not pressed for disk space and processing the current cube doesn't take too long, you should keep your existing aggregations.

If you choose to replace your existing aggregations, you are given the same three choices for data storage you had originally: MOLAP, ROLAP, and HOLAP (see Figure 22-14). If you choose to add to your existing aggregations, your current storage type is retained.

Finishing the Wizard

The Usage-Based Optimization Wizard then goes through the same process the Storage Design Wizard uses to determine the aggregations that should be used. (Refer back to the "Setting Aggregation Options" section and Figure 22-3 for more information about this step).

The very last step of this wizard asks you if you want to process the cube. If you don't want to process it now, the wizard saves the aggregations so that they can be processed later. Unless processing the cube takes a long time, I suggest doing it immediately because you may not be able to use it until after it is processed.

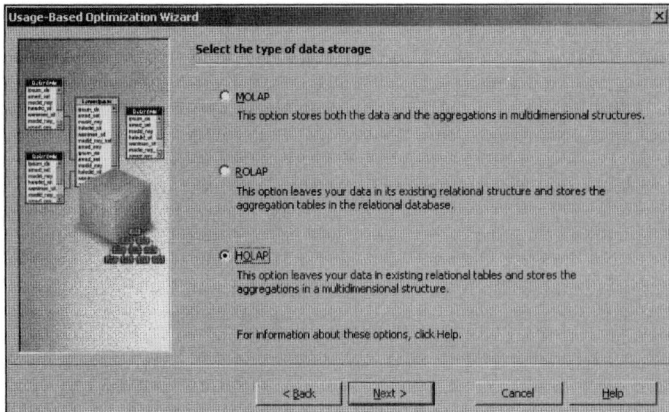

Figure 22-14: Choosing a new data storage type for your aggregations

Summary

In this chapter, I talked about how to improve your cube's performance. By storing aggregations, you can make a big difference when it comes to solving queries. However, the key to finding the optimal combination of aggregations depends on knowing how you plan to use your cube. Analyzing data from past queries is a good source of information, as well as your own ability to identify the types of queries that should be optimized. Once you have this information, you can use the tools in OLAP Manager to build a better cube.

In the next chapter, I wrap up this part of the book by explaining how to secure the information in your OLAP database. In some cases, unrestricted access to the information in your OLAP database isn't a problem. On the other hand, it may be a mistake to make all of this information public because your competitors can take advantage of it.

Chapter 23

Security Considerations

THIS CHAPTER DISCUSSES how you can secure the information in your OLAP cube and make as much or as little of it available to other users as you want. Security is always a prime concern when you have a resource as valuable to your organization as a data warehouse or an OLAP cube. Without proper security, your competitors may be able to exploit your own information against you.

Basic Security Concepts

Unlike SQL Server, OLAP security is based solely on the Windows 2000/NT security system. This means that it can take advantage of the facilities already built into Windows 2000/NT. Before I get into a detailed discussion of OLAP security, I want to spend a few minutes discussing some basic concepts of Windows security.

Only an intro. This section is intended to introduce you to a few basic security terms and concepts used in a Windows networking environment. It is not meant to be a comprehensive discussion of these features. Please refer to *Windows 2000 Server Administrator's Bible* by Randall Hinsberg (IDG Books Worldwide, 2000) for the complete details about Windows security.

User Names

A *user name* is a unique identifier associated with a person who accesses a Windows server. Each user name has a secret password associated with it.

Authentication

Authentication verifies that you are allowed to use a particular user name. Typically, the authentication process begins by requesting both your user name and password and then verifying that the pair is valid. If the user name isn't defined to the server or if the wrong password is supplied, a security violation occurs and you are denied access.

Authorization

A *resource* is an item that you wish to access. This may be a server, a file, or an OLAP database. Often, resources are arranged in a hierarchy, such as a file that is contained inside a directory. Even though you may have permission to access a particular file on a particular server, you can't access the file if you don't have access to the server.

Just because your user name and password are fine doesn't mean that you are allowed to access any resources. Your user name must be authorized to access a resource. An administrator, using another user name, can authorize your access to the resource.

Permissions

Permissions are the types of access you may be granted to a resource. Some common permissions are *read*, *write*, and *execute*. If your user name has read permission to a specific file, you may read any portion of the file you wish – but you are prevented from writing to the file.

Security Groups

Because a resource – like a server – may have a large number of user names that can access it, granting access to each individual user name becomes tedious. It's even more tedious to grant access to each of the individual resources on the server. Security groups were developed to make things easier. A *security group* is a unique identifier that represents a collection of user names; you can use it in place of a user name when granting access to a resource.

If your user name is included in a security group, you are considered a member of that particular security group. Thus, a resource such as a server may have a security group called StandardUsers. This group is granted access to a number of different resources, such as directories, printers, and so on. When the system administrator creates your user name, and he or she adds you to the StandardUsers group, you automatically are authorized to access any of the resources that the group is authorized to access.

Specifying security groups. Because a security group can be used anywhere a user name is used, you can specify that one security group is a member of another security group.

Roles

A *role* is a way of creating a security resource for an application. While the application itself can be considered a resource, it is very desirable to control individual functions inside the application using Windows security.

For example, in an order entry program, you may create a role for clerks called "Clerk" and one for supervisors called "Supervisor". The Supervisor role may enable the user to access any function in the program, while the Clerk role may not enable the user to access the price override function. The actual security logic is included in the program and consists of subroutine calls to verify that your user name is a member of a particular role.

Security in OLAP Services

There are two levels of security in OLAP: OLAP administrators and OLAP users. OLAP administrators are granted full access to the databases on the server and all of the cubes contained in them. OLAP users are granted limited access to an OLAP database through a set of roles that the OLAP administrator defines.

The basis for security. OLAP security is based on Windows 2000 Server security, so you must install OLAP Services and your OLAP databases on an NTFS-formatted disk drive. FAT-formatted disk drives do not support Windows security, and the files you place on them are open to anyone. This means that anyone with access to your server can make a copy of the files that make up your OLAP database.

FAT versus NTFS. FAT disk drives are slower than NTFS-formatted disk drives. So even if security isn't a problem, you should use NTFS disk drives to get better performance.

Managing OLAP Users

Only OLAP administrators are permitted to access the OLAP Manager utility. This is handled by normal Windows security. Your user name must be a member of the Windows security group called OLAP Administrators. To control the list of user names associated with this group, you need to use the *Active Directory Users and Computers* utility.

USING THE ACTIVE DIRECTORY USERS AND COMPUTERS UTILITY

To run the Active Directory Users and Computers utility, go to the Start menu and choose Program → Administrative Tools → Active Directory Users and Computers (see Figure 23-1). This utility displays information in the same format as the OLAP Manager. The left side of the form displays a tree view of the various objects you want to manage, while the right side displays details about the currently selected object.

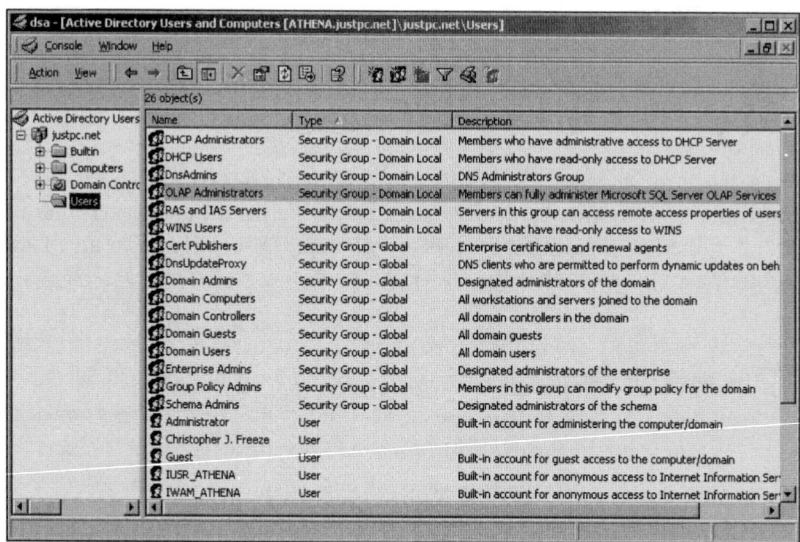

Figure 23-1: Running the Active Directory Users and Computers utility

 **More about security tools.** This chapter explains how to set up security for OLAP Services using a Windows 2000 Server. While you need to do the same things on Windows NT Server 4.0, you use different utilities. For more information about these security tools, read *Windows NT Server 4.0 For Dummies* by Ed Tittel (IDG Books Worldwide, 1999).

 **About MMC.** Both the OLAP Manager and the Active Directory Users and Computers utility (as well as SQL Server Enterprise Manager) are based on the Microsoft Management Console (MMC). Most of the administrative tools you use in Windows 2000 are based on MMC. Once you get familiar with some of the tools, using the rest of the tools is pretty easy.

FINDING THE USERS IN THE GROUP

To see the list of users associated with the OLAP Administrators group, expand the domain in the tree view and select the Users icon. Then double-click the line containing OLAP Administrators in the details side of the form. This displays the Properties window for the OLAP Administrators group. Select the Members tab to see the user names that are included in the group (see Figure 23-2).

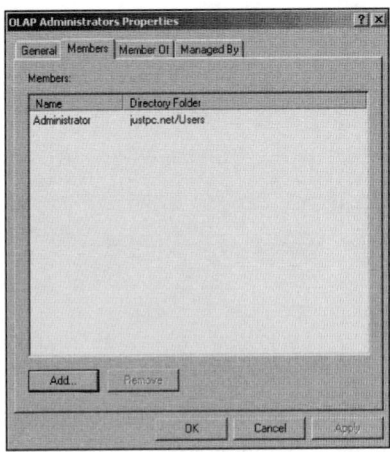

Figure 23-2: Looking at the members of the OLAP Administrators group

 **Sign on as Administrator.** You must be signed onto the server as Administrator, or any other user name that is a member of the Administrators or Domain Admins group, in order to see the list of users associated with a security group.

ADDING USER NAMES AND GROUPS

You can add a new user name to the security group by pressing the Add button at the bottom of the Properties window. This displays the dialog box shown in

Figure 23-3. All of the user names that are available on the system are listed here. Simply select the user names and groups you want to add to the OLAP Administrators group and press the Add button. These user names and groups are copied into the bottom half of the form. If you decide not to add a user name or group, simply select the name in the bottom half of the form and press Remove. Once you're satisfied with the list, press OK and the users are added to the previous form. Press OK or Apply on the OLAP Administrators Properties window to accept the changes or Cancel to abort the changes.

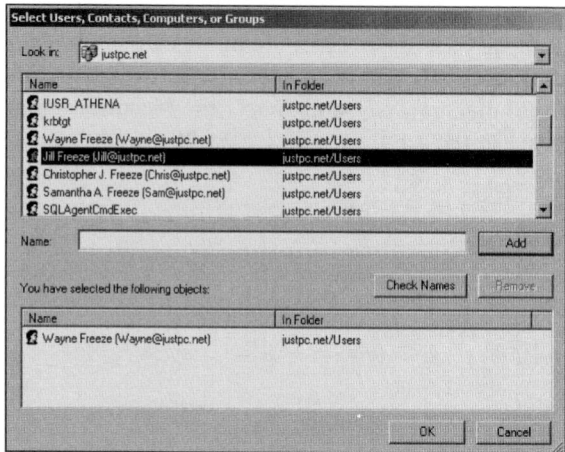

Figure 23-3: Selecting user names and groups to add to the OLAP Administrators group

REMOVING A USER NAME OR GROUP

To remove a user name or group from the OLAP Administrators group, simply select the name from the list of names in the Properties window and press Remove (see Figure 23-4). A message box is displayed asking you if you really want to make the change. Press Yes to delete the name from the member list. Then press OK or Apply to make the change or Cancel to abort the change.

Creating OLAP Roles

Before someone other than an OLAP administrator can access a cube, you must use the OLAP Manager utility to define one or more roles for each OLAP database. As the roles are defined, you can add the list of user names and groups that can access the role. Then these roles are mapped onto the database, which determines the real level of access.

CREATING A NEW DATABASE ROLE

To create a role using the OLAP Manager, expand the Database icon to which the role will belong. Then expand the Library icon beneath the Database icon to list the existing roles. Right-click the Roles icon and select New Role. This displays the Create a Database Role dialog box shown in Figure 23-5.

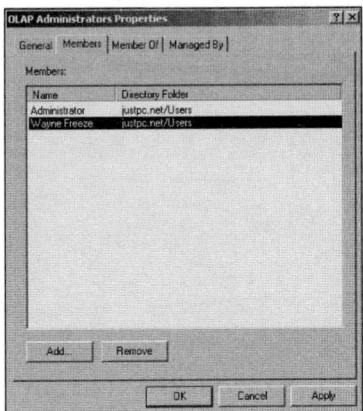

Figure 23-4: Removing a user name from the Members list

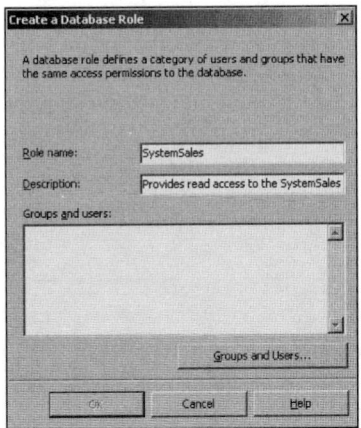

Figure 23-5: Creating a new database role

You start the process by choosing a unique name for this role and giving it a longer description that describes it purpose. Then, you can add a list of user names and groups that are associated with this role by pressing the Groups and Users button at the bottom of the form. This displays the Add Users and Groups dialog box (see Figure 23-6).

By default, this dialog box shows only a list of security groups that you can add. By pressing the Show Users button, the list of all users that you can add is appended to this list. To see the user names in a particular security group, select the group and press the Members button. A separate dialog box is displayed containing the list of members in that group.

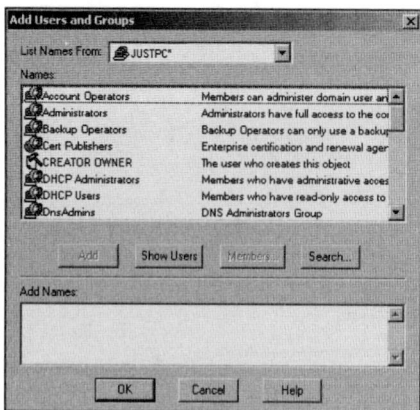

Figure 23-6: Adding user names and groups to the role

As you decide which user names and security groups you wish to add to the role, press the Add button to copy the names to the bottom part of the form. If you make a mistake, simply highlight the name or names you wish to delete and press the Del key. When you find the list of user names and security groups you wish to add to the Role, press OK. You are returned to the Create a Database Role dialog box and the names you selected are added to the role. Press OK on this dialog box to save your changes.

Implementing OLAP Security

There are only two practical ways you can associate users with a role. If you have a single administrator in charge of Windows and OLAP security, create a security group that contains a list of users who are permitted to access a role. Then add that security group to the role. Essentially, you only use one tool (the Active Directory Users and Computers utility) to manage both Windows and OLAP security. If you have one individual who is responsible for Windows security and another who is responsible for OLAP security, simply enable the OLAP administrator to explicitly add each user to a role. This way is better because the OLAP administrator need not worry about learning to use the Active Directory Users and Computers utility.

EDITING A DATABASE ROLE

Once you create a database role, you can add and delete users in a particular role by using the Edit a Database Role dialog box. You open this dialog box by expanding the Roles icon to list the roles that are defined in the database, right-clicking the role you wish to modify, and selecting Edit. A dialog box identical to the Add a Database Role dialog box appears (see Figure 23-7), except you are not permitted to change the name of the database role.

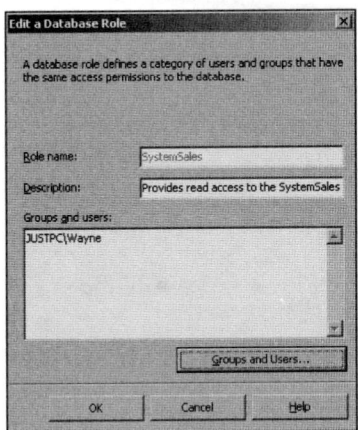

Figure 23-7: Editing a database role

To delete a user name in the Edit a Database Role dialog box, simply highlight the user name and press the Del key on the keyboard. You can add more names by pressing the Groups and Users button. The same Add Users and Groups dialog box that you saw previously is displayed. Once you finish making changes, press OK in the Edit a Database Role dialog box to save the changes. Of course, pressing Cancel returns you to OLAP Manager without making any changes.

Managing OLAP Roles

Once you create your database roles, you need to assign the roles to the cubes. You do this by using the Manage Roles dialog box. To open this dialog box, run OLAP Manager and select the cube you wish to manage. Right-click the cube's name and select Manage Roles from the popup menu, which displays the Manage Roles dialog box (see Figure 23-8).

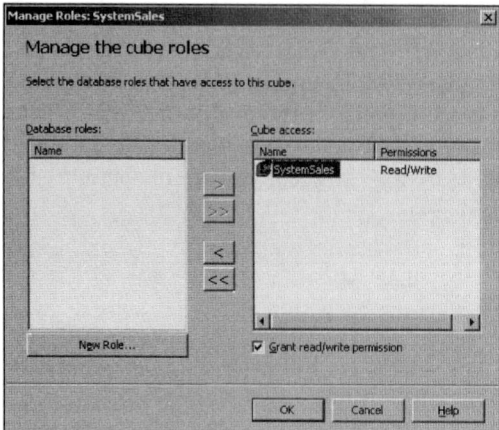

Figure 23-8: Associating a database role with a cube

Shortcut. Press the New Role button below the list of database roles to launch the Create a Database Role dialog box.

On the left side of the dialog box, is a list of database roles that are not used. On the right is a list of roles that are granted access to the cube and their security permissions. To add a database role to the cube, simply select the role and press the > button. To add all of the roles to the cube, press the > button. You remove a role from the cube the same way. Select the role you want to remove and press the < button. To clear all of the roles from the cube, press the << button.

You can change the security permissions associated with a role by using the Grant read/write permission checkbox below the Cube access list. By default, all database roles are assigned read permission. To change the permission to read/write, select the role you which change and place a checkmark in the checkbox. This changes the permission to read/write. To change the permission back to read, simply remove the checkmark.

Once you finish mapping the database roles to the cube, press the OK button to save your changes or the Cancel button to leave things as they are.

Write-Enabling the Cube

Until now, I talked about cubes as static objects that never change except when they are loaded or updated from the data warehouse. However, it is possible to change values in individual cells. By default, you can't update the cells in a cube, but if the cube is write-enabled and you are a member of a role that has Read/Write access to the cube, you can change a value.

 Of all the tools I discuss in this book, only Excel has the ability to update a cell value — and then only if you create a macro to do it.

All changes that are made to a write-enabled cube are saved in a relational database table and applied after the cube is loaded. This is known as the *write-back table*. The OLAP administrator can use the OLAP Manager to delete the data in the write-back table in an effort to convert the cube back to read-only, browse the data in the table, or convert the write-back data to a partition.

Write-Enabling a Cube

To write-enable a cube, right-click the cube and select Write-Enable from the popup menu. The dialog box shown in Figure 23-9 is shown. Values automatically are selected for the data source and for the table that holds the write-back changes. You can choose other values if you want by selecting a different data source from the drop-down box. Or you can create a new data source by pressing the New button. You can change the table name by typing a new name in the Table name text box. Pressing OK automatically creates the write-back table and enables the cube for write access.

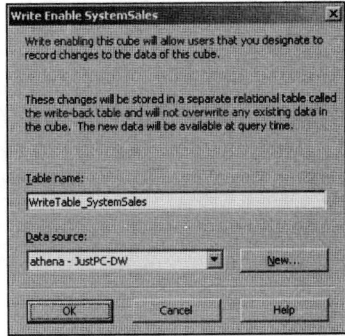

Figure 23-9: Using the Write Enable dialog box

Browsing Write-Back Data

You can browse the data in the write-back table by right-clicking the cube and selecting Write-Back Options → Browse Write-Back Data. This displays a simple form containing the data in the write-back table (see Figure 23-10).

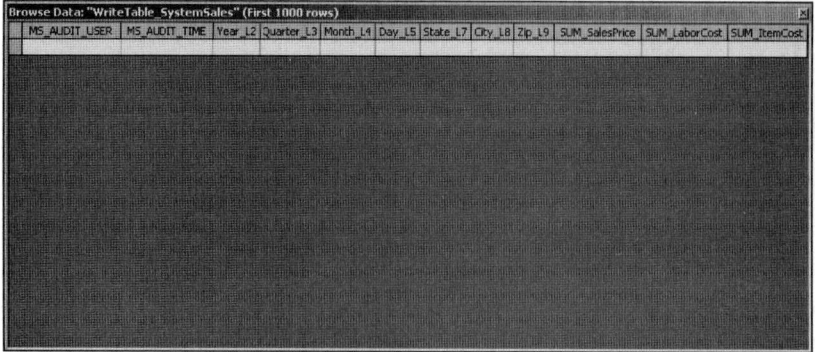

Figure 23-10: Browsing write-back data

Converting Write-Back Data to a Partition

If you have the Enterprise Edition of SQL Server, you can create a cube with multiple partitions. If your cube is write-enabled, you can convert the data in the write-back table into a partition by right-clicking the cube and selecting Write-Back Options → Convert to Partition from the popup menu.

Disabling Write Access

If you want to disable write access to your cube, right-click the cube and choose Write-Back Options → Delete Data from the popup menu. This displays a message box asking if you really want to delete all of the write-back data and convert the cube back to a read-only situation. Press Yes to proceed or No to cancel the operation. Note that pressing Yes changes all users with read/write permission to the cube to read and causes any programs that attempt to write to the cube to fail.

Cell-Level Security

With *cell-level security*, you selectively enable or disable access to a particular cell or group of cells in a cube. This is a very powerful concept because it enables you to create different levels of access within a single cube. You can prevent some users from drilling down beyond a certain level or choose to hide an entire dimension.

 **Service Pack 1.** Cell-level security requires the Service Pack 1 (or newer) for OLAP Services. You can download this patch by going to www.Microsoft.com/sql and following the links to the service pack information. Note that there is also a Service Pack 1 for SQL Server itself. While you aren't required to enable cell-level security, it does correct a number of bugs in SQL Server 7 itself.

How Cell-Level Security Works

Cell-level security is based on roles and access rules. An *access rule* consists of an MDX expression that returns TRUE or FALSE and a permission. The permission can be CellRead, CellReadContingent, or CellWrite. Each time the user tries to access a cell or set of cells in the cube, the OLAP server evaluates the access rules to determine whether or not to grant access. If the MDX expression in the access rule returns TRUE, the user accessing the cube has access to the cells. If it returns FALSE, then access is denied.

If the user is denied access to a cell, a value of #N/A is returned.

CELLREAD AND CELLREADCONTINGENT

The CellRead permission permits access to a cell if the MDX expression is TRUE and denies access to a cell if the MDX expression is FALSE. The MDX expression evaluates only the cell being accessed.

The CellReadContingent permission evaluates not only the cell being accessed, but also all of the other cells used to derive the value in the cell. If the user can't access one of these underlying cells, CellReadContingent denies access – even if the user has access to the cell being accessed.

CELLWRITE

The CellWrite permission also implies the CellRead permission. Thus, if the MDX expression evaluates to TRUE, the user is allowed to write to the cell.

Setting Cell-Level Security

While cell-level security looks like an interesting feature, it currently has one big disadvantage. You can set cell-level security only by writing a program. While the program itself isn't that difficult to write, it violates one of the fundamental principles of this book – no programming needed. You can visit Microsoft's Web site at www.Microsoft.com/sql and follow the links to OLAP and cell-level security. They provide some examples of how to write such a program.

Summary

This chapter covered the security features of OLAP Services. For the most part, all you really need to do is enable or disable read access for a particular cube for a particular set of user names. How you do this is up to you. The important thing is that you do it. Operating a server without security is just asking for problems.

While I'm impressed with cell-level security, I'm disappointed that the only way to access the security is through a program. I believe that Microsoft eventually will include a way to manage it from OLAP Manager; if they don't write one, I might. Stop by my Web site at www.JustPC.com and follow the links to this book's Web page for more information.

This chapter wraps up how to create an OLAP database. In the next part of the book, I focus on how to use Excel to analyze your cubes. Excel PivotTables provide an excellent way to view cubes and analyze the data in them. However, there's more to using PivotTables than just employing a different Cube Browser. You can control the formatting by using all of Excel's powerful formatting tools. You can create PivotCharts, which are a graphical form of a PivotTable, and you can publish your PivotTables and PivotCharts to the Internet.

Part VII

Analyzing the OLAP Database with Microsoft Excel

Chapter 24

Creating Basic Excel Worksheets

IN THIS CHAPTER

- ◆ Connecting Excel to your data warehouse

- ◆ Extracting data from your data warehouse

- ◆ Performing common operations

THIS CHAPTER DISCUSSES how to create basic Excel spreadsheets using data from the data warehouse and the OLAP database. You'll finally learn how to tap into these vast resources using a tool you probably have worked with for years.

Connecting Excel 2000 to Your Data Warehouse

You can have the most incredibly populated data warehouse in the world, but it literally does you no good if the people responsible for making key corporate decisions aren't able to do anything with this data. Sure, your database administrator can run you virtually any report, but your best decisions may not come as a result of the traditional reports you may order. There is much value in the fact that now any manager or corporate decision maker can use a familiar tool, Excel 2000, to explore hunches or ideas as they come to mind. No more waiting for the report to generate — you can get the answers you need immediately. This is important because, as the old adage goes, "Time is money."

Obviously, getting Excel 2000 to talk to your data warehouse is the first step you need to take in this process. However, the good news is that once the connection is mapped properly the first time, you need to do little more than select a special menu item to access the data warehouse during subsequent work sessions.

Getting Started

To begin connecting Excel 2000 to your data warehouse, launch Excel and then select Data→Get External Data New Database Query. This launches Microsoft Query's Choose Data Source window shown in Figure 24-1.

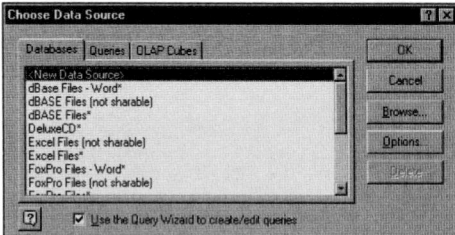

Figure 24-1: The Choose Data Source dialog box enables you to access a variety of data sources.

Naming the Data Source

In the Database tab, select the New Data Source option and then click OK. The Create New Data Source dialog box appears. Your first order of business is to give the data source a meaningful name (see Figure 24-2). Remember to name it something you should recognize in a heartbeat from a huge list of Microsoft's predefined options.

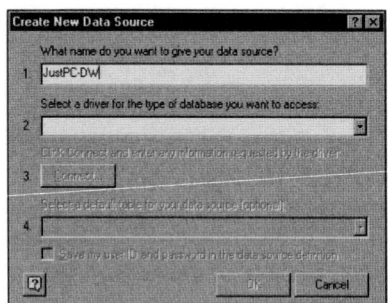

Figure 24-2: Entering a name for your new data source

Selecting a Driver

Once you select a name, you are asked to select a driver for the type of data source you want to access. While there is an enormous number of options to choose from (FoxPro, Oracle, and ODBC drivers, to name a few), look for SQL Server. Click that option, and then press the resulting Connect button.

Looking for drivers? You can find most of the Microsoft drivers under "M" due to their Microsoft prefix. SQL Server is an exception to that rule. For some odd reason it lacks the standard Microsoft prefix, so you need to look under the "S" options instead.

Logging into the Database Server

The SQL Server Login dialog box opens, prompting you to enter the database server's name, as well as any necessary user IDs and passwords (see Figure 24-3). Press the Options button to expand the Server Login dialog box, and then use the Database drop-down box to choose the database you want to map into Excel. Once you select the desired database, click OK. A *Connecting to data source* message appears for several seconds as your workstation attempts to establish the connection.

Missing a database? Only the databases you have security permission to access appear on this list. If you do not see the database you're looking for, speak with your database administrator to possibly have your permissions edited.

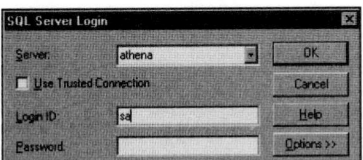

Figure 24-3: You need a server name, login ID, and password to continue defining the data source.

Finishing the New Data Source

When a connection is finally established, you return to the Create New Data Source dialog box. The Create New Data Source dialog box gives you the opportunity to set a default table for the data source; but flexibility with data analysis is our main objective, so I suggest you leave it blank. You also have the opportunity to tell Microsoft Query to save your user ID and password along with the data source definition.

 **Security alert.** While saving your user ID and password with your data source may save you time by not requiring you to enter a user ID and password each time you access the newly defined data source, it can pose some potential security threats. Anyone that has physical access to your workstation will automatically have access to your data source. Unless you are absolutely certain that no one else can assess your workstation, the safest thing is to just leave the option blank.

Click the OK button to return to the Choose Data Source dialog box. Because your data source is fully defined now, simply click the Close (X) button to exit the dialog box.

Extracting Data from the Data Warehouse

Now it's finally time to retrieve data from that data source you defined. You do this by defining a new database query. To begin the process from within Excel, select Data → Get External Data → New Database Query. You should recognize the resulting dialog box, Choose Data Source, from Figure 24-1. Select the name of the data source you defined and then press OK. The Connecting to data source message appears. If you have not told Excel to save your user ID and password with the data source definition, you are prompted to enter that information now. Then be sure to press the Options button so you can select a specific database to work with.

Choosing Your Query Fields

Pressing the Options button takes you to the Query Wizard screen shown in Figure 24-4. The *Available tables and columns* pane on the left side of the dialog box enables you to pick and choose the data you want to include in your query. To add a column or table to your query, click it and then press the > button. You can delete a query element by clicking its name in the *Columns in your query* pane and then pressing the < button. You can remove all of the columns by pressing the << button. Remember to click those plus signs to reveal "hidden" columns nested underneath the various tables!

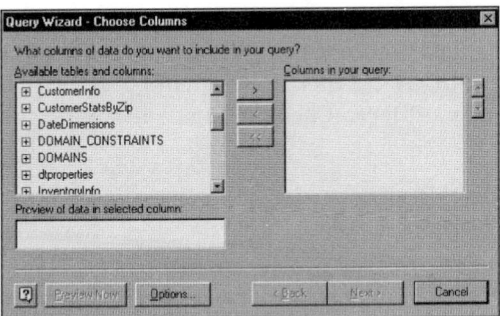

Figure 24-4: The Query Wizard makes it a whole lot easier to extract the data you need.

Filtering Your Data

Once you choose all of the fields you want to include in your query, click the Next button. This takes you to the Query Wizard's Filter Data dialog box. By filtering your data, you can grab just the subsections you need. This may be the only way to reduce mammoth data warehouses to sizes small enough to manipulate and analyze. Filtering data before you extract it is often more efficient than pulling in database records and filtering them in Excel. Not only is it faster this way, but you can still employ filters in Excel to perform more in-depth analysis of a specific chunk of material.

Limiting the data. Because Excel 2000 can import only around 65,000 records, you may need to use the filter at this level to cut down the amount of data you import. If you're a small company that has maybe 10,000 customers, you needn't worry. However, if you're working with data from a larger corporation (such as ATI Technologies) that may have millions of registered customers, then you definitely need to use the filters to narrow the number of records you're trying to import.

For example, when considering placing an ad in a certain newspaper, you may want to extract only database records of customers from the newspaper's circulation zip codes. This way, you may be able to target ads that meet the customer base's previous buying patterns. If you have very few customers in the zip code under consideration, you may opt for a larger, more generalized ad that makes both your presence and your offerings hard to miss.

To begin using the Query Wizard's filtering tool, click the name of the field to which you want to apply the filter. (In the previous example, that would be the zip code field.) Use the first drop-down box on the left to specify the condition of the filter (for example, if the record is equal to, less than, or greater than). In the second drop-down box, type in the specific criteria (such as the exact zip code you want to extract or the specific state from which you want records returned) by which you want each record to be filtered (see Figure 24-5). Then apply and/or qualifiers to define additional conditions the records must meet. Click the Next button to move to the next step in the Query Wizard.

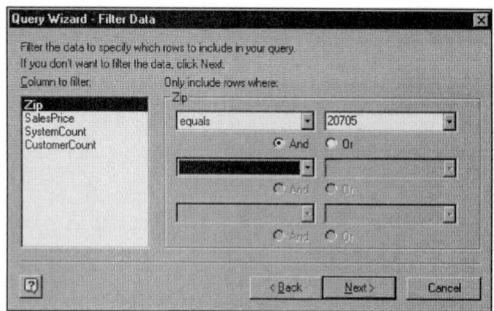

Figure 24–5: The Query Filter helps you pull out the specific records you want to analyze.

Sorting It All Out

The Data Query Sort Order tool enables you to group your records and put them in the desired order. For example, you can sort by state in ascending order first to place customers from the same state together. Then you can sort by the total amount spent at JustPC in descending order to locate your five best customers in each state.

Sorting records by multiple criteria is a lot easier than it sounds. To follow through with the preceding example, use the Sort by drop-down box to select the State column of the data warehouse and check the Ascending option. In the Then by drop-down box, choose SalesPrice and check the Descending option. The resulting Data Query - Sort Order dialog box resembles the one pictured in Figure 24-6. Once the desired sorting criteria is defined, click Next to continue.

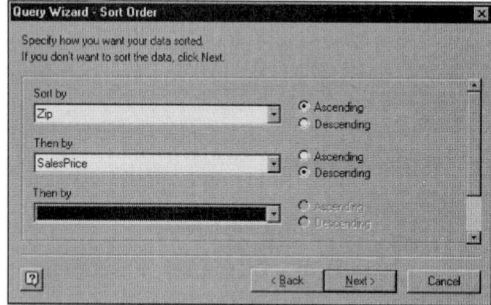

Figure 24–6: The Sort Order dialog box helps you put your records in order.

The Final Steps in Defining Your Query

As its final request, the Data Query Wizard asks you what it should do with the resulting data. As you can see in Figure 24-7, your choices include:

◆ Return data to Microsoft Excel

◆ View data or edit query in Microsoft Query

◆ Create an OLAP cube from this query

In order to begin analyzing the data in Excel 2000, choose the Return data to Microsoft Excel option.

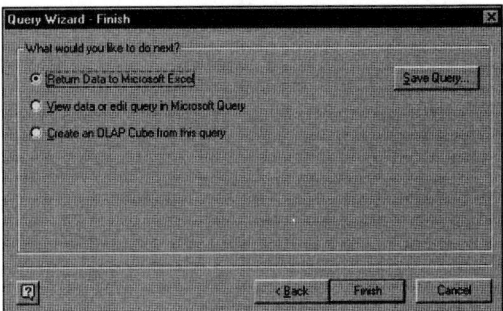

Figure 24-7: In this last screen, tell the wizard where you want the data.

Executing and Saving the Query

To execute the query you defined without saving it, simply press Finish and the data is brought into Excel. However, if this is a query you anticipate running often as your data warehouse undergoes constant changes and updates, you may want to save the query to save time down the road. You can save the query by clicking the Save Query button on the right side of the final wizard screen. This transfers you to a standard Save As dialog box in which you can name the query. Simply press Save Query to make the query available in the future under the specified name.

Importing the Data from Your Data Warehouse

After pressing the Save Query button, a Returning External Data to Microsoft Excel dialog box (similar to the one pictured in Figure 24-8) appears. From here, you import the data into the current Excel worksheet, a new worksheet, or a PivotTable report. The data appears in the current worksheet by default; however, you can make another selection simply by clicking its radio button.

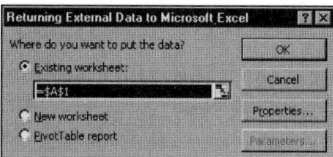

Figure 24-8: The Returning External Data to Microsoft
Excel dialog box gives you options as to where you
want the resulting data placed.

Setting External Data Range Properties

By setting a few key external data range properties, you can virtually eliminate the
need to reformat imported data. Though as you can see in Figure 24-9, many of the
default settings already do the job without you needing to change them.

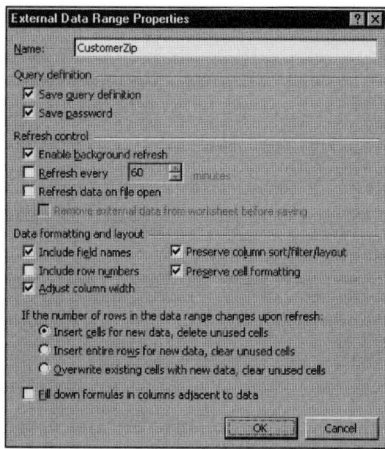

Figure 24-9: The External Data Range Properties dialog box
opens when you press the Properties button.

The only change you may want to consider making is to set the data refresh
options. If your data changes at frequent intervals throughout the day and your
workstation can sustain a constant server connection, this may be a great tool for
making the most current, up-to-date corporate decisions. Your choices include
enabling a background refresh (the default) that updates the data as soon as it
changes; telling Excel to refresh the data at intervals you define (using the arrow
button to choose the desired number of minutes); and instructing Excel to fetch
updated data each time you open the file.

When you finish setting the external data range properties, click OK. To close the
Returning External Data to Microsoft Excel dialog box, click OK again (or for the
first time if you declined setting external data range properties).

About refreshing. Frequent data refreshes may bog down your computer's performance as the refresh vies for CPU resources. Unless you really need current data in order to make accurate and/or beneficial decisions, you may want to pass on frequent data refreshes. Besides, odds are your data won't change so dramatically during your work session that it affects your ultimate decisions anyway.

Introducing the External Data Toolbar

Once the data is returned to your Excel worksheet, a floating External Data toolbar (see Figure 24-10) may appear to assist you in working with the data query results. If the toolbar does not open on its own, you can call on it by right-clicking inside any of Excel's toolbars and then selecting the External Data toolbar. From that point on, you can edit the data query, change the data range properties, and refresh the data by pressing a single button – no multi-menu selections needed!

Edit Query

Query Parameters

Cancel Refresh

Refresh Status

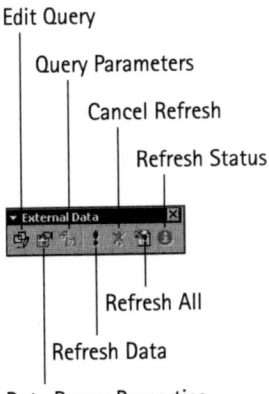

Refresh All

Refresh Data

Data Range Properties

Figure 24-10: The External Data toolbar simplifies many external data operations.

And what's really nice about this toolbar is that it floats. If it should get in the way of your work, you can move it effortlessly by clicking the toolbar's dark blue title bar and dragging it into a new position.

Running a Saved Query

Running saved queries is a common occurrence when the query you execute routinely includes columns that change on a regular basis. For example, the best five customers in each state may change at a moment's notice if you're tapping into your central ordering data warehouse. Sure you can tell Excel to refresh the data for you at specified intervals, but rerunning the query is a good way to conserve system resources while providing an accurate snapshot of your data.

To run a saved query, simply launch a blank worksheet. Run the query by selecting Data → Get External Data → Run Saved Query. The Run Query dialog box shown in Figure 24-11 launches. Click the name of the saved query you want to run and then press the Get Data button. The new results are output to the current Excel worksheet.

Replacing results. If you want to replace the previous results of the data query with the new ones, simply open the worksheet you wish to replace and then select Data → Refresh from Excel's menu bar. Or you can press the Refresh Data button on the External Data toolbar.

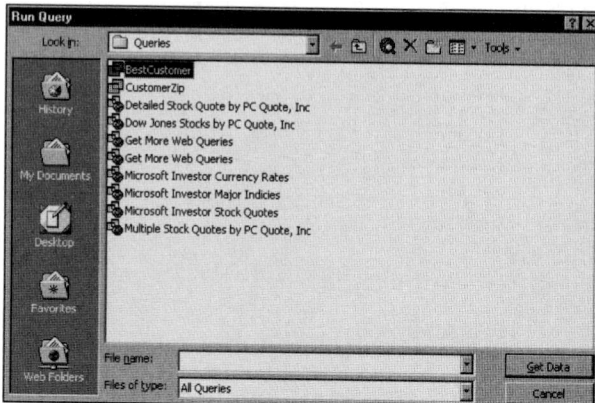

Figure 24-11: The Run Query dialog box closely resembles a standard Microsoft Office 2000 Open dialog box.

Performing Common Analysis Functions in Excel

Now on to the easy part – performing standard Excel operations against the data warehouse results provided by your data query. With the depth and breadth of material residing in a SQL Server database, standard Excel operations such as sorting, filtering, subtotaling, consolidating, and grouping are more valuable and informative than ever before. At last, you have a truly meaningful use for all those slick features that make Excel one of the most powerful data-analysis tools on the market today!

Sorting Your Data

Initially, you may wonder why anyone would sort data in Excel when you can do it in the data query definition. The primary difference lies in the flexibility of data analysis. By sorting the data in Excel, you can import the records from, say, every customer in every state and then have Excel subtotal the sales from each state for you. Because sorted data queries can't perform specific operations such as subtotaling, it may be just as efficient to keep the majority of the work in Excel proper. It also gives you the flexibility to arrange the data any way you want, any time you want.

To begin sorting data within Excel, either open the results of a previously run data query or perform a new data query to populate a fresh worksheet. For maximum control, I suggest you choose the Sort command from Excel's Data menu. It produces a Sort dialog box, as shown in Figure 24-12.

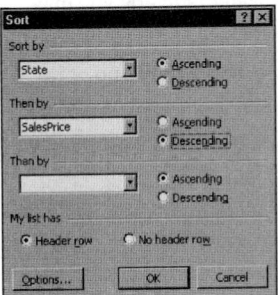

Figure 24-12: The Excel Sort dialog box resembles the Data Query Wizard's Sort Order dialog box.

Work your way through each of the drop-down boxes to select the field you want to sort by and whether you want the records to appear in ascending or descending order. Note that my sort (shown in Figure 24-12) groups the customers by state in ascending alphabetical order by state. Then it requests that customers with the highest dollar amount spent appear first within each state so I can pinpoint the best customers in each state. Press OK to begin sorting by the criteria you defined.

Sort on a single field. To perform a sort using a single field, you can bypass the Sort dialog box altogether. Just click the name of the column by which you want to sort, and then use the Sort buttons on Excel's Standard toolbar to shift the data into the desired position. Click the AZ button to sort the selected field in ascending order, or press the ZA button to sort in descending order. Keep in mind you can sort only one field this way. If you try to perform a second sort using the Sort buttons, it overrides the first sort. You need to call on the Sort dialog box for more complex jobs.

Filtering Your Data Using AutoFilter

Like performing a sort, you also can filter data by defining it in the data query. But again, you may benefit from including a wide range of records in your data query and then using Excel to wheedle the data down into more manageable chunks. Because filtering data is a bit more complicated than sorting it, you definitely will appreciate working with AutoFilter on this one.

Begin the data filtering process by choosing the Filter → AutoFilter commands from Excel's Data menu. Note that tiny arrow buttons now appear next to each column label (see Figure 24-13). To filter the data, click the arrow button immediately to the right of the field by which you want to filter and select the item from the list you want to keep from the drop-down menu.

TIP

AutoFilter shortcut. If you plan to make use of AutoFilter regularly, you may want to go ahead and add a button for it on Excel's Standard toolbar. You can do this by clicking the Add/Remove arrow button at the right end of the Standard toolbar. Select the Add/Remove menu item to open the list of buttons available to you. Click AutoFilter to select it, and then click outside the menu to close it. The AutoFilter button now appears on your Standard toolbar, making it a snap to open and close AutoFilter any time you want.

	Zip	SalesPrice	SystemCour	FirstName	LastName	CustomerI	Stat	CustomerTypeDesc
2	20010	1789.7756	1	Janet	Adams	4583	DC	Small Busi
13	20791	1675.2422	1	Cathy	Adams	3021	MD	Small Busi
20	20818	1542.0507	1	Bo	Adams	6888	MD	Small Busi
22	20818	11221.196	7	Hugh	Adams	1222	MD	Small Busi
23	20818	11266.0446	7	Grant	Adams	3454	MD	Small Busi
36	20849	4889.4186	4	Paul	Adams	10910	MD	Small Busi
40	20850	4534.2471	3	Scott	Adams	8659	MD	Small Busi
41	20850	5196	3	Lewis	Adams	56	MD	Small Busi
49	20866	3928.346	3	Julian	Adams	12826	MD	Small Busi
56	20878	2603.43	2	Jeremy	Adams	11924	MD	Small Busi
57	20878	3611.0551	2	Pamela	Adams	4421	MD	Small Busi
62	20895	6724.7098	5	Lisa	Adams	15016	MD	Small Busi
73	21042	8775.482	6	Carl	Adams	776	MD	Small Busi
88	20705	5730.7955	4	Dennis	Adderley	10241	MD	Small Busi
99	20818	4772.3512	3	Edward	Adderley	6913	MD	Small Busi
100	20830	6242.2474	4	Frank	Adderley	4990	MD	Small Busi
101	20841	1158.3471	1	Elvis	Adderley	2317	MD	Small Busi
103	20841	2794.2326	2	Patrice	Adderley	10882	MD	Small Busi

Figure 24-13: AutoFilter's arrow buttons function like standard drop-down boxes.

The AutoFilter list includes a list of the values displayed in the column. Selecting any of these values will automatically hide all other values in the column. You can also select (Blanks) and (NonBlanks), which will hide all blank cells and all non-blank cells, respectively. Selecting (All) will restore all of the values that were previously hidden by AutoFilter. Two of the options (Top 10...) and (Custom...) are discussed in more detail below.

CREATING YOUR OWN TOP 10 LIST

Selecting (Top 10...) from the AutoFilter drop-down box, will display the dialog box shown in Figure 24-14. This dialog box is used to automatically hide all of the values in the column except for the ones that meet the criteria specified in the Top 10 AutoFilter dialog box. You can do any of the following:

◆ Whether you want the top or the bottom records in the selected field

◆ Whether you want the top or bottom 10 (the default number); you can use the arrow buttons to adjust the number to meet your specific needs

◆ Whether you want the results figured by item or by percentage

Once the desired settings are in place, click OK to apply the filter as defined.

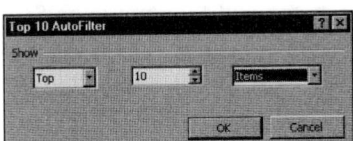

Figure 24-14: The Top 10 AutoFilter name is a bit misleading because the feature can do so much more.

CUSTOMIZING YOUR AUTOFILTER OPTIONS

For more complex or multistep filtering, you may want to customize your AutoFilter. To do this, click the primary field you want to work with, click the AutoFilter arrow button, and then select Customize from the list. The Customize AutoFilter dialog box shown in Figure 24-15 appears.

Use the drop-down boxes on the left to set a condition for the filter (such as equals, greater than, and so on). In the drop-down boxes on the right, choose the values to which the records should be compared. If, for example, you want to produce a list of customers who spent more than $2,500 with JustPC, enable AutoFilter and use the SalesPrice arrow button to choose the Customize option. Once in the Customize AutoFilter dialog box, choose *is greater than* for the first drop-down box, and then enter 2500 into the second drop-down box. When you finish setting the desired options, click OK to apply the filter.

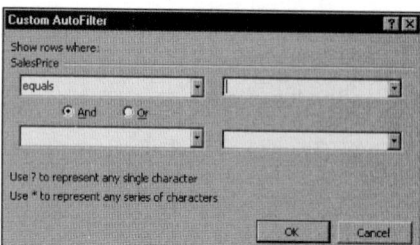

Figure 24-15: The Customize AutoFilter dialog box gives you maximum filtering capabilities.

Creating Subtotals for Your Data

When many people hear the word "subtotal", money pops into mind – especially for those of us who have spent significant time generating balance sheets or budgets. In Excel 2000, however, the Subtotal tool can do much more. To follow through with our JustPC example, you can use the Subtotal function to find the number of customers in each town or zip code; the average amount of money spent by customers from a certain area; and so on.

The first thing you need to do before setting your Subtotal options is to sort the worksheet by the field you want to subtotal. If you plan to count the number of customers from each zip code, click the zip column name and then press the Sort Ascending option. From there, you need to click Data, Subtotals to launch the Subtotal dialog box (pictured in Figure 24-16). Use the *At each change in* drop-down box to select the field containing the data you want to group by (Zip, in the case of our example). The *Use function* drop-down box is where you specify what kind of subtotal you're looking for – Count, Average, Minimum, and so on. And finally, the *Add subtotal to* drop-down box is where you tell Excel which data to perform the selected operation on (CustomerID instructs Excel count the number of customers from each zip code). Click OK to have Excel calculate the subtotals you requested. You can remove the subtotals later on by simply opening the Subtotal dialog box again and pressing the Remove All button.

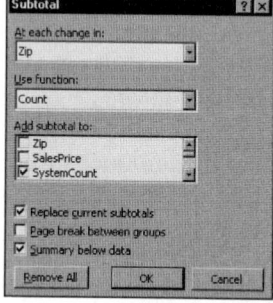

Figure 24-16: The Subtotal dialog box can count, add, and average, and do a bunch of other things as well.

Summary

This chapter introduced many ways you can set up Excel 2000 to perform data analysis using your SQL Server 7 data warehouse. You learned how to connect Excel to your data source, how to define database queries that retrieve the data you want, and how to perform basic Excel operations of the data you import.

In the next chapter, you learn how to build simple PivotTables using the OLAP database. I start by explaining what a PivotTable is and how it can help you tap into the wealth of information hidden in your OLAP database. I go on to demonstrate how to connect to your OLAP server, as well as how to manipulate and format your PivotTables.

Chapter 25

Building Simple PivotTables

IN THIS CHAPTER

- ◆ Introducing PivotTables
- ◆ Getting data from your OLAP server
- ◆ Creating a simple PivotTable
- ◆ Slicing and dicing your PivotTable

WHILE YOU CAN IMPORT data from your data warehouse directly into Excel, the true power of using Excel to analyze your data lies in connecting it to OLAP Services. You can use Excel PivotTables to view your OLAP cubes.

Introducing OLAP PivotTables

An Excel PivotTable provides a way to look at multidimensional data (see Figure 25-1). In the past, PivotTables were created with data from a worksheet. In Excel 2000, you can link to an OLAP cube defined in OLAP Services. Unlike regular Excel PivotTables, OLAP PivotTables are stored on the OLAP server. This means you can process larger sets of data than you can process in a regular Excel PivotTable. However, this also means that the only way you can use an OLAP cube in Excel is as a PivotTable or PivotChart.

The PivotTable is broken into four main areas:

- ◆ Data Area
- ◆ Row Area
- ◆ Column Area
- ◆ Page Area

The data area holds measures from your cube, while the remaining areas hold information from dimensions. The row and column areas hold the dimensions that you want to examine in detail on the PivotTable, while the page area holds dimensions whose values are fixed. Each of the areas can hold one or more fields.

Page Area   Column Area

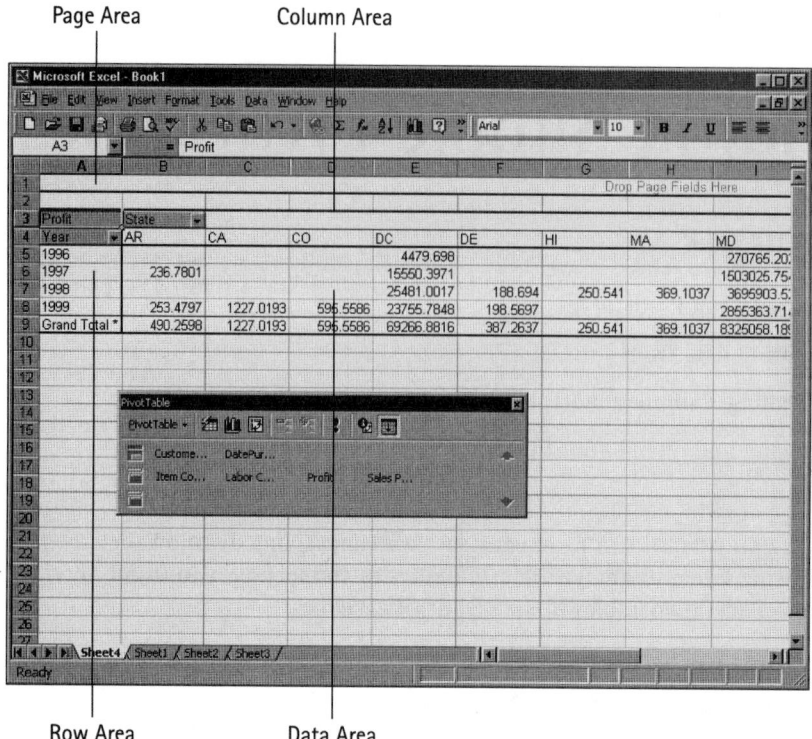

Row Area   Data Area

Figure 25-1: A typical Excel PivotTable

The OLAP server does most of the processing of the data, leaving Excel to handle the formatting and presentation of the cube's data. Each time you change the way the data is displayed in your PivotTable, Excel requests a fresh copy of the data from the OLAP server.

There are other minor differences in terms of how Excel handles OLAP PivotTables, when compared to regular PivotTables, but none are really significant. Mostly they result from limitations imposed by using OLAP Services, not Excel, to perform the data aggregation. For instance, you can't define new calculated fields in your PivotTable. You must define them in the cube itself. Because this is how the Cube Browser works, you should just think of Excel as a more powerful version of the Cube Browser.

Getting Data from Your OLAP Server

You use the same basic technique for getting data from your OLAP server as you do for getting data from the data warehouse. The Get External Data function performs both tasks. However, due to the nature of OLAP Services, you see a few different dialog boxes along the way.

Choosing a Data Source

To load data into an Excel PivotTable, choose Data → Get External Data → New Database Query from Excel's main menu. This displays the Choose Data Source dialog box. Select the OLAP Cubes tab, as shown in Figure 25-2.

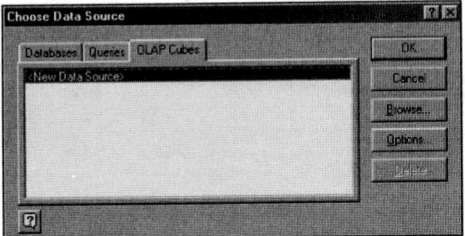

Figure 25-2: Getting external data from your OLAP cube

If you already defined an OLAP data source that you want to use, you can select it and continue with the next section, "Adding the Cube to Your Worksheet." Otherwise, you need to select <New Data Source> and press OK to display the Create New Data Source dialog box.

DEFINING AN OLAP DATA SOURCE

In the Create New Data Source dialog box, you need to name your data source and select an OLAP provider (see Figure 25-3). The name you choose for your data source shouldn't conflict with any other data sources you create. Then you need to select an OLAP provider. Choose Microsoft OLE DB Provider for OLAP Services. This should be the only provider on the list.

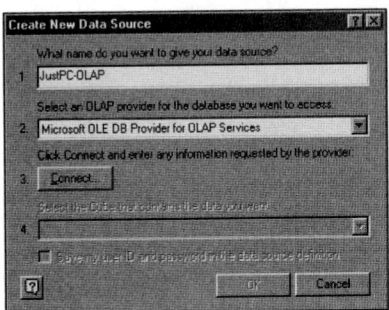

Figure 25-3: Creating a new data source

ESTABLISHING A MULTIDIMENSIONAL CONNECTION

Once you select your provider and name the data source, press the Connect button to connect to the database. This displays the Multi-Dimensional Connection Wizard shown in Figure 25-4. Select OLAP Server and specify the name of your OLAP server.

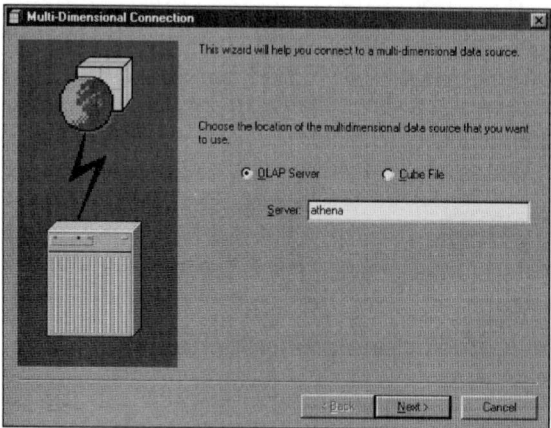

Figure 25-4: Specifying the location of your OLAP server

CHOOSING YOUR OLAP DATABASE

In the next step of the wizard, you need to choose the name of your OLAP database (see Figure 25-5). Pressing Finish returns you to the Create New Data Source window shown in Figure 25-3. Select the cube you want to use and press OK to finish creating your data source.

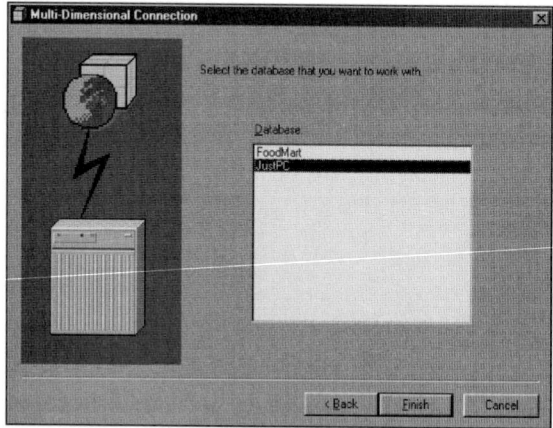

Figure 25-5: Choosing the OLAP database you want to use

About saving. You can opt to save your database login information with the data source. Don't do it. This information is stored on your computer in an unencrypted file so anyone could read the file and get your passwords.

Adding the Cube to Your Worksheet

Now that you've selected the cube you want to analyze, you need to add it to your worksheet and select layout and options. The Get External Data Source Wizard jumps to the last step of the PivotTable and PivotChart Wizard (see Figure 25-6).

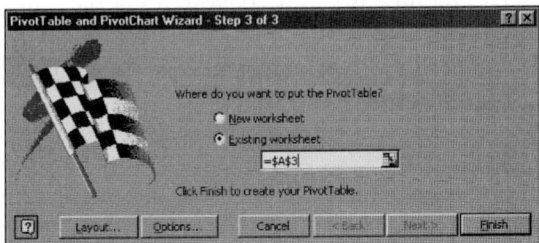

Figure 25-6: Placing your PivotTable in your workbook

PLACING YOUR PIVOTTABLE

You have two options for placing your PivotTable. You can place it on the current worksheet starting with a particular cell or you can create a new worksheet with your PivotTable. I prefer to place PivotTables on separate worksheets because it makes it easier for me to deal with multiple PivotTables in a single workbook.

SETTING THE PIVOTTABLE'S INITIAL LAYOUT

Pressing the Layout button on the PivotTable and PivotChart Wizard displays the window shown in Figure 25-7. Using this window, you can define the initial layout of your PivotTable. While you don't have to set up your PivotTable this way, it does make it easier to use once the data is loaded.

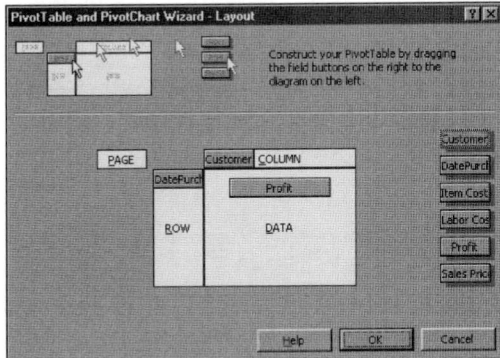

Figure 25-7: Defining the PivotTable's initial layout

You can see a list of the data fields that can be displayed in the PivotTable on the right side of the window. To add a field to your PivotTable, simply click the field and drag it onto an area of the PivotTable where you want the field displayed. You can drag dimension fields only onto the Column, Row, and Page areas and measures only onto the Data area.

You can drag multiple fields onto each of the areas; however, they must be the right fields for the area. I suggest that you only drag one field into the Data area until you are more comfortable using PivotTables.

Once you're satisfied with the layout of your PivotTable, press the OK button to return to the last step of the PivotTable and PivotChart Wizard.

SETTING PIVOTTABLE OPTIONS

Pressing the Options button displays the PivotTable Options window (see Figure 25-8). Not all of the options available for regular Excel PivotTables are available for OLAP PivotTables.

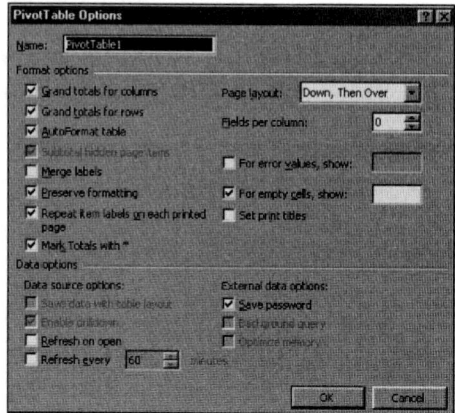

Figure 25-8: Setting options for your PivotTable

TIP

Exercise your options. You can display this same option window by selecting PivotTable → Table Options from the floating PivotTable toolbar.

You can choose to display grand totals for both columns and rows by checking or unchecking the *Grand totals for columns* and *Grand totals for rows* checkboxes. When you close the PivotTable Options window, Excel applies your changes to the PivotTable.

The *AutoFormat* checkbox instructs Excel to reapply the AutoFormat you select when you change the view of your table.

Subtotal hidden page items isn't available with OLAP based PivotTables.

Checking *Merge labels* on the form displays the total labels in the PivotTable of a single cell that stretches across the range of levels corresponding to the subtotal. This makes it easier to read the information in your PivotTable.

The *Preserve formatting* option preserves how you format the PivotTable as you change its layout or refresh the data. If you don't check this option, you may lose the formatting.

Repeat item labels on each printed pages does exactly what it says and is recommended when you print your PivotTables.

You also can choose to add an asterisk to the end of any total label by checking *Mark Totals with *.

The *Page layout* option controls allows you to control how your PivotTable will be printed if it occupies more than a single page. Your PivotTable will be broken into a series of columns and rows that are one page wide and one page high. Then the multiple pages can be either printed one column at a time (Down, Then Over) or one row at a time (Over, Then Down).

You can choose which values are displayed for missing data and invalid data by placing a checkmark in the *For empty cells, show:* and *For error values, show:* checkboxes and then specifying a string for display in the cell. Note that these values are for display purposes only and are not included in any calculations.

When checked, the *Set print titles* option repeats the titles at the start of each column and row on each page sent to the printer.

In the Data source options section of the dialog box, you can tell Excel to refresh the data in your PivotTable automatically when the PivotTable is opened. Or you can let Excel automatically refresh the data at intervals you specify. Setting either of these options can be useful in some cases, but I wouldn't bother because Excel automatically loads the most current data from the cube each time you change how it is displayed. You can also instruct Excel to save your password to the database along with the PivotTable, so you don't need to supply the password each time you open the workbook.

FINISHING YOUR PIVOTTABLE

Once you select the options you want, press OK to save the values. Then press Finish to build the PivotTable. Excel starts the OLAP query to build your PivotTable. Depending on the size of the cube and the hardware you have, it may take a few moments to finish. When the query is completed, Excel displays a PivotTable similar to the one in Figure 25-9.

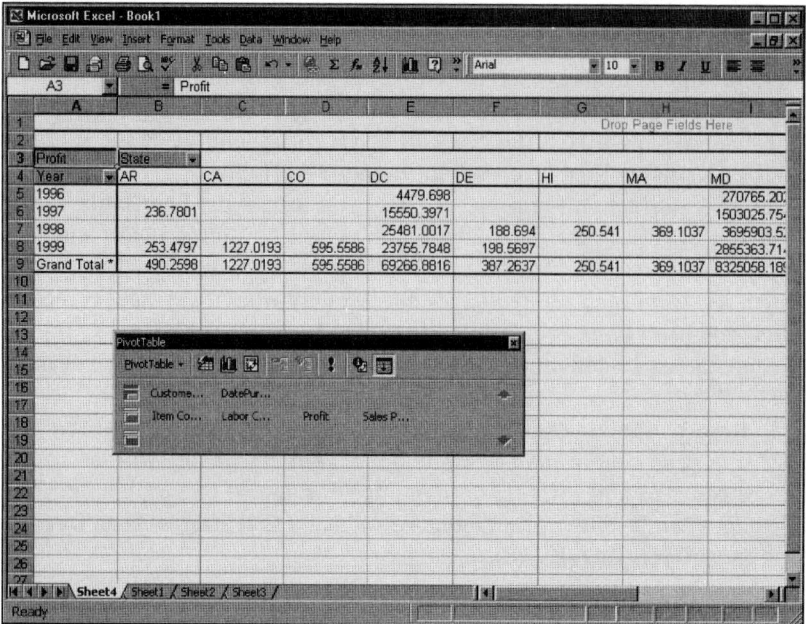

Figure 25-9: Displaying your PivotTable

Exploring Your PivotTable

Like all PivotTables, OLAP PivotTables show you only summary information when you first create them. However, like the Cube Editor, you easily can drill-down into the cube to see the how the data is derived. You also can drag-and-drop various columns, rows, and pages around the PivotTable until you find the information you want.

PivotTable Fields

There are two types of PivotTable fields. In Excel, these are known as *data fields* and *non-data fields*. They are displayed in the data area and the non-data area on the floating toolbar (see Figure 25-10). Pressing the Show/Hide Fields button toggles the display of the fields on the bottom of the toolbar.

The icon at the start of each row indicates the type of fields that are stored in that row. The data area contains fields that you can display in the data area of the PivotTable. These fields are known as *measures* in the cube. The non-data area contains dimension fields from the cube. If your cube has more than three rows of fields, the scroll buttons are enabled so you can scroll through the available fields.

To change your PivotTable, simply drag a field from the toolbar onto the PivotTable in the appropriate area. Excel automatically queries the OLAP server to get the requested information.

Hide Details

Show Details

Non-Data Area   Show/Hide Fields

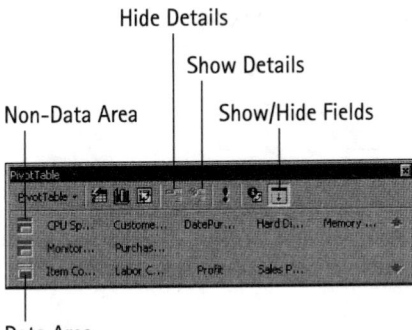

Data Area

Figure 25-10: Using the undocked PivotTable toolbar

 **TIP**

Easy reading. Sometimes you may find a PivotTable with multiple fields in the data area easier to read if you place all of the dimensions in the row area and don't include any in the column area. Each data area would appear in its own column, making it easier to compare values for the same combination of dimensions.

Slicing Your Cube

When you first load your cube into Excel, all you see is summary information. The dimensions you assign to be columns, rows, and pages when you create the PivotTable are displayed on the worksheet. The dimensions that you don't assign anywhere are implicitly assigned to the page area. This means that the information displayed in the PivotTable reflects all possible values for these other dimensions.

When analyzing the data in your PivotTable, you often may want to restrict the data in the page area so that you can look at other information more closely. This is analogous to carving a slice from the center of the cube, and it known as *slicing the cube.*

Figure 25-11 shows a PivotTable based on sales information from the JustPC application. While the values for each year and state are shown in the data area of the PivotTable, the cube was sliced using the Customer Type dimension so that you can view only individual customers.

To select a particular value for a dimension in the page area, press the drop-down arrow to display a list of values in the dimension (see Figure 25-12). Then select the value you want to use to restrict the dimension. You can expand the plus signs to choose a more specific value. When you find the value you want, press OK to close the selection window. Excel then sends a query to the OLAP server to get a fresh copy of the data with the new restrictions applied and displays the newly requested information in the PivotTable.

If you choose the first value, in this case All Customer Type, you remove all restrictions on this particular dimension and the PivotTable is updated accordingly.

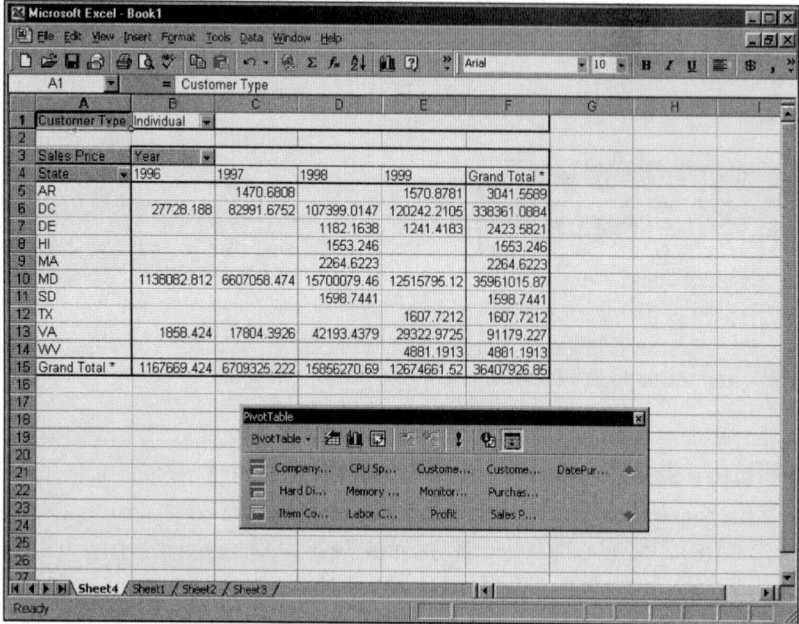

Figure 25-11: Looking at sales by year and state for individual customers

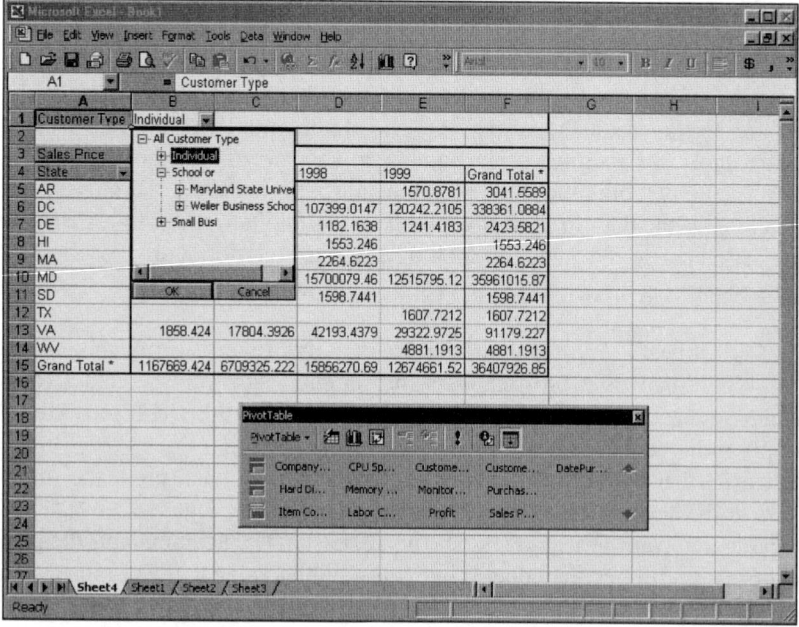

Figure 25-12: Choosing a slice of your cube

 **About values.** You can select only a single value for each dimension in the page area.

Drilling Down into Your Cube

Looking at the summary information in the data area can be interesting, but usually you want to see the underlying data values that make up a particular value in the data area. This process is known as *drilling down* into your cube.

When you drill-down into your cube, you take a dimension in the row or column area and expand one or more of the values to expose the new lower level in the hierarchy. You can do this by pressing the down arrow next to the field and selecting the values you want to include in the display (see Figure 25-13).

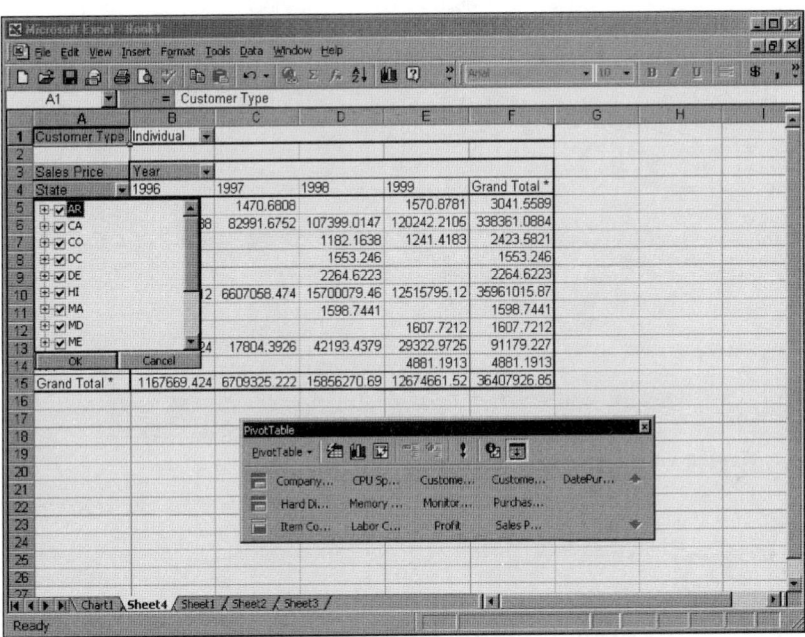

Figure 25-13: Drilling down for more detailed information about a customer's location

Inside the display, the highest level of your dimensions is listed. By clicking the plus sign next to one of the values, you expose the child values on the next level. You can repeat this process until you reach the lowest level.

Beside each value you can place one checkmark, two checkmarks, or no checkmarks. You cycle through the checkmarks by clicking the box. One checkmark means that the value is displayed, while two checkmarks denote that all of the values at the next lower level are displayed. Of course, no checkmarks mean that the value isn't displayed.

Another way to expand a row or column is to double-click a cell in the row area or column area. Consequently, all of the child cells at the next lower level are displayed. You also can select the cell that you want to show the details for and press the Show Details button on the toolbar.

In Figure 25-14, I expanded the Customer Location dimension to include only Washington, D.C., Maryland, and Virginia. It also shows the cities in Virginia of the individual customers.

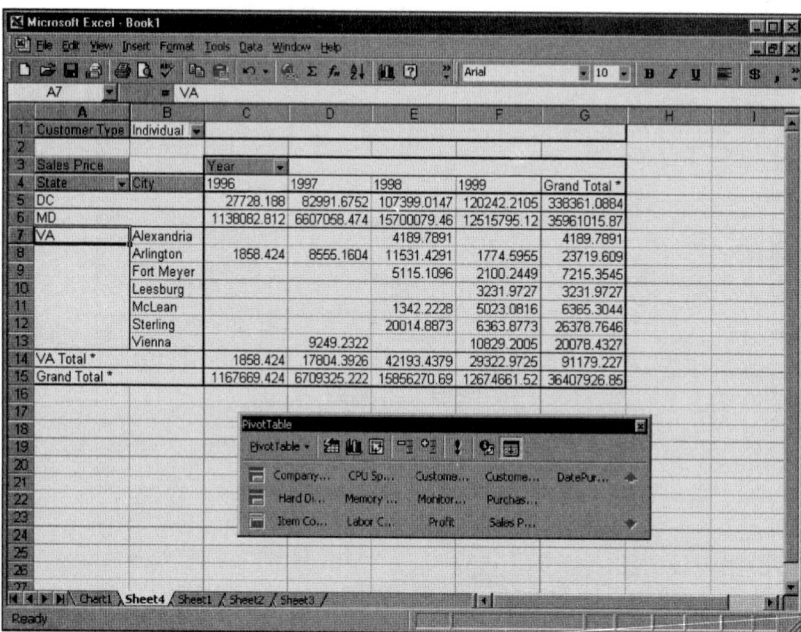

Figure 25-14: Viewing Virginia cities for individual customers

Summary

This chapter showed you how to create a PivotTable in Excel using a cube on the OLAP server. It also covered some basic operations to perform with your cube, such as slicing the cube to look at a more specific subset of data and drilling down to see the more detailed information in the cube.

In the next chapter, I continue my discussion of PivotTables by covering how to format the data and detailing some tricks that make data analysis much easier.

Chapter 26

Extracting Information from PivotTables

IN THIS CHAPTER

- ◆ Formatting PivotTables
- ◆ Computing other statistics
- ◆ Offline access to a cube

ONCE YOU CREATE YOUR OLAP-based PivotTable, it's time to try extracting information from it. Extracting information from a PivotTable can be easy or hard; it really depends on the data in the cube. However, Excel includes a number of tools that can make it easier to use your PivotTable that, in turn, can help you find the information you seek.

Exploring the PivotTable Toolbar

Like all toolbars in Excel, the PivotTable toolbar can be *docked* with the other toolbars at the top of the worksheet or *undocked* and floating somewhere on your screen. While most toolbars contain the same options when undocked, the PivotTable toolbar displays the fields available from the OLAP cube (see Figure 26-1).

Formatting a PivotTable

A common problem with most Excel worksheets is that they can be difficult to read, especially if you have a lot of data. To combat this problem, Excel includes an AutoFormat tool that enables you to choose from a variety of standard PivotTable formats. Once an AutoFormat is applied, it automatically adapts to changes to your PivotTable. This is very useful because manual formatting changes are often lost when you add another field to the table or change how the information is displayed.

ADDING AN AUTOFORMAT
You can press the Format Report button or choose PivotTable → Format Report from the PivotTable toolbar. This displays the AutoFormat dialog box as shown in Figure 26-2. To apply the AutoFormat, simply choose a style and press the OK button.

391

PivotTable
Menu Items

Hide
Detail

Show
Detail

Field settings

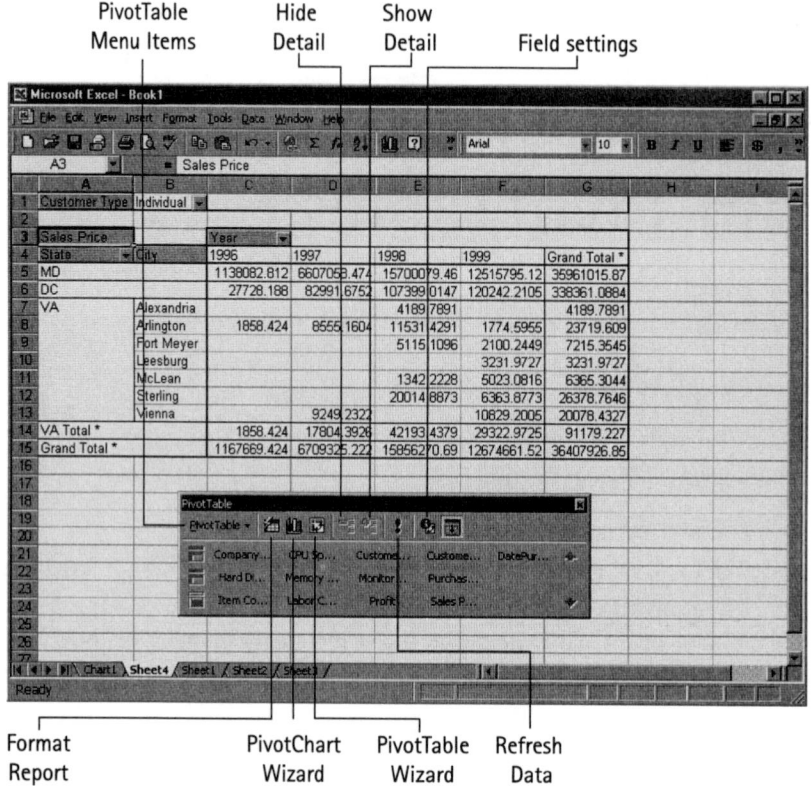

Format
Report

PivotChart
Wizard

PivotTable
Wizard

Refresh
Data

Figure 26-1: Using the undocked PivotTable toolbar

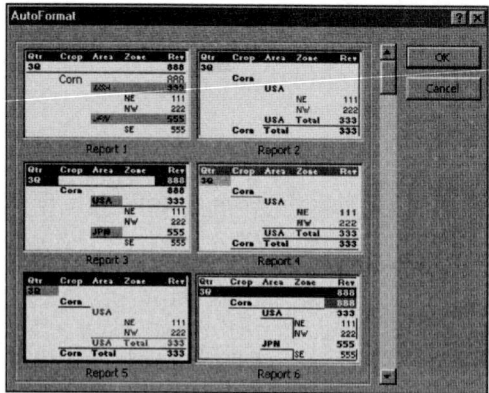

Figure 26-2: Choosing a format for your PivotTable

You can choose from 10 report styles and 10 table styles. Report styles merge your column dimensions with the row dimensions to create a document in which the labels run down the left side of the document (State and Year), and the data is displayed as a series of columns on the right side (Sales Price, Profit, Item Cost, and Labor Cost). This can be seen in Figure 26.3.

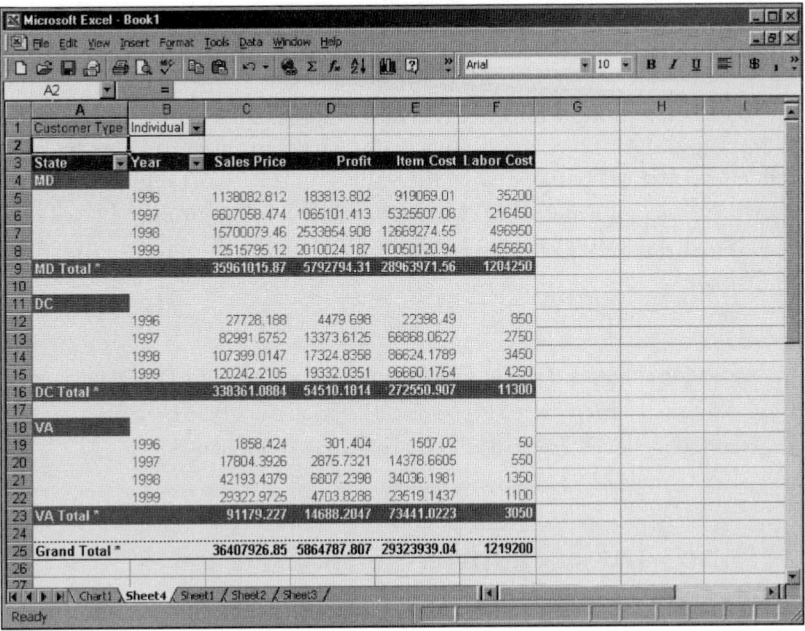

Figure 26-3: Using a report style to convey multiple measures

Table styles, on the other hand, format your PivotTable as a two-dimensional table with labels above and to the left of the data values. Like the report styles, you can choose from a number of different styles.

Matters of style. The report styles can make a PivotTable with multiple measures displayed in the data area much easier to read, while the table styles lend themselves to displaying information in a more compact format.

REMOVING AN AUTOFORMAT

To remove the AutoFormat, simply choose PivotTable → Table Options from the floating PivotTable toolbar and uncheck the AutoFormat field. This removes all of the AutoFormat formatting from your PivotTable and restores it to Excel's default formatting. You can elect to apply an AutoFormat of none or PivotTable Classic from the AutoFormat dialog box to return your PivotTable to normal.

PivotTable and PivotChart Wizards

Clicking the PivotTable Wizard button creates a new PivotTable using the same data source as your current PivotTable. You may find this useful if you want to create a new PivotTable to examine your data differently from your current Pivot-Table. Clicking the Chart Wizard icon creates a new PivotChart. Chapter 25 provides more information about this feature.

Recalculate

Pressing the Recalculate button on the PivotTable toolbar gets a fresh copy of the cube's data from the OLAP server. This isn't really necessary in most cases because it is impossible to delete or change any of the values on the PivotTable. However, if you process your cube using the OLAP Manager, while working on the PivotTable, you should press the Refresh button on the PivotTable toolbar to get the latest contents of the cube.

Accepting changes. If you make a change to your cube using OLAP Manager, the changes aren't reflected in your Excel PivotTable until you get a fresh copy of the cube. A quick way to do this is to press the Recalculate button.

Field Settings for Measures

The PivotTable Field dialog box enables you to tweak how the information from a particular field is displayed in your PivotTable. To display the dialog box, double-click the field's display name in the PivotTable or select the field and choose PivotTable → Field Settings from the floating PivotTable toolbar (see Figure 26-4).

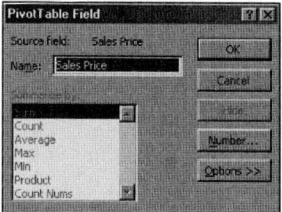

Figure 26-4: Reviewing field settings for a measure

Some of the settings in the dialog box are disabled because they are available only when you access a non-OLAP data source.

Changing the value in the Name text box doesn't change the underlying data values displayed in the PivotTable or data field the values are derived from – but it does make the PivotTable easier to use for others who are unfamiliar with your cube. By default, the initial value for Name is the same as the name of the source field.

CHOOSING A NUMBER FORMAT

If you have a numeric value, you can press the Number button to display the Format Cells dialog box (see Figure 26-5). This value is used as the default format for that data field. When compared with the chart in Figure 26-3, the chart in Figure 26-6 is much easier to read. The only thing I did was to change the default number format to Currency.

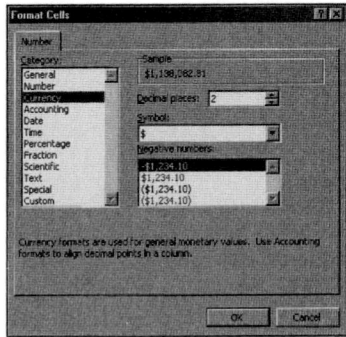

Figure 26-5: Setting a default numeric format for a data field

State	Year	Sales Price	Profit	Item Cost	Labor Cost
MD	1996	$1,138,082.81	$183,813.80	$919,069.01	$35,200.00
	1997	$6,607,058.47	$1,065,101.41	$5,325,507.06	$216,450.00
	1998	$15,700,079.46	$2,533,854.91	$12,669,274.55	$496,950.00
	1999	$12,515,795.12	$2,010,024.19	$10,050,120.94	$455,650.00
MD Total *		$35,961,015.87	$5,792,794.31	$28,963,971.56	$1,204,250.00
DC	1996	$27,728.19	$4,479.70	$22,398.49	$850.00
	1997	$82,991.68	$13,373.61	$66,868.06	$2,750.00
	1998	$107,399.01	$17,324.84	$86,624.18	$3,450.00
	1999	$120,242.21	$19,332.04	$96,660.18	$4,250.00
DC Total *		$338,361.09	$54,510.18	$272,550.91	$11,300.00
VA	1996	$1,858.42	$301.40	$1,507.02	$50.00
	1997	$17,804.39	$2,875.73	$14,378.66	$650.00
	1998	$42,193.44	$6,807.24	$34,036.20	$1,350.00
	1999	$29,322.97	$4,703.83	$23,519.14	$1,100.00
VA Total *		$91,179.23	$14,688.20	$73,441.02	$3,050.00
Grand Total *		$36,407,926.85	$5,864,787.81	$29,323,939.04	$1,219,200.00

Figure 26-6: Changing a general, formatted number to currency can make a big difference in how your PivotTable looks.

You can override this value by explicitly setting a format on the PivotTable itself; but if you change how your PivotTable is displayed, you may find that your table is only partially formatted.

CUSTOM CALCULATIONS

While you can't define your own calculated fields in your OLAP PivotTable, Excel provides a list of custom calculations that help you translate your data from a simple number into a more meaningful value. This part of the dialog box normally is hidden, but you can display it by pressing the Options button (see Figure 26-7).

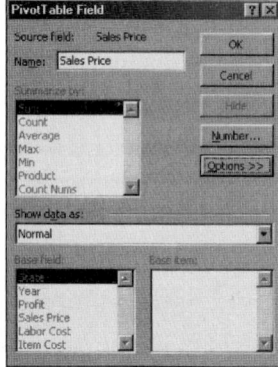

Figure 26-7: Defining a custom calculation

Simply select the type of custom calculation you want to apply in the *Show data as:* drop-down box. Then specify any other parameters that may be required to perform the calculation. You can choose from any of these custom calculations:

- **Normal** displays the value as retrieved by the OLAP query. Selecting this option undoes any custom calculation you previously selected.

- **Difference from** computes the difference between the current cell value and one of the values from the chart. You choose the value by selecting an item from the Base field section that contains the value. Then select one of the values in the Base item section of the dialog box.

- **% of** computes the relative percentage between the value in the current cell and another cell in the PivotTable that you specify by choosing values for the Base field and Base item sections.

- **% difference from** computes the difference between the current cell value and the value specified by the Base field and Base item and displays it as the relative percentage of the base item.

- **Running total in** computes a running total for the specified data field.
- **% of row** computes the cell's display value as the relative percentage of the total for the row.
- **% of column** computes the cell's display value as the relative percentage of the total for the column.
- **% of total** computes the cell's display value as the relative percentage of the grand total for the PivotTable.
- **Index** computes the cell's display value according to the following formula: `((value in cell) x (Grand Total)) / ((Row Total) x (Column Total))`

Using the JustPC database, I created a PivotTable that shows the relative percentage of sales for each state by year. By choosing the *% of column* custom calculation, you can easily see that over 97 percent of the sales were to customers in Maryland (see Figure 26-8). While you can extract this information directly from the dollar amounts, computing the percentages really drives the point home.

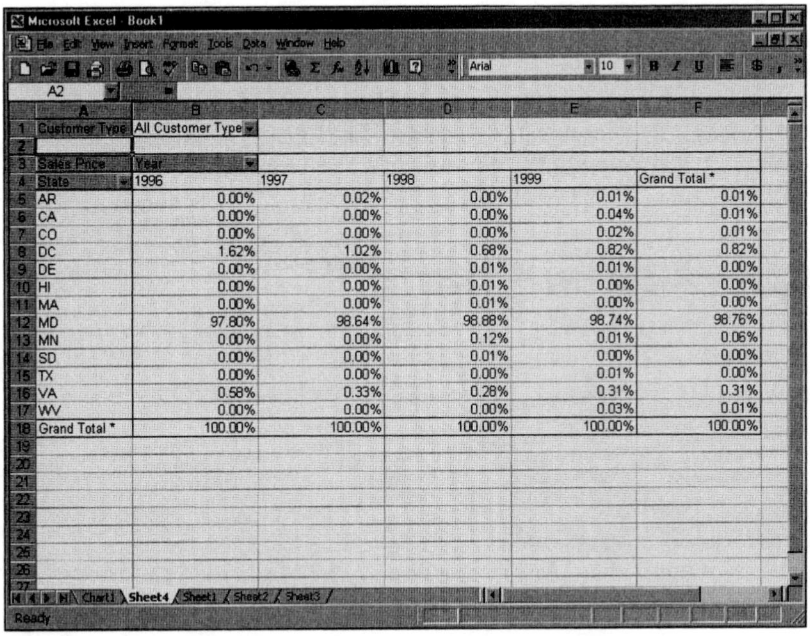

State	1996	1997	1998	1999	Grand Total *
AR	0.00%	0.02%	0.00%	0.01%	0.01%
CA	0.00%	0.00%	0.00%	0.04%	0.01%
CO	0.00%	0.00%	0.00%	0.02%	0.01%
DC	1.62%	1.02%	0.68%	0.82%	0.82%
DE	0.00%	0.00%	0.01%	0.01%	0.00%
HI	0.00%	0.00%	0.01%	0.00%	0.00%
MA	0.00%	0.00%	0.01%	0.00%	0.00%
MD	97.80%	98.64%	98.88%	98.74%	98.76%
MN	0.00%	0.00%	0.12%	0.01%	0.06%
SD	0.00%	0.00%	0.01%	0.00%	0.00%
TX	0.00%	0.00%	0.00%	0.01%	0.00%
VA	0.58%	0.33%	0.28%	0.31%	0.31%
WV	0.00%	0.00%	0.00%	0.03%	0.01%
Grand Total *	100.00%	100.00%	100.00%	100.00%	100.00%

Figure 26-8: Viewing the relative sales for each state

Field Settings for Dimensions

You also can tweak how dimension fields are displayed in your PivotTable using the PivotTable Field dialog box (see Figure 26-9). You change the display name of the field by changing the value in the Name text box.

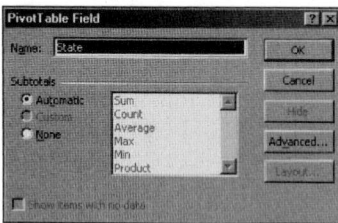

Figure 26-9: Choosing settings for dimension fields

You also can decide whether to display subtotals for the field by choosing the Automatic or None radio buttons. Because the subtotals are extracted from the OLAP cube, you can't choose a custom setting. By default, the subtotals are displayed.

AUTOSORT AND AUTOSHOW

Pressing the Advanced button displays the PivotTable Field Advanced Options dialog box, as shown in Figure 26-10. This dialog box contains three sets of options, one of which (Page field options) is disabled for OLAP cubes. The remaining options – AutoSort and AutoShow – control how the information is displayed in your PivotTable.

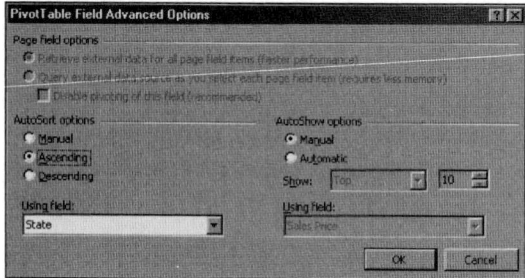

Figure 26-10: Setting AutoSort and AutoShow options

AutoSort controls how the individual cells are displayed within the particular field. You can choose to sort your data based on the values in the dimension column or data column. Choosing Manual restores the sort order to the way in which you retrieved it from the OLAP cube.

AutoShow enables you to show or hide rows or columns based on the values in a particular field. With this option, you can specify the number of rows you want to display and choose whether they should have the highest or lowest values in the table. Choosing Manual displays all of the rows or columns that you normally see.

In Figure 26-11, I chose to display only the top three rows for the State dimension based on the profit data field. I also specified that the data be sorted in ascending order by profit.

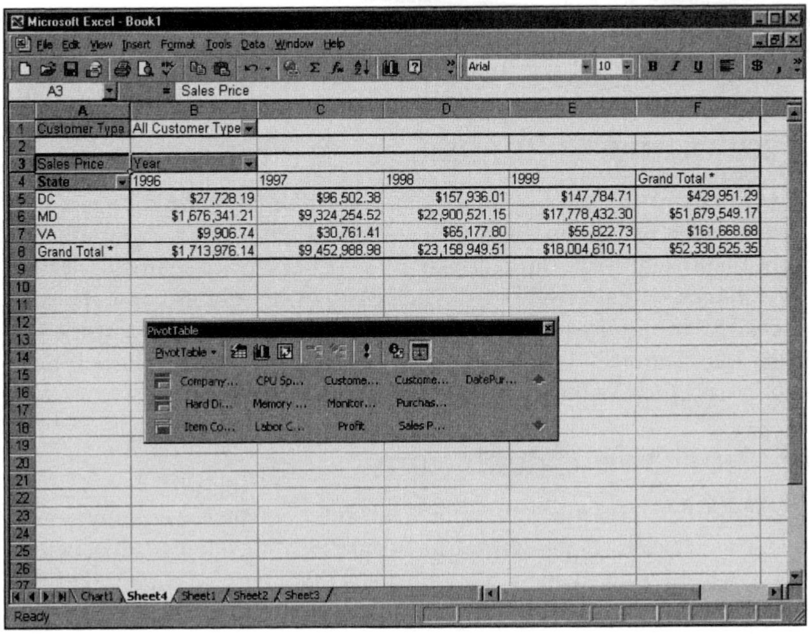

Figure 26-11: Choosing the top three states for JustPC

Tweaking Your PivotTable

While many of the standard Excel tools don't work with an OLAP PivotTable, there are a lot of tools that do work with it. These can help you improve the readability of your PivotTable. This is especially true when you want to print your PivotTable or publish it to the Internet.

Moving Rows and Columns

While you can use AutoSort to order your values within a dimension, you also can drag-and-drop a column or a row from one place in the PivotTable to another. This technique provides an alternate order to your PivotTable that AutoSort can't provide.

To drag-and-drop a row or column, first turn off AutoSort; otherwise you are prevented from making any changes. Next, click the heading for the row or column you wish to move. You may drag the cell anywhere within its current level. If there are any lower levels from the hierarchy displayed beneath the cell you are moving, they automatically are moved along with the cell.

Saving changes. Changing your view of the cube may cause your changes to be lost, so exercise care when making these changes.

Hiding Rows and Columns

You can hide rows and columns easily in your PivotTable by selecting the row or columns to be hidden and choosing Format → Row → Hide or Format → Column → Hide from the main menu. You can redisplay a hidden row or column by selecting the rows or columns on either side of the hidden rows or columsn and choosing Format → Row → Hide or Format → Column → Hide from the main menu. While you may lose this information if you change how the PivotTable is displayed, these options may be easier to use than the Show and Hide Details buttons.

Adding Your Own Calculations

You can't modify the calculations in your PivotTable, but there isn't any reason why you can't use the PivotTable values in calculations outside the PivotTable. I find this useful when I want to add a set of numbers that aren't summarized as part of a field.

No grand total? Disable *Grand totals for columns* and *Grand totals for rows* when trying to include multiple values from the PivotTable in an external formula. This prevents you from adding a grand total.

Printing PivotTables

Printing a PivotTable is identical to printing a worksheet. All of the same tricks including setting the print area (File → Print Area) and previewing your output (File → Print Preview) work the same way for PivotTables as for regular worksheets.

 **More than one page?** If your PivotTable will occupy more than one sheet of paper, you should check the Set print titles options in the PivotTable Options dialog box (choose PivotTable → Table Options from the PivotTable toolbar). This option will display the column labels on each page making it easier to read.

Offline Access to Your Cube

In order to access your OLAP cube, you must be connected to an OLAP server. However, this isn't always practical. To address this problem, Excel enables you to save your cube to a local file. This means that you don't have to be connected to the OLAP server to edit your PivotTable. You can perform most of the functions locally and then reconnect to the server to refresh your cube as needed.

Getting a Local Copy of Your Cube

To get a local copy of your cube, select Client-Server Settings from the PivotTable toolbar and press the Create local data file button. This displays the Create Cube File Wizard shown in Figure 26-12.

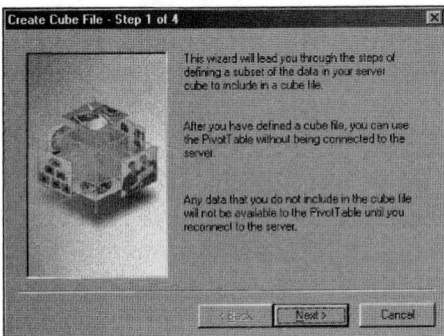

Figure 26-12: Creating a local cube file

SELECTING THE DIMENSIONS

In the second step of the wizard, you are prompted to select the dimensions and levels you want to incorporate into your local cube (see Figure 26-13). Remember that if you don't select a dimension or level, then it does not appear in your local cube.

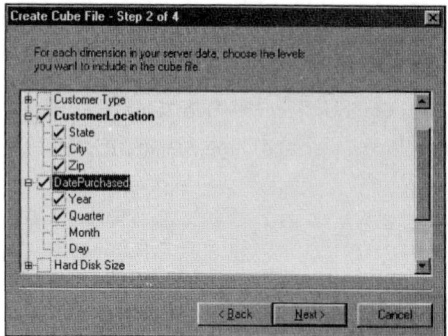

Figure 26-13: Selecting dimensions and levels for your local cube

All of the dimensions available from the OLAP server are listed. By default, the dimensions and levels you currently are using in your PivotTable are selected. Dimensions that have a checkmark next to them are included in your local cube. If the dimension name is shown in bold, all of the levels below it are selected; otherwise the top level itself is selected, and possibly some of the lower levels. You can click the plus sign to see the levels that are actually selected.

SELECTING TOP-LEVEL INFORMATION

The third step of the wizard asks you to select the amount of detail that should be included for that level (see Figure 26-14). As with the previous step, the values that are preselected are those values that currently appear in your PivotTable. If you don't select a piece of information (as with the previous step), it isn't there when you access your local cube.

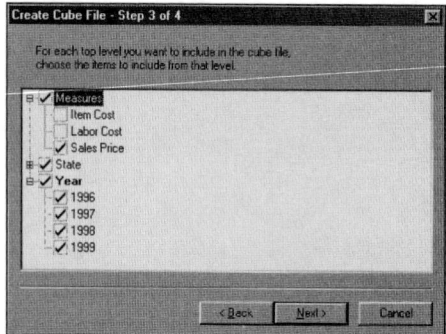

Figure 26-14: Selecting the amount of top-level information for your local cube

FINISHING THE WIZARD

In the last step of the wizard, you simply press the Finish button to start building the cube. The wizard then sends a query to the OLAP server requesting the information for the cube. While the query is running, the dialog box shown in Figure 26-15 tracks the progress of the query. You then are prompted for the name of your local cube file to save it on your local system.

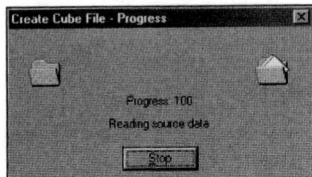

Figure 26-15: Querying the OLAP server for data for your local cube

Reconnecting to the Server

To switch back to using the OLAP server, select the Server-based data option on the Client-Server Settings dialog box. Excel automatically queries the OLAP server, gets a fresh copy of the data, and resumes querying the OLAP server each time you change the cube. However, this data is not used to update the local cube.

You easily can switch back and forth between the OLAP server and your local cube file by using this dialog box. If you want to refresh your local cube, just press the Edit local data file button and go through the previous steps of the wizard. This is also a good time to review your selected dimensions and levels to see if you have all the information you really need.

Summary

OLAP PivotTables are powerful tools for analyzing your data. Using AutoShow, you easily can identify the top 10 levels on which you should focus your attention. Using custom calculations, you can change your PivotTable from a series of absolute values to relative values. Again, this makes unusual situations easier to identify.

In the next chapter, I discuss how to create PivotCharts, which are graphical views of your PivotTable. Sometimes it is easier to identify data trends using a graph than any other way and Excel provides a number of different graphs from which you can choose.

Chapter 27

Charting Information from PivotTables

IN THIS CHAPTER

◆ Creating a PivotChart from a PivotTable

◆ Manipulating PivotCharts

◆ Formatting your PivotCharts

THIS CHAPTER DISCUSSES some common charts that you can derive from PivotTable data and how you can use them for data analysis. In addition, I show you how to polish the appearance of your charts so you can use them in PowerPoint presentations, on the Web, and so on.

Creating a PivotChart from a PivotTable

Which has greater impact — a table pointing out that $1.7 million of a company's sales came from its home state while just over $148,000 came from a neighboring state, or a chart (like the one shown in Figure 27-1) that graphs the amount of business coming from each neighboring jurisdiction? The numbers themselves may not tell you much, but the graph enables you to see that the majority of your out-of-state business comes from one place — making that location the best candidate for business expansion. It's that kind of deduction that makes the interactive nature of PivotTables and PivotCharts so valuable when it comes to data analysis.

Generating a PivotChart from a PivotTable is a snap. All you need to do to get started is click inside one of the PivotTable's data fields. The floating PivotTable toolbar expands, displaying a button for each field in the PivotTable. Press the PivotTable drop-down arrow button to open a special PivotTable menu. From there, simply click the PivotChart menu item. A basic column graph, like the one pictured in Figure 27-1, is added onto your workbook as a tab called Chart1 (as opposed to Sheet1).

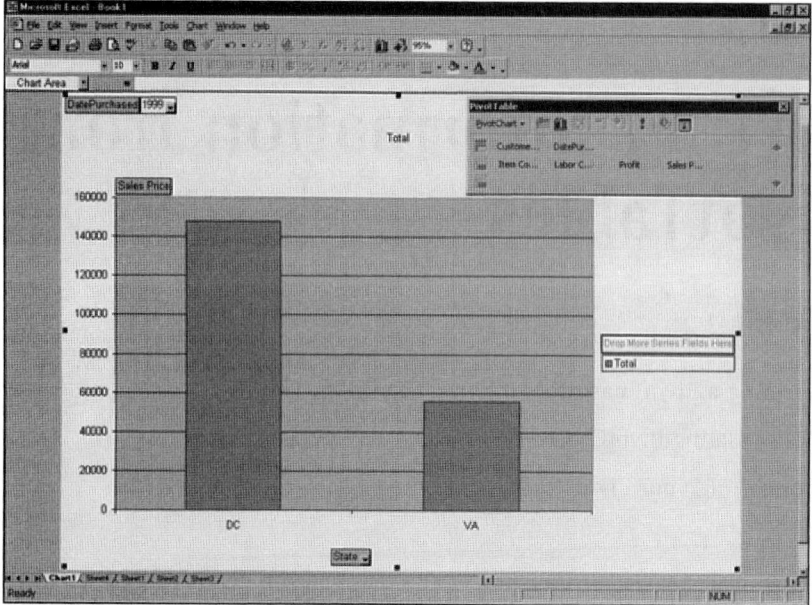

Figure 27-1: Learn at a glance how much of your business comes from Maryland and Virginia.

Building a PivotChart Using an OLAP Cube

Of course, not all the information you want to analyze is readily available in PivotTable form (not to mention in manageable chunks). Therefore, you may want to know how you can generate PivotCharts from an OLAP cube. Sound complicated? Not as complicated as you may think.

Being able to break down massive quantities of information into a more manageable OLAP cube gives you incredibly flexible, yet controlled, data analysis possibilities within Excel. For example, with flexible data analysis, you can discover whether your field person in a given state is the real cause of poor sales. Or you can tell just how much in profits the electric company's prolonged power outage cost you by examining business activity during the exact time of the outage. As a result, it has never been easier to wrap your hands around large chunks of data and make informed business decisions.

Simplifying Tasks Using the PivotTable and PivotChart Report Wizard

As always, Microsoft's step-by-step wizards go a long way toward simplifying even the most complicated of tasks. The PivotTable and PivotChart Wizard is no exception. To begin using the wizard, launch a blank Excel 2000 workbook and then choose the PivotTable and PivotChart Report option from the Data menu. Step 1 of the PivotTable and PivotChart Wizard appears (see Figure 27-2).

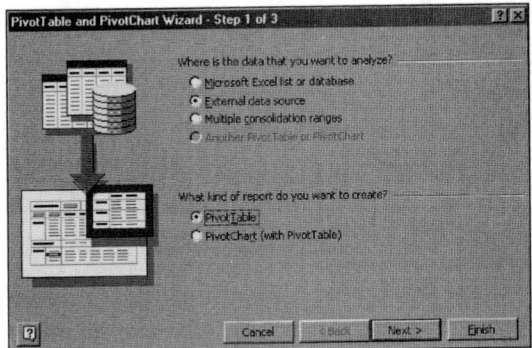

Figure 27-2: The PivotTable and PivotChart Wizard prompts you to tell it the location of the data you want analyzed.

The first part of the step asks you to specify where the data you wish to analyze is stored. We want to work with an existing OLAP cube, so choose the External data source option. In the same step, you also are asked to pick which type of report you want—PivotTable or PivotChart (and PivotTable). Choose the bottom option—PivotChart (with PivotTable)—and then press Next to proceed to the next step.

Step 2 (refer to Figure 27-3) asks you where the desired external data is stored. Click the Get Data... button. That takes you to the familiar Choose Data Source screen you worked with in Chapter 22. Open the OLAP Cubes tab, click the name of the OLAP cube you're looking for, and then press OK.

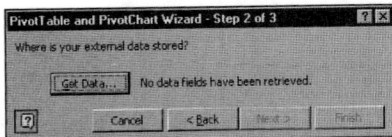

Figure 27-3: Step 2 tells you to retrieve the data.

This moves you to the final step in the wizard (see Figure 27-4). Tell the wizard to place the returned data in the current worksheet, and then click Finish to exit the wizard. Again, the wizard works a few moments before returning a blank PivotChart.

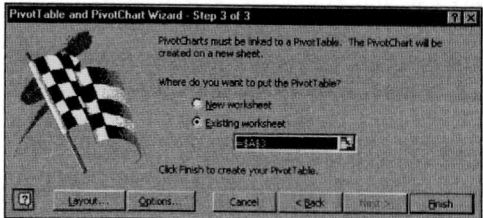

Figure 27-4: The final step in the PivotTable and PivotChart Wizard

Default type. Remember that the default graph type is a simple column chart, like the one in Figure 27-1. I show you how to change it later in this chapter.

The empty PivotChart shown in Figure 27-5 is the blank canvas on which you begin painting various scenarios. By taking the time to experiment with multiple arrangements of the data, you may uncover links and information that literally have the potential to change the way you do business forever. This may seem overly dramatic, but sound data-analysis tools in the hands of business-savvy decision-makers can make all the difference in the world.

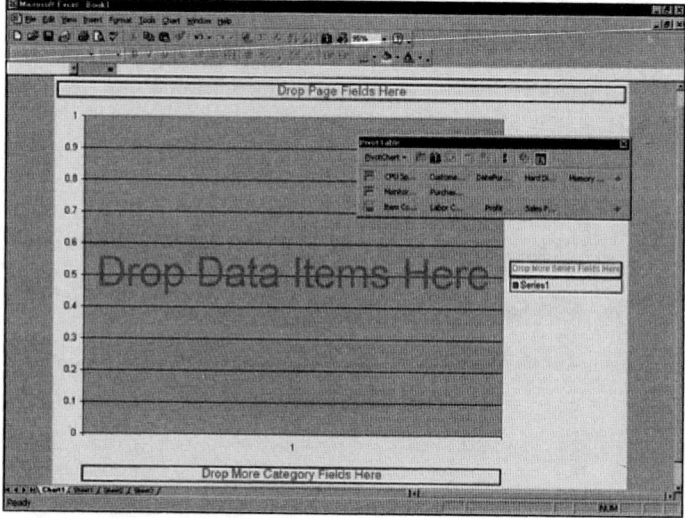

Figure 27-5: Your clean PivotChart slate

Manipulating PivotCharts

Before we get deeper into working with charts, let's take a few moments to refresh our memories with the proper chart terminology. As you read about them, some of these terms may come back to you courtesy of your grade school math education. (Hey, if you're anything like me, you've surely forgotten at least some of them by now!)

◆ The *x-axis* is displayed along the bottom of the chart.

◆ The *y-axis* is displayed along the left edge of the chart.

◆ The *z-axis* adds depth to the chart.

◆ *Legends* tell you how to find the different series of data plotted on the chart.

◆ The *chart title* describes what the chart tells you.

◆ An *axis title* provides additional information about the values.

◆ A *data table* (in our case, PivotTable) provides additional information about the data that generated the chart.

Once the blank PivotChart and all the applicable data fields from the OLAP cube you want to analyze are in place, you can begin turning the PivotChart into something useful. You accomplish this by using the floating PivotTable toolbar shown in Figure 27-6. In looking at the toolbar, notice that there are two basic types of data fields — data area fields that you can drag inside the chart and non-data area fields that can occupy the outer edges of the chart.

Non-Data Area Fields

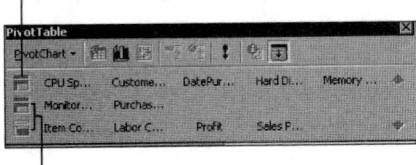

Data Area Fields

Figure 27-6: The floating PivotTable toolbar makes locating the fields you want to work with a breeze.

Now, let's take a closer look at how to configure a meaningful chart from these fields using the data fields from the sample JustPC OLAP cube. Say you want to analyze the profits of various items in your company's product line in relation to one another. Start by clicking the Profit button in the data area field section of the PivotTable toolbar and dragging it into the center of the chart. Simply drop the button into place. You see one large blue block, representing the company's total profits to date for all products. That number on its own, however, says very little; you need to put some other data fields into place in order to draw any meaningful conclusions.

To continue building a useful PivotChart, drag-and-drop the DatePurchased button into the box immediately to the right of the chart. This button enables you to examine company profits during a very specific period of time — ranging from a single day to the total length of time the company has been in business. While this, too, provides some interesting information, it still is not quite as valuable as it could be.

Next, try dragging the CPU Speed button into the data field box at the bottom of the PivotChart. At last, you can draw some useful conclusions! For instance, this view of the information can help you decide when to cut a specific speed of CPU from your product line due to lack of profits.

Drilling Down to the Finer Details

Now that you're comfortable putting data fields in their proper places, it's time to learn how to fine-tune your views of the data. As you attempt to determine the best location in which to place a certain data field on the PivotChart, there are some things you should keep in mind. To illustrate my point, let's use the DatePurchased field as an example. If that non-data area field is placed at the top of the PivotChart, you are able to look at only a single unit of time (for example, the company's entire history or a specific year, quarter, month, or day) at any given time. However, if that same field is placed at the bottom or to the right of the PivotChart, you can pick and choose how much (or how little) of the data you view at a time (for example, multiple years). Having said all that, you also want to get comfortable picking and choosing the specific data you want to display in your chart. For data fields residing at the top of the chart, you face an "either-or" situation. You can either choose to view all of that field's data (the default), or you can select a single chunk of time. To get started, simply click the data field's drop-down arrow button and then use the plus signs to drill your way down to the desired unit of time you wish to analyze (see Figure 27-7). Choose the appropriate unit of time and click OK to close the menu box.

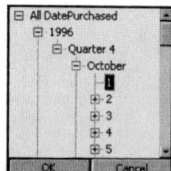

Figure 27-7: When located at the top of the PivotChart,
the DatePurchased field menu looks like this.

If, on the other hand, the same DatePurchased field is located on the bottom or to the right of the PivotChart, you can make multiple selections. For example, suppose you want to compare the sales during the holiday shopping season of each year of business. You do so by clicking your way through the network of plus signs for each year and placing a checkmark in the October checkbox for each year of data available (see Figure 27-8). Such analysis may reveal the success of an aggressive advertising campaign, or the comparative growth of profits through the years. The possibilities are almost endless!

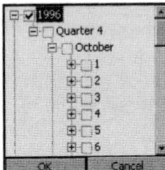

Figure 27-8: If placed in the proper location, you can compare specific chunks of time with one another.

Remember to click OK to put your options in place, or press Cancel to abort the mission. The more you play with PivotCharts and their data fields, the more quickly you uncover valuable bits of information.

Formatting Your PivotCharts

It's entirely possible that once you make your big discovery, you'll want to share it with others. With Excel 2000, you can do this in a variety of ways. You can print out the PivotChart, include it in a PowerPoint presentation, or publish it to the Web either statically or interactively. Of course, each of these mediums has its own aesthetic requirements in order to make a chart look its best – but many formatting needs remain the same.

Choosing a Chart Type

As I pointed out earlier, the default chart type for PivotCharts is a simple column chart. While this is a fine choice for most types of data you come across, other chart types may be more suitable to the task at hand.

What's the right type? All the charting theory in the world is no substitute for visual appeal. Just because theory suggests one type of chart is better than another for a specific graph doesn't guarantee it is true. If the chart conveys the information you want in a clear, concise manner, then follow your gut when choosing a chart type. As the saying goes, "There's an exception to every rule."

Here is a list of chart types available in Excel and the information they display. Each of these chart types has at least two subtypes that provide slightly different ways of looking at your data. Familiarizing yourself with this information can make the task of choosing an appropriate chart type a whole lot easier.

- ◆ *Column charts* compare one or more series of data in which each value represents a column (or field) of data.

- ◆ *Bar charts* are column charts turned on their side.

- ◆ *Line charts* plot one or more series of data as lines across the chart.

- ◆ *Pie charts* show how much each value in a series relates to the series as a whole.

- ◆ *XY charts* compare two series of data by drawing a point at the location specified by the corresponding values from each series.

- ◆ *Area charts* display how values in a series change over time by using a solid area under each value. You can use multiple series in a single chart.

- ◆ *Doughnut charts* resemble pie charts, except they can display data from multiple series.

- ◆ *Radar charts* display one or more series of data by plotting each value relative to a center point.

- ◆ *Surface charts* plot two series of data at right angles to each another.

- ◆ *Bubble charts* are similar to XY charts, but they compare three sets of data instead of two. The third data value determines the size of the bubble marker.

- ◆ *Stock charts* display stock market information using values for high, low, close, and volume with traditional stock market formats.

- ◆ *Cylinder charts* resemble column and bar charts, but they use cylindrical shapes.

- ◆ *Cone charts* also resemble column and bar charts, but use conical shapes.

- ◆ *Pyramid charts* are similar to column and bar charts, but use pyramid shapes.

You can select one of these charts, by right-clicking on the charting area and selecting Chart Type from the popup menu. This will display the dialog box shown in Figure 27-9. Simply choose the chart type and subtype you want to use to display your data.

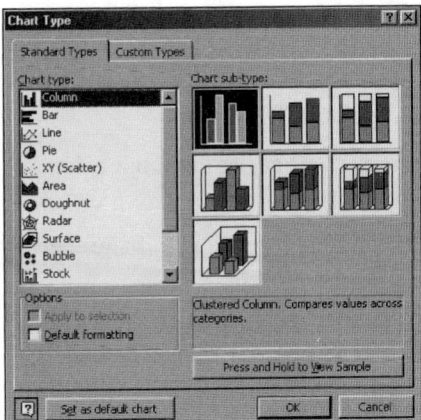

Figure 27-9: Choosing a chart type and subtype

Tweaking the Chart for Best Results

If the chart takes up a central position on a PowerPoint slide, an overhead transparency, or a Web page, bigger may be better (at least from a visibility standpoint). But if you intend to use the chart as part of a Word document's narrative, then judicious sizing may be everything. You surely don't want to overpower the text of your document. Size and other chart enhancements can go a long way toward achieving the desired effect.

For example, it's entirely possible that after creating a PivotChart you decide it doesn't quite meet your needs. Maybe the title is too small or the labels along the y-axis aren't formatted properly. Perhaps the chart is too large to fit with the Word document into which you plan to import it. These things are easy to change by using the proper dialog boxes. To get started, simply move the cursor over one of parts of the chart listed below and right-click to display the popup menu for that part of the chart. Then choose Format from the popup menu to display a Format dialog box for that chart object.

- ◆ *Axis* borders the plot area and provides a scale for the values drawn in the chart.

- ◆ *Chart area* refers to the entire chart.

- ◆ *Chart title* is a text field displayed at the top of the chart.

- ◆ *Data label* is a text field that displays the value associated with a data marker.

- ◆ A *data marker* can consist of a bar, column, point, slice, bubble, or other graphical object corresponding to a single data value.

- ◆ *Data series* is the collection of data markers corresponding to a set of data.

Data table contains the data used to create the chart.

◆ *Error bars* indicate the potential degree of error for a series.

◆ The *floor* is the bottom part of the plot area in a 3-D chart.

◆ *Gridlines* are lines drawn on the chart to make it easier to match a data marker with information displayed along the axes.

◆ *Legend* is a box that associates the name of a data series with its graphical representation.

◆ *Plot area* is the section in the chart containing the data series and bounded by the axes.

◆ *Trendlines* are lines derived from a data series that attempt to project where the data series is headed.

◆ A *wall* is a vertical part of the plot area in a 3-D chart.

The Format dialog boxes for the different chart objects have many tabs in common. For example, some of the tabs you should already know how to use, such as font, number, and alignment. However there are other tabs such as Patterns, Scale, and Shape that perform unique functions for a chart, which can make a big difference in your chart's appearance. Do you know that you can choose the color or set the pattern used to display many of these objects? While it may seem trivial, it's not when you're trying to create a slide show that's clearly visible from the back of an auditorium, or when you need to print clearly legible handouts of the chart. These formatting dialog boxes come in two flavors: *line oriented* and *area oriented*. You can even change the scale used on each axis, which may be helpful when you don't like the scale Excel chooses.

TIP

Adjusting the scale. On the Scale tab of the Format Axis dialog box, you can adjust the scale up or down to amplify your findings. If the scale is small and the values are close in size, the smaller scale more effectively helps the reader detect subtle differences. If, on the other hand, you want your data to appear more even than it actually is, nudging the scale up gives the chart a more level appearance. I'm not encouraging you to lie — I'm merely pointing out that the way data is presented can have intangible effects all of their own.

Most of the options are associated with a data series. Just click anywhere on the line or bar representing the data series and select Format Data Series from the popup menu to display the Format Data Series dialog box. On the Shape tab, you can choose the shape of the columns or bars in a bar chart. This enables you to turn an ordinary column chart into a pyramid chart. You also can change the order of the series and tweak how the data series is presented on the chart. With 3-D charts, you can adjust your viewing angle. You can even add error bars on some charts, showing the degree of confidence you have in the value.

MAKING CHART LINES MORE VISIBLE BY SETTING LINE PATTERNS IN A DATA SERIES

When it comes to charts (or anything else for that matter), one size usually does not fit all. Line charts, scatter charts, and radar charts make extensive use of lines, so they can be harder for readers to see if they're used as a slide or scaled down to fit multiple pages on a sheet of paper. Luckily, Microsoft thought of this potential dilemma and offered a solution.

Right-clicking over a point in a line chart, choosing Format Data Series, and then selecting the Patterns tab on line charts, scatter charts, and radar charts displays the dialog box shown in Figure 27-10. Typically, both the line and marker are set to automatic; however, you may want different values. For instance, you can make the line weight heavier so that it shows up better on a projection screen. You also may want to choose a color to correspond to each source of data so that a viewer instantly can see which line belongs where when you publish a chart to a Web page. You need to right-click each individual data line to set the desired options because you can set only one line's attributes at a time.

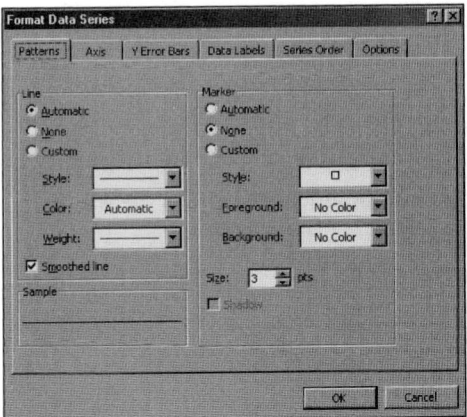

Figure 27-10: You can change how a line is drawn for a data series by changing its pattern in the Format Data Series dialog box.

In addition to choosing the color, style, and weight of the line itself, you also can *smooth* the line. Smoothing replaces the sharp angles that occur at various data points along a line with a rounded curve. Just check the *Smoothed line* checkbox in the Format Data Series dialog box. This often makes the line more visually appealing. You may also find this very useful when plotting data from a series of points in a scatter chart.

You also can select the marker you want to display on each data point in the series. Just as you do with lines, you choose from a set of standard styles such as diamonds, squares, and triangles. You can even choose one color for the foreground (outside edge) of the marker or the background (interior) of the marker. Even the size of the marker can be controlled and displayed with a shadow for a 3-D effect.

Use those markers! Consider using markers on line charts when the chart is to be viewed from far away, or when you intend to print multiple charts on a single piece of paper. These markers can enhance the chart's visibility greatly.

ADDING COLOR TO YOUR CHARTS BY SETTING AREA PATTERNS

When you attend a slide presentation in an auditorium full of people, it may be impossible to see where one slice of a pie chart begins and the other ends. Color variance may be the solution for presenters and audience members alike.

Using the Format Data Series dialog box, you can change how areas, such as the plot area and pie slices, are displayed with techniques similar to those found in line patterns. While you can choose the color of the area and control how the border is displayed around the area, the most powerful option is defining how the area itself is filled.

How will your chart be used? When designing your chart, it's important to keep in mind how it will be used. In general, it's better to use light and soft colors in the background and bright or dark colors in the foreground. This makes your chart much easier to read because it emphasizes the line and columns on the chart, rather than the stuff behind them. If the chart's primary purpose is to be printed out in black and white, focus your attention on pattern fills as opposed to color because patterns may be easier to identify on paper than various shades of gray.

ACHIEVING A DRAMATIC EFFECT USING GRADIENT FILL

We've all seen the fancy PowerPoint slides in which one rich color flows gently into another, creating an effect that exudes professionalism. Well you can add more than basic colors and patterns to your PivotCharts, too.

To begin applying this effect, right-click the plot area of your PivotChart and select Format Plot Area from the resulting shortcut menu. Click the Fill Effects button on the Patterns tab to display the Fill Effects dialog box shown in Figure 27-11. On the Gradient tab, you can choose to create an effect in which one color changes into another color. There are three basic options: One color, Two color, and Preset. *One color* creates a gradient using various shades of that color. *Two colors* create a blended gradient using the two specified colors. *Preset* allows you to choose from many different predefined gradients, including some that involve more than two colors for a rainbow effect.

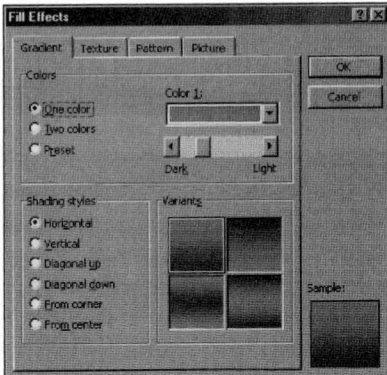

Figure 27-11: You can specify a gradient fill for the plot area.

Using the *One color* option, you can gradually change your chosen color into another color that is either lighter or darker than itself. You also can choose how light or dark the second color is by moving a slide bar from dark to light. Moving the slider to either end results in a white or black second color.

In *Two color* mode, you can explicitly choose the two colors used. In *Preset*, you can choose from a set of already defined gradients. Here you find bold rainbow effects, stunning sunrise color schemes, and the like. In many cases, you can't duplicate the preset pattern because more than two colors are used.

A Color for Every Mood

While it may sound corny on the surface, don't underestimate the power of suggestion. Everyone knows that colors such as red, orange, and yellow project a warm image, while blues and greens project a cooler image. The same goes for textures, which I present in the next section. A wood grain background is great for presenting construction statistics, while water is clever for displaying surfing vacation destination numbers. With the right colors and textures in the background, you can communicate a whole mood along with the data itself. Remember, however, that these colors are only good for full-color presentations or printouts; grayscale printouts virtually eliminate the very effect you're trying so hard to achieve.

Once you choose the desired gradient colors, you need to select which shading style you want to use. The styles determine how the color change is made. You can select from a variety of styles. Pick the one that best fits your chart, without making it look too cluttered.

TEXTURE FILL: MORE THAN JUST COLOR

Imagine a fancy marble texture for a classy company chart, or a denim effect for a blue jeans manufacturer. Whether your chart is destined for the Web or a live presentation, texture fills can add depth and character to your charts.

Selecting the Texture tab on the Fill Effects dialog box enables you to choose from an assortment of predefined textures. Simply click the texture you want to use and then click OK to return to the Format Data Series dialog box.

Consider the source (for the output). While the textures in Texture Fill look nice on your display and on a high-quality color printer, they can look pretty bad on a monochrome laser printer.

COMBINING COLOR AND PATTERNS TO ACHIEVE A UNIQUE EFFECT

If you want to design a series of charts in your college's school colors, or simply have a preferred color scheme for your company, the Pattern tab enables you to combine them in dozens of ways ranging from polka dots to stripes (in any conceivable direction) to zigzags.

The Pattern tab enables you to specify two colors and a pattern that is used to fill the area you select. I usually choose my colors in the drop-down boxes at the bottom of the tab, and then I pick a pattern. That way I can tell which patterns work best because all of the pattern swatches change to reflect my chosen colors.

Lazy lasers. Most charts look best when printed on a color printer. It's difficult to distinguish between the various colors used in a chart on a lazer printer. However, you can make your printed charts look better by using a Pattern Fill on the various chart objects instead of color. The key here, however, is selecting contrasting colors so that the effect doesn't appear muddy. Sure you can use the defaults if your only output is from a standard printer; but with a little forethought, you can plan ahead and choose colors that work well electronically and on paper.

CREATING PERSONALIZED EFFECTS WITH PICTURE FILL

If your chart objects don't stand out when using gradients, textures and patters, consider using a picture. On the Picture tab of the Fill Effects dialog box, you can choose a graphic image to fill an area. You can stretch a picture so that one picture fills the entire area, or you can stack as many pictures as you want to fill the area.

 **It's a matter of size.** If you choose to stack pictures, the last picture may not be complete depending on the data value. You also can specify a scale factor so that each picture represents so many units of the value axis.

Imagine the possibilities! Your corporate logo, or maybe even your star product, can become an integral part of your charts.

You also can use Picture Fill on a 3-D chart using standard columns or bars. However, it does not work with 3-D shapes such as pyramids or cylinders. You have the option to apply the pictures to all sides of the chart, or just to the sides you select.

 **You're surrounded!** If you don't display the picture on all sides of your PivotChart, then the color that was displayed on the chart object before using Picture Fill continues to be used. To change this color, simply change it using the Format Data Series dialog box, Pattern tab to change the color as described earlier. Then use the Picture Fill dialog box to reselect the picture.

 **A picture is worth a billion dollars.** While you can use Picture Fill to create interesting background images, it also can be used to fill in the bars in a bar chart. By selecting Stack and Scale → Format and specifying the Units/Picture on the Picture tab, you can use graphics such as dollar bills to represent money, cars to represent auto production, and insects to represent software bugs.

LIVEN UP YOUR CHARTS BY CHOOSING DIFFERENT SHAPES

Tired of the same old columns and bars? If you want something a little out of the ordinary, then you may want to explore your options when it comes to changing the shape of your chart elements.

Choosing a new shape in a 3-D column or bar chart involves nothing more than right-clicking over the bar chart, choosing Format Selected Data Series from the shortcut menu, and choosing the Shape tab (see Figure 27-12). Simply click the shape you want and press OK to apply your selection.

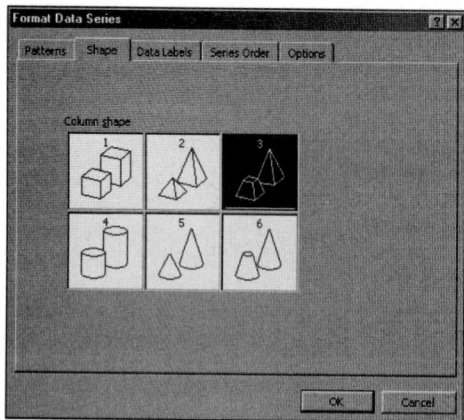

Figure 27-12: If you want a pyramid chart instead of a normal bar chart, simply choose a different shape in this dialog box.

Putting the Finishing Touches on Your PivotChart

Now that your PivotChart looks the way you want it to, it's time to put on some finishing touches such as adding a title, some data labels, and a legend (if they don't already exist). You begin defining these elements in the same manner: by right-clicking anywhere inside the chart's area, and then choosing the Chart Options item from the resulting shortcut menu. Once in this dialog box, just follow the directions to begin working with the desired element.

Giving Your PivotChart a Title and Data Labels

First, make sure you're looking at the Chart Options Titles tab. It should resemble the tab pictured in Figure 27-13. If you're stuck with the basic default column chart, you see three text boxes ready to be filled. In the Chart title box, enter the name you want to give your chart. In the background, Excel automatically places the title onscreen and centered above the chart.

Next, press the Tab key to move to the Category (X) axis text box. (Notice that a preview of the title you entered appears on the preview screen that occupies the right half of the tab.) This enables you to label the fields represented across the bottom of the PivotChart.

Finally, press the Tab key to label the values displayed on the left side of the PivotChart using the Value (Y) axis text box. Click OK to save the title and labels you entered.

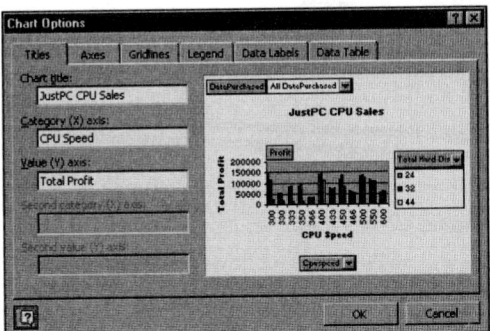

Figure 27-13: The Titles tab enables you to label your chart and its major elements to make its purpose even clearer.

CHANGING THE APPEARANCE OF THE TITLE AND LABELS

As you look at your PivotChart, you may discover that you want to enlarge the title a bit, or you want the data labels smaller to look a bit less overpowering. Luckily, making these adjustments is a piece of cake. Simply right-click the element you want to format and then choose the Format [name of chart element] item. A three-tabbed dialog box opens, giving you ample opportunity to change the title's color, type font, and size – as well as its position on the page in relation to the chart.

The first tab, the Patterns tab, is where you define the attributes of the area occupied by the selected chart element. In other words, use this tab to give the title a background of its own, and/or to apply a border to the chart element. The default settings here are probably good enough for the majority of cases. However, you may want to consider modifying them if you're trying to achieve a more artistic effect.

The second tab, the Font tab, you should recognize from your dealings with Excel and Word. This is where you specify the font and type size used, as well as the color and any special effects you want to apply to the text.

Finally, there's the Alignment tab. Not only can you specify where the text appears onscreen (centered, flush right, and so on), but you also can rotate the text to change its orientation altogether. To do this, simply click the red diamond in the Orientation screen and drag it to the desired angle. If you want the text to appear vertically, just click the vertical text side of the Orientation window – no clicking and dragging needed!

When you're satisfied with how the chosen label looks, press OK to dismiss the dialog box and move on to the next chart element you want to format.

Getting Your Chart in Line

If you're measuring multiple pieces of data across the bottom of your chart, vertical gridlines may come in handy. With these gridlines, the viewer easily can determine where one cluster of data ends and another one begins.

To set vertical gridlines, right-click anywhere inside the chart's area and choose Chart Options. Inside the Gridlines tab, you see a section devoted to Category (X) axis. Place a checkmark next to the Major gridlines option so Excel can differentiate among clusters of data.

 **Minor gridlines, major headaches?** While minor gridlines may be helpful for more exact analysis on the y-axis, they also can do more harm than good in certain circumstances. For instance, if the values reflected on the y-axis cover a wide range of numbers, then the gridlines may clutter the chart without providing any benefit. If the range of numbers is narrow, however, the minor gridlines may help the viewer derive more exact data from the chart.

Legend(ary) Enhancements

If you added a second series field to your chart, Excel probably created a legend for you. To modify the appearance of this legend, just right-click over it and then choose the tab you wish to work with. Here again you have a Pattern tab that enables you to dictate the legend's background, a Fonts tab that enables you to define text attributes, and a Placement tab that enables you to specify where you want the legend to appear in relation to the chart.

Summary

This chapter taught you how to convert your text-based PivotTables into a more visual form of data analysis: PivotCharts. In addition to generating PivotCharts, you learned how to manipulate these charts to convey various bits of information, as well as how to ready these charts for either electronic or printed distribution.

In the next chapter, I present one of the most interesting enhancements to Excel 2000 — the ability to publish interactive Excel elements to the Web. That's right, rather than having a static Web page, you can manipulate many Excel elements using little more than a Web browser!

Chapter 28

Interactive Data Analysis on the Web

IN THIS CHAPTER

- ◆ Placing interactive spreadsheets on the Web
- ◆ Seeing live data charts on the Web
- ◆ Manipulating PivotTables on the Web

THIS CHAPTER DISCUSSES some ways you can make information available on the Web for people to analyze from near or far. In addition, you learn how to manipulate that data yourself.

Excel and the Web

While Excel 97 had the ability to save documents in HTML format and publish them to the Web, it had many limitations that prevented this feature from being truly useful. For example, readers could not interact with the document in any way. The result was a static Web page much like a typical text-based page.

With Excel 2000, these limitations are gone once and for all! Not only can you save workbooks as HTML documents, but you also can enable people to manipulate them using their Web browser! They can sort and filter data over the Web, and turn static information into meaningful data right before their very eyes. What a wonderful decision-making tool for corporate executives!

The possibilities are almost endless. For example, you can make company sales stats available on an internal or password-protected Web page so various sales teams can see how they're doing in relation to one another. Nothing like a little friendly competition to keep things moving! And because the information is interactive, staff can compare one team to another, one salesperson to another, and so on. Or you can place important statistics on a private Web page in which your board of directors can access it to stay abreast of the organization's progress.

Using Web Folders to Publish Pages with Ease

Publishing Web pages used to be such a hassle. You messed with FTP servers, typed in cryptic commands, and so on. Surely there was an easier way – and there is, thanks to Office 2000.

Web Folders, a new feature of Office 2000, enable you to access files on a Web server just like you find them on your local hard disk. This feature makes publishing an Excel document to the Web a trivial matter. Of course, you need the proper information (such as server names, passwords, and directory names) from your network administrator or Webmaster to access the Web server and get your Web Folders properly mapped – but that, too, should be a simple task.

Once all of the setup work is complete, publishing to the Web is as easy as simply saving a document. Finally!

Saving Excel Documents for Use on the Web

Before you can publish a spreadsheet to the Web, you need to make sure it's in a format that Web browsers can read – as opposed to requiring the reader to download the file and view it using Excel 2000. This universal Web page publishing format is known as *HyperText Markup Language (HTML)*.

To save an Excel document in HTML format, simply click File → Save As Web Page on the menu bar. A window, like the one shown in Figure 28-1, appears.

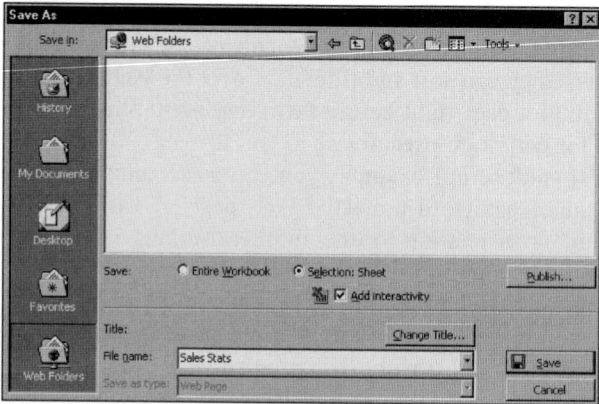

Figure 28-1: Saving your Excel document as a Web page closely resembles saving a standard spreadsheet.

When you save your Excel document in HTML format, you have a number of decisions to make. First, you can save a static version of a single worksheet, or the entire workbook. The static versions of these documents can't be manipulated using a Web browser, but they may be fine for publishing most documents in which the object is to communicate information and not to provide data for analysis by others. You simply select the entire workbook or the current selection. Then click Save to save the document or click Publish to display the dialog box shown in Figure 28-2.

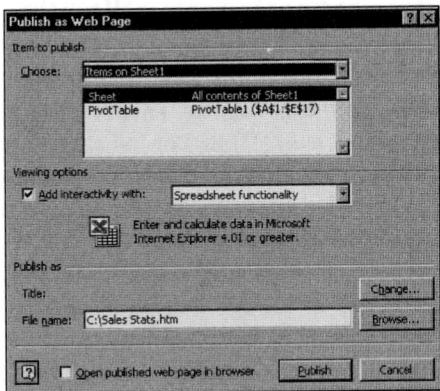

Figure 28-2: This dialog box simplifies the task of publishing your Excel document as a Web page.

If you select an individual object such as a chart or worksheet, you can check the *Add Interactivity with:* box to enable people with Web browsers to work interactively with your worksheet, chart, or PivotTable.

 **Stalled interactions.** If you want to incorporate this interactivity into your document, you need to make sure that the Excel Web Components and Office Server Extensions are installed on your Web server. If they aren't, interactivity is not available.

The Publish as Web Page dialog box enables you to choose the level of functionality for interactive documents; otherwise, it does the same basic job that the standard Save as dialog box does. If you want to view PivotTables interactively over the Web, you must publish the document and select PivotTable functionality from the *Add Interactivity with:* drop-down box in the Viewing options section.

 **Gee, that's obvious.** If everyone who accesses your interactive Excel components has Excel 2000 on their computers, you also can make your workbook available in .XLS format on your Web site. That way, users with Internet Explorer 4.1 or greater can automatically start Excel inside the browser when they reference the workbook.

HTML Formatting Issues for Interactive Documents

In Excel 2000, you can save workbooks in HTML format and reload them into Excel without any loss of data. However, this doesn't mean that your HTML version of the document looks identical to the native version of the document. This is because Excel enables you to do some tasks that are impossible in HTML. For instance, you can't display rotated text in HTML so any cells containing rotated text are displayed as horizontal text. Table 28-1 lists some of the key differences between HTML documents and regular documents. You should take all of this into consideration when designing your document for the Web.

TABLE 28-1 KEY HTML LIMITATIONS

Feature	Discussion
Rotated text	Is displayed horizontally
Dotted or dashed borders	Are displayed as a single solid line
Conditional formatting	Is not used; default format is used instead
A single cell with multiple fonts	Is displayed using the default font
Graphics	Are lost if you publish the entire worksheet
Drawing objects	Are lost
Cell comments	Are lost
Outlining information	Is lost
3-D charts	Are converted to 2-D charts
Surface charts	Are converted to column charts
Custom positioning and sizing of chart objects	Are lost; defaults are used instead
References to other worksheets	Are converted to a value

Accessing Excel Documents on the Web

Accessing workbooks on the Web is easy; just fire up your Web browser and open the document. There are, however, some major differences in how the various static and interactive documents work.

Viewing Static Documents on the Web

To view a static Excel document using your Web browser, simply enter the URL into your browser's address bar. If you're viewing an entire workbook, you may see a display like the one shown in Figure 28-3. This loads the base Web page and displays a list of worksheets and charts available at the bottom of the document — similar to the way the tabs for the worksheets and charts are displayed at the bottom of the workbook in Excel. Clicking the name of a worksheet displays the worksheet, chart, or PivotTable in the area above.

	FY 95		FY 96	
Defense Discretionary	$	274.00	$	266.00
Foreign Aid	$	20.00	$	18.00
Medicaid	$	89.00	$	92.00
Medicare	$	177.00	$	191.00
Net Interest	$	232.00	$	241.00
Non-Defense Discretionary	$	252.00	$	249.00
Other Mandatory	$	179.00	$	162.00
Social Security	$	333.00	$	347.00
Welfare	$	44.00	$	67.00

	FY 95		FY 96	
Federal Spending				
Defense Discretionary	$	274.00	$	266.00
Welfare/Medicaid	$	133.00	$	159.00
Net Interest	$	232.00	$	241.00
Non-Defense Discretionary	$	272.00	$	267.00
Other Mandatory	$	179.00	$	162.00
Social Security/Medicare	$	510.00	$	538.00

Figure 28-3: Viewing a static workbook using your Web browser

While a single Web page can hold one worksheet, PivotTable, or chart, an entire workbook needs to generate multiple Web pages — one for each sheet. Given that, saving the workbook in HTML format results in more information than you may expect. Excel automatically creates a base Web page with the name you specify for the workbook. Then it creates a directory with the name of your workbook followed by files to hold the individual Web pages. These files correspond to each of the worksheets and other elements in your workbook.

 **I've been framed!** Viewing an HTML-formatted workbook requires a browser that supports frames. Therefore, many older browsers and most lightweight browsers may have a problem viewing your workbook.

Using the Spreadsheet Component

The Office Web Components enable you to access a worksheet and make changes to it while using a Web browser (see Figure 28-4). While this facility is not nearly as powerful as Excel itself, it certainly is useful when you want to create some worksheets for others to use. For example, you can use this function to enable someone to enter data and calculate information for an employee expense report, and then send the Web page to someone else for processing. Or if you offer a payment plan for your customers, you can enable them to type in the amount they want to finance and have the monthly payments calculated for them. Take a look at Table 28-2 to get an idea of just how powerful these interactive Web features are.

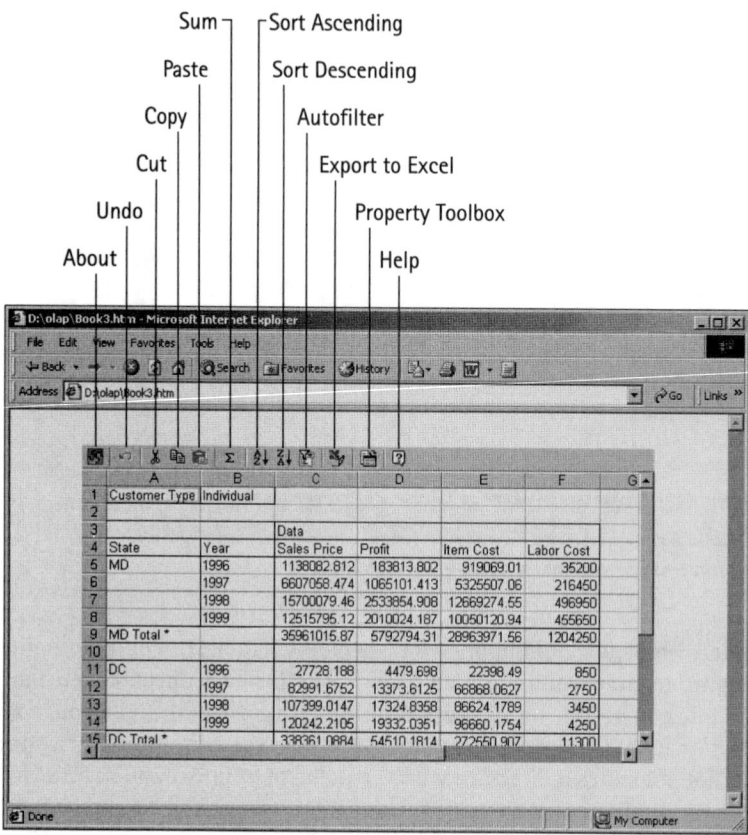

Figure 28-4: Viewing an interactive worksheet over the Web.

TABLE 28-2 INTERACTIVE SPREADSHEET BUTTONS

Button	Function
About	Displays an About menu for the Office Web Components.
Undo	Reverses the previous change.
Cut	Copies the data to the clipboard and deletes it from the worksheet.
Copy	Copies the data to the clipboard.
Paste	Copies data from the clipboard to the worksheet.
Sum	Adds a series of values.
Sort Ascending/Sort Descending	Enable you to sort the data in a worksheet in ascending or descending order.
AutoFilter	Enables you to hide rows in your worksheet based on the information you provide.
Export to Excel	Starts an Excel session using the data from the Web site.
Property Toolbox	Displays a dialog box of the same name.
Help	Accesses the help subsystem.

I've done all that work for nothing? One disadvantage of using a Web page to distribute a worksheet is that users can't save the results of their data manipulation. While they can send the Web page to someone or export the page into Excel, the original Web page itself remains untouched. Of course, many people look at this as a big advantage — especially if the data is sensitive in nature.

As you can see in the preceding table, the typical Undo, Cut, Copy, Paste, Sum, and Sort buttons are available in the Web-based worksheets as well. The AutoFilter function enables you to choose which rows to display in a table. Think of it as an oversimplified database filter. AutoFilter is especially useful when you have large tables and you only want to see a subset of the values. For example, an interactive, online Olympic spreadsheet that lists athletes by sport, country of origin, and so on enables you to use AutoFilter to view only gymnasts, only United States athletes, and so on. As long as the fields exist, you can sort and filter by them.

ENLISTING MORE ADVANCED FUNCTIONALITY

One of the buttons mentioned above that merits further investigation is the Properties Toolbox button. The Spreadsheet Property Toolbox dialog box (see Figure 28-5) enables you to perform many of the more advanced functions that you can access within Excel but that, by their complex nature, are difficult to work with using a simple Web browser. These functions normally are available by right-clicking and selecting from a shortcut menu in Excel, or by accessing one of Excel's many toolbars. Table 28-3 gives you a quick glance at the settings available on the Property Toolbox.

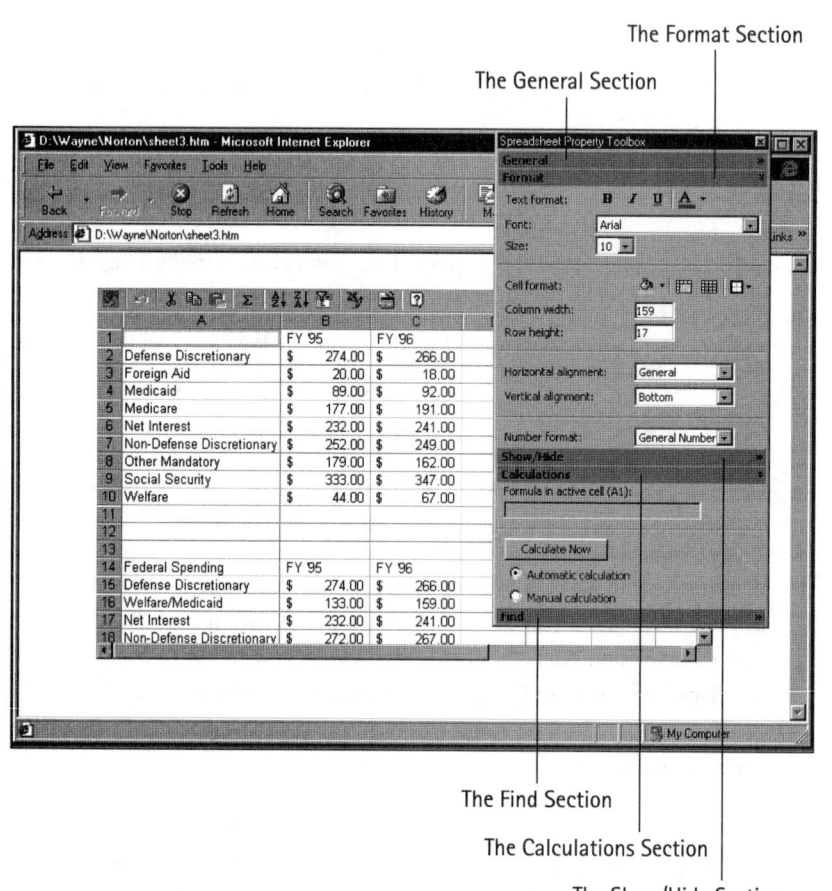

Figure 28-5: The Spreadsheet Property Toolbox enables you to change many of the elements on the online worksheet.

TABLE **28-3** SPREADSHEET PROPERTY TOOLBOX SETTINGS

Option	Function
General section	Supplies an Undo button and a button to access the help facility.
Format section	Enables you to change the characteristics of a cell and its data.
Show/Hide section	Enables you to change how the worksheet is displayed in your browser.
Calculations section	Displays the current value or formula in a cell and recalculates the values in the worksheet.
Find section	Displays a simple find command that can find a text string in the worksheet.

Probably the two must useful sections of the Property Toolbox are the Format and Calculations sections. The Format section enables users to make basic changes in the selected cells' format. This includes changing the font (color, size, and font name); merging cells and setting borders; setting the row height and column width for a cell; specifying alignment; and specifying the number format used to display numeric information.

The Calculations section shows the name of the current cell and its contents. You can click the Calculate Now button to force the spreadsheet to recalculate the results on the spot, or choose to let the Office Web Component recalculate the values in the worksheet automatically or on demand.

Get Live Visual Results with the Chart Component

If you thought the ability to manipulate data on the Web was neat, you'll be thrilled to see that you can incorporate the same level of interactivity into online charts!

Interactive charts use the Office Web Components to display a chart and a worksheet containing the data used to create the chart (see Figure 28-6). All of the functions of the interactive worksheets are available so you can change the data in the chart. Any changes to any of the cell values charted immediately are reflected in the chart.

Saving changes. Any changes you (or anyone else) make to the Web page are not saved. As soon as you leave the site, the data is restored to its original state. If you find that you need to make more permanent changes, you have to do it locally in Excel and then overwrite the existing Web file with the newly modified one.

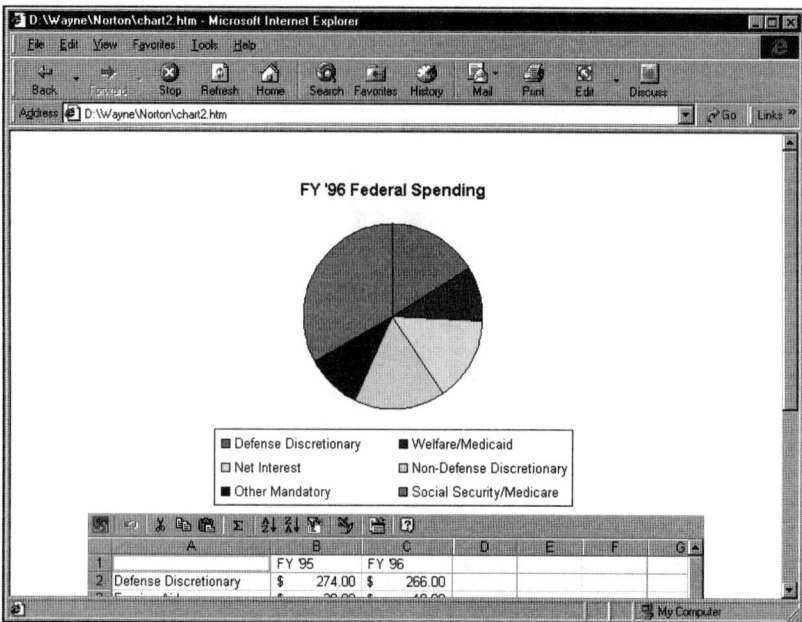

Figure 28-6: Viewing an interactive chart on the Web

While you can't change the chart type or any of the chart's characteristics, you can change the number of data points displayed in the chart. For example, inserting a new row adds a new set of values to the chart. Of course, you must add the new row after the first row and before the last row in the chart because you can't change the range of cells included in the chart.

You also can use the AutoFilter feature of the worksheet to select or hide rows (see the section "Filtering Your Data Using AutoFilter" in Chapter 24 for more information about how to use AutoFilter). Any hidden rows are not displayed in the chart, giving you a truly customized view of the data. You can build one large chart containing a lot of information so users have access to all of the information they need. Then they can use the AutoFilter feature to focus on smaller subsets of the information, rather than forcing you to build several smaller charts (an unnecessary task few of us have time for). For example, a company may publish a chart about the productivity of its sales force, which you can break down further to discover who sold the most units of a particular item or which sales team had the biggest percentage of sales for the month.

Flexible Data Analysis Using the PivotTable Component

The ultimate Web-based data analysis tool is Excel's PivotTable Component (see Figure 28-7). This tool enables you to manipulate the PivotTable just as if you were using Excel. You can drag-and-drop fields into different positions on the

PivotTable and it automatically is updated to display information as the reader wants to see it. You can select which values you want to see in a particular field by clicking the drop-down arrow button at the end of each field.

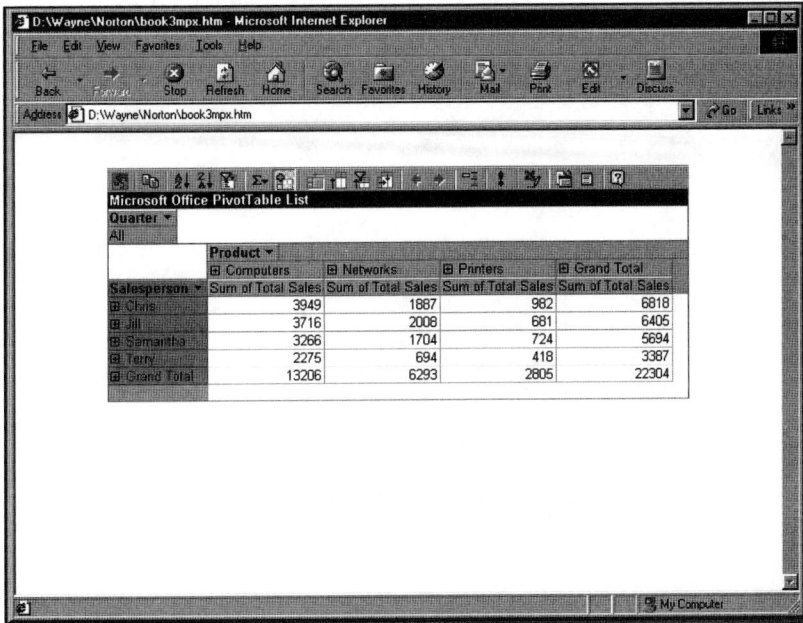

Figure 28-7: Viewing an interactive PivotTable on the Web

The only drawback to using PivotTables over the Web is that you cannot create a new PivotTable; you can only manipulate one that already is published to the Web with PivotTable functionality. Of course, it's still a powerful and dynamic analytical tool for managers and just about anyone else who wants to put a different spin on the data that's available.

TIP

Appearance matters. The way you present information can make all the difference in the world as to how the data is perceived and received. Whenever I contemplate publishing an interactive worksheet, I spend a fair amount of time playing with the data first to make sure that the information I making available can't be used against me. I'm not suggesting anyone blatantly lie, but who doesn't want to paint themselves in the most favorable light possible? If the data looks worse one way than another, consider publishing a static worksheet or remove the problem fields from the worksheet so users can't use them.

In addition to creating and manipulating PivotTables, the PivotTable Component enables you to manipulate PivotCharts (see Figure 28-8). The PivotTable Component displays both the PivotChart with the PivotTable beneath it. Unlike Excel in which you can manipulate the values directly on the chart, you have to manipulate the PivotTable below the PivotChart to change the information on the PivotChart.

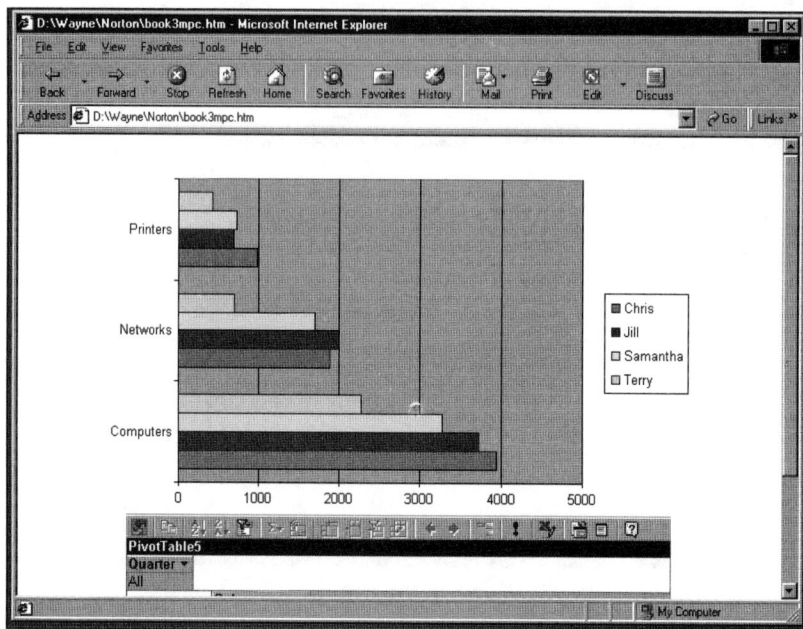

Figure 28-8: Viewing an interactive PivotTable on the Web

Summary

It's one thing to be able to analyze data at your own desk, but it's truly amazing when you can contemplate analyzing live data while on a business trip or while visiting a branch office at the other end of the country. This chapter attempted to give you a taste of the powerful Office 2000 Web components that make this data analysis revolution possible. You saw not only how to publish interactive Excel components to the Web, but you also discovered what you can and cannot do over the Web. Best of all, you saw just how easy it is to analyze data on the Web versus in Excel proper – without requiring your readers to have Excel 2000 on their machines!

Appendix A

What's on the CD

THIS APPENDIX DISCUSSES the JustPC application I used throughout the book. While JustPC is a fictitious business, its database is far more complex than the traditional databases discussed in a database book. I did this purposely to demonstrate many of the problems that you'll encounter in a real business.

The data supplied on the CD-ROM is totally synthesized. Thus, if you examine the data closely, you see such things as duplicate telephone numbers, only one Internet service provider, and so on. I did this to prevent the legal problems that could arise from using live data. As I go through the database, I indicate which data fields are suitable for data analysis and which are not. After all, you wouldn't want to set up a really complex query to have it fall apart when you find that 25 different customers in different states share the same phone number.

What Is JustPC?

JustPC is a small mom-and-pop retail business that operates in the state of Maryland, just outside of Washington D.C. As you may guess from its name, JustPC's primary business is selling personal computers. While this business is relatively small, it has served over 10,000 customers since it opened its first store in 1996. Currently, it operates three stores located in Maryland. With 1998 sales of over $23 million it is a thriving business and 1999 looks even better. One of the biggest reasons JustPC has been able to survive in this highly contested business field is the use of state-of-the-art technology to assist it in performing its normal business data processing. Part of the advantage of this technology is that it enables JustPC to perform extensive data analysis to make better business decisions.

The JustPC Database

The JustPC database is built using Microsoft SQL Server 7 running on a Windows 2000/NT Server platform. Like most relational databases in the real world, the JustPC database includes a large number of tables that store its data in a highly normalized fashion. For simplicity, the database is broken into five major sections: Customer Information, Inventory Information, Sales Information, Accounts Payable/Receivable Information, and Personnel/Payroll Information.

Realistic Database Design

This database design is supposed to represent a database used by a small- to medium-sized business. Each table contains information needed to operate JustPC. Don't assume that this database design is appropriate or complete for a real business. If you spend a few minutes looking at the database design, no doubt you'll identify several new fields and perhaps a few new tables that should be included. You also might come up with several ways to simplify the database design.

However, this is nearly always true of any database in production. In a real business, a database is not designed at one time, but over a period of years as new applications are added and existing applications are enhanced. I've never met a database administrator whose fondest wish was to throw away all of the existing databases and replace them with a completely integrated design.

Remember that the primary purpose of this database is to provide a foundation for the examples in this book. I tried to achieve a balance between having too complex a database design and making it too trivial to convert the database into a data warehouse. You'll have to deal with many challenges like this one when creating your own data warehouse, so I hope I made the right decisions.

Customer Information

The Customer Information section of the database is important because JustPC's customers are key to its success. Each customer that does business with JustPC is assigned a unique customer identifier, known as the CustomerId. This value is used as a key to the Customers table, as shown in Table A-1. Any information that is directly related to a customer is stored here, including the customer's name, address, and CustomerType. (See Table A-2 for a list of the valid CustomerType values.)

TABLE **A-1 FIELDS IN THE CUSTOMERS TABLE**

Field	Description
CustomerId	A value that uniquely identifies a particular customer
CustomerType	A broad classification of customers into different categories (See Table A-2 for the available customer types.)
FirstName	The first name of the customer
LastName	The last name of the customer
CompanyName	The name of the organization associated with the customer; only valid when CustomerType is not IN

Field	Description
Street	The street address of the customer
City	The city where the customer is located
Zip	The zip code of the customer's location
Phone	The telephone number of the customer
EMailAddress	The customer's e-mail address

 The data in the Customers table was prepared so that the data in the CustomerType, CompanyName, City, State, and Zip fields are meaningful for data analysis. While other fields may contain information, no attempt was made to ensure that the data would be suitable for analysis. For instance, several unrelated customers may have the same telephone number.

TABLE A-2 CUSTOMER TYPES

CustomerType	Description
CO	A major corporation
ED	An educational institution, such as a school or college
IN	An individual consumer, not associated with a business or other organization
MB	A medium-sized business
NP	A not-for-profit organization
SB	A small business

Inventory Information

The Inventory Information section of the database contains data about the collection of materials used to build computers and the accessories sold to a customer (see Table A-3). Inventory items are broken into a series of general types (as shown in Table A-4). Each item is assigned a list price that is changed for the item if it is sold independently. However, if the item is sold as part of a system, the price is discounted.

The DateAvailable and DateUnavailable fields are used to indicate when a part can be sold. This information enables me to keep historical information about past inventory items, which is critical for data analysis purposes.

The Suppliers table (see Table A-5) contains information about where to purchase various inventory items. It holds information about the sales representative and the mailing address of the supplier.

The Suppliers table described in Table A-6 contains information about the various offerings of the supplier. This table translates an InventoryId value into a part number recognized by the supplier. The table includes additional information about the cost of the item and the last time that the information was updated.

TABLE **A-3** FIELDS IN THE INVENTORYITEMS TABLE

Field	Description
InventoryId	A value that uniquely identifies an item in the inventory
Description	A short description of the inventory item
InventoryType	Groups similar types of items together (See Table A-4 for the available inventory types.)
SpeedSize	Holds the speed of a CPU on a motherboard; the size of a hard disk or memory, modem speed, network card speed, monitor size, and so forth
QuantityOnHand	The number of the item currently in stock
ReorderPoint	When QuantityOnHand drops below this level, you should reorder the item
ListPrice	The price that you should charge for the item, if sold by itself.
DateUpdated	The date this information was changed last
DateAvailable	The date the item first became available
DateUnavailable	The date the item ceased to become available

While the data structures in the InventoryItems table are fairly realistic, the number of items kept in the table are probably fewer than a real-life, mom-and-pop computer store would keep. I did this to simplify the data analysis later on because the extra entries only add bulk to the reports and do not demonstrate any new techniques.

TABLE A-4 INVENTORY TYPES

InventoryType	Description
CA	Complete case with keyboard, mouse, floppy, and so on
CD	CD-ROM
CM	Complete multimedia, with sound card, speakers, CD-ROM, and so on
CP	CPU and motherboard
DI	Display monitor
FD	Floppy diskette drive
HD	Hard disk
ME	Memory
MO	Modem
OS	Operating system software
SO	Sound card
SP	Speakers
SW	Software application
VI	Video card

TABLE A-5 FIELDS IN THE SUPPLIERS TABLE

Field	Description
SupplierId	A value that uniquely identifies a supplier
SupplierName	The name of the supplier
ContactName	The name of the sales representative
Address	The street address of the supplier
City	The city where the supplier is located
State	The state where the supplier is located
Zip	The supplier's zip code
Phone	The telephone number of the sales representative

 The data in the Suppliers table isn't used in any of the examples in the book. It is included for completeness in the database design.

TABLE A-6 FIELDS IN THE SUPPLIES TABLE

Field	Description
SupplierId	A value that uniquely identifies a supplier of an inventory item
InventoryId	The InventoryId value from the InventoryItems table
SupplierPartNumber	The part number used by the supplier for the specified inventory item
Cost	The current cost of the item from the supplier
DateUpdated	The last time this entry was updated in the database

Sales Information

Sales information is generated when a customer purchases something in the inventory. This process is known as an *order*. When a customer places an order, each of the line items is stored independently from the order in three different tables depending on the type of order entry. There are three basic types of orders:

- *Accessories* are hardware and software items pulled directly from the InventoryItems table.

- *Labor* represents the cost of labor for fixing a problem on someone's existing computer.

- *System* contains the information for a complete computer system.

The common information for all three types of orders is stored in the Orders table (see Table A-7), while the line item information is stored in different tables based on the type of the order entry. It is possible that entries can and will be made in each of these tables for a single order. In order to identify the information in each table uniquely, a field called Seq is included to make each of the rows unique.

The OrderAccessories table (see Table A-8) contains fields that describe the item sold, its cost, and the cost to install it. Note that the SalesPrice field doesn't include sales tax and the LaborRate is different from the employee's salary. The Warranty field indicates that work was done as a warranty repair—at no charge to the customer.

The OrderLabor table (see Table A-9) is very similar to the OrderAccessories table, but it represents information for a strictly labor order entry. This most likely is a diagnostic charge for identifying a hardware problem, removing a virus from a computer, or reinstalling previously purchased software.

The OrderSystems table (see Table A-10) and the Systems table (see Table A-11) work together to record information about a particular computer system. The entry in OrderSystems serves to record the purchase information, plus assign a serial number to the system. This serial number is used as an index into the Systems table where all of the individual components of the system are listed. This information enables the service technician to determine the exact parts originally installed on the computer when the computer is brought in for service under warranty.

The Stores table (see Table A-12) tracks information about each store in the company.

 The Order Information section and the Customer Information section of the database form the basis for most of the examples used in this book. A large amount of effort went into making the data in these sections interesting.

TABLE A-7 FIELDS IN THE ORDERS TABLE

Field	Description
OrderId	A value that uniquely identifies an order
CustomerId	A reference to the customer placing the order
EmployeeId	A reference to the employee handling the order
DateOrdered	The date the order is placed initially
StoreId	A reference to the store where the order is placed initially
DateDelivered	The date the order is received by the customer
TotalSale	The total amount of the sale
SalesTaxRate	The sales tax rate used to calculate the sales tax for the order
SalesTax	The total sales tax for the order
Shipping	The cost to ship the order to the customer
SpecialInstructions	A text field that hold comments about the order

TABLE A-8 FIELDS IN THE ORDERACCESSORIES TABLE

Field	Description
OrderId	A value that uniquely identifies an order
Seq	A sequence number that differentiates among multiple entries in the OrderAccessories table for a single order
InventoryId	A reference to the inventory item that is sold
SpecialInstructions	Any special instructions from the customer
Warranty	True means the accessory is replaced under warranty.
LaborBillable	The amount of time billed to the customer for installation
LaborRate	The amount of money billed for each hour of installation time
LaborCost	The total cost of labor
EmployeeId	A reference to the employee who installs the part
SalesPrice	The price the customer pays for this item
ItemCost	The cost of the item
Quantity	The number of items ordered

TABLE A-9 FIELDS IN THE ORDERLABOR TABLE

Field	Description
OrderId	A value that uniquely identifies an order
Seq	A sequence number that differentiates among multiple entries in the OrderLabor table for a single order
SpecialInstructions	Any special instructions from the customer
Warranty	True means the labor is charged to the warranty
LaborBillable	The amount of time billed to the customer for installation
LaborRate	The amount of money billed for each hour of installation time
EmployeeId	A reference to the employee who installs the part

TABLE A-10 FIELDS IN THE ORDERSYSTEMS TABLE

Field	Description
OrderId	A value that uniquely identifies an order
Seq	A sequence number that differentiates among multiple entries in the OrderSystems table for a single order
SystemId	The serial number associated with a computer system
SpecialInstructions	Any special instructions from the customer
EmployeeId	A reference to the employee who installs the part
SalesPrice	The price the customer pays for this item
LaborCost	The cost of labor for the system

TABLE A-11 FIELDS IN THE SYSTEMS TABLE

Field	Description
SystemId	The serial number associated with a computer system
InventoryId	A reference to one of the inventory items included in the computer system
Quantity	The number of the specified inventory item included in the computer system
ItemCost	The cost of the inventory item

TABLE A-12 FIELDS IN THE STORES TABLE

Field	Description
StoreId	A number associated with each store location
Street	The street address of the store
City	The city where the store is located
Zip	The zip code of the store's location
Phone	The telephone number of the store
DateOpened	The first day the store is open for customers

Accounts Payable/Receivable Information

The AccountsPayable table (see Table A-13), the AccountsReceivable table (see Table A-14), and the TransactionTypes table (see Table A-15) all track financial information about JustPC.

TABLE **A-13** FIELDS IN THE ACCOUNTSPAYABLE TABLE

Field	Description
TransactionId	A reference number associated with the financial transaction
TransactionType	A field that indicates the type of transaction
SupplierId	A reference to the supplier in the Suppliers table that receives the payment
InvoiceNumber	The invoice number from the supplier
DateInvoiced	The date the supplier's invoice is generated
DatePaid	The date JustPC sends the money to the supplier against its invoice
Amount	The amount of money paid to the supplier
Comments	Any comments about the transaction

TABLE **A-14** FIELDS IN THE ACCOUNTSRECEIVABLE TABLE

Field	Description
TransactionId	A reference number associated with the financial transaction
TransactionType	A field that indicates the type of transaction
OrderId	A reference to an order placed by a customer
DateInvoiced	The date JustPC invoices the customer
DatePaid	The date JustPC sends the money to the supplier against its invoice
Amount	The amount of money the customer receives
Comments	Any comments about the transaction

TABLE A-15 TRANSACTION TYPES

InventoryType	Description
AP	Accounts payable transaction
AR	Accounts receivable transaction

 These tables are included to make the database design complete. However, no sample data is included for them.

Personnel/Payroll Information

This section contains two tables, the Employees table (see Table A-16) and the Payroll table (see Table A-17). The Employees table holds information about an employee, such as name, address, and job title. The Payroll table holds information about the employee's wages and payroll deductions. Each entry in the table represents the information for a single paycheck for a single employee.

TABLE A-16 FIELDS IN THE EMPLOYEES TABLE

Field	Description
EmployeeId	A value that uniquely identifies an employee
FirstName	The first name of the employee
LastName	The last name of the employee
Street	The street address of the employee
City	The city where the employee lives
State	The state where the employee lives
Zip	The zip code where the employee lives
Phone	The telephone number of the employee

Continued

TABLE **A-16** FIELDS IN THE EMPLOYEES TABLE *(Continued)*

EMailAddress	The employees's e-mail address
PayRate	The amount of money per hour the employee earns
JobTitle	The employee's job title
DateHired	The date the employee starts working for JustPC
DateLeft	The date the employee leaves the company

TABLE **A-17** FIELDS IN THE PAYROLL TABLE

Field	Description
EmployeeId	A value that uniquely identifies an employee
DatePaid	The date the payroll check is issued
HoursWorked	The total number of hours the employee works in this pay period
PayRate	The amount of money per hour the employee earns
FederalTax	The amount of federal taxes that are withheld from this paycheck
StateTax	The amount of state taxes that are withheld from this paycheck
SocialSecurity	The amount of Social Security taxes that are withheld from this paycheck

 A real human resources system includes more tables and more detailed information about each employee. However, for the purposes of this book, you can assume that the only meaningful data in these tables is the EmployeeId, and the related FirstName and LastName fields. The rest of the fields do not contain any significant information.

Loading the JustPC-DB Database

The JustPC-DB database is located on your CD-ROM in the x:\OLAP\Database\ JustPCDB.Zip file. This file contains a SQL Server database backup of the entire

JustPC-DB database. This includes all of the database structures and all of the sample data. Note that the size of the backup file is approximately 30 megabytes; you should allow about 40 to 50 megabytes of space for the database files and logs.

Unzip the file onto your hard disk and follow these steps to load the JustPC-DB database:

1. Choose Start → Programs → SQL Server 7.0 → Enterprise Manager from the task bar.

2. In Enterprise Manager, select the icon associated with the database server where you want to install the database.1

3. Right-click the icon beneath the database server and select All Tasks → Restore Database from the popup menu.

4. The Restore database dialog box is displayed. On the General tab of the Restore database dialog box, select Restore From Device (see Figure A-1).

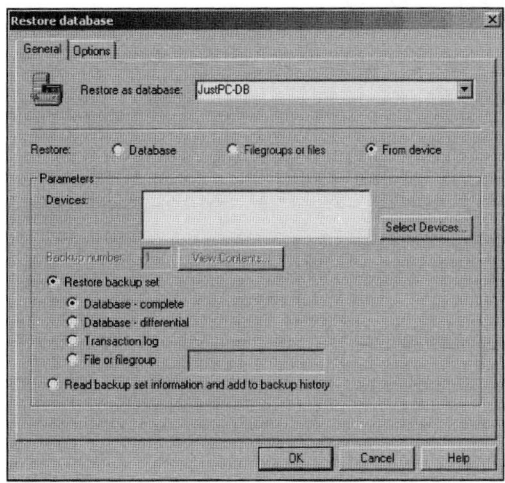

Figure A-1: Restoring the JustPC-DB database

5. In the Parameters section, press the Select Devices button. This displays the Choose Restore Devices dialog box shown in Figure A-2.

6. Press the Add button to display the Choose Restore Destination dialog box shown in Figure A-3.

7. Enter the fully qualified file name of the JustPC-DB database backup or press the button to the right of the file name text box to display a directory tree. Press OK to accept the file name.

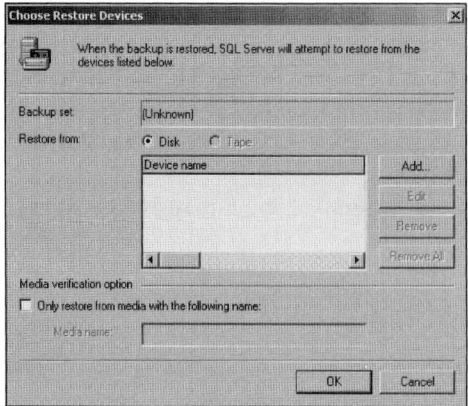

Figure A-2: Selecting the database backup file

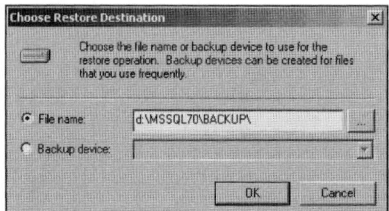

Figure A-3: Enter the database backup file name.

8. Press OK on the Choose Restore Devices dialog box to return to the Restore Database dialog box.

9. In the Restore Database dialog box, type **JustPC-DB** as the name of the database in the Restore as database text box.

10. Select Restore backup set and Database – complete in the Parameters section of the dialog box and press OK to begin the restore process.

This installs a complete copy of the JustPC-DB database.

Loading JustPC-DW

Just follow the steps listed above, but substitute the file x:\OLAP\Database\ JustPCDW.zip for the database file and restore it to the database JustPC-DW. Note that this database is only about half the size of the JustPC-DB database.

Glossary

Access 2000 An easy-to-use tool to develop database applications. Part of the Microsoft Office 2000 suite

Aggregate The process of combining the values of a single column across a set of rows. Typical aggregation functions are COUNT, MAX, MIN, and SUM.

Alias An alternate name for a column or table that exists only for the duration of a query

ANSI SQL A standard for the *SQL* language from the American National Standards Institute (ANSI). The current version of the standard is referred to as SQL-92.

Application A collection of programs and *databases* that enable a *user* to solve a problem

Application Log A file containing SQL Server status information in a Windows 2000/NT system

Atomic An object that can't be subdivided. See also *Atomic Field.*

Atomic Field A field whose contents can't be broken down further. (For example, a data is not atomic because you can break it down into day, month, and year, while a month is atomic because you can't break it into smaller pieces.) See also *Atomic.*

Authentication The process of establishing a *user's* identity. This usually involves providing a user name and a secret password to the operating system or SQL Server to prove that you have access to the functions associated with the user name.

Authenticated User A person who passes the *authentication* test

Authorization The process of determining the access rights to functions and data that an *authenticated user* is allowed to perform

Axis One dimension of a *cube*

Backup A copy of the information in a database taken at a given point in time. You use backup to *recover* the information in the database.

Base Table A real table in the database that is referenced in a view

Batch Job A process in which a non-interactive program is executed, typically when no one is around to control its execution

Business Logic The set of *business rules* used to operate a business or other organization

Business Rules A set of instructions that implements a business procedure. For example, the set of steps that a payroll clerk must follow to compute the amount of money an employee is paid is considered a business rule. Business rules often are implemented as part of a *program* (or set of programs) that runs on a computer.

Cache A buffer that holds frequently used information. In a database system, a cache typically resides in the computer's memory and holds information from the database's disk storage.

Calculated Member A *member* of a *cube* that is computed on the fly based on already existing data in the cube

Cell The intersection of a *row* and a *column* in a *table* that contains a single value. In a *cube*, a cell represents the intersection of all of the *dimensions*.

Child A *member* in the next lower *level* of a *hierarchy*. This member represents a subset of the information in its *parent*.

Client The user side of a multi-computer application. For example, Query Analyzer, Excel, and MapPoint can be client programs for a SQL Server database.

Client/Server A programming technique in which a *client* program makes requests of a *server* program. In the case of SQL Server, the *client* program running on the user's computer generates requests for information or supplies commands to the *database server*, which processes them and returns the results to the calling application.

Clustered Index A special type of index used to determine the order of the rows in a table. A table can contain only one clustered index.

Codify This technique replaces a field in a database with an encoded value. That encoded value is used as a key to another table in which the original field is extracted. This typically is used when dealing with "standard" text fields. For example, the text field JobTitle can be codified into an integer field called JobTitleCode. Using JobTitleCode in your database ensures that all employees have the same value for their job title. JobTitleCode is much smaller than JobTitle, so you also save space in the database.

Column A field in a relational database table

Commit The act of saving a set of changes in a database. You can abandon the changes by performing a *Roll Back*.

Composite A field that can be broken into multiple subfields

Composite Index An index that uses multiple columns as the key value

Connection A link between the client program and the *database server*

Cross–Tabulation Report A report that aggregates every combination of two or more data fields

Crosstab Report See *Cross-Tabulation Report.*

Cube A set of data organized by *dimensions* and containing *measures*. The data generally is extracted from a *data warehouse* and is analyzed by tools such as Excel *PivotTables*.

Cube Browser A tool included in the OLAP Manager that enables you to view the data in a cube

Cube Editor A tool included with the OLAP Manager that enables you to view and change the structure of a cube

Data Dictionary A repository that contains detailed information about every field, table, and view in a database and how they are related to one other

Data Element Another name for *column*

Data Mart A concept identical to a data warehouse, but smaller in scope. Rather than encompassing all of the data in an organization, a data mart may contain only information about a single department or application.

Data Scrubbing The processing of analyzing data for consistency before data is loaded into a data warehouse

Data Source The source of the data loaded into a *dimension* or *member* of a cube

Data Transformation Services A tool in SQL Server that enables you to move and transform data from one database to another. This tool is extremely useful when you are extracting data from your production database to your data warehouse.

Data Type Defines the storage mechanism for a *column*. It also determines the set of basic operations that can be against the column. Some common data types include CHAR, which holds strings of characters, and INT, which holds numeric values.

Data Warehouse A central repository containing data that is made available to satisfy unstructured requests for information by end users. The data generally is extracted from production applications and summarized to minimize the amount of work needed to satisfy the request.

Database A collection of *tables*, *indexes*, and other *database objects* that are used by one or more *applications* stored inside a *database server*

Database Administrator A database administrator is the person responsible for the design and maintenance of a database. Besides creating and changing the database, this person also is responsible for such tasks as database backup and database recovery.

Database Client The computer used to access a *database server*. Typically, this computer runs a tool, such as Query Analyzer to perform *query* operations against the database, or a custom application that enables the user to add, delete, and modify information in the database.

Database Diagram A graphical representation of a subset of the *database objects* contained in a database

Database Object A *table*, *column*, *index*, *trigger*, *view*, *constraint*, *rule*, *stored procedure*, or *key* in a database

Database Owner The *user name* of the individual responsible for the *database*. This individual is also known as the *database administrator*.

Database Query See *query*.

Database Replication The process whereby the contents of one database are synchronized with another database

Database Server The computer containing the set of *databases* and the software that services requests from *database clients*

DBA See *database administrator*.

DBO See *database owner*.

Decision Support System (DSS) An application designed to help people make better business decisions. Typically a decision support system uses a data warehouse as the source of the data to be analyzed.

Dimension A part of the cube used to organize the *members* in the cube. A dimension has one or more *levels* used to group data values. For instance, a time dimension has the all level at the top, followed by a years level containing the set of years, and a months level containing the months in a particular year.

Dimension Table A table in a data warehouse used to index the values in a fact table

Drill-Down The act of expanding the information displayed from a cube to see the next level of detail

Domain A collection of computers in a Windows environment in which the computers all share a common security database

English Query A tool included in Microsoft SQL Server 7 that enables you to enter queries using English-like questions and sentences

Equijoin A join operation with two or more tables in which one field in one table must equal another field in another table

Excel 2000 A part of the Microsoft Office 2000 suite of programs that can analyze tabular data using worksheets and multidimensional data using PivotTables and PivotCharts

Export The process of moving data from a database to a file

Expression An algebraic formula that can involve constants, columns, functions, and arithmetic operators. Often used in SQL statements

Fact Table A central table in a data warehouse whose primary key values link back to dimension tables. The remaining values typically describe a transaction, such as a purchase, within an organization. Sometimes these values are summarized according to the dimensions included in the table to reduce the amount of data stored.

Field An alternate name for *column* or *data element*

Filter An expression used to identify a series of records in a query

Foreign Key A *column* or set of columns whose value must match the *primary key* of another *table*

Full Backup A complete *backup* of a database. Can restore the entire contents of a database without using any other backups

Function A routine that performs a task often involving calculations and returns a value based on zero or more parameters.

Hierarchy An arrangement of the *members* in a *dimension* into *levels* based on *parent-child* relationships. For example, a time dimension is broken into years, years are broken into months, and so on.

HOLAP See *Hybrid OLAP database.*

Hybrid OLAP Database (HOLAP) A Hybrid OLAP database uses techniques from a MOLAP database and a ROLAP database to provide better performance than either approach.

Identifier A string of characters used to uniquely describe a database object such as a *column* or *table*

Identity Column A column in a table that contains a system-generated, monotonically increasing value, which is guaranteed to be unique within the table

IIS See *Internet Information Server.*

Import The process of copying data from a file to a *database*. This is the opposite of *export.*

Incremental Update The process whereby rows are added, rather than replaced, in a table

Index A database facility that stores details about the location of *rows* containing a specified *key* value. This *database object* allows the *database server* to retrieve rows from a *table* faster than without the index. Indexes usually are created based on typical searches performed by users to increase performance.

Internet An international network that permits computers to communicate among each other using the TCP/IP suite of protocols

Internet Information Server (IIS) Microsoft's high-performance Web server that runs on a *Windows 2000/NT Server* system

Intranet An internal network for an organization that is based on the tools and protocols used by the Internet

Job See *batch job.*

Junction Table The table in the middle of a *many-to-many relationship*

Key A *column* or set of columns whose content is used to identify one or more *rows*. See also *primary key, foreign key,* and *index.*

Level Level describes the amount of detail displayed in a dimension. The lower the level, the more detail is displayed.

Login An identifier that gives an individual access to a *database server.* A login is mapped to a particular *user name* when accessing a specific *database.*

Many-to-Many Relationship A relationship between two *data elements* in which a particular value for one field implies that the second field can have a particular range of values. While the second field implies that the first field also can have a range of values. For example, an author may write many books, while a book may be written by many authors.

MapPoint 2000 This application is a member of the Microsoft Office 2000 suite and is used to analyze geographic data.

MDX See *MultiDimensional eXtensions.*

Measure A numeric column included in a *fact table.* Typically contains information that you can analyze

Member An item in a *dimension* that represents one or more occurrences of data. The combination of a member and its parent values must be unique.

Metadata A collection of attributes that describe your database – including the data type of each column, the format that you should use to present the data, a description of the data, plus any other useful information in understanding how the data is created and how you should use it.

MOLAP See *Multidimensional OLAP database.*

MultiDimensional Extensions (MDX) A language used for building queries that access a cube

Multidimensional Database (MOLAP) A multidimensional database stores information in a collection of large multidimensional arrays. This makes it easy to locate a specific piece of information quickly. However, this structure is extremely time-consuming to load.

Nested Query A Select statement that contains one or more *subqueries*

Normalization The process of designing a database according to a set of well-defined rules that minimize duplication of information

Null A condition that exists when a *column* doesn't have a value. Do not confuse this with an empty string, whose value is a string of characters with a length of zero.

ODBC See *Open Database Connectivity.*

OLAP See *online analytical processing.*

OLAP Manager A utility that enables you to manage an OLAP server; it contains tools that enable you to design and populate OLAP cubes.

OLAP Server A type of *server* designed to store *multidimensional databases* and to process queries against the data

OLAP Services A facility in Microsoft SQL Server that includes tools such as the *OLAP Manager* and the OLAP server which responds to requests for *Multidimensional OLAP databases*

OLE DB An object-oriented programming interface to access a *database* or other data source that supports Microsoft's COM technology

OLE DB Consumer A program that requests information from a data source using an *OLE DB provider*

OLE DB Provider A program that responds to requests for information from an *OLE DB consumer*

One-to-Many Relationships A relationship between two *data elements* in which a particular value for one *field* implies that the other field can have a range of values. While the second field implies that the first field can have only one value. For example, there is a one-to-many relationship between a mother and her children. A mother may have many children, while a child has only one mother.

One-to-One Relationship A relationship between two *data elements* in which a particular value for one *field* implies that the other field has a particular value and vice versa. For example, there is a one-to-one relationship between a person and that person's social security number.

Online Analytical Processing (OLAP) A database technology that enables you to view multidimensional structures for data analysis

Open Database Connectivity (ODBC) A technology developed by Microsoft that permits Windows programs to access different database systems. *OLE DB* superceded this technology.

Operator A symbol that performs computations, comparisons, and other tasks within an *expression*

Package The collection of information defined to Data Transformation Services that is used to *import* or *export* data from your database

Parameter A value or expression passed to a function

Parent A *member* in the next higher *level* in a *hierarchy*. The parent represents the aggregation of the values of all of its *child* members.

Partition A storage container for data and aggregations of a cube. Every cube has at least one partition. Note that multiple partitions only come with some editions of SQL Server.

Partial Backup An incomplete *backup* of your database. A partial backup records the changes made since another backup was taken. Its primary advantage is that it runs much faster than a *full backup*. To completely recover your database, you need a *full* backup and any other partial backups that were taken after the full backup was taken.

Pass-Through Query A query that is passed through the current server untouched onto another server for execution

Permission The ability to perform a specific function inside a *database*. Each user must have the proper *authorization* in order to use the resource specified by the permission.

Pivot The process of exchanging one dimension for another in a *cube* or *PivotTable*

PivotTable A facility in *Excel* that enables you to analyze multidimensional data. You can extract the data locally from a *worksheet* or remotely from a *database server* or *OLAP server*.

PivotTable Service A tool on a *client* computer that communicates with an *OLAP server* to provide data for a *client application* such as *Excel*

Precalculate The process of performing *aggregations* on *multidimensional* data in anticipation of future queries

Primary Key The *column* or columns in a *table* that uniquely identify a *row*

Private Dimension A *dimension* used only by a single *cube,* as opposed to a *shared dimension* that is common to multiple cubes

Processing The act of loading data into the cube. This is required each time a cube is created, when its structure is changed, or when the data in the data warehouse changes.

Production Application An application that implements *business logic* to help an organization perform its primary goals

Publisher The source of data in the replication model

Query A request to retrieve, insert, update, or delete information in a *database*

Query Optimizer A part of the *database server* that analyzes a database *query* to determine the most efficient way to execute the query

Rapid Application Development Tool A tool that enables you to build applications quickly, at the cost of execution efficiency

Record A collection of fields containing related information that is treated as a single entity; also known as a *row* in a *table*

Recovery The process of rebuilding a *database* based on database *backups* and *transaction logs*

Refresh The set of operations that deletes the data from a cube and loads the cube with a fresh set of data from the data warehouse. See also *process.*

Relational Database A *database* that appears to the user as a simple collection of *tables* in which each table consists of a series of *columns* or *fields* across the top and a series of *rows* or *records* down the side. The underlying data structures used to hold the data are totally invisible to the user.

Relational OLAP Database (ROLAP) A Relational OLAP database stores its information in a relational database. This has the advantage of being easy to load, but it can be time-consuming to search.

Relationship A situation whereby a *foreign key* in a table is linked to a *primary key* in another table. A relationship may be *one-to-one, one-to-many,* or *many-to-many.*

Repeating Group A variable that contains multiple occurrences of information. This is similar to an array with dynamically defined bounds. An example of a repeating group is book authors in which there may be one, two, three, or more authors depending on the particular book.

Replication Model See database replication.

Repository See *data dictionary.*

ROLAP See *Relational OLAP database.*

Role A predefined set of *permissions* in the *database.* When a *login* ID is assigned to a role, it inherits all the permissions associated with the role.

Row A collection of *columns* stored in a *table*

Schema A description of the *database* using a language such as *SQL.*

Server A server side of a client-server application. This program responds to requests from *client* applications.

Shared Dimension A dimension in an *OLAP database* that is common to multiple cubes

Slice and Dice The act of moving and combining dimensions while selecting one or more individual level values in a cube to see data from different viewpoints

Snowflake Schema A database design in which one or more dimensions surround a fact table and one or more tables represent each dimension. See also *Star Schema.*

SQL See *Structured Query Language.*

SQL Server Microsoft's high performance database management system. Includes a number of tools such as the Query Analyzer, Enterprise Manager, English Query, and OLAP server

SQL Statement A single *query* written in the *SQL* language

Star Schema A database design in which one or more dimensions surround a fact table and a single table represents each dimension. See also *Snowflake Schema.*

Strategic Application Deals with the long-range business goals of an organization. A *data warehouse* is an example of a strategic application. See also *tactical application.*

Structured Query Language (SQL) A language originally developed by IBM in the 1970s that has become the standard language for accessing relational *databases*

Subquery A Select statement nested inside another *SQL statement*

Subscriber The destination of data in a replication model

Table The only database object that contains business data. It provides a view of this data with a series of *columns* and *rows*. Each column of data corresponds to a *field*. A row also is known as a *record*.

Table Scan The process whereby the database server must read every row in a table to satisfy a *query*

Tactical Application Deals with the day-to-day issues of running an organization. A payroll application is an example of a tactical application. See also *strategic application.*

Transaction A logical unit of work that consists of one or more changes to a *database*. Either all or none of the steps in the transaction are completed. The classic example of a transaction is transferring money from one account to another, in which the funds are subtracted from the source account and added to the destination account. If only half of the transaction is completed, the database is in error.

Transaction Log A file containing a list of changes made to the *database*. You can use this information to undo changes made to the database or you can combine it with a *backup* file to recover *transactions* made after the backup was made.

Underlying Table See *base table.*

Unique Index An index in which each row must have a unique *key* value

User Name An *identifier* associated with a *login* that is used to determine an individual's *permissions* in a *database*

View A virtual *table* created through the use of a *SQL* Select statement. A view appears to the user exactly as a table for all read operations and some write operations, depending on how the view was created.

Virtual Cube A logical cube created from existing dimensions and measures of one or more physical cubes. A virtual cube is similar in concept to a view.

Virtual Dimension A logical dimension created from an existing dimension in a cube

Visual Basic A rapid application development tool often used to build database applications

Visual Basic Script A version of Visual Basic that runs inside another application, such as Data Transformation Services, which enables you to customize a task

Windows A family of operating systems from Microsoft

Windows 98/95 An operating system designed to support interactive processing. Currently, there are three versions of Windows 98/95: Windows 98 Second Edition, Windows 98, and Windows 95.

Windows 2000 Professional An operating system designed to support interactive processing. This operating system replaces Windows NT Workstation.

Windows 2000/NT Server An operating system designed to support various *servers*, such as database servers or Web servers

Windows NT Workstation An operating system designed to support interactive processing; typically used by power users

Wizard A sequence of dialog boxes that prompt a user for information that is used to perform a complex task

Index

Symbol & Numbers

463

IDG Books Worldwide, Inc.
End-User License Agreement

4. <u>Restrictions on Use of Individual Programs</u>. You must follow the individual requirements and restrictions detailed for each individual program in the What's on the CD-ROM Appendix of this Book. These limitations are also contained in the individual license agreements recorded on the Software Media. These limitations may include a requirement that after using the program for a specified period of time, the user must pay a registration fee or discontinue use.

By opening the Software packet(s), you will be agreeing to abide by the licenses and restrictions for these individual programs that are detailed in the What's on the CD-ROM Appendix and on the Software Media. None of the material on this Software Media or listed in this Book may ever be redistributed, in original or modified form, for commercial purposes.

5. <u>Limited Warranty</u>.

(a) IDGB warrants that the Software and Software Media are free from defects in materials and workmanship under normal use for a period of sixty (60) days from the date of purchase of this Book. If IDGB receives notification within the warranty period of defects in materials or workmanship, IDGB will replace the defective Software Media.

(b) IDGB AND THE AUTHOR OF THE BOOK DISCLAIM ALL OTHER WARRANTIES, EXPRESS OR IMPLIED, INCLUDING WITHOUT LIMITATION IMPLIED WARRANTIES OF MERCHANTABILITY AND FITNESS FOR A PARTICULAR PURPOSE, WITH RESPECT TO THE SOFTWARE, THE PROGRAMS, THE SOURCE CODE CONTAINED THEREIN, AND/OR THE TECHNIQUES DESCRIBED IN THIS BOOK. IDGB DOES NOT WARRANT THAT THE FUNCTIONS CONTAINED IN THE SOFTWARE WILL MEET YOUR REQUIREMENTS OR THAT THE OPERATION OF THE SOFTWARE WILL BE ERROR FREE.

(c) This limited warranty gives you specific legal rights, and you may have other rights that vary from jurisdiction to jurisdiction.

6. <u>Remedies</u>.

(a) IDGB's entire liability and your exclusive remedy for defects in materials and workmanship shall be limited to replacement of the Software Media, which may be returned to IDGB with a copy of your receipt at the following address: Software Media Fulfillment Department, Attn.: *Unlocking OLAP with Microsoft® SQL Server™ and Excel 2000*, IDG Books Worldwide, Inc., 10475 Crosspoint Blvd., Indianapolis, IN 46256, or call 1-800-762-2974. Please allow three to four weeks for delivery. This Limited Warranty is void if failure of the Software Media has resulted from accident, abuse, or misapplication. Any replacement Software Media will be warranted for the remainder of the original warranty period or thirty (30) days, whichever is longer.

(b) In no event shall IDGB or the author be liable for any damages whatsoever (including without limitation damages for loss of business profits, business interruption, loss of business information, or any other pecuniary loss) arising from the use of or inability to use the Book or the Software, even if IDGB has been advised of the possibility of such damages.

(c) Because some jurisdictions do not allow the exclusion or limitation of liability for consequential or incidental damages, the above limitation or exclusion may not apply to you.

7. **U.S. Government Restricted Rights**. Use, duplication, or disclosure of the Software by the U.S. Government is subject to restrictions stated in paragraph (c)(1)(ii) of the Rights in Technical Data and Computer Software clause of DFARS 252.227-7013, and in subparagraphs (a) through (d) of the Commercial Computer – Restricted Rights clause at FAR 52.227-19, and in similar clauses in the NASA FAR supplement, when applicable.

8. **General**. This Agreement constitutes the entire understanding of the parties and revokes and supersedes all prior agreements, oral or written, between them and may not be modified or amended except in a writing signed by both parties hereto that specifically refers to this Agreement. This Agreement shall take precedence over any other documents that may be in conflict herewith. If any one or more provisions contained in this Agreement are held by any court or tribunal to be invalid, illegal, or otherwise unenforceable, each and every other provision shall remain in full force and effect.